THE
FundLine Advisor

The Essential Mutual Funds Handbook for Canadian Investors

Richard Croft & Eric Kirzner

HarperBusiness
HarperCollins*PublishersLtd*

Canadian Cataloguing in Publication Data

Croft, Richard, 1952-
The fundline advisor

"A HarperBusiness book"
ISBN 0-00-638600-8

1. Mutual funds - Canada.   2. Mutual funds - Canada - Rankings.
I. Kirzner, Eric, 1945-   .   II. Title.

HG5154.5.C76 1996   332.63'27   C96-930731-4

The material in this publication is provided for information purposes only. Laws, regulations, and procedures are constantly changing, and the examples given are intended to be general guidelines only. This book is sold with the understanding that neither the authors nor the publisher is engaged in rendering professional advice. It is recommended that legal, accounting and other advice or assistance be obtained before acting on any information contained in this book. Personal services of a competent professional should be sought.

The authors, publisher, and all others directly or indirectly involved with this publication do not assume any responsibility or liability, direct or indirect, to any party for any loss or damage by errors or omissions, regardless of the cause, as a consequence of using this publication, nor accept any contractural, tortious, or other form of liability for its contents or any consequences arising from its use.

96 97 98 99 ❖ HC 10 9 8 7 6 5 4 3 2 1

Printed and bound in the United States

Contents

List of Figures

Recommended Asset Mixes for 1997

List of Tables

To my wife Barbara,
and my children
Christopher, Loa and Machaela
—R.C.

To my wonderful family:
my wife Helen,
my daughters Diana and Jennifer,
and my son-in-law Jordan

—E.K.

Acknowledgments

Writing a book of this nature is a daunting task. The objective was to write a book that is different—a one-stop top-down guide to investment planning that takes you from the asset mix decision all the way to the FundLine—an understandable approach for mixing and matching mutual funds within a porfolio. At the end of the day, you end up with a well-balanced portfolio that does not sacrifice performance.

A successful book requires a great deal of support. A special thanks to Toronto-based Vincent and Associates who supplied much of the data in the appendix, to Southam Communications who worked closely with us to develop our performance and consistency indexes, and to our editor Don Loney and the entire staff at HarperCollins.

Also, a special thanks to ManuLife Securities, who have supported me in my work as a consultant and mutual fund analyst, and to the mutual fund companies for their support and input in the development of the FundLine.

—R.C.

Faith, Fortune and the FundLine

We cannot escape the fact that our financial well-being is critical to our overall well-being. People in a strong financial position are more confident, make clearer decisions and, although we have no ready statistics to make the point, probably live longer. A weak financial position, on the other hand, can strain your family life, cause anxiety at work and force you to make decisions that are not always in your—or your family's—best interests. So, like it or not, we need some level of financial independence.

Most Canadians understand this. A recent study by Decima Research showed that "87% of Canadians agree that saving for retirement is very important." Talk to most baby boomers and they will take that position one step further. They simply don't believe the government, principally through Canada Pension and Old Age Security, will be able to provide any measure of support in their retirement years. The more skeptical baby boomers believe that the Canada Pension Plan will be empty of funds by the time they retire.

The point is, we understand the importance of establishing a set of objectives, putting in place a long-term plan and periodically re-examining our position with so-called financial checkups. *Unfortunately, many don't do it!*

Statistics from that same Decima study showed that 50% of Canadians make only a token effort to review their finances, and those who do, do so less than once a year. Even more startling was the fact that only 25% of Canadians regularly contribute to a Registered Retirement Savings Plan. So, what's the problem? We understand what is needed, yet many of us fail to act.

We think there are a couple of reasons for this. Issue number one for most individuals is not knowing where and how to start. And often, when seeking advice from those in the financial services industry, individual investors end up with more problems than solutions. You may find, for example, that a stockbroker will tell you why this stock or that bond is a good investment, but not be specific on how it fits within your long-term financial objectives and risk tolerances. A financial planner, on the other hand, might provide excellent tax advice and a reasonable financial blueprint, yet not be able to recommend the right investments to get you to where you want to go.

Interestingly, for individuals who fall into this camp, we have some straightforward advice. This book is geared to you, because it will provide the foundation on which to build a long-term investment plan. It will do so within the context of your sensitivity to risk and your personal financial circumstances. For those of you in this category, we are confident this will be the only book you will need.

Issue number two, and a difficult one, concerns the investor who distinguishes *investing* from *investment planning*. These individuals have a more sophisticated knowledge, or think they do, about the financial markets. For them, investing is as simple as Will Rogers once advised: "Buy a stock that goes up. If it doesn't go up, don't buy it."

These individuals invest to earn a profit. Fair enough! But making an investment with little or no thought as to how it fits within your personal financial circumstances is akin to investing in a vacuum. And we believe this "vacuum block" can lead individuals down a road to speculative excess that may be more damaging to the pocketbook than if they never invested at all.

We define this investment strategy as the "lottery syndrome," and if you think you fall into this category, read the rest of this chapter carefully. It is important that we explain why it is critical you get off this road and back onto a proper investment planning path. Establish some goals, construct a balanced portfolio to meet your personal circumstances, and then, when you are well on your way, go ahead and make some of those short-term investments with promise.

The Lottery Syndrome

On a recent trip to the Montreal Exchange, we were invited to talk with some of the traders, walk around the Exchange floor and, along the way, gain some insight into the workings of a modern stock exchange. Long known as an aggressive exchange, with many up-and-coming new companies, the Montreal Exchange is a place where more than a few companies have risen from obscurity to achieve financial success.

But the company on the minds of exchange traders and personnel on the day we visited was not a Montreal Exchange-listed company, but one listed on the Alberta Stock Exchange. The price of the company's stock had doubled, from about 18 cents when the day began to 37 cents per share at the close of trading, some six hours later.

This company was making news because of a new procedure it had developed for locating breaks in cable lines used to transmit data. Rather than having to search tediously for the cable break, this company had developed—or purchased—a technology that could quickly pinpoint where a break had occurred. Having ascertained the exact location of a break, the company could implement a service call and fix the problem.

Finding underground cable breaks does not seem like much of a story on the surface—pardon the pun—but add the word "Internet" to the discussion and this obscure player on the fringes of the World Wide Web could become an overnight success. At least, that was the story line, and for this Internet play, 37 cents per share was the price of admission.

Yes, at the Montreal Exchange this day, we found secretaries, receptionists and, of course, traders talking about this company's potential. And as you might imagine, most had bought shares. We noted with interest how much better the story got with every new person we encountered. Why, some went so far as to suggest that at a point in the future this company might even have real earnings to boast about! Earnings are not much of a concern during the early stages of a speculative frenzy, but the notion that earnings may at some point exist provides a measure of comfort for those who have already paid the 37-cents-per-share admission price.

For those of us who prefer to deal in fundamentals—an approach that is not particularly useful when dealing with a speculative frenzy—we noted with interest the firm's apparent lack of earnings and rather suspect balance sheet. So, despite the hype, we recognized that this was simply another stock story on the lips of some very astute traders who, for the most part, would be selling their shares to you at an even higher admission price.

If we have piqued your interest with this story, then you have fallen into the first and, we think, most critical investment trap. Don't worry, though—it's a trap most individual investors fall into on a regular basis. We think of it as the "lottery syndrome," the blind search for performance driven by the hot story of the week. You buy into this investment because you see potential and fear missing a great opportunity. We believe that individual investors caught up in this search for performance see the trees without noticing the financial forest.

We believe the so-called lottery syndrome is just one reason 80% of individuals fail to reach their financial objectives. And it isn't that your "search for performance-minded investments" is wrong. It isn't! Nobody makes an investment expecting to lose money. But when we make investments without any thought about what role they play in our long-term financial plan, then we are investing poorly. In short, we have set no objectives.

Without a defined set of goals, investors are really just playing the market. Buy at one price; sell when you have a profit or, more likely, when you can no longer stomach the losses. So entrenched is this view among investors that many follow the same philosophy when investing in mutual funds. In this case we refer to it as trying to "time the market." Most are no more successful in the mutual fund business than they are in the penny stock game.

Statistics tell us that most individual investors buy and sell at exactly the wrong time. We cite, as the most recent example of this phenomenon, the $2 billion in net mutual fund redemptions (i.e., net redemptions being the total dollar value of mutual fund units redeemed in a given month, net of the total dollar value of new mutual fund purchases) that took place in February 1995. This happened just when the stock and bond markets were at rock bottom, and just before both began a rally that extended well into 1996.

And don't think that this perception of bad timing is lost on professional investors. So established is the perception that individual investors find themselves on the wrong end of the financial roller coaster at exactly the wrong time, that professional investors have designed *sentiment indexes* to track the movements of individual investors. One such indicator is the aforementioned rate of new mutual fund redemptions relative to new mutual fund purchases. Indicators like this are referred to as *contrarian indicators*, which simply stated means you do the opposite of what the index is telling you.

On Prophets and Profits

Every day in the financial press you can read quotes from well-known market analysts explaining why the markets did this or that the previous day. In magazines, we find interviews with money managers who will gladly provide their views about what the future holds. And during the RRSP season, virtually every fund company will send managers across the country armed with economic forecasts and explanations of their strategy for the coming year. The more aggressive the forecast, the more enticing the message.

This reminds us of an article written by Kenneth Fischer in a 1987 issue of *Forbes* magazine. For those not familiar with the name, Mr. Fischer is a money manager living in California and author of the book *Super Stocks*. More important, he is a proponent of "value investing" and "contrarian market timing." Put another way, he likes to find stocks that are out of favor with the general market, but "undeservedly unpopular."

In the *Forbes* article, Fischer recalled the time at the beginning of his investment career when he was attending an American Electronics Association conference. During a dinner contest, attendees were asked to predict the close on the Dow Jones Industrial Average at the end of the next day. Eager to participate, the dinner guests turned in cards with their name and forecast.

He noted that the person next to him predicted the Dow would plunge by 35 points. At the time the Dow was around 800. A 35-point decline, in percentage terms, was considered significant. When asked why he expected such a crash, he replied that he hadn't the foggiest idea what the Dow would do the next day. However, he went on to explain, "If an individual is correct in predicting a small move, the crowd will simply consider that person lucky. On the other hand, if the extreme call wins, people will be dazzled."

As one would expect from such a story, the market did fall by 29 points, and his colleagues were indeed dazzled. In fact, by the afternoon, folks bombarded the winner, looking for some insights that could help them forecast the next crash. He obliged them all, says Fischer, embellishing his "analysis" as he retold the tale. In fact, by that evening he had convinced himself that he had known about the decline all along, and became indignant when Fischer reminded him that his call was based on showmanship.

And so another prophet was born.

Unfortunately, this story parallels many of the predictions of supposedly shrewd forecasters who ply their trade in the financial marketplace. But just so that we understand the pitfalls of prophecies, follow with us, along the trail of the hot and not-so-hot forecasters. As a case in point, take Joe Granville.

Joe Granville was the predominant forecaster in the 1970s. A master technician, Joe spoke with evangelical enthusiasm, and when he uttered a buy or sell recommendation, he could move markets.

Indeed, at one point, because Granville's prognostications wielded so much influence on the stock market, the U.S. Securities and Exchange Commission (SEC) launched an insider trading investigation. Believe it or not, the SEC was investigating whether subscribers to Granville's newsletter were privy to insider information.

The SEC argued that because Granville's recommendations caused the stock market to react violently, anyone with knowledge about his next recommendation could buy before the general public was made aware.

Talk about a catch-22! Here was Granville, earning a considerable income from the sale of his newsletter, but all of it premised on his subscribers getting the information first. If the SEC was convinced that the forecasts in the newsletter were in fact inside information, he would have to inform the news services at the same time he informed his subscribers. Which, of course, defeated the purpose of the newsletter.

Fortunately or unfortunately, depending on which side of the fence you sit, the issue became a moot point by the 1980s. Granville, never being one to sit on the fence, talked of the great crash through most of the 1980s, and by doing so missed one of the greatest bull markets of all time. Even the October 19, 1987, stock market crash did nothing to relieve the pain suffered by Granville's followers. Fact is, at the lowest point following the crash, stocks were still up more than 100% from the point at which Granville began his doom-and-gloom crusade.

The Next Wave

When Granville's roller coaster was going downhill, Robert Prechter was starting the slow ride to the top. What's most interesting about Prechter and the timing of his ascent was that he believed in many of the same things Granville did. Both, for example, believed that the ebb and flow of the stock market was driven by human psychology. And they are, to a large extent, probably right!

Now, we have to tell you that neither of us has ever been a great supporter of the so-called tale of the chart. We note a comment made some years ago in a *Barron*'s article that technicians do two things well: 1) they always have a reason a particular chart pattern didn't lead to the result they expected, and 2) they know where to buy graph paper cheap.

And just to add some flair to our rather skeptical view, think about the beginning of the 1980s, when Granville was touting doom and gloom and Prechter was predicting the next major bull market rally. Presumably, they were both looking at the same charts.

In any event, two factors set Prechter apart for most others. The first was his unwavering faith in the principles of what is called the "Elliot Wave" and the second was his belief in precise prophecies. These he took to the extreme, where he would not only predict market direction, but also price points at which the direction would change.

And that, too, worked for a while—up to the October 1987 crash, something Prechter failed to see coming. Which, more than anything, defines the art and science of forecasting. The science comes from reading historical chart patterns—the art is in the timing. To make a name for yourself in the forecasting business, be on the right side of the market, at a major turning point.

To the Crash, to the Crash . . .

Enter Elaine Garzarelli. Her claim to fame was her uncanny prediction of a stock market crash that came just two weeks prior to October 19, 1987.

At the time, as a money manager at Shearson Lehman Hutton Inc. (she is no longer employed as a money manager at Shearson and is currently an independent money manager), she took the bulk of her clients out of the stock market during the first week of October 1987. In fact, records show that Garzarelli predicted, on October 13, 1987, that a serious stock market crash was imminent.

Somehow forgotten by the Garzarelli faithful were her predictions immediately following the stock market crash. According to her charts, the October 19th setback was only the beginning. She predicted—and was quoted on major news wires no less—that another 300-point post-crash *decline* would come to pass, beginning on Tuesday, October 20. In hindsight, the market never went any lower, and because of her stubbornness, she missed one of the great buying opportunities of the 1980s.

Interestingly, it was some six months before Garzarelli got her clients back into the stock market. And even with 20/20 hindsight at our disposal, it's not clear that Garzarelli did her clients any great favor. In most cases they would have been just as well off holding their positions through the crash and into the next year. But then again, Ms. Garzarelli is still widely quoted and still manages a significant cache of money.

From our vantage point, the forecasters' hall of fame is not a crowded room.

The Rush for *Windows*

Rather than continue with our own retrospective on past performance, allow us to fast-forward to the present and make what we believe is one final compelling argument against following the crowd!

In the first six months of 1995, the shares of Microsoft went from $60 (prices in U.S.$) per share to, on July 17, 1995, $109 per share. This was some high-octane performance driven by expectations for the August 24, 1995, launch of *Windows 95*, the most hyped-up piece of software ever to come down the programmers' turnpike.

But here's the question: "On July 17, 1995, with the stock at $109 and investors anticipating the billions of dollars in profits that would flow to Microsoft in the first year—the company having just reported record second-quarter profits in 1995—do you buy the stock?"

Again forgetting the "buy on the rumor, sell on the news" cliché, many people did! Within two days (July 19, 1995) of hitting the $109 per share price, the stock fell to an intra-day low of $88^3/4, and closed at $94^1/2 for a two-day loss of 13.3%.

Now with that backdrop, we find in the July 20, 1995, edition of *The Wall Street Journal*, the following articles:

> *Item*: "The Street had been talking about a possible 20%-25% correction in technology prices since the beginning of the year. After yesterday's decline, a widely watched semiconductor index still stands at more than double its low of the past year, although it's down more than 8% from the peak."

> *Item*: How low do some of the most bearish investors think technology stocks could go? "One big bear on technology, who asked not to be named, pointed out that Microsoft's

200-day moving average is around 75 (it ended at $94^1/2$, off $7^1/4$). Some pros believe the 200-day average of a stock's price action represents the short-term floor for its price."

Item: Part of what spooks Mr. Kassen and lots of other investors is that Intel and Microsoft, for example, are two of the most widely owned stocks in the U.S. at the moment. Indeed, they have been trading at or near records recently. "Look at the number of managers with 40% or 70% of their funds in technology," he says. "You have to wonder. They can't get any bigger. And are there more buyers out there who can take those kinds of positions?"

Now ask yourself, do you buy the stock at this point? In the real world—not including Wall Street and Bay Street—nothing much had changed. Microsoft was going to, and in fact did, release *Windows 95* on time. On July 20, Microsoft was still running on all cylinders and, in fact, not many analysts had reduced their 1996 earnings estimates. And then, had you bought at $109 per share, do you buy more when it falls to $$88^3/4$?

With the benefit of 20/20 hindsight, most investors would have no difficulty justifying a decision to buy the stock. However, without the benefit of that so-called crystal ball, the decision to buy or sell hangs on your ability to forecast the future, at a time when the future is clouded by conflicting reports in the financial press.

Solving the Investment Dilemma

We think there is a better approach, one that is not driven by a decision to buy or sell Microsoft, or any other stock for that matter. Concentrate, instead, on establishing some reasonable long-term performance objectives within the context of your ability to tolerate risk—something, we believe, that is the most important, and difficult, financial decision you will ever make.

Having made a decision to establish a plan, get in the practice of having regular financial checkups. And we're not talking about making small changes to the portfolio on a daily basis, or scanning the newspapers for the most recent stock and mutual fund quotes. We're talking about set intervals, like once a year, or perhaps semi-annually or quarterly. And, most important, should your personal circumstances change. In other words, often enough to keep your fingers on the pulse and satisfy yourself that, for the long term, you are moving in the right direction.

And while that too may seem overwhelming, fear not, because *we're here to help!* By purchasing this book, you've just taken the first step toward a top-down investment management program that we believe will guide you along the road to financial freedom.

The FundLine Advisor is more than just a book about mutual funds. Think of it as your one-stop shopping guide to investment management. Updated every year, this book will provide you with an annual financial checkup and, more than that, will act as your guide every step along the way. We will show you how to get ahead with your money and provide you with the tools to help you get your money working for you, rather than you working for it.

We will help you to see the big investment picture and not get caught up in the emotions of the moment; to buy when everyone is standing on the sidelines; to know how to invest for the long term and what to invest in. In short, we will take you step-by-step through the world of investing with a long-term investment plan that will meet your objectives and let you sleep at night.

These are the principles on which this book is built. You will, in the chapters that follow, learn all you need to know about personal investing and portfolio construction. And you won't have to predict changes in the business cycle, the direction of interest rates, the outlook for inflation or whether or not Microsoft stock will rise or fall.

We'll help you establish long-term goals, walk you through a lesson in risk management and examine the need for self-discipline. And having developed a reasonable long-range investment plan, we'll construct a portfolio to get you from here to there, using a top-down approach that focuses on you, rather than on your investments.

The Croft–Kirzner Approach

Defining Your Investment Goals
Chapter 1

Understanding Risk
Chapter 2

Defining Your Tolerance for Risk
Chapter 3

Learning the Mutual Fund Basics
Chapters 4 through 8

Building Your Personal Mutual Fund Portfolio
Chapters 9 through 12

When it comes to selecting specific investments, you can pick and choose from our list of Best Bet Funds in each category, judged not solely on the basis of past performance, but in terms of risk-adjusted performance. The funds were chosen using two criteria:

1. The proprietary Croft-Kirzner Rating that evaluates funds on the basis of risk-adjusted performance and consistency. To be included in this category, the funds must have at least a three-year track record, although we occasionally provide honorable mentions—without providing a score—for funds with specific objectives that we think will pay off in the year ahead.

2. An examination of each fund in terms of investment style and the approach of the fund's management, as defined by our exclusive FundLine. In other words, the FundLine provides the basis to mix and match funds within your portfolio, providing solid returns with the least amount of risk.

As for the ongoing management of your portfolio, you need to simply purchase the yearly updates to this book. In these updates, we will provide our ideal asset mix in terms of what percentage you should commit to each asset class for the year ahead, and update the Best Bet list of funds in each category.

You Be the Guide

You may choose to read each chapter in sequence, to make sure you understand the fundamentals that support our approach to investment planning. For example, Chapter 2, "Understanding Risk," provides an in-depth discussion of risk. Chapter 4, "Mutual Fund Categories," looks at the essentials of mutual fund investing and discusses the merits of load versus no-load funds.

If you are a fairly sophisticated investor, you may want to skip the fundamentals and move right through the chapters that lay out your personal investment plan. Either way, we'll be there by your side.

For our Best Bet Funds list (see Appendix), we used statistics gleaned from Southam's database of funds. Of course, we cut the potential candidates down from more than 1,250-plus to fewer than 100, all having—with rare exceptions—at least a three-year track record. We want to recommend only the top funds in each category and then provide the tools to mix and match investment styles within your portfolio.

As mentioned, we are using the proprietary Croft-Kirzner rating system to rank funds from 1 (Best) to 5 (Worst) based on a risk-adjusted performance and their consistency relative to their benchmark. But we caution that our rating is but one step in the process. While the rating defines how well a fund manager has balanced risk and return in the past, it examines each fund on its own merit and not within the context of a portfolio.

That's where the FundLine comes in. The FundLine examines each fund from 24 different perspectives, including where the fund fits within a specific asset class, what geographic region the fund focuses on (i.e., Latin America, Europe, Far East, North America, etc.) and what type of investment style is practiced by management.

To properly construct a portfolio of funds, you want to mix and match top-performing funds that fill as many of those categories as possible. By doing that, you will have a personalized portfolio diversified by asset class, geographic region, fund objectives and management style—in short, a well-balanced personalized portfolio that should remain strong through all the different phases of a business cycle. We'll also give you some advice on how to fine-tune your portfolio using our economic outlook (Chapter 12), which will be updated annually.

For even a casual observer, the results of not planning for the future and investing wisely should be obvious. Looking for government handouts during your retirement years is not a very appealing alternative—especially when you can create your own situation with some judicious planning now.

The issue is not whether to invest; it is how to overcome the real or imagined hazards of investing. Don't walk away from the capital markets because the game is too complex. It needn't be!

PART I

Your Investment Persona

CHAPTER ONE

Personal Investing: Pillars and Perils

Investor Personalities

We believe the first step in any sensible investment program and, we might add, one of the more difficult aspects of investment management, is gaining some understanding of your investment personality. *Your investment personality dictates how well you can tolerate risk and, more important, lays the foundation for you to quantify the trade-off between risk and return.*

For example, conservative investors are more interested in not losing money than in earning big returns. Aggressive investors, on the other hand, are willing to forgo safety of principal and income in search of greater profits. Seems simple enough, but in reality most investors fall somewhere between these two extremes. Even conservative investors have to be willing to assume some risk, and some aggressive investors may not have the financial wherewithal to handle the roller coaster action of the stock market. There are, as you might expect, trade-offs. Our approach is to look at investment management the same way a professional money manager looks at it. And to that end, we present four personal investment cornerstones as seen in Figure 1.1.

Figure 1.1: PERSONAL INVESTMENT CORNERSTONES

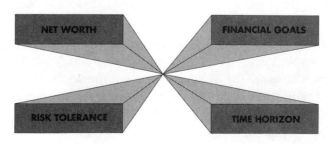

(Note: Pension fund managers think of "Net Worth" as "Assets under Administration." "Financial Goals" becomes the "Required Rate of Return." "Risk Tolerance" for the professional pension fund manager is evaluated using actuarial studies to determine cash inflows and outflows, year over year. The final issue is "Time Horizon," which for a pension fund manager is unlimited. As individual investors, we have a more defined time horizon.)

We offer six distinct investment personality categories, and present at the end of Chapter 3 an optimum asset mix for each. The asset mix is the second step down the road to independent financial freedom.

1. *Safety* investors are uncomfortable with risk. They lean toward investments that provide regular returns, even if these returns are low. Their attitude toward financial planning is apprehensive and, at times, pessimistic. Whereas others dream of wealth when they invest, safety investors are motivated by the dread of poverty.

2. *Safety/Income* investors are concerned about safety, but often require a specific income stream to meet their financial obligations. They recognize the need for a trade-off. Safety/Income investors want to make certain their principal investment is secure, but share a keen interest in the income that can be generated by that principal investment. We find many retirees who may be living off a fixed income and require the receipts from their portfolio to supplement their living standards in this investment category.

3. *Income/Growth* investors focus their attention primarily on the income side of the investment equation. However, unlike Safety/Income investors, the portfolio's income stream is not usually considered a critical supplement to their standard of living. At least not yet! Often we find that Income/Growth investors will reinvest the income stream into more securities within the portfolio, effectively dollar-cost averaging their investment program. Income/Growth investors understand that financial security depends on some growth being attained within the portfolio and, to that end, will spend a great deal of time understanding just how much return is required to meet their long-range financial objectives. They often set more reasonable goals that, for the most part, can be attained with their investment style.

4. *Growth/Income* investors understand that risk is a natural part of investing. With this in mind, they set out to structure the perfect portfolio, which is usually a balanced investment scheme. The assets are chosen for their ability to survive the ups and downs of the business cycle. There is one drawback, however: the portfolio is designed to be left alone. Balanced investors are often so absorbed with day-to-day survival that they neglect tomorrow's opportunities.

5. *Growth* investors are not at all concerned about income. Usually, this group of investors has a long time horizon and often a sizable net worth. The objective here is to maximize the potential growth within the portfolio, with reasonable risks. Growth investors have an appreciation about the trade-off between risk and return, and are willing to assume higher levels of risk as long as they are rewarded with greater returns.

6. *Aggressive/Growth* investors are the quick-draw artists of the investment world, fingers often poised to move from one opportunity to another. They switch from asset to asset, thriving on risk, seeking the thrills that accompany a profitable trade, and are willing to accept, or some would say, *ignore,* the risks associated with that type of investment philosophy. Aggressive/Growth investors are often young, have a reasonable income base and, although they tend to look for results over the short term, are seeking some long-term guidance.

These classifications provide us with a general overview of an investor's ability to tolerate risk. However, knowing how much risk individual investors can tolerate is only part of the task. Equally important is the need to outline specific investment goals and objectives and to examine your current net worth and income stream in order to define your goals within the context of your current financial position and time horizon. Only by understanding these four factors can you lay the foundation on which to build a long-term investment plan.

The Personality of Investing

Successful long-term investing requires a balancing act between risk and return, something we'll spend more time on in Chapter 2. For now, it's important to understand that every step up the performance ladder requires the investor to take on more risk. The goal is to 1) decide how far up the performance ladder we need to go, and 2) make sure that each step taken requires as little risk as possible.

Start this process by examining your current financial objectives. The question, of course, is where do you see yourself in 10 years? Retired and enjoying the finer things in life? Nestled in the home of your dreams? Content and pleased with the accomplishments of the past and your aspirations for the future? Or maybe you'll be climbing the career ladder and developing a successful foundation in the vocation of your choice. Perhaps your dreams include traveling to faraway places—cruising the oceans of the world in the lap of luxury, or maybe hop-scotching from country to country by air; seeing the world as you want to, with time on your side. Financial security is obviously important, but you may not feel qualified to properly manage your affairs. You've watched helplessly as inflation eats away at your savings; gotten angered as the tax man nickel-and-dimes away chunks of your earnings, so that for every step forward, you seem to be taking two steps back. But, believe it or not, you can take some decisive steps toward financial independence. The first step is to assess your current financial condition to determine your current net worth. But before firing up the calculator, you should decide whether or not to include your principal residence. The bottom line is that you need now and always will need a place to live. Of course, you may decide to rent at some point in the future. In that case, you may want to sell your principal residence and invest the tax-free profits into upgrading your lifestyle. Or, you may prefer to retain your residence and simply utilize other forms of disposable income to meet your financial requirements. If you fall into the former camp, and are clear about your long-term plans, then by all means, include the principal residence as part of your net worth. For those of you who fall into the latter camp, or simply have no plans to sell the family homestead, we suggest you do not include the family home as part of your net worth. Write down your net worth score on the chart below.

Rating Your Net Worth	**Points**
Your net worth is $5,000 or above, but less than $25,000	1
Your net worth is $25,000 or above, but less than $50,000	3
Your net worth is $50,000 or above, but less than $100,000	5
Your net worth is $100,000 or above, but less than $250,000	7
Your net worth is $250,000 or more	10
Net Worth Score	_____

Note: Ratings and scores are tabulated in Chapter 3.

Setting Your Financial Objectives

Many factors affect not only the way we view money, but the way we invest. At the outset, many of us are unclear about our financial goals, because most of us have never been taught just how important goals are in the context of investment management. We think goals are critical, because they define for us the required performance objectives.

As you might expect, there is a wide range of investment objectives. They include such things as growth of capital, protection of principal, levels of income and tax considerations. There are also short- and long-term goals, such as the future education needs of our children, retirement planning, saving for a house or simply improving our lifestyle. Take a few minutes with the family and think about some of the financial objectives you want to accomplish. Everything is on the table at this point, from a vacation in Hawaii or a new car to, perhaps, a cabin cruiser—name your own dream! Of course, aside from your financial objectives, there are issues you need to address, including retirement and, if you have children, some commitment for their college tuition. So write down your goals in order of importance and in terms of timing. For example, a trip to Hawaii may be a short-term goal, especially if you hope to take the trip within say the next five years. In fact, any goal that is to be reached within the next five years should be included on your short-term list; goals with a longer horizon should be included on the long-term list. Your children's education is a longer-term goal, and obviously retirement planning deserves some special attention.

Near-Term Goals (less than five years)

Short-Term Goals	Years to Goal	Goal Amount	Current Net Worth	Amount Required

Long-Term Goals (more than five years)

Long-Term Goals	Years to Goal	Goal Amount	Current Net Worth	Amount Required

Having put together a list of potential goals, try to rank them in terms of importance and then put some realistic costs on them. For example, your retirement income should be at least 70% of your current income and, to be safe, you should adjust that number to reflect the impact of inflation. Inflation is a tricky subject to tackle, especially when attempting to forecast cost increases over long periods of time. In recent years, for example, the cost of a college education has increased at more than twice the rate of inflation. That has led some financial advisors and planners to attach an above-average assumed rate of inflation to the current tuition level, sometimes in the 7% per annum range. While we agree that it is important to factor some reasonable inflation assumptions into future education costs, we're not sure that 7% is a reasonable long-range forecast. At a 7% rate of increase, a university education that costs $10,000 today will cost about $20,000 in 10 years' time, or $40,000 by the year 2016. If your child is two feet tall at one year of age, and four feet tall at age six, that equates to a 14% annual growth rate. If we maintained that assumption for the next five years, your child would be over eight feet tall at age eleven, and should be receiving scholarship offers to play collegiate basketball. Past trends, then, are not necessarily indicative of the future. For example, if government cutbacks mean fewer students can afford to attend college or university, that will eventually create cash-flow problems at these institutions and may bring back some good old-fashioned cost-cutting measures and, by extension, some competitive tuition fees. Fixing your rate of return assumes that you never need to review your investment objectives and goals. But the fact is that, over time, they change. A regular annual review is in order and, of course, if personal circumstances change—like a death in the family, marriage, divorce, the birth of a child—you will need to take a few moments to re-think your priorities. Finally, it is always important to keep some funds set aside for emergencies. A good rule of thumb is to have enough savings to meet three to six months' worth of expenses. With that in mind, below is a goal calculation worksheet which can help you determine how much you need to set aside for specific goals. You will need to use some of the numbers from the tables at the end of this chapter to help you complete the worksheet.

GOAL CALCULATION WORKSHEET #1

1 Name your goal:

2 How much money does this goal require? _____ (in today's dollars)

3 How much have you already saved for this goal? _____

4 How long do you have to meet this goal? _____ (in years)

5 Projected value of current investments _____ (enter factor from Table 1.1)

6 Future value of current savings _____ (multiply line 3 by line 5)

7 How much additional capital is required? _____ (subtract line 6 from line 2)

8 Calculate annual savings required _____ (enter factor from Table 1.2)

9 Annual savings required to meet goal _____ (multiply line 7 by line 8)

10 Monthly savings required to reach your goal _____ (divide line 9 by the number 12)

GOAL CALCULATION WORKSHEET #2

1	Name your goal:	Buy a car	
2	How much money does this goal require?	$35,000.00	(in today's dollars)
3	How much have you already saved for this goal?	$10,000.00	
4	How long do you have to meet this goal?	5	(in years)
5	Projected value of current investments	1.47	(enter factor from Table 1.1)
6	Future value of current savings	$14,700.00	(multiply line 3 by line 5)
7	How much additional capital is required?	$20,300.00	(subtract line 6 from line 2)
8	Calculate annual savings required	0.19	(enter factor from Table 1.2)
9	Annual savings required to meet goal	$3,857.00	(multiply line 7 by line 8)
10	Monthly savings required to reach your goal	$321.42	(divide line 9 by the number 12)

(Source: adapted from *Worth Magazine*)

The Magic of Compounding

Having established some financial goals and assessing their costs, we need to look more closely at rates of return, because how much you need to earn on your investments, and over what period of time, dictates how far up the performance ladder we need to go.

And that also plays a role in helping to establish financial goals that are reasonable. We can't say, for example, that we want to be a millionaire someday. It may be possible to reach that goal, but how much do we need to set aside, over what period of time and at what rate of return? Having figured that out, is it realistic? Having sustainable expectations is important, because we need to establish some successes in order to maintain a solid footing on our way to financial independence. Failing to meet unrealistic expectations can be discouraging, and that can have a negative impact on your long-range plans.

Realities and Expectations of Compounding

One of the world's wealthiest bankers, Baron Rothschild, was once asked if he could name the Seven Wonders of the World. As was his style, the answer was brief and to the point: "I cannot recall all the world's Seven Wonders, but let me suggest to you the eighth wonder of the world. It can be utilized by each and every one of us to get what we want. It is compound interest."

The concept of compound interest is not that difficult. Suppose you place money in an investment that pays interest compounded annually. During the first year, you would earn interest on the principal. However, in subsequent years, you would earn interest not only on the original principal, but also on the interest earned in the first year. For example: Assume that you invested $1,000 today, at 10% interest, compounded annually. At the end of the first year, your investment would have grown to $1,100. This represents the original investment ($1,000) plus $100 ($1000 x 1.10) interest earned on the principal. Assume you reinvested the entire amount for another year; the investment would appreciate to $1,210 ($1,100 x 1.10). During the second year, you earned $100 interest on the original investment, plus $10 interest on the interest earned in the first year. The amount at the end of two years can be broken down as follows:

Original investment	$1,000.00
First year's interest	100.00
Second year's interest on original investment	100.00
Second year's interest on interest	10.00
Total Return	**$1,210.00**

Reinvestment for the third year would produce $1,331.00 ($1,210 x 1.10). The third year's interest of $121 accounts for $100 on the original principal, plus $21 on the interest earned during the first two years. The interest-on-interest component of the investment is what causes the snowballing effect on the growth of money.

To underscore the importance of this, assume the original $1,000 investment was left to compound for 50 years. The investment would have grown to $117,390.85. The interest payable in the 50th year would be made up of $100 on the original principal, plus $10,671.89 on the $105,781.96 interest earned during the first 49 years.

The Million-Dollar Goal

Suppose you had set aside an extra $1,000 five years ago. Now suppose you left it in a savings account earning, say, 6% interest, compounded annually. That money would be worth $1,338.23 today. By placing it in a term deposit earning 10% interest, compounded annually, that $1,000 would have grown to $1,610.51 today.

Forget about finding an extra $1,000, and instead commit to saving, say, $100 a month at 8% interest. In five years, that $100 per month will be worth $7,347.68. Shop around at a few more financial institutions, and you might get 10% interest on $100 per month. At that rate, your savings program would net you $7,743.71 after five years. The longer that money is left to compound, the more dramatic the effect on the value of your portfolio. Setting aside $100 per month for 10 years at 8% interest leaves you with a nest egg of $18,294.60; at 10% interest, you would have $20,484.50. Once you start saving, the condition becomes contagious, which is why we suggest you set up a regular savings plan and stick to it. And it's important that your savings do not force you to change your lifestyle. Save an amount that you can live with, and over time it will become second nature. Now let's see what is required for our millionaire status. Let's begin with a savings program of $200 per month, at an interest rate of 10% per year. At that rate, it will take you 37.75 years to reach your million-dollar goal. Earn 12% on your $200 per month, and it takes just under 33 years to reach that goal. If you can save $400 per month and earn 12% per year, it will take you just over 27 years to reach $1 million; at 10%, it will take just under 31 years.

The Rule of 72

We trust you get the picture. It is one thing to plan for the future, but it is quite another to understand what it will take to meet those goals. Needless to say, there are a number of formulas that can be used to calculate the future value of a lump sum of money put aside today.

But while formulas can be useful in determining the value of an investment at some point in the future, they are not a tool that you carry with you to the local bank or trust company. As you probably guessed, then, there is an easier way to calculate the future value of a fixed investment today. It is known as the "Rule of 72." Simply stated, if you divide the number 72 by the return on a particular investment, it will tell you how many years it will take for your money to double. For example, if the current rate of return was 9%, your funds would double in 8 years (72 divided by 9 = 8). If the interest rate is 12%, your original investment would double every 6 years (72 divided by 12 = 6). Now, assuming you invested $10,000 in a bond fund that, historically, has been compounding at 10% a year; how soon will your money double? The answer is 7.2 years (72 divided by 10). How about this? Suppose you have $10,000, and you want to double this amount in 10 years to fund your retirement nest egg. What compound rate of return must you earn? Divide 72 by the number of years, and you get 7.2%. To double it in 5 years, you'll have to earn an annual return of 14.4% on your investment (72 divided by 5). Simplicity at work, yet the Rule of 72 illustrates some powerful investment principles, most notably the magic of compounding. It also drives home the advantages of mutual funds, where dividends and interest can be automatically reinvested into additional shares. Interest makes your investments grow; compound interest makes them grow faster. And how about the role 72 plays in assessing the impact of changes in the level of your potential return? Money compounding at 6% annually will take 12 years to double; compounding at 12% it will double in half the time. The flip side of this compounding debate is the impact inflation can have on your investments. And there, too, the Rule of 72 plays a role. An inflation rate of 3% means that a dollar today will be worth roughly 50 cents in 24 years. A 5% inflation rate means that your cost of living will double every 14.4 years. Tell that to a 40-year-old who is just beginning to establish a retirement fund.

Rating Your Financial Objectives

Retirement planning is a bit more complex in that the goal is usually a longer-term issue. Then there is the question of whether your investment portfolio is compounding inside or outside an RRSP or some other tax-sheltered investment vehicle. Moreover, the accumulation of wealth is but the first step in the investment process. Once you have accumulated enough wealth to retire, you need to maintain an investment portfolio in order to generate sufficient income so as to protect your principle while also providing a certain level of income.

RETIREMENT PLANNER

1	Current income	_____	
2	Annual retirement income goal	_____	(in today's dollars)
3	How many years to retirement?	_____	
4	Inflation factor	_____	(factor from Table 1.4)
5	Annual retirement income goal (inflation adjusted)	_____	(multiply line 2 by line 4)
6	Amount required to support retirement income	_____	(multiply line 5 by 10)
7	How much have you currently set aside for this goal?	_____	
8	Projected value of current investments	_____	(enter factor from Table 1.1 or Table 1.3)
9	Future value of current savings	_____	(multiply line 7 by line 8)
10	How much additional capital is required?	_____	(subtract line 9 from line 6)
11	Calculate annual savings required	_____	(enter factor from Table 1.2)
12	Annual savings required to meet goal	_____	(multiply line 10 by line 11)
13	Monthly savings required to reach your goal	_____	(divide line 12 by 12)

SAMPLE RETIREMENT PLANNER

1	Current income	$50,000.00	
2	Annual retirement income goal	$40,000.00	(today's dollars)
3	How many years to retirement?	20	
4	Inflation factor	1.64	(factor from Table 1.4)
5	Annual retirement income goal (inflation adjusted)	$65,600.00	(multiply line 2 by line 4)
6	Amount required to support retirement income	$656,000.00	(multiply line 5 by 10)
7	How much have you currently set aside for this goal?	$150,000.00	

8	Projected value of current investments	2.92	(enter factor from Table 1.1 or Table 1.3)
9	Future value of current savings	$438,000.00	(multiply line 7 by line 8)
10	How much additional capital is required?	$218,000.00	(subtract line 9 from line 6)
11	Calculate annual savings required	0.02	(enter factor from Table 1.2)
12	Annual savings required to meet goal	$4,360.00	(multiply line 10 by line 11)
13	Monthly savings required to reach your goal	$363.33	(divide line 12 by 12)

(Source: adapted from *Worth Magazine*)

For most of us, the longest-term financial goal is our retirement. And, in all likelihood, we will be drawing on our retirement income long after having met our shorter-term goals. The point being, our retirement goal will be financed with income left over after meeting our shorter-term goals.

With that in mind, we need to determine the compound annual rate of return you require to meet your retirement objective (refer back to the last line on your retirement planner).

Required Rate of Return	Score
If required compound return is 6% or less	1
If required compound return is more than 6%, but less than or equal to 8%	5
If required compound return is more than 8%, but less than or equal to 10%	10
If required compound return is more than 10%, but less than or equal to 11%	15
If required compound return is greater than 11%	20

Financial Objective Score _____

Summary

Defining your goals is an important part of investment planning. Armed with this information, you have an understanding of where you want to get to. Chapter 3 will help you to evaluate how much risk you are willing to assume in order to attain your stated goals.

As long as you are willing to move forward with an understanding that risk and return are two sides of the same investment coin, then you will become a successful long-term investor—perhaps even in spite of yourself!

Table 1.1: COMPOUNDING FACTORS FOR CURRENT SAVINGS (NOT TAX SHELTERED)

Year	4%	5%	6%	7%	8%	9%	10%	11%
1	1.02	1.03	1.03	1.04	1.04	1.05	1.05	1.06
2	1.04	1.05	1.06	1.07	1.08	1.09	1.10	1.11
3	1.06	1.08	1.09	1.11	1.12	1.14	1.16	1.17
4	1.08	1.10	1.13	1.15	1.17	1.19	1.22	1.24
5	1.10	1.13	1.16	1.19	1.22	1.25	1.28	1.31
6	1.13	1.16	1.19	1.23	1.27	1.30	1.34	1.38
7	1.15	1.19	1.23	1.27	1.32	1.36	1.41	1.45
8	1.17	1.22	1.27	1.32	1.37	1.42	1.48	1.53
9	1.20	1.25	1.30	1.36	1.42	1.49	1.55	1.62
10	1.22	1.28	1.34	1.41	1.48	1.55	1.63	1.71
15	1.35	1.45	1.56	1.68	1.80	1.94	2.08	2.23
20	1.49	1.64	1.81	1.99	2.19	2.41	2.65	2.92

Table 1.2: FACTORS TO DETERMINE HOW MUCH ADDITIONAL CAPITAL IS REQUIRED

Year	4%	5%	6%	7%	8%	9%	10%	11%
1	1.00	1.00	1.00	1.00	1.00	1.00	1.00	1.00
2	0.50	0.50	0.50	0.49	0.49	0.49	0.49	0.48
3	0.33	0.33	0.33	0.32	0.32	0.32	0.31	0.31
4	0.25	0.25	0.24	0.24	0.24	0.23	0.23	0.23
5	0.20	0.20	0.19	0.19	0.19	0.18	0.18	0.17
6	0.17	0.16	0.16	0.16	0.15	0.15	0.14	0.14
7	0.14	0.14	0.14	0.13	0.13	0.12	0.12	0.12
8	0.13	0.12	0.12	0.11	0.11	0.11	0.10	0.10
9	0.11	0.11	0.10	0.10	0.09	0.09	0.09	0.08
10	0.10	0.10	0.09	0.09	0.08	0.08	0.08	0.07
15	0.07	0.06	0.06	0.05	0.05	0.05	0.04	0.04
20	0.05	0.05	0.04	0.04	0.03	0.03	0.03	0.02
25	0.04	0.04	0.03	0.03	0.02	0.02	0.02	0.02
30	0.03	0.03	0.03	0.02	0.02	0.02	0.01	0.01
35	0.03	0.02	0.02	0.02	0.01	0.01	0.01	0.01
40	0.03	0.02	0.02	0.01	0.01	0.01	0.01	0.01

Table 1.3: RETIREMENT FACTORS FOR CURRENT SAVINGS (TAX SHELTERED)

Year	4%	5%	6%	7%	8%	9%	10%	11%
1	1.04	1.05	1.06	1.07	1.08	1.09	1.10	1.11
3	1.12	1.16	1.19	1.23	1.26	1.30	1.33	1.37
5	1.22	1.28	1.34	1.40	1.47	1.54	1.61	1.69
7	1.32	1.41	1.50	1.61	1.71	1.83	1.95	2.08
9	1.42	1.55	1.69	1.84	2.00	2.17	2.36	2.56
11	1.54	1.71	1.90	2.10	2.33	2.58	2.85	3.15
13	1.67	1.89	2.13	2.41	2.72	3.07	3.45	3.88
15	1.80	2.08	2.40	2.76	3.17	3.64	4.18	4.78
17	1.95	2.29	2.69	3.16	3.70	4.33	5.05	5.90
19	2.11	2.53	3.03	3.62	4.32	5.14	6.12	7.26
21	2.28	2.79	3.40	4.14	5.03	6.11	7.40	8.95
23	2.46	3.07	3.82	4.74	5.87	7.26	8.95	11.03
25	2.67	3.39	4.29	5.43	6.85	8.62	10.83	13.59
27	2.88	3.73	4.82	6.21	7.99	10.25	13.11	16.74
29	3.12	4.12	5.42	7.11	9.32	12.17	15.86	20.62
31	3.37	4.54	6.09	8.15	10.87	14.46	19.19	25.41
33	3.65	5.00	6.84	9.33	12.68	17.18	23.23	31.31
35	3.95	5.52	7.69	10.68	14.79	20.41	28.10	38.57

Table 1.4: INFLATION FACTORS

Year	1.00%	1.50%	2.00%	2.50%	3.00%	3.50%	4.00%
1	1.01	1.02	1.02	1.03	1.03	1.04	1.04
2	1.02	1.03	1.04	1.05	1.06	1.07	1.08
3	1.03	1.05	1.06	1.08	1.09	1.11	1.12
4	1.04	1.06	1.08	1.10	1.13	1.15	1.17
5	1.05	1.08	1.10	1.13	1.16	1.19	1.22
6	1.06	1.09	1.13	1.16	1.19	1.23	1.27
7	1.07	1.11	1.15	1.19	1.23	1.27	1.32
8	1.08	1.13	1.17	1.22	1.27	1.32	1.37
9	1.09	1.14	1.20	1.25	1.30	1.36	1.42
10	1.10	1.16	1.22	1.28	1.34	1.41	1.48
11	1.12	1.18	1.24	1.31	1.38	1.46	1.54
12	1.13	1.20	1.27	1.34	1.43	1.51	1.60
13	1.14	1.21	1.29	1.38	1.47	1.56	1.67
14	1.15	1.23	1.32	1.41	1.51	1.62	1.73
15	1.16	1.25	1.35	1.45	1.56	1.68	1.80
16	1.17	1.27	1.37	1.48	1.60	1.73	1.87
17	1.18	1.29	1.40	1.52	1.65	1.79	1.95
18	1.20	1.31	1.43	1.56	1.70	1.86	2.03
19	1.21	1.33	1.46	1.60	1.75	1.92	2.11
20	1.22	1.35	1.49	1.64	1.81	1.99	2.19
21	1.23	1.37	1.52	1.68	1.86	2.06	2.28
22	1.24	1.39	1.55	1.72	1.92	2.13	2.37
23	1.26	1.41	1.58	1.76	1.97	2.21	2.46
24	1.27	1.43	1.61	1.81	2.03	2.28	2.56
25	1.28	1.45	1.64	1.85	2.09	2.36	2.67
26	1.30	1.47	1.67	1.90	2.16	2.45	2.77
27	1.31	1.49	1.71	1.95	2.22	2.53	2.88
28	1.32	1.52	1.74	2.00	2.29	2.62	3.00
29	1.33	1.54	1.78	2.05	2.36	2.71	3.12
30	1.35	1.56	1.81	2.10	2.43	2.81	3.24

CHAPTER TWO

Understanding Risk

*"I want a very careful Investment Advisor—one who doesn't
take the slightest risk," warned the would-be client.*

"I'm your man, sir," said the advisor. "Can I have my fee in advance?"

Introduction

When a scientist combines hydrogen, sulphur and oxygen in particular proportions under controlled laboratory conditions, he produces sulphuric acid. This is a scientific fact, applicable on earth under known conditions. This formula began as theory and was followed by empirical observation that the result was always the same.

However, in the financial world, there is no such certainty. Over long periods of time (25-plus years), stocks have yielded higher returns than bonds, and bonds have outperformed Treasury bills (T-bills). This is likely to be the case in the future.

What is uncertain, however, is what will happen in shorter time periods, under different economic conditions. For example, during periods of high interest rates, Treasury bills may realize more significant returns than stocks. In periods of low interest rates, the reverse may be true. Differences in yield are also unpredictable. The returns on all financial assets are impacted by unpredictable and uncertain future events, which implies that past performance data for mutual funds and benchmark indexes must be interpreted with caution. There is no guarantee that the future will reflect the past.

What careful analysis of past data does, however, is provide clues to the future. We can discover those funds and their fund managers that did indeed reward their investors with returns appropriate for the risk class, and justified their management fees and fund commissions. The key is to understand risk and be able to discuss it in the context of performance.

Understanding Risk

Risk is a formidable concept—hard to define, more difficult to quantify. Yet it is arguably the single most important aspect of investing. Why? Because risk defines how volatile investments will be, and in terms of portfolio management, the kind and quantity of risk you are willing to accept will have a dramatic impact on your eventual rate of return.

Understanding the principles of risk and, more important, your level of risk tolerance, will help you avoid making investment decisions when emotions are running high. You will be less likely to sell because of fear, or to buy on a whim. This is the premise behind the Risk Assessment Profile you will fill out in Chapter 3.

In the end, solid long-term investment planning requires an understanding of what we like to think of as the "investor's sleep quotient." How much risk can you tolerate without lying awake at night worrying about your investments?

When we talk about quantifying investment risk, we are really talking about volatility. Even novice investors recognize that short-term bond funds are relatively safe investments. In terms of volatility, the price of most short-term bond funds will not fluctuate widely and will provide monthly dividend reinvestments. The price today will not be that much different from what it was yesterday, last week, last month or, in some cases, last year.

Still, even a low-risk investment has a cost. The fact that short-term bond funds do not fluctuate widely also means that unit holders will not likely reap the benefits of huge capital gains from one year to the next. In short, you must accept limited potential reward in order to attain safety of principal.

Further, we have to understand that there is no such thing as a risk-free investment. Even with Government of Canada Treasury bills, bank accounts or money market mutual funds, you must, as we have seen, accept the low probability of real capital growth.

On the other hand, if you invest in highly leveraged commodities or financial futures, you would be justified in expecting your assets to increase at a more rapid pace than your short-term bond fund. But then the risk in the futures market also means that you could lose your entire investment, and then some.

It isn't enough to know how various securities will perform at different stages in the business cycle. Beyond looking at the expected rate of return, we have to look at the variability of those returns, or the odds that you would actually earn that rate of return. As you might expect, analysts evaluate those odds by looking at the "variability of returns," which is how we define risk.

Understanding how much the total return for a particular asset is likely to vary from one year to the next is as important as the return itself. It is one thing to say you want to earn 15% a year; it is quite another to say that you do not want to lose your principal. There has to be some middle ground, some form of risk/reward trade-off. Unfortunately, most investors avoid any discussion of risk because, for the most part, they know very little about it. Because we think it is so important, we will spend some time in this chapter defining risk, both statistically and in terms of real-world investing.

Types of Risk

Risk is not just a question of how we view a particular investment, or whether that investment will return a set amount. Risk also takes into account such things as the business cycle, tax burdens and inflation. Indeed, there are a number of risk factors that can be quantified:

1. **Business risk** covers a number of issues, but primarily means a decline in the earning power of the corporation. On a company-specific level, this risk could take the form of a strike, a rise in fuel costs (which would impact the airline industry) or perhaps, as was the case with Exxon, an oil spill. It also includes the risk that a business cannot meet its obligations and defaults.

2. **Market risk** affects virtually all shares and any other investment asset that has an active secondary market. October 19, 1987, was a classic case of market risk. Because the market sold off sharply, virtually all shares declined, whether or not there was any change in a company's long-term prospects. The bond market works much the same way. When the level of interest rates changes, it affects the price of all bonds, whether they are issued by governments or corporations.

3. **Liquidity risk** is the risk of not being able to sell your investment quickly. A house is a good example of an asset that is not liquid, because there is no active secondary market in which to sell it. In other words, when selling your house, you need to find an agent—unless, of course, you are going it alone—and the agent needs to ferret out prospective buyers. That all takes time. So assets such as houses or collectibles, for which there is no secondary market, have poor liquidity.

An active secondary market simply means that there are always investors willing to buy and sell your investment. With stocks and mutual funds, for example, there are always willing buyers and sellers, and the prices they are willing to pay are always posted. As such, you can instantly sell your stocks or mutual funds with a simple phone call, and can receive cash for the sale usually within three business days.

4. **Inflation**, which, as we have already seen, affects the performance of nearly all investments.

5. **Interest rate risk** is the risk that the price of your security will fall as interest rates rise.

6. **Political risk** can come from the domestic side, with tax increases, changes in tariffs, or subsidy policies. It can also come from other parts of the world if national security or world stability is threatened.

Table 2.1: TYPES OF RISK

Investments	Business Risk	Market Risk	Liquidity Risk	Inflation Risk	Interest Rate Risk	Political Risk
Stocks and Equity Funds	Yes	Yes	No	Yes	Yes	Yes
Gov't Bond Funds	No	Yes	No	Yes	Yes	No
Corporate Bond Funds	No	Yes	No	Yes	Yes	Yes
Treasury Bills/Money Market	No	No	No	Maybe	Maybe	No
GICs	No	No	Maybe	Maybe	Maybe	No
Precious Metals Funds	No	Maybe	No	Maybe	Maybe	Yes

By using the broader definitions of risk, it is clear that T-bills and money market funds are not risk-free investments. How much importance you attach to "inflation risk" or "liquidity risk" will tell you how well these investments suit your needs. In many ways, while you are guaranteed your principal repayment and any interest along the way, you could still end up, after factoring inflation into the picture, with a negative real after-tax return.

Fortunately, because we can define risks, we can examine how each type of risk affects each asset class, and by how much. Depending on the particular security and the investor's time horizon, the impact can be quite different. Prudent investors strive to reduce risk by extending their time horizon, by spreading their investment dollars across a number of asset classes and through other diversification techniques, including spreading their dollars across geographic regions and investing in different investment management styles. And the easiest way to implement those risk-reduction techniques is through an investment in mutual funds.

Mutual funds are ideal for the investor who wants diversification and professional management, but who doesn't want to keep track of a whole bunch of different investments. But it's not as easy as it sounds, because you are still stuck with the problem of selecting the right funds. Just consider, for example, the following information that you could have gathered from data in *The Financial Post*'s Mutual Funds Performance Survey:

Over the 10-year period August 1, 1985, through July 31, 1995, the Altamira Capital Growth Fund, a Canadian RRSP-eligible equity mutual fund, earned an annual compounded rate of return for its holders of 9.6% before load fees. What that tells us is that a $10,000 investment made on August 1, 1985, would have grown to $25,009 by July 31, 1995, assuming, of course, you reinvested all of your dividend and capital gain distributions in Altamira Capital Growth Fund.

Over this same period, Prudential Growth Fund of Canada, an equity fund with similar characteristics, earned 10.2% compounded annually; $10,000 grew to $26,413. Furthermore, a portfolio of Canadian stocks as measured by the Toronto Stock Exchange 300 Composite Total Return Index showed an 8.6% return; $10,000 would have grown to $22,819. An investment in three-month Canadian Treasury bills yielded 8.9%; $10,000 would have become $23,457.

There are some obvious conclusions. First, both of these equity mutual funds compensated investors for the time value of money—each outperformed an investment in Canadian Treasury bills. Second, the managers of both funds earned their management fees (at least partially) by outperforming a randomly selected portfolio of Canadian equities as measured by that TSE 300 Composite Index. The Prudential Growth Fund of Canada appeared to have been, in retrospect, the better investment for an investor who actually held the shares for those 10 years, as it yielded a higher return than the Altamira Capital Growth Fund.

Useful information to be sure, but if we are to look only at returns, then our analysis is incomplete. Looking to the future, do we conclude that Prudential Growth Fund of Canada is now a *better buy* than Altamira Capital Growth Fund? Did its performance justify the risk inherent in the fund's portfolio over the previous 10 years? Were there, in fact, other mutual funds in the RRSP-eligible Canadian equity classification that dominated both? A deeper and more critical analysis would have been necessary before informed decisions could be made on which, if either, fund to invest in.   **– R.C.**

Performance Analysis

Suppose you are examining the past performance of XYZ, a balanced mutual fund (see Chapter 4, "Mutual Fund Categories"). The company has earned a 10-year annual compounded rate of return of 16%. Assume that the average balanced mutual fund has realized a rate of return over the same period of 12.5%. An initial reaction is to conclude that XYZ outperformed the average balanced fund, so it must be the better buy.

However, XYZ may have had a riskier portfolio than the average, and its net asset value (NAV) may have tended to fluctuate much more than the typical fund. And that means that if you had to sell XYZ at the wrong time, you could end up receiving a relatively low price. Furthermore, XYZ may very well be more vulnerable to market downturns than the average balanced fund.

The objective in mutual fund analysis is to evaluate a fund's past performance and compare that performance with funds that have the same objective, then measure the performance of all funds with the same objective against an appropriate benchmark index.

With that in mind, here are some essential factors that professionals consider when evaluating mutual fund performance.

How do you select from among the long and growing list of available mutual funds? You need both information and a consistent way of analyzing what you get. Your two major sources of mutual fund information are the prospectuses of the funds and the published performance data as found in the various newspapers and periodicals as mentioned below.

The prospectus, which you can obtain from the mutual fund itself, will outline the general investment philosophy of the fund managers, the current structure of the investment portfolio, sometimes identified by industry, (and for global and international funds, the geographic breakdown of its investments), the management fees and the names of the fund advisors.

The performance data, published in the financial press, provides for each of the thousand or so Canadian open-ended mutual funds, descriptive and analytic data, including the initial launch date of the fund, RRSP eligibility, total assets, net asset value per share, maximum entry and/or exit load fees, the tenure of the fund manager, annual compounded rate of return over various time periods, some measure of volatility or standard deviation (remember, the higher the volatility the wider the swings in net asset values and returns) and other useful material. These data are essential to compare mutual funds for decision making.

The underlying data, and indeed most or all of the calculations, can be found in Canadian publications such as *The Financial Post*'s monthly Mutual Funds Performance Survey, the quarterly Survey of Funds and *The Globe and Mail Report on Business* monthly Report on Mutual Funds. Southam newspapers also produce monthly fund inserts for a number of their regional publications, which we expect will eventually include the Croft-Kirzner Performance Index and the Croft-Kirzner Consistency Index.

In the Mutual Fund Tables, funds are classified by objectives, as stated by the fund management or the prospectus. The Canadian performance-ranking publications normally list the surveyed funds by these stated investment objectives, allowing investors to conduct their analyses on a comparative basis within fund groupings.

Although there is some consistency among the services with respect to data supplied, none of the services provides everything. Generally, either *The Financial Post*, *The Globe and Mail* or the Southam mutual fund inserts will provide enough for your needs. However, it may be necessary to utilize other services if you require some special analytic information.

The Return Side of the Investment Equation

The historic performance of mutual funds should reflect both the returns and the risk. The appropriate measure of return is straightforward; it is simply the annual compounded rate of return. Compounded annual rate of return includes the change in net asset value, plus dividend and capital gain distributions, which we assume the investor reinvests in additional units. The objective, then, is to determine the annual compounded rate of return over a specific time period.

For example, suppose that the initial net asset value of Fund A was $10.00, and you purchased 100 units; your initial investment, then, is $1,000. Assume that over the next 10 years, the dividends and capital gain distributions allow you to purchase an additional 80 units, and at the end of that 10-year period, the net asset value per share is $28. Your investment is now worth $5,040, since you own 180 units of $28.00 per unit. For those who like mathematics, the annual compounded rate of return is calculated as:

$$\$1,000 \ (1 + R)^{10} = \$5,040$$
$$R = .1756 \text{ or } 17.56\%$$

The annual compounded rate of return for this fund, which we denote as R, is then 17.56%.

No sales charges, commissions or loads are considered in the calculations that are presented in the published performance tables. However, if you are ambitious, you can translate the pre-load returns to an after-load basis by subtracting the load from the initial investment, compounding the remainder at the annual growth rate of the fund and then calculating the rate of return on the terminal value relative to the total initial investment.

For example, if Fund A had a 4% load and earned 17.56% compounded for 10 years, the after-load return is reduced to 17.10%.

The internal rate of return is fine, and certainly the impact a load has on the performance numbers is relevant, but all returns should be evaluated in light of the risk undertaken.

Richard: "Why worry about the risk of a fund? Looking back, if my mutual fund earned 17.56% per year for 10 years and my $10,000 investment grows to over $50,000, and the average fund—or a benchmark index—in the same category only earned 13% per year ($10,000 only grew to $33,946), then why be concerned about risk? My fund has done well and made me a lot of money!"

Eric: "What if you had had to sell three years ago when the market hit bottom? You would have received a very low price. High performers are usually the most volatile, meaning that their net asset values move in wide swings.

"If you are analyzing past performance to identify fund managers (or teams of managers) who exhibit above-average performance, then risk measures are very important. A fund manager who achieves a high rate of return over a specific period may have done so through sheer luck or by holding an extremely risky portfolio. That same manager may perform poorly in the future, independent of market performance, or may suffer large losses when the market is weak.

"On the other hand, fund managers who have earned above-average returns consistently, with only modest or average volatility, may have earned those returns through skill. And although there is no guarantee those same managers will perform like that in the future, there is at least past evidence of superior portfolio management skills. What you are looking for, then, is consistency—a fund that performs reasonably well during both favorable and unfavorable times.

"Keeping with the consistency theme, consider what would happen if a fund advanced by 25% and then fell by 25%. How have you done?"

Richard: "Well, logic would tell me that I broke even."

Eric: "Not on your life! You have lost over 6%! Look at the arithmetic! If you invest, say, $10,000, you end up with $12,500 after the fund rises 25% ($10,000 x 1.25 = $12,500). Now, with your fund worth $12,500, you lose 25%, and you end up with $9,375 ($12,500 x .75 = $9,375). The same result holds true if you first lose 25% and then gain 25%—you still get $9,375.

"Funds with wide swings are dangerous. The idea is to find funds that perform consistently and satisfactorily in both up and down markets, which means that we need to look at the average annual returns in order to provide an appropriate measure of comparison from one year to the next."

Measuring the Risk/Return Trade-off

You cannot avoid risk. Even a decision to do nothing has an impact on the performance of your portfolio. The choice is not to find risk-free investments, but rather to understand what types of risk you are willing to assume. But to make that decision, we must understand the trade-off between risk and return.

Beta

A number of definitions are used by investors when they approach risk. Stock market investors are probably most familiar with the term "beta." In nontechnical terms, beta is an indicator of how a fund's value has fluctuated relative to past changes in an appropriate benchmark (an equity fund, for example, might be compared with the Toronto Stock Exchange 300 Composite Total Return Index).

The higher the fund's beta, the greater the degree of fluctuation for a given change in the overall market. We assume, by definition, that the benchmark index (the TSE 300 Composite Total Return Index, in this example) has a beta of 1. A Canadian equity fund with a beta of 2 would be expected to advance twice as fast as the benchmark index in an uptrend and fall twice as fast in a downtrend.

A high beta equity fund, therefore, would be expected to realize high rates of returns when the stock market was strong, but relatively large losses when the market was weak. A low beta fund would be expected to have relatively lower rates of returns when the market was strong, but suffer smaller losses when the market was weak.

However, beta has some drawbacks, particularly when looking at a portfolio that includes a broad cross-section of assets. Here, we are more concerned with the degree of risk in each asset class (i.e., bonds, precious metals, real estate, etc.) than with the risk of a particular fund relative to its benchmark index.

Standard Deviation

To measure the variability of returns for specific funds, we enter the realm of standard deviation. Simply stated, standard deviation is the amount that a fund's price has varied from its mean or average price over a given period of time. It differs from beta in that it measures the volatility of a specific investment, and not specifically how that investment performs relative to some benchmark index.

Standard deviation is a useful measure of risk for investors who hold small, nondiversified portfolios of investments, including mutual funds. It is simple to calculate and relatively easy to understand. The information is supplied by most financial newspapers, although, to be fair, the financial press usually provides only a broad measure of standard deviation by simply classifying funds as either average, above average or below average in this risk measure relative to all of the funds in the same objective category.

Finally, there is one other caveat; standard deviation is based on past results.

STANDARD DEVIATION OR BETA?

Conventional wisdom is that if the portfolio represents merely a part of the investor's total assets, then market risk or beta is appropriate. If the portfolio represents the client's sole asset, then total risk or standard deviation should be used.

Mathematical Mumbo Jumbo or Vital Statistics?

With some apologies to all of you, we think it is important to at least show you how standard deviation is calculated. And to do that, we need to define and illustrate a few statistical tools. To keep things as simple as possible, we will look at the Trimark Canadian Fund and examine how the *Southam Source Disk* calculates standard deviation. The following percent changes in net asset values were recorded over a 36-month period ending July 1995.

Table 2.2: TRIMARK CANADIAN FUND MONTHLY RETURNS

Period	Monthly Return	Value of $10,000
Aug-92	2.71%	10,271.10
Sep-92	1.25%	10,399.80
Oct-92	2.51%	10,660.62
Nov-92	-0.37%	10,621.61
Dec-92	4.12%	11,059.64
Jan-93	3.01%	11,392.20
Feb-93	-4.67%	10,859.85
Mar-93	1.66%	11,040.55
Apr-93	-4.88%	10,502.11
May-93	0.30%	10,533.82
Jun-93	-0.36%	10,495.80
Jul-93	2.66%	10,774.56
Aug-93	6.23%	11,446.25
Sep-93	-5.75%	10,787.98
Oct-93	2.21%	11,026.61
Nov-93	-0.06%	11,019.66
Dec-93	-1.92%	10,807.97
Jan-94	-2.06%	10,585.00
Feb-94	5.17%	11,132.14
Mar-94	3.39%	11,509.97
Apr-94	1.49%	11,681.47
May-94	5.71%	12,348.36
Jun-94	-1.04%	12,220.06
Jul-94	5.05%	12,836.93
Aug-94	-1.28%	12,672.75
Sep-94	1.50%	12,863.34
Oct-94	3.17%	13,271.50
Nov-94	3.43%	13,726.44
Dec-94	5.46%	14,476.18
Jan-95	5.52%	15,275.12
Feb-95	0.41%	15,337.29
Mar-95	2.06%	15,653.86
Apr-95	1.43%	15,878.18
May-95	-2.64%	15,459.63
Jun-95	1.42%	15,678.38
Jul-95	-1.09%	15,507.64
Average Period Return	*1.27%*	

Having done those calculations, we then calculate an arithmetic mean, or as it is more commonly referred to, an "average." An average is simply the sum of all the monthly returns divided by the number of observations, which in this case is 36. The average can be found at the bottom of Table 2.2.

Variance and Standard Deviation

Variance and standard deviation define for us how far the monthly returns for the Trimark Canadian Fund varied from the average monthly return, which we know to be 1.27%. For example, in August 1992, the Trimark Canadian Fund returned -1.09%; or, put another way, Trimark deviated from its average return by -2.36%. Table 2.3 looks at the deviations from the average monthly return for the 36 periods.

Table 2.3: DEVIATIONS AND DEVIATIONS^2 FROM AVERAGE—TRIMARK CANADIAN FUND

Period	Monthly Return	Deviation	Deviation^2
Aug-92	2.71%	1.44%	0.02%
Sep-92	1.25%	-0.02%	0.00%
Oct-92	2.51%	1.24%	0.02%
Nov-92	-0.37%	-1.64%	0.03%
Dec-92	4.12%	2.85%	0.08%
Jan-93	3.01%	1.74%	0.03%
Feb-93	-4.67%	-5.94%	0.35%
Mar-93	1.66%	0.39%	0.00%
Apr-93	-4.88%	-6.15%	0.38%
May-93	0.30%	-0.97%	0.01%
Jun-93	-0.36%	-1.63%	0.03%
Jul-93	2.66%	1.38%	0.02%
Aug-93	6.23%	4.96%	0.25%
Sep-93	-5.75%	-7.02%	0.49%
Oct-93	2.21%	0.94%	0.01%
Nov-93	-0.06%	-1.33%	0.02%
Dec-93	-1.92%	-3.19%	0.10%
Jan-94	-2.06%	-3.33%	0.11%
Feb-94	5.17%	3.90%	0.15%
Mar-94	3.39%	2.12%	0.05%
Apr-94	1.49%	0.22%	0.00%
May-94	5.71%	4.44%	0.20%
Jun-94	-1.04%	-2.31%	0.05%
Jul-94	5.05%	3.78%	0.14%
Aug-94	-1.28%	-2.55%	0.07%
Sep-94	1.50%	0.23%	0.00%

Oct-94	3.17%	1.90%	0.04%
Nov-94	3.43%	2.16%	0.05%
Dec-94	5.46%	4.19%	0.18%
Jan-95	5.52%	4.25%	0.18%
Feb-95	0.41%	-0.86%	0.01%
Mar-95	2.06%	0.79%	0.01%
Apr-95	1.43%	0.16%	0.00%
May-95	-2.64%	-3.91%	0.15%
Jun-95	1.42%	0.14%	0.00%
Jul-95	-1.09%	-2.36%	0.06%

Average Monthly Return	**1.27%**
Variance = (sum of deviations^2) / 36	**0.09%**
Standard Deviation = square root of variance	**3.01%**

To compute the "average deviation" for each fund, our natural impulse is to simply add up the 36 deviations and divide by the number of observations. However, if we do that for the Trimark Canadian Fund, we end up with zero, suggesting that the fund never varied from its mean, which clearly is not the case. Of course, that the sum of the deviations equals zero defines the central tendency of an average. The sum of deviations around an arithmetic mean or average should always equal zero. The way around this problem is to square the deviations and then sum the resulting numbers. By doing that, we convert the negative deviations into positive numbers, and the larger the deviation, the larger will be the squared value of it. The squared deviations can also be found in Table 2.3.

With the squared deviations from Table 2.3, we can now calculate the variance for our Trimark Canadian Fund. Variance is simply the sum of the squared deviations divided by the number of observations:

$$\text{Variance} = 3.26\% \quad 36 \text{ observations} = .091\%$$

The standard deviation is simply the square root of the variance:

$$\text{Standard Deviation} = \sqrt{.00091} = .0301 \text{ or } 3.01\%$$

Statistically, 68% of all observations in a normal distribution are expected to lie within one standard deviation of the mean. We would expect, given a normal distribution of returns, that in 68% of all observations, the monthly return of the Trimark Canadian Fund will fall between +4.28% (1.27% average plus 3.01% standard deviation = +4.28%), or -1.74% (1.27% average return minus 3.01% standard deviation = -1.74%).

The true test of how well the model works can be seen by looking at observations within two standard deviations of the average. We would expect that in 95% of all cases, the monthly performance of the Trimark Canadian Fund will fall within two standard deviations of the average. Using the Trimark Canadian Fund example, two standard deviations represent a monthly return that could be as high as 7.29% (6.02% *plus* 1.27% average), or as low as -4.75% (1.27% average *less* 6.02%). Note that in Table 2.3, over the 36 monthly returns, Trimark Canadian Fund never exceeded either the upside or downside boundary as defined by our two standard deviations from the mean.

Understanding standard deviation gives us an idea how much the price of a fund might vary from one month to the next. We think that adds an important element to the discussion for investors who want to know not only what the performance numbers look like, but what the manager had to do to achieve those results. However, use care when looking at a fund's historical standard deviation, because like past performance numbers, historical measurements only tell you what happened—not what may happen in the future.

Correlation

By now you've probably learned more than you ever wanted to know about statistics. And you're probably thinking, why? Are these stats really necessary?

If it helps, we understand your concerns and appreciate your indulgence. We also believe that it is imperative that you become familiar with the fundamental concepts in this discussion, because these are the principles that underpin a number of our performance measurement systems—specifically, how we rank mutual fund performance on a risk-adjusted basis.

With that in mind, we ask you to consider one other concept: correlation. Simply stated, correlation defines how closely the performance of one fund tracks the performance of another. For example, suppose that we had two funds in our portfolio, and the performance of each fund was identical (see Table 2.4).

Table 2.4: PERFECT POSITIVE CORRELATION OF FUND A AND FUND B

Period	Fund A Monthly Return	Fund B Monthly Return	Value of $10,000.00
Aug-94	1.00%	1.00%	10,100.00
Sep-94	0.50%	0.50%	10,150.50
Oct-94	0.00%	0.00%	10,150.50
Nov-94	-1.00%	-1.00%	10,049.00
Dec-94	2.00%	2.00%	10,249.97
Jan-95	1.50%	1.50%	10,403.72
Feb-95	1.00%	1.00%	10,507.76
Mar-95	0.50%	0.50%	10,560.30
Apr-95	0.00%	0.00%	10,560.30
May-95	-1.00%	-1.00%	10,454.70
Jun-95	2.00%	2.00%	10,663.79
Jul-95	1.50%	1.50%	10,823.75

	Fund A	Fund B	Combined Fund A and Fund B
Average Return	0.67%	0.67%	0.67%
Standard Deviation	1.03%	1.03%	1.03%

Every month, Fund A went up by a certain percentage; so did Fund B, and by the same percentage. At the end of this 12-month period, your portfolio generated an average monthly return of 0.67%, and over that period had an annual standard deviation of 1.03%.

If the goal of diversification is to reduce risk and enhance return, why own the second fund? Because both funds are generating exactly the same return at exactly the same time, we gain nothing in terms of risk reduction or performance enhancement. Obviously, there is more to diversification than blindly buying more than one fund.

That's where the final piece of statistical information comes into play—correlation. Simply stated, correlation mathematically defines how closely one fund tracks the performance of another fund. Correlation can vary between +1 (perfect positive correlation) and -1 (perfect negative correlation). Of course, while Table 2.4 shows two funds that have demonstrated perfect positive correlation, that is not something we would expect to see in the real world. Most often, two funds have a positive or negative correlation that falls somewhere between the +1 and -1 extremes.

With that in mind, we would like you to take a look at Table 2.5. In this table, we examine two funds, A and Z, that have demonstrated perfect negative correlation.

Table 2.5: PERFECT NEGATIVE CORRELATION OF FUND A AND FUND Z

Period	Fund A Monthly Return	Fund Z Monthly Return	Value of $10,000.00
Aug-94	1.00%	-1.00%	10,000.00
Sep-94	0.50%	-0.50%	10,000.00
Oct-94	0.00%	0.00%	10,000.00
Nov-94	-1.00%	1.00%	10,000.00
Dec-94	2.00%	-2.00%	10,000.00
Jan-95	1.50%	-1.50%	10,000.00
Feb-95	1.00%	-1.00%	10,000.00
Mar-95	0.50%	-0.50%	10,000.00
Apr-95	0.00%	0.00%	10,000.00
May-95	-1.00%	1.00%	10,000.00
Jun-95	2.00%	-2.00%	10,000.00
Jul-95	1.50%	-1.50%	10,000.00

	Fund A	Combined Fund Z	Fund A and Fund Z
Average Return	0.067%	0.067%	0.00%
Standard Deviation	1.03%	1.03%	0.00%

By combining Funds A and Z in Table 2.5, we bring to light a good news/bad news scenario. The good news is that in terms of standard deviation (0.0%), you now own a riskless portfolio. The bad news is that your portfolio is going nowhere!

The idea, of course, is to find two real-world funds that are not perfectly correlated either positively or negatively, and more to the point, fine-tune that combination so that we 1) reduce risk, and 2) maintain an optimum level of performance.

With that in mind, we want to once again look at the monthly returns of the Trimark Canadian Fund. In this case, we've assumed that while the long-term returns from the Trimark Canadian Fund are attractive, the deviation in monthly returns is too high. In other words, we want to reduce the risk in the portfolio without losing all of the performance.

To accomplish this, we have decided to add another fund to the portfolio, which in this case is the Dynamic Income Fund. The Dynamic Income Fund carries substantially less risk than the Trimark Canadian Fund, and as might be expected, the returns are also not as stellar as the Trimark Canadian Fund.

Table 2.6: TRIMARK CANADIAN FUND AND DYNAMIC INCOME FUND

Period Return	Trimark Canadian Fund	Dynamic Income Fund	Value of $ 10,000.00
Aug-92	2.71%	-0.58%	10,106.80
Sep-92	1.25%	0.31%	10,185.84
Oct-92	2.51%	1.61%	10,395.36
Nov-92	-0.37%	-0.83%	10,333.14
Dec-92	4.12%	1.78%	10,638.12
Jan-93	3.01%	1.02%	10,852.11
Feb-93	-4.67%	0.66%	10,634.25
Mar-93	1.66%	1.40%	10,797.38
Apr-93	-4.88%	0.68%	10,570.96
May-93	0.30%	1.64%	10,673.39
Jun-93	-0.36%	-0.85%	10,608.55
Jul-93	2.66%	-0.53%	10,721.48
Aug-93	6.23%	1.39%	11,129.92
Sep-93	-5.75%	0.57%	10,841.60
Oct-93	2.21%	-0.32%	10,944.10
Nov-93	-0.06%	-0.28%	10,925.28
Dec-93	-1.92%	0.11%	10,826.57
Jan-94	-2.06%	0.28%	10,730.05
Feb-94	5.17%	2.42%	11,137.20
Mar-94	3.39%	0.86%	11,374.31
Apr-94	1.49%	1.49%	11,543.62
May-94	5.71%	-0.55%	11,841.27
Jun-94	-1.04%	1.44%	11,864.78
Jul-94	5.05%	2.45%	12,309.77
Aug-94	-1.28%	-0.19%	12,219.47
Sep-94	1.50%	-0.15%	12,302.32
Oct-94	3.17%	0.19%	12,508.88
Nov-94	3.43%	1.70%	12,829.29
Dec-94	5.46%	1.89%	13,300.90
Jan-95	5.52%	-0.38%	13,642.86
Feb-95	0.41%	-0.75%	13,619.60
Mar-95	2.06%	1.50%	13,862.17
Apr-95	1.43%	0.00%	13,961.49
May-95	-2.64%	0.84%	13,836.05
Jun-95	1.42%	1.25%	14,020.27
Jul-95	-1.09%	1.52%	14,050.49
	Trimark	**Dynamic**	
Average	1.27%	0.65%	0.96%
Standard Deviation	3.05%	0.97%	1.70%

Note from Table 2.6 that we have reduced the risk in this portfolio by 44.2% (standard deviation of 1.70% versus 3.05%), while reducing the average monthly performance by only 24.2% (average monthly return of 0.96% versus 1.27%). What that demonstrates is the risk-reduction aspect of diversification across asset classes (i.e., a Canadian equity fund and a Canadian bond fund).

Investors can further reduce risk by diversifying not only across asset classes, but by geographic region and investment style (and that is the rationale behind the FundLine, which we discuss in Chapter 11).

With a well-diversified portfolio, you will end up meeting your financial goals with as little risk as possible.

CHAPTER THREE

Assessing Your Tolerance for Risk

The Importance of Risk

When it comes to buying mutual funds, the main criterion is certainly performance. Unfortunately, most investors look at performance with little or no regard to risk—which isn't surprising, given that performance is so much easier to quantify.

If performance were the only criterion when screening potential fund candidates, then it would simply be a case of matching your required rate of return (see Chapter 1) with a fund that has generated that rate compounded over, say, the past five or 10 years.

For example, suppose that the required compound annual rate of return over the next 20 years to meet, say, your retirement needs, was 10%. With a scan of the *Southam Source Disk*, we would screen only those funds with at least a 10-year track record and then simply buy into a fund whose compound rate of return exceeds 10%. Mission accomplished!

Of course, as you might imagine, things are never really that simple. The problem is that our tolerance for risk defines for each of us how well we can adapt to the ebb and flow of our investment return, and how much of an impact those changes have will define for us our ability to maintain investments for longer periods of time.

Need proof? Read on!

The Power of Positive Investing

Consider, for a moment, the mountain charts that accompany mutual fund marketing literature— the ones that graphically display what a $10,000 investment made 10, 20 or 30 years ago would be worth today. If nothing else, they emphasize the "power of positive investing." Figure 3.1, for example, charts the growth of a $10,000 investment in the Marathon Equity Fund. If you had invested $10,000 in the Marathon Equity Fund on January 1, 1987, it would have grown to $36,931.11 by December 31, 1995. That translates into a 15.62% compound annual return.

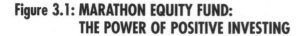

**Figure 3.1: MARATHON EQUITY FUND:
THE POWER OF POSITIVE INVESTING**

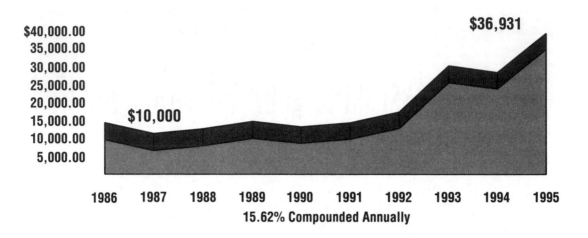

The Marathon Equity Fund was recently capped at just over $300 million in assets. What that means is you can no longer buy into the fund. Too bad, because this is an excellent mutual fund with a stellar track record. We chose this fund as an example to define both sides of the risk/reward equation for a couple of reasons:

1. Over the past five years—January 1991 through to December 1995—the fund returned 32.9% compounded annually. That was good enough to earn top marks in the performance parade of Canadian small cap funds. More important, those returns were good enough to attract the attention of the financial press and excite more than a few investors looking to catch a ride on the next hot-performing fund.

2. It provides an insightful commentary on the importance of balancing risk and return.

Riding the Bumps Along the Way

What's not apparent on those long-term mountain charts is the wild roller-coaster ride, something that can be seen in Figure 3.2. You can see how investors can get tripped up. There are advantages to having a competent financial advisor holding your hand through the rough stretches.

**Figure 3.2: MARATHON EQUITY FUND:
RIDING THE ROLLER-COASTER**

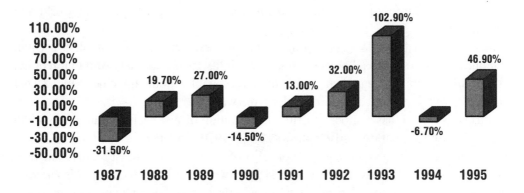

To make the point, allow us to draw your attention to the period beginning in January 1987 and ending in December 1991. Convincing an investor to put money into this fund at the beginning of 1987 should have been relatively easy. After all, stocks had been booming through most of the 1980s, and small cap stocks were particularly hot. Small companies, which is what the Marathon Equity Fund invests in, were in the 1980s routinely being bought out by larger companies, and that was regularly providing shareholders with double-digit returns.

Given such a strong period of growth, a mountain chart depicting the returns for most equity funds would have looked like the side of Mount Everest—at a time, we point out, when the attractiveness of guaranteed investment certificates (GICs) was beginning to wear thin.

Investors who bought $10,000 worth of the Marathon Equity Fund in January 1987 and held the fund until the end of December 1991 (some five years later) saw the value of their investment rise to $10,075.50. And that assumes the investor had the sum and substance to remain in the market after the 1987 stock market crash.

We like to think of Figure 3.2 as "real-world investing." And just to add some real-world grist to this mill, we would submit that after the October 1987 collapse in stock prices, most investors would have been rushing for the sidelines, asking themselves why they ever abandoned GICs.

In real-world terms, nothing is as frustrating as watching the value of your portfolio stagnate. And as that frustration grows, investors begin to lay blame and, like our example in the Introduction, tend to cast all mutual funds in the same light.

In this real-world discussion, we would expect by the end of this five-year cycle that very few long-term investors would still be holding this fund, and more than likely would have sold out at the worst possible moment.

Two Conflicting Points of View

What we have, then, are two conflicting points of view: our mountain charts that characterize the power of positive investing, and our annual return chart that sets out the real-world roller-coaster experience.

In order to bridge these two conflicting points of view, we need to establish a balance between our long-term financial objectives and our ability to tolerate risk. And that requires a diversified investment strategy that 1) builds a reasonable mountain chart, and 2) helps smooth out the real-world highs and lows along the way.

In our view, strategic asset allocation fits the definition of just such a strategy. Asset allocation is to the 1990s what diversification was in the 1970s and 1980s.

Diversification, as in owning a large portfolio of stocks, is the most significant reason given for buying mutual funds. The reason is simple, writes Sheldon Jacobs in his *Handbook for No-Load Fund Investors:* "There are two basic risks in owning stocks—1) the risk the market will go down, and 2) the risk an individual company will do poorly. Diversification can eliminate the latter risk. And since the wise investor is risk averse, it makes sense to avoid taking any risk that is unnecessary."

As the world becomes more complicated, the risks of investing increase. In 1994, when interest rates began to rise, the bond market and stock market tumbled, and with them virtually all bond and stock funds.

On the other hand, international stock and bond funds fared a little better. Of course, money market funds continued to spin positive returns. We believe a well-constructed asset allocation portfolio can address those concerns by striking a reasonable balance between your financial objectives and your risk tolerances. The next step along this road, then, is to gain some insight into your investment personality.

Your Risk Assessment Profile

Market conditions constantly change. Over time, securities will be affected by economic circumstances. These changes must be met with decisive action. Take the case where an investment performs poorly and its price drops sharply. You don't want to let your losses accumulate when you would have been in a better position by simply selling and looking elsewhere.

That decision, however, is also a matter of the investor's personality. Veteran money managers will tell you that many investors are reluctant to sell when faced with a loss. Many investors find it difficult to admit to a mistake, or believe (falsely) that they do not incur a true loss until a security is sold.

On the other side of the risk/return coin, you have to be able to maintain your positions for the long term, being careful not to take profits quickly. Many of the same investors who will let their losses run will just as quickly take a profit. There is, of course, some psychological satisfaction in making money. But over the long term, this reduces your chances for gains. All too often it takes you out of a market that is performing well. In this case, a little patience is its own reward.

Our personal investment profile looks at risk and return as two sides of the same coin. We established your return requirements in Chapter 1, and with the Risk Assessment Profile we can gain some insight into your ability to tolerate risk.

By totaling the scores from Chapters 1 and 3, we establish a kind of policy statement, which, for lack of a better term, is your benchmark asset mix. Indeed, we will use that to gauge the performance of our annual asset mix relative to your personal benchmark. More about that in Chapter 9.

For now, take some time to read the questions in the Risk Assessment Profile. Answer each of them as honestly as you can and, where required, work together with your spouse. Investment planning should be a family affair.

Please indicate how much importance you attribute to each of the following considerations. Use the scorecard below each question to rate your response.

RISK ASSESSMENT PROFILE

1. Liquidity

How important is it that you have access to your investment capital in case of emergencies or other investment opportunities?

It is extremely important	1
It is important	2
It is slightly important	4
It is not important at all	5
Score:	_____

2. Safety

After one year of investing, and assuming you were holding blue chip investments, how much would the value of your long-term investment capital have to decline before you would sell it and take a loss?

I would sell if my investment declined by 5%	1
I would sell if my investment declined by 15%	2
I would sell if my investment declined by 52%	3
I would sell if my investment declined by 50%	4
I would not sell my investment	5
Score:	_____

3. Current Income

How important is it that you receive an income stream from your investments over the period of your investment horizon?

It is extremely important	1
It is important	2
It is slightly important	4
It is not important at all	5
Score:	_____

4. Future Gains

How would you describe your reaction to financial news that may have a detrimental effect on your invesments?

I would likely sell my investments	1
I would be fearful and consider selling my investments	2
I would be uncomfortable, but would hold my investments	3
I would remain calm and definitely hold my investments	4
Score:	_____

5. Portfolio Variability

How important is it that you never experience a loss in your portfolio during any given time period?

It is extremely important	1
It is important	2
It is slightly important	4
It is not important at all	5
Score:	_____

6. Performance Reviews

What performance numbers are you most concerned about?

Monthly performance numbers	1
Quarterly performance numbers	3
Annual performance numbers	5
Score:	_____

7. Speculation

Within the past five years, how often have you invested money in speculative investments?

I have never invested speculatively	1
I have invested speculatively once	2
I have invested speculatively twice	3
I have invested speculatively three or more times	4
Score:	_____

Risk as a Function of Time

If you are like most investors, you want to see your capital grow. Of course, just how substantial your growth objectives are depends, to a large extent, on how well you tolerate the risk of owning stock. Because what you may not know is that stocks are one of the few investment assets that can deliver growth over the long term.

We trust you see the problem. Too many individual investors looking for growth are preoccupied with safety of principal, and because of that are not willing to assume the risk that accompanies an investment in equities. They simply cannot afford, or are not willing to accept, the volatility associated with equity investments.

What we are really talking about when discussing risk is the potential of loss. And within that context, equity investments are risky, because over short periods of time there is a reasonable chance that you could lose money. However, if you are willing to take a longer-term view to investing, the risk of loss diminishes dramatically.

Robert S. Bell, the principal player in *Bell Charts*, a company that publishes data on mutual funds, in a recent study examined the monthly performance of two key North American stock market indexes from December 31, 1981, to September 30, 1995. The two indexes in question were the Toronto Stock Exchange (TSE) 300 Total Return Index (i.e., the TSE 300 Composite Index, assuming all dividends are reinvested), and the U.S.-based Standard and Poor's 500 Total Return Index, reflected in Canadian dollars.

This time period "provided us with statistics for 153 different annual time periods, 141 two-year periods, 129 three-year periods, 105 five-year periods and 45 ten-year periods," wrote Bell. We think the results are interesting.

According to Bell, "looking at the action for the TSE over the 153 one-year time frames, we see that the index declined 22.9% of the time. The worst one-year decline was -18.5%. Conversely, the best 12-month period was +86.9% and the average was +12.9%." Despite the high average annual return, there is a better than one-in-five chance of losing money over any given one-year time period.

If you look at the TSE Total Return Index over the two-year time periods, the results were dramatically different. There was less than a one-in-fifteen (6.4%) chance of losing money in any given two-year period, and the worst two-year loss for the TSE was only -3.7%.

Interestingly, over the five-year and 10-year time periods, the TSE never recorded a single losing period, even if you bought at the peak during any given month. The worst 10-year period for the TSE 300 Total Return Index since December 1981—including 45 different 10-year time periods—was a +7.8% compounded annual return. Downside risk went from -18.5% (worst one-year time period) to +7.8% (worst 10-year time period) by simply extending the time frame of reference from one year to 10 years.

Of course, these performance numbers are for the benchmark TSE Total Return Index and do not take into account the performance of Canadian equity fund managers. Good managers add performance value, a factor that will further skew the time horizon statistics.

Tables 3.1 and 3.2 examine the statistics for the TSE Total Return Index and the S&P 500 Total Return Index. "In each case, notice how the risk of losing money declines sharply over time," says Bell.

Table 3.1: TSE TOTAL RETURN INDEX (SINCE DECEMBER 31, 1981)

	1 year	2 years	3 years	5 years	10 years
Best period (% return)	86.9%	32.8%	30.7%	27.8%	13.5%
Worst period (% return)	-18.5%	-3.7%	-7.2%	0.2%	7.8%
Average (% return)	12.9%	10.9%	10.2%	9.4%	9.7%
Number of plus periods	118	132	118	105	45
Number of negative periods	35	9	11	0	0
% chance of losing money	22.9%	6.4%	8.5%	0.0%	0.0%

Table 3.2: S&P 500 TOTAL RETURN INDEX (SINCE DECEMBER 31, 1981)

	1 year	2 years	3 years	5 years	10 years
Best period (% return)	55.7%	38.1%	33.4%	30.8%	18.3%
Worst period (% return)	-22.8%	-1.1%	-2.3%	6.2%	14.4%
Average (% return)	18.1%	16.7%	16.5%	15.2%	16.0%
Number of plus periods	138	139	127	105	45
Number of negative periods	15	2	2	0	0
% chance of losing money	10.9%	1.4%	1.6%	0.0%	0.0%

The upshot, says Bell, is to hold: "Too many investors sell after a period of weak performance and are not there when the fund or the markets recover. They have moved on to the hot performer of the previous year, only to participate in the ensuing correction. It is quite possible to own nothing but the best-performing funds in Canada and still lose money. The winners are the buy-and-hold investors."

We are not suggesting, then, that equity investments carry no risk. What we are suggesting is that your time horizon has a great deal to do with risk, and by extension how much equity you can tolerate in your investment program.

Time Horizon

How long do you plan to hold your investments? If you are planning to retire some 20 years down the road, then you would expect to hold your investments for 20 years. Similarly, if you are putting together a portfolio to save for a down payment on a house five years in the future, your time horizon is five years.

Less than 2 years	0
Between 2 and 5 years	3
Between 5 and 10 years	6
Between 10 and 20 years	10
More than 20 years	15
Score:	_____

Risk Assessment Profile Total Score: _____ *(Total of 1 through 7)*

YOUR PERSONAL INVESTOR PROFILE

Category	Source of Information	Total Score
A: Net Worth	Chapter 1	_____
B: Financial Objectives	Chapter 1	_____
C: Risk Assessment Profile	Chapter 3	_____
D: Time Horizon	Chapter 3	_____

Total Score (A + B + C + D) _____

What Does It All Mean?

The final tally is effectively your "Personal Investment Profile." But remember, financial circumstances and goals change, so take the time to re-evaluate your situation at periodic intervals.

Your Personal Investment Profile is structured as an aggressiveness index, and provides the foundation on which to establish your personal asset mix. The higher the score, the more aggressive the asset mix. The first step when constructing a long-term portfolio is deciding how much emphasis should be given to each asset class.

With that in mind, we start the process by defining your "policy statement." That is simply the average weighting we would expect you to hold in each asset class. Your policy statement is defined as the midpoint in the asset mix chart depicted in Figure 3.3.

You will also note two other percentages, a maximum and a minimum, wrapped around the policy statement. These are simply the maximum and minimum commitments you should make to each asset class at any point in time. Each year this book will be updated, and each year we may suggest you over-weight, under-weight or maintain your policy statement for the year ahead.

By doing this, we hope to enhance your returns when the economy is strengthening and reduce your risk when the economy is slowing down. In other words, it's another way of trying to smooth your ride through the ups and downs of the business cycle.

Figure 3.3: YOUR PERSONAL INVESTMENT PROFILE

Safety

Your Score: < 15   Your Category: ☐

	Equities			Fixed Income			Cash	
Min	Policy	Max	Min	Policy	Max	Min	Policy	Max
0%	10%	20%	60%	75%	90%	10%	15%	30%

Safety / Income

Your Score: 15-24   Your Category: ☐

	Equities			Fixed Income			Cash	
Min	Policy	Max	Min	Policy	Max	Min	Policy	Max
10%	20%	30%	50%	65%	80%	10%	15%	25%

Income / Growth

Your Score: 25-34   Your Category: ☐

	Equities			Fixed Income			Cash	
Min	Policy	Max	Min	Policy	Max	Min	Policy	Max
20%	35%	50%	30%	50%	70%	10%	15%	25%

Growth / Income

Your Score: 35-44   Your Category: ☐

	Equities			Fixed Income			Cash	
Min	Policy	Max	Min	Policy	Max	Min	Policy	Max
30%	50%	70%	25%	40%	55%	5%	10%	15%

Growth

Your Score: 45-54   Your Category: ☐

	Equities			Fixed Income			Cash	
Min	Policy	Max	Min	Policy	Max	Min	Policy	Max
40%	60%	80%	20%	30%	40%	5%	10%	15%

Aggressive Growth

Your Score: > 55   Your Category: ☐

	Equities			Fixed Income			Cash	
Min	Policy	Max	Min	Policy	Max	Min	Policy	Max
50%	75%	100%	0%	20%	30%	0%	5%	10%

Remember, your personal policy statement is simply the first step in the selection of an ideal portfolio. In Chapter 10, using our proprietary Croft-Kirzner FundLine, we'll add other dimensions of diversification by breaking down this asset mix into specific geographic regions and investment styles. And finally, of course, we'll provide a list of our Best Bet Funds for the year ahead, based on our own Croft-Kirzner Performance and Consistency Index.

PART II

Mutual Fund Basics

CHAPTER FOUR

Mutual Fund Categories

There are more than 1,000 mutual funds established in Canada, ranging from the traditional equity and bond funds to the more esoteric aggressive growth and specialty funds. The introduction of these new and interesting funds has meant the expansion of investment choices, but it has also made the mutual fund selection process more complex and difficult.

The Basic Features of Mutual Funds

Mutual funds provide four major investment features:

- *Diversification within an asset class*: With one transaction, you can own a portfolio of common stock or government bonds. Well-thought-out fund combinations can provide diversification across geographic boundaries (i.e., U.S. equity funds, international equity funds, global bond funds) and diversification by management style, as in aggressive growth versus a fundamental value style.
- *Convenience*: Mutual funds provide a vehicle that allows investors to buy in dollar amounts rather than 100-share lots. The fact that investors can begin with small initial investments and make periodic contributions—or systematic withdrawals—are advantages not found with other investment vehicles.
- *Mutual funds are cost-effective*: Buy a portfolio of 15 stocks or put together five bonds with staggered maturities, and transaction costs add up. At an average price of $15 a share, and a 100-share board lot of each, this translates into a $45,000 portfolio, out of reach for many. Instead, by purchasing shares in a Canadian equity fund you get a portion of a large, already fully diversified investment portfolio. Mutual funds, then, bring size to the equation, and that allows for a cost advantage that individual investors simply cannot compete with.

- And, finally, *mutual funds provide access to the skills of a professional money manager*.

Other mutual fund features include a variety of entry and exit plans, tax-shelter plan eligibility (with some exceptions), liquidity, transferability and record keeping.

But there are costs to these benefits. One of the costs is direct and visible. The fund manager levies an advisory fee, charged monthly against the fund's assets, and there may be a load or commission when you buy the shares.

The Two Types of Investment Funds

An investment fund is the financial term used to define the role of an investment company. An investment fund (mutual fund) is, then, a company that invests in other companies (i.e., equity funds) or other fixed-income investments (i.e., bond funds). There are two types of investment funds: open-end funds and closed-end funds.

Open-End Funds

Open-end funds (usually referred to as mutual funds) sell units or shares to the public on a continuous basis and invest the proceeds in a portfolio of securities according to a published statement of objectives or investment policies. The "open-end" designation means that the mutual fund corporation can keep issuing new shares to purchasers.

Mutual funds are also required to buy back (redeem) shares on demand. You buy and sell the shares of open-end funds at what is called the "net asset value per share" (NAVPS), subject to a front-end and/or back-end load or commission, if any. Some funds are specifically no-load, and in cases where there is a load, it is negotiable.

The fund managers invest in a portfolio of securities (such as Canadian money market securities, Canadian stocks, foreign stocks and so on) in accordance with the fund's stated objectives and investment policies. Mutual fund units are purchased either through your stockbroker or financial planner, or from the company itself. The minimum initial purchase required is normally $500, with subsequent purchases in the order of $100.

There are more than 1,000 open-end mutual funds situated in Canada, classified by various types of objectives. These objectives range from equity funds that invest strictly in common shares to money market funds that invest in money market instruments.

Closed-End Funds

In contrast to an open-end mutual fund, closed-end funds are investment company pools for which the number of shares outstanding is fixed (i.e., closed). Since closed-end funds do not sell shares continuously to the public, the shares are traded on the secondary market. You buy and sell in the same manner that you buy and sell publicly traded shares of companies— through a stockbroker—by placing buy and sell orders in the auction market. Closed-end investment funds fit in somewhere between holding companies and mutual funds.

Like the open-end fund, the closed-end investment company invests its assets in a portfolio of securities according to an investment plan or strategy. Closed-end funds are typically specialized, holding portfolios in such specific areas as precious metals, foreign countries and foreign currencies. Some, however, hold diversified portfolios of primarily Canadian securities.

Since closed-end fund shares are traded rather than redeemed, the price is determined in the secondary market. Historically, closed-end fund shares have traded at discounts to the net asset value per share. In Canada and the U.S., for example, the discount on foreign country funds has averaged as high as 20% in recent years.

Why do closed-end funds shares typically trade at a discount? The discount reflects:

- the cost of liquidating the portfolio and distributing the proceeds to investors
- the implicit management/advisory fees or other expenses of the fund
- the preference for brokers to sell open-ended mutual funds
- the lack of promotion for closed-end funds, and
- the fact that closed-end funds are not awarded the favorable tax treatment of their open-ended counterparts in some countries. As a result, embedded tax liabilities may be inherited by the purchasers in the form of unrealized underlying stock appreciation.

You can buy shares in closed-end funds through your stockbroker. The shares are traded in the same manner as common shares, and commissions will run 1% to 3% of the value of the transaction, depending on the size of your purchase. Net asset values for Canadian closed-end funds are published in *The Globe and Mail*'s *Report on Business*, Saturday edition.

Mutual Fund Categories

The Canadian reporting services group funds into categories fairly consistently, although there are some minor variations. In general, the funds are categorized as follows:

Money Market Funds

One of the most versatile investment vehicles is the money market fund (MMF). These unique funds invest in money market securities of various maturities. Although there are a large number of money market instruments, the most popular are Treasury bills, issued by the Government of Canada and the provinces; bankers' acceptances; short-term government and high-quality corporate bonds; and the promissory notes of companies with very high credit ratings—a product called commercial paper. These are all considered low-risk investments for which the possibility of a default is relatively remote.

Unlike traditional mutual funds, however, the MMFs (with a few exceptions) attempt to maintain a fixed net asset value per share by using the amortized cost method for valuing some or all of their assets. Traditional mutual funds have floating NAVPS and calculate the value of their portfolio each day (a process called "marking to market").

Money market funds pay only interest, so all distributions are likely to be treated as interest income. Normally, income is distributed through additional shares or units rather than through cash payments.

In addition, MMFs invest virtually all of their assets in money market instruments, including Treasury bills, certificates of deposit, deposit receipts, government short-term bonds and commercial paper.

Bond or Mortgage Funds

Fixed-income funds have virtually all of their assets in fixed-income securities, including bonds, mortgages and money market instruments. The primary objective is stable and regular income.

Dividend Income Funds

Dividend income funds are mutual funds that invest in high-yield preferred and common shares of blue-chip Canadian companies. Some funds also invest a small proportion of their portfolio in fixed-income securities such as money market funds, bonds and debentures. The principal investment objective is to generate investment income for the unit holder. Capital growth may occur, as well, in a favorable interest rate environment.

Although dividend income funds are generally much more stable than equity funds, they will, and do, fluctuate in value. For example, as interest rates rise, the market value of the preferred and common shares and other securities held in the fund will often fall. Furthermore, if unit holders decide to redeem their units at such a time, this could force the fund manager to sell securities at a loss to meet redemptions, further reducing the net asset value per share.

The key investment feature of dividend income funds is the dividend income produced—and the way in which those dividends are taxed. As a unit holder, you are entitled to your proportionate share of the dividends and interest earned on the fund's portfolio, as well as any capital gains (losses) incurred in the fund's trading of securities before their maturity. Normally, dividend income fund distributions are made with additional shares or units rather than cash payments.

Dividend income is given preferential tax treatment at the personal level. That is what makes dividend income and dividend income funds so attractive. The dividend tax credit is discussed later in the chapter.

Balanced Funds

The fund manager maintains a balanced portfolio of stocks and bonds, normally within a specified range. The primary objective is stability of returns. Balanced funds are either formalized where the portfolio is fixed in some proportion, such as 40% bonds and 60% equities; or semi-discretionary, where proportions can be changed when the advisor deems it wise.

Equity Growth Funds

The funds of an equity growth portfolio are invested in shares that are expected to have above-average earnings and growth potential.

Aggressive Equity Growth Funds

These funds pursue a strategy of investing in very aggressive common shares and look for unusually high growth.

Gold or Precious Metal Funds

These funds hold gold and other precious metals and/or gold mining shares.

Global and International Funds

These are funds that invest a substantial portion of their assets in securities outside the country of domicile. International funds are those that limit their investments to markets and countries outside the domestic country. They might even restrict their investment activities to a specific region, country or continent. In contrast, global funds have no geographic bounds; they invest anywhere that their management believes a bargain can be found—including the host country. Global funds thus offer greater diversification than international funds because of the lack of restriction on investment activities. However, an investor can combine ownership of a diversified domestic portfolio with ownership of international funds to replicate a global portfolio, and can define international allocations among different countries using *single country funds*—funds that invest all of their assets in a specific country.

Specialty Funds

Funds that invest in a defined industry or asset including gold, high technology and oil and gas.

Real Estate Funds

These are funds that invest all or most of their assets in real estate.

Index Funds

These are funds whose objective is to replicate the performance of some market index, such as the TSE 300 Composite Index. The fund manager's objectives are to acquire the portfolio at as low a cost as possible, then maintain the portfolio through adjustments to reflect the changes to the index due to substitutions, mergers and takeovers. (We'll provide a more in-depth discussion on index funds in Chapter 5.)

Labor-sponsored Mutual Funds

Labor-sponsored funds were first developed in 1984 by the Canadian Federation of Labour. The oldest is the Quebec-based Fonds de Solidarité.

Labor-sponsored mutual funds are designed to encourage venture capital investment in small- and medium-size Canadian businesses in part through tax incentives offered to investors. Like other mutual funds, they represent a pool of capital acquired from investors and allocated to a portfolio. However, they can only be sponsored by organized labor organizations.

Labor-sponsored mutual funds, then, invest in small- and medium-size emerging companies, many of which are not publicly traded. As a result, valuation of the portfolio is generally based on security appraisals or market estimates rather than market prices. Unlike most other mutual funds, labor-sponsored mutual funds price their units or shares monthly, rather than daily.

We look at labor-sponsored funds from three perspectives: 1) as a conduit for venture capital, 2) as a questionable investment for a conservative investor, and 3) as an investment vehicle.

And while the government-sponsored tax breaks are attractive, they have a price: a government-imposed penalty if certain investment requirements are not met, a board of directors that must reserve a seat for a labor union and a system that used to classify investors by type. Prior to the April 1996 federal budget, investors who were retired or who were 65 years of age or older could redeem their labor-sponsored investment fund after only two years and still retain their tax credits. Other investors had to hold the fund for a minimum of five years. In the April 1996 federal budget, Finance Minister Paul Martin eliminated the advantage for senior citizens.

In what looks suspiciously like a pyramid structure, any run on these funds after the minimum five-year holding period without sufficient new money coming in to meet those redemptions would mean that those investors who were the last to enter the game might become the first casualties. Of course, performance of the investments within the fund will go a long way toward determining the retention rate of those early investors.

On the cost side, most labor-sponsored funds come with a back-end load, which means that investors pay a fee to exit the fund. The fee usually starts at 6% of assets after one year, and declines by 0.75% each year thereafter. In most cases there is no exit fee if you hold the fund for at least eight years.

The Essentials of the Tax Picture for Labor-Sponsored Funds

Having provided some investment caveats, we have to say that the tax deductions are attractive. On a $3,500 investment, you are immediately entitled to a 20% federal tax credit (up to a maximum of $700), regardless of where you live in Canada. As well, some provinces—notably Ontario, Prince Edward Island, New Brunswick, Nova Scotia and Saskatchewan—offer an additional 20% tax credit (to a maximum $700, except Saskatchewan, where the maximum is $700), which means that outside an RRSP, your out-of-pocket cost for a $3,500 investment can be as low as $2,100.

There is one additional issue to bear in mind, and that is the imposition of an alternative minimum tax. Likely not to be a concern for most investors, the tax credits would have no value for individuals faced with paying a minimum tax. Under that scenario, Revenue Canada will add back certain credits and subtract deductions in order to arrive at the alternative minimum tax.

That aside, the sales spin really picks up steam when you look at buying the labor-sponsored fund inside an RRSP. In this case, you are entitled to additional savings. Effectively, your initial investment of $3,500 is deposited into an RRSP and is immediately eligible for the basic RRSP deduction. Depending on the provincial tax rate, investors earning more than $30,000 would receive approximately $1,400 in additional RRSP tax credits, while investors earning more than $68,000 receive as much as $1,855 in additional RRSP tax credits.

A $3,500 labor-sponsored fund investment inside an RRSP can mean as much as $1,400 in federal and provincial tax credits, and an additional $1,855 (the maximum potential benefit) in RRSP tax credits. The net after-tax investment, then, is $245 for those in the highest tax bracket, and approximately $700 for individuals earning between $30,000 and $68,000 (depending on the province in which the investor resides).

Another aspect of labor-sponsored funds remains up in the air. At least that's the read we get after talking with a number of accountants. Here's the scenario. You are an Ontario resident (one of the provinces that allow the maximum deductions) and purchase a $3,500 labor-sponsored fund outside an RRSP. Under the new rules, you will receive a 20% federal tax credit ($700) and a 20% provincial tax credit ($700). Your net out-of-pocket cost is $2,100.

Some eight years later, you decide to sell the labor-sponsored fund and the value at the time of sale is $2,600. The question is: Do you 1) have a capital loss of $900 (i.e., $3,500 initial unit value less $2,600 receipts at point of sale = $900 loss), or 2) have a capital gain of $500 (i.e., $2,600 receipt at point of sale - $2,100 out-of-pocket expense = $500 profit)? At this time, we have no definitive answer. However, if we were betting advisors, we would tend to error of the side of caution, and assume Revenue Canada will take the position that you would in fact have a capital gain.

Understanding the Investment Issues for Labor-Sponsored Funds

Obviously, the tax implications are what make labor-sponsored funds an attractive alternative. And should the labor-sponsored fund actually spin some positive returns over the five years, you would end up with a capital gain and only a portion of the accompanying tax liability. You pay tax only on capital gains above the $3,500 initial investment.

On the other hand, if the fund were to lose 10% compounded annually (not an unreasonable assumption), the value of your investment at the end of five years would be $2,066.72. Assuming your actual out-of-pocket cost after federal and provincial tax credits is $2,100, you would have a total out-of-pocket loss of $33.28. If you redeem your labor-sponsored fund at that point you pay a back-end load of approximately $46.50 (approximately 2.25% of current value of fund $2,020.22). On your initial out-of-pocket cost of $2,100, you would get back $2,020.22. And that does not take into account the lost-opportunity cost attached to your initial investment!

Here's where we have a problem. The labor-sponsored fund could lose 7% compounded annually, leaving you with $2,380.12 (after back-end load charges). On paper you have lost $1,119.88 ($3,500 investment less $2,380.12 at redemption = -$1,119.88), but in actual fact, after accounting for the tax credits, you have $280.12 in after-tax profits. That is a net return of 2.5% compounded annually on your initial $2,100 out-of-pocket investment (assuming you received the maximum provincial tax credit at the point of purchase).

A typical investment in a first-year GIC yielding 6% will return about 2.9% to investors in the highest tax bracket. That the after-tax return on a GIC is about the same as the return on a labor-sponsored fund that lost 7% compounded anually, illustrates, in our opinion, the problem with tax-driven investments.

While on the Subject of Taxes . . .

After seeing how tax treatment can skew the investment landscape, we need to spend some time understanding the impact taxes have on more traditional investments. Your return from balanced funds, for example, will be a combination of interest income, capital and dividend distributions and appreciation in the NAVPS—each taxed in its own way. The interest income is taxed as ordinary income. Seventy-five percent of the capital gain distribution is included in income and taxed as ordinary income, while dividend income is subject to the gross-up and dividend tax credit treatment.

Each year you will receive a statement setting out your share of the interest and dividends earned on each fund's portfolio, as well as any capital gains (losses) incurred in the fund's trading of securities before their maturity. All interest, dividend and capital gain income received from the fund, whether it be by cheque or through reinvestment in additional shares, is taxable income. Occasionally a fund makes distributions in excess of its income. These are identified as returns of capital and are not taxable when received. However, they will reduce your cost base of the units, eventually culminating in a larger capital gain.

Your interest income is treated as ordinary income and is taxed in the normal manner. Dividend income is treated as dividend income and is afforded the special treatment that dividend income receives in Canada.

Here is how it works. Dividends received from taxable Canadian corporations are grossed up by 25%, and then a dividend tax credit is applied, computed as 16.67% of the dividend. The net effect of this gross-up and credit is to reduce the effective tax rate to well below that paid for comparable interest income.

The dramatic impact of the dividend tax credit is shown in the accompanying table, which contrasts the tax treatment of $1,000 earned on a term deposit with $1,000 earned in the form of a dividend payment. The amounts are calculated for a Canadian taxpayer who is in the highest marginal tax bracket (taxable income of about $60,000 or more), although the differential is universal (see Table 4.1).

Table 4.1: CALCULATING THE DIVIDEND TAX CREDIT

Income	Interest	Dividend
	$1,000.00	$1,000.00
Gross-Up (25%)		250.00
Taxable Income	1,000.00	1,250.00
Federal Tax (29%)*	290.00	362.50
Federal Dividend Tax Credit (16.67% of $1,000)		166.70
Federal Tax Payable	290.00	195.80
Provincial Tax Payable	159.50	107.69
Total Tax Payable	449.50	303.49
Income after Tax	550.50	696.51
Effective Marginal Tax Rate	44.95%	30.35%

*These calculations are approximations only for illustrative purposes. They ignore federal and provincial surtaxes.

Capital gains can occur in two ways: the fund may make capital gains distributions based on profitable trading of securities; alternatively, if you sell your units for an amount in excess of your original cost (as adjusted for returns of capital), you will also incur a capital gain. Capital gains are subject to the 25% exclusion rule; that is, only 75% of an eligible gain need be included in income. Capital gains may be offset by allowable capital losses. The amount included is taxed at the marginal tax rate.

> **What is a dividend?**
> A dividend is money paid by a company to its shareholders. Common dividends are paid to common shareholders and represent a return on invested capital and are paid out of after-tax profits. Common dividends may fluctuate based on the profitability of the company. Preferred dividends are paid to preferred shareholders and "usually" remain fixed for the life of the preferred shares. Preferred dividends are also paid out of after-tax profits.

Loads and Other Costs

There are two types of potential costs borne by fund holders: loads or sales charges payable at purchase (front end) and/or at sale (back end), and management fees. Sales charges are levied by what are called load funds; firms that charge no sales fees are called no-load. The issue of fees for mutual funds is becoming extremely complex.

Part of the problem is the blurring between loads, sales fees and management fees.

Mutual fund loads or commissions are designed as compensation to the broker or agent for advising and arranging the transaction. They come in a variety of packages and options, and since there is no universal truth as to which is best, it is important to understand exactly what you are paying and what you are paying for. The load should also be considered in light of the management fee.

To clarify, loads are sales commissions; management expenses are the charges of the fund manager, including advisory fees, distribution expenses and other operating expenses. These may also include a form of sales commission. Read on.

Both load and no-load groups charge management fees that average, at least for Canadian equity funds, about 2.15% and are deducted from the NAVPS. Load funds, on average, charge slightly higher management fees, as well.

Front-end loads are still widely used in the load category. These are paid at the time of purchase and are calculated on the total investment. If you invest $10,000 in a mutual fund and pay a 5% front-end load, you will pay $500 in commissions.

This represents a load of 5.26% as a percentage of the $9,500 that goes to the purchase of units. Although loads can be as high as 9% (or 9 divided by 91 x 100 = 9.9% effectively), they are negotiable and can normally be reduced depending on the size of your order and your bargaining skills. The most you are likely to pay is 6%, but 3% to 4% is closer to the norm.

Back-end loads or deferred charges have proliferated recently. This option allows you to pay a commission on redemption, typically on a scaled-down basis reflecting the number of years you hold the fund. Therefore, the load is reduced the longer your holding period, falling to zero after a set number of years (normally seven or eight).

For example, the load may be 5.5% if you redeem in the first year, tapering off to nothing if you hold for more than seven years. This deferred method sounds like the way to go, except that there are catches. The management fees are usually higher for the back-end load, so the reduced commission associated with holding the fund is balanced—although not necessarily equally—against the increased management fee paid. Sometimes the fee is based on market value rather than cost, and thus you could, potentially at least, end up substantially increasing the effective fee.

Over 40% of the Canadian mutual funds charge no loads at all (part of the no-load group). The no-load group consists primarily, but not exclusively, of banks and trust companies; they charge no sales commissions, but instead sell their products through registered salespersons within their branches or through arrangements with brokers.

A portion of the management fee, typically 50%, with many no-load funds may be paid as a commission to staff or selling brokers. These are so-called trailer fees. So you really are paying some sort of sales fee, whether or not you use a financial advisor, broker or mutual fund agent—it is simply a matter of what you want to call it!

Many funds are now offering choices, as in choose your poison. In some cases, AGF being the classic example, fund companies will offer as many as three different classes of shares or units in the same fund, each providing a different combination of sales commissions and management fees. Options are good, but make sure you understand what you are paying for!

That being said, loads and fees are not critical criteria for selecting funds—your choice should be based on expected return and volatility. However, in choosing among similar funds, it depends on your holding period and strategy. If your investment strategy is to set an asset mix, buy mutual funds to match your needs and hold them for the long term, the more suitable fee package will normally be to pay the front-high load and the lower annual management fee. If your style tends to involve substantial trading and turnover, the no-load fund with high management fee approach will often yield the best result.

Operating Expenses

The fund's operating expenses can be measured as total operating costs per $100 of assets. Although studies indicate that, in general, high expense ratio funds tend to slightly underperform low expense-ratio funds, the relationship is not a strong one and is likely to be dominated by other factors. Investors are thus cautioned that a low expense ratio does not necessarily imply above-average performance.

Behind the Numbers—A FundLetter Analysis of Canadian Equity Fund Performance

The Load/No-load Issue
The recent formation of the no-load fund mutual fund group within the Canadian mutual fund industry has focused attention on the load/no-load issue again.

Both load and no-load groups charge management fees that average, at least for Canadian equity funds, about 2.15%. Load funds on average charge slightly higher management fees, as well. How differently do they perform?

A landmark study published by the U.S. Securities and Exchange Commission (SEC) in 1962 concluded that funds with load charges performed no better than no-load funds, and slightly worse after the load. Loads were fixed in those fledgling development days of the mutual fund industry, and ran as high as 9.9% on an effective basis. Now commissions are negotiable, and rarely should you pay the top rate.

To check things out, we analyzed performance in the Canadian equity fund category. The results were interesting. Over the past five years, the average no-load fund slightly outperformed the average load fund by about 16 basis points per year (0.16%). Putting it on a practical footing, a $10,000 investment in the typical no-load fund grew to $13,401, while a similar investment in the average load fund grew to only $12,634, assuming a 5% load.

However, over the past 10 years, capturing three market cycles, load funds outperformed the no-loads by a substantial margin—more than sufficient to overcome the load and leave an incremental profit.

For example, that same $10,000 investment in the no-load fund grew to $22,443, an annual compounded rate of return of 8.42%, compared with $23,933 for a load fund at 5% commission (an annual rate of return of 9.11%). At a 3% commission, the $10,000 grew to $24,436 (a 9.34% annual rate of return). The typical load fund passed the no-load fund in approximately the seventh year. For both categories, the top-performing funds in terms of return were in the $100 to $500 million category.

So the recent period favored the no-load group, the more extended period the load group.

Table 4.2: CANADIAN EQUITY FUND PAST PERFORMANCE

Category	Total Investment	Amount Allocated to Units	Five-year Ending Value	Ten-year Ending Value	Ten-year Annual Returns
Load at 5%	$10,000	$9,500	$12,634	$22,933	9.11%
Load at 3%	10,000	9,300	12,900	24,436	9.34%
No-load	10,000	10,000	13,401	22,443	8.42%

The bottom line? There are lots of criteria for selecting Canadian equity funds, of which load is only one. Nevertheless, everything else being equal, if you have a short investment horizon (i.e., six years or less), concentrate your research on the no-load group. But if your investment horizon exceeds six years, take a close look first at the load group.

* The FundLetter is a monthly newspaper published by the Hume Group in Toronto (subscription information at 1-800-733-4863). The FundLetter focuses on issues and investments within the mutual fund industry, and the contributing editors make specific recommendations on where to invest. Richard Croft and Eric Kirzner are both contributing editors to the FundLetter.

How many funds in your portfolio?

Another approach is to buy a portfolio of different mutual funds spanning the safety, income and growth objectives. The "family of funds" concept is catching on quickly. The largest mutual fund organizations offer a number of different mutual funds—as many as 30 different ones—that capture the entire objectives spectrum. The notion is that once you have entered the "family" by buying one of the funds, you should be able to revise your portfolio holdings by switching within the family—in some cases at no cost. So, if you wish, you can build your initial portfolio structure with a single fund organization and vary the composition as you see fit.

But some fund organizations offer yet another option—portfolios of their underlying funds that provide diversification on their own. Typical portfolios range from strict income orientation (100% bond and mortgage funds) to heavy growth emphasis (100% equity and real estate funds).

With the advent of the "family of funds" concept, investors can now re-balance their own portfolio with reasonable costs. The purchase of one of the funds within the family enables you to periodically revise your portfolio holdings by allowing you to switch to another fund within the family—in some cases at no cost.

In Summary

The Good News
- Diversification: many funds have diversified portfolios; difficult to replicate on your own.
- Asset allocation: you can pursue strategic, dynamic and tactical programs with mutual funds.
- Professional management.
- Record keeping.
- Wide range of choices: you can do most of your financial planning with mutual funds.
- Lots to choose within categories.
- Periodic purchase plans; dollar-cost averaging.
- Numerous withdrawal options: ratio, fixed period, constant dollar.
- Usually small initial purchase ($100 to $1,000); small subsequent purchases, some as low as $25.
- Dividend reinvestment options are extremely valuable.

The Bad News
- Some mutual funds perform poorly.
- Some don't stick to objectives.
- Many are inconsistent.
- Hidden fees are buried in advisory fees.
- Sales reps may be motivated by commission rather than your interest.
- Abuses: cross-selling; twisting; mutual commissions: distributor gifts
- Improper valuation.
- Internal cross-trading within fund families may be a problem.
- Misleading sales promotions: use of skewed charts, truncated axes.
- Some registered representatives are poorly trained in the skills of effectively mixing and matching funds.
- Hidden switch costs.

CHAPTER FIVE

Equity Funds

The Risk of Avoiding Stocks

We believe that equity assets, or, if you prefer, *stocks*, should play a role in virtually all investment portfolios. Just how big a role depends on your specific long-range goals and your ability to tolerate the ups and downs of the business cycle.

Notwithstanding those caveats, the fact remains that stocks are a superb investment. Just how good are the performance numbers? Well, over the past 70 years, stocks have been the number one performing investment asset, outperforming all other investments hands down.

Peter Lynch, one-time portfolio manager of the giant U.S.-based Fidelity Magellan Fund and author of *Beating the Street*, discusses the relative performance of stocks and bonds in the preface of his book. Using the *Ibbotson SBBI Yearbook*, Lynch examines "Average Annual Returns for the Decades 1926-1989"—a summary of returns you would have received using different types of investment vehicles: the 500 stocks in the Standard and Poor's Composite Index, a portfolio of small-company stocks, long-term U.S. government bonds, long-term U.S. corporate bonds and short-term U.S. Treasury bills.

Over the seven decades reviewed in the Ibbotson study, only once (1930-1940) did U.S. bonds outperform U.S. stocks. "By sticking with stocks all the time," writes Lynch, "the odds are six to one in our favor that we'll do better than the people who stick with bonds." And the performance numbers are, well, mind-boggling. "Over the entire 64 years covered in the study, a $100,000 investment in long-term U.S. government bonds would have been worth $1.6 million; the same amount invested in the S&P 500 would be worth $25.5 million."

The key to this discussion is the notion that equity assets must be held for the long term. In the Ibbotson study, we are talking about a 70-year time period, which clearly does not fit within the investing life of an individual. But even over much shorter periods, equity assets have performed admirably. For example, if we look at the five-year track record of Canadian equity funds, not one fund lost money. The worst of the group[1]—looking at the five-year period ending December 31, 1995—returned 3.0% compounded annually; the best returned over 34% compounded annually. According to mutual fund studies, the average holding period for any mutual fund, including funds that hold equities, is 17 months. And therein lies the problem: individual investors too often sell too quickly and usually at exactly the wrong time.

At this stage, we know that individual investors attempt to time the market. There are, as we have seen, two reasons for this: 1) the need to move in and out quickly, looking for a fast buck from some speculative investment, and 2) the fear of a stock market collapse like the one we witnessed in October 1987 and again in October 1992. A more recent example that should still be fresh in the minds of Canadian investors is the sell-off in both bonds and stocks leading up to the 1995 Quebec referendum.

Assuming we have been able to convince you of the risks associated with the lottery syndrome, let's for a moment focus on the fears of a stock market collapse.

We trust that the argument to hold stocks in your portfolio is compelling. And we understand that to do so means riding the ups and downs of the business cycle and assuming some risk along the way. We also know that, given a choice, most investors would prefer to avoid risk. If we could play Monday-morning quarterback with our investments, we would all make fortunes in short order—with no risk!

Unfortunately, investments are made with an eye toward the future, which tells us that buy-and-sell decisions are driven by expected changes in the economy, or are based on developments that might or might not happen within specific companies. This is another reason why so many investors prefer to avoid stocks in their portfolio. It's simply too hard, despite being overloaded with information, to keep abreast of the ebb and flow of the financial markets.

Let's face it—most investors have neither the time nor the inclination to pore over financial statements and economic trends in search of the diamond in the rough of investment ideas. And while brokerage firms pay top dollar to research analysts whose job it is to forecast the performance of the stock market and/or the earnings of specific companies, many brokers will tell you that even *they* don't have the time to read all the material.

And frankly, we're not sure this type of analysis is the primary issue within the context of your personal investment plan. While we believe that research analysts help maintain efficient financial markets, we question the relevance of short-term earnings forecasts within the context of a long-range investment plan.

We would argue that there are more important issues to contend with. We believe that individual investors should spend less time searching for the next Microsoft or the newest wave in mutual funds or the next state-of-the-art tax shelter, and instead make a commitment to understanding their own investment personality and develop a cover-all-the-bases investment plan designed from the top down.

---

[1] *The worst-performing Canadian equity fund, according to the* Southam Source Disk, *during this five-year period was the Admax Canadian Select Growth Fund; the best-performing Canadian equity fund in terms of the five-year compound annual return was the Marathon Equity Fund.*

Equity Funds Defined

An equity fund is structured to invest primarily in shares of common stock. A Canadian equity fund, for example, invests in the shares of Canadian companies and is considered to be an eligible investment for your Registered Retirement Savings Plan.

There are also equity mutual funds that invest in the common shares of companies outside of Canada, which can be broken into a number of broad categories, including:

1. **U.S. Equity Funds:** Mutual funds that invest primarily in the common shares of U.S.-based companies. Not an eligible RRSP investment, except within the 20% foreign content rules.
2. **International and Global Funds:** Mutual funds that invest primarily in the common shares of companies outside Canada. These funds may invest primarily in U.S. stocks, or may focus on other regions around the globe, such as the emerging markets of Latin America and the Far East, as well as mature markets such as Japan and Europe. There is a fine line that distinguishes between international and global funds. International equity funds invest in stocks in countries outside Canada. Global equity funds, on the other hand, invest in stocks in countries outside Canada as well as in stocks domiciled in Canada.
3. **Special Equity Funds:** Sometimes referred to as sector funds, these mutual funds invest in specific industries or sectors of the economy. Examples include the science and technology sector, precious metals and health care, to name a few. We think this is one of the growth areas in the mutual fund industry, and would expect to see more of these specialty funds in the future.

We can also distinguish equity funds in terms of their specific objectives, as defined in the fund's prospectus. Some equity fund managers, for example, focus primarily on large cap stocks; others have a mandate to invest in the shares of small companies with, say, a market capitalization of less than $250 million.

More important, some funds require the manager to maintain a fully invested position, while others allow greater latitude. We don't come down on one side of this debate or the other. There are pros and cons to both positions.

A fully invested fund is useful because it forces the manager to implement an investment strategy that focuses on industries and security selection. That fits well with our asset allocation theme (see Chapter 9). By establishing the asset mix, we are determining 85% to 90% of our overall return. We are depending on the individual fund managers to provide their expertise on security and industry selection that impacts on the remaining 10% to 15% of our overall return.

On the other hand, a manager who has the discretion to move in and out of the market—i.e. from stocks to cash, etc.—as the business cycle dictates can add value if he is good at market timing. However, equity managers who are not fully invested impact your overall asset mix in ways you might not have anticipated.

Consider, for example, the All-Canadian CapitalFund which "seeks long-term growth of capital and income, invests in companies with better-than-average growth potential and a policy of regularly paying dividends, [and] invests primarily in common shares but can also invest in Treasury bills, bonds and preferred shares." The managers—Michael A. Parente, J. L. Michele Spicer and Paul A. Graham—have the latitude to move from equities into cash and bonds as market conditions dictate. In fact, at the end of March 1996, the fund's portfolio was holding 43% cash.

Suppose your asset mix looks something like Table 5.1, in which you want 40% of your portfolio in Canadian equity. If you buy the All-Canadian CapitalFund to represent your Canadian equity component, you are not getting full measure for your money. Because the All-Canadian CapitalFund has only 57% of its money invested in Canadian equity, you don't have 40% of your portfolio in Canadian equity. In fact, you only have about 23% of your overall portfolio actually invested in Canadian stocks (i.e., 40% from Table 5.1 as a percentage of 65% actually invested in Canadian equity by the All-Canadian CapitalFund). All things being equal, we would prefer to hold, in this case, a Canadian equity fund that was fully invested in Canadian stocks. And while all the managers have some latitude as to how much cash they can hold at a point in time, we prefer that a Canadian equity manager maintain at least 90% of the portfolio invested in Canadian equity. More about this in Chapter 9.

Table 5.1: SAMPLE ASSET MIX

Asset Mix	Percentage
Canadian Equity Assets	40%
U.S. Equity Assets	10%
Fixed-Income Assets	35%
Cash Assets	15%

Since the All-Canadian CapitalFund holds 35% of its assets in cash, your actual asset mix, assuming other factors remain constant, would look like Table 5.2:

Table 5.2: SAMPLE ASSET MIX

Asset Mix	Percentage
All-Canadian CapitalFund	23%*
U.S. Equity Assets	10%
Fixed-Income Assets	35%
Cash Assets	32%

* 57% (fund's position in Canadian equity) x 40% (percentage of asset mix represented by Canadian equity assets) = 23% exposure to Canadian equity

Of course, the easiest way to buy Canadian equity assets, and know that the fund is always 100% invested in Canadian shares, is to purchase an index fund, something that has been growing in popularity south of the border.

Equity Index Funds—The North and South Debate

When it comes to trends in the Canadian mutual fund industry, much can be learned from our friends south of the border; not because American fund companies are better than their Canadian counterparts, but because trends are often defined by a time line, and in that regard, Americans have been at it longer. And like most things in the business community, trends in the U.S. usually find their way into Canada.

I raise this issue because I am seeing a small but growing movement among Canadian mutual fund investors toward so-called equity index funds. And I find that disturbing, because it's clear to me that the cost savings associated with Canadian equity index funds are not sufficient to justify what amounts to a guarantee of underperformance.

Now, you can argue, as some in the financial press have, that this is simply a case of what goes around comes around. In the 1960s and early 1970s, when the mutual fund industry was in its infancy, investors were sold on the risk-reduction advantages of diversification. Mutual funds simply provided a more efficient cost-effective way to structure an equity portfolio.

As the industry matured and more companies entered the market with new funds, investors began to comparison-shop. Since all broad-based equity funds offered diversification, the allure of one fund over another came down to performance, and that set the stage for the now-famous mountain charts that appear in most mutual fund marketing literature.

Then, in 1976, about the time investors were focusing on money management skills as the primary reason for buying a particular fund, along came the Vanguard Group and the launch of their now-famous Vanguard Index Trust 500 portfolio.

At the time, the concept of indexation was a radical idea! Here was a fund whose objective was to match the performance of the benchmark index, which in this case was the Standard and Poor's 500 Total Return Index. No performance promises, no attempt to highlight the skills of the money manager; just a simple guarantee, low-cost structure and instant diversification.

What Vanguard did was redefine—or shall we say revisit—the way mutual funds were sold, and in doing so set the stage for what today is a widespread debate as to how much value one should attach to management expertise.

The management of Vanguard will tell you that performance by nature is fickle. Too often last year's hot manager becomes this year's outcast. As such, the costs associated with performance in many cases outweigh the benefits. The fact that the Vanguard 500 fund now lays claim to more than U.S.$10 billion in assets illustrates how critical an issue this is to U.S. mutual fund investors.

— R. C.

The Canadian Experience

Canadian equity index funds have been around since 1983, the first to enter the game being the Great West Life Equity Index Fund. However, to be fair, this is not a pure play on the TSE 300 Composite Index because the fund's objective is to buy the 250 largest companies in the TSE 300 Composite Index. It doesn't say the manager has to buy certain percentages of each stock, percentages that correspond to the percentage weighting within the benchmark index. It simply restricts the manager as to which 250 stocks he can purchase.

The Green Line Canadian Index Fund, on the other hand, is a pure index investment, designed to track the performance of the TSE 300 Composite Index. In this case, the manager attempts to match the weightings of stock in his portfolio to their representative weighting within the TSE 300 Composite Index.

When examining the merits of an index fund, analysts talk in terms of tracking error, which essentially defines how closely the index fund tracks the performance of the benchmark index. How well the manager mirrors the index defines for an investor how well the manager is doing his job. The question of performance, then, becomes a moot point. You won't do any better than the benchmark index, but you shouldn't do any worse, either.

Given the rise in the number of Canadian equity index funds, there is little doubt that Canadian investors share many of the American views on the subject. Like our U.S. cousins, we, too, are asking if the long-term performance numbers are sufficient to justify high management fees. Of course, that assumes that Canadian equity index funds are delivering on their promise of low fees, and that issue is not clear.

When investors buy traditional equity funds, they are buying the manager's performance record, so the fees for traditional equity funds, presumably, compensate a manager for outperforming the benchmark index. But here's where the pay-for-performance debate gets ugly, and supports the movement toward equity index funds.

When you look at the five-year track record for Canadian equity funds, you have to ask yourself: "Where's the performance?" Only 21 out of 109 Canadian equity funds with a minimum of a five-year track record matched or beat the 8.4% compound annual return generated by the TSE Total Return Index.

If we take an unweighted average of all Canadian equity funds with at least a five-year track record, the numbers pale in comparison: 6.9% compounded annually versus 8.4% for the TSE 300 Total Return Index.

If we look at a weighted average (i.e., larger funds, where most investors are putting their money, have a greater impact on the average than do smaller funds), of all Canadian equity funds with a five-year track record, the performance numbers come in at 8.3% compounded annually, which is just slightly less than the TSE 300 Total Return Index.

Over shorter periods, the pay-for-performance arguments are even harder to justify. Only 40 out of 118 Canadian equity funds had better three-year performance numbers than the TSE 300 Total Return Index. And over the past year, only 33% (50 out of 150 Canadian equity funds) of

Canadian equity funds beat the TSE Total Return Index. On the surface, those numbers present a powerful case for index funds.

However, if you scratch below the surface, the numbers tell a much different story. In the first place, of the five Canadian equity index funds with five-year records, none was able to equal the performance of the TSE 300 Composite Total Return Index (including dividends reinvested). The best of the lot, the Green Line Canadian Index Fund, had a five-year compound annual return of 5.5%, three full percentage points below the five-year compound annual return on the TSE 300 Total Return Index.

The other Canadian index funds performed even more poorly: First Canadian Equity Index Fund came in at 4.8% compounded annually over the past five years; Great West Life Equity Index Fund returned 4.5% compounded annually over the same period; the Mutual Canadian Index Fund returned 4.5% compounded annually; and last on the list, the N.N. Canadian 35 Index returned 3.6% compounded annually.

Moreover, in terms of performance, the Green Line Canadian Index Fund—which we said was the best-performing Canadian index fund—ranked 71st out of 118 Canadian equity funds in terms of five-year performance numbers. It is the same story among the other Canadian equity index funds.

Fund Name	Rank on the Basis of Five-Year Compound Annual Return
First Canadian Equity Index	81st out of 118
Mutual Canadian Index	84th out of 118
Great West Life Equity Index	85th out of 118
N.N. Canadian 35 Index	100th out of 118

Based on these performance stats, two issues seem clear: 1) not all Canadian index funds are created equally, and 2) based on past performance, it appears that Canadian equity index funds guarantee a record of underperformance.

Of course, there is another side to this argument. Fund companies will tell us, quite correctly, that an index has no costs attached to its performance. For the fund company, even though the fund is indexed, there is the cost of buying the securities represented in the index, and there is an annual administrative fee.

In the end, however, the motive for buying an index fund comes down to cost. You might be willing to accept a lower standard if management fees for the index fund are substantially below the average for all Canadian equity funds. But here, too, most Canadian index funds fall down.

Interestingly, the average management-expense ratio (MER) for the five Canadian index funds is 1.83% (ranging from a low of 1.01% for the Green Line Canadian Equity Index Fund to a high of 2.25% for N.N. Canadian 35 Index). Compare that with the 1.96% average MER for the 109 Canadian equity funds that have at least a five-year track record, and the pay-for-performance argument begins to blur.

Even assuming the lowest cost structure—i.e., Green Line Canadian Index Fund with an MER of 1.01%—you have to ask just what are you paying for. And, in the best-case scenario, you are paying one percentage point per year for the right to simply track an index. Perhaps rather than asking what costs we should attach to performance, we should ask: "What costs should we save at the expense of guaranteed underperformance?"

Another issue that we cannot understand is the notion that investors should pay a load to buy an index fund. Yet, of the five Canadian index funds with five-year track records, two of them charge loads. The Mutual Canadian Index Fund has a front-end load that can be as high as 3.8%, and the N.N. Canadian 35 Index Fund has a back-end option that can be as high as 5%.

And consider this: the two Canadian equity index funds that charge a load also hold portfolios that track the Toronto 35 Index. In this case, one has to wonder why investors would not simply buy the Toronto 35 Index Participations (TIPs) that trade on the TSE. Toronto Index Participations are essentially a closed-end fund that hold the 35 stocks in the Toronto 35 Index. There is, of course, a brokerage commission attached to buying TIPs, the same cost as would be the case with any stock. However, the annual administrative fees are only 0.25%.

Mind you, TIPs are not as convenient as a mutual fund. For example, you have no mechanism to provide for reinvestment of the dividends. But you have to ask if that inconvenience is worth it as opposed to the management fees and load charges inherent in the two mutual fund alternatives.

Coming Full Circle

Having looked at the cost issues attached to Canadian equity index funds, we have come full circle in the pay-for-performance debate. In our opinion, the performance among traditional Canadian equity funds is well worth the cost of admission. In fact, you pay a high price in terms of performance for the benefit of shaving a small amount off your management-expense ratio.

Investment Objectives and Styles

Scanning the *Southam Source Disk*, we see a number of specific fund objectives related to Canadian equity funds. Objectives range from the very basic "the objective of the fund is to provide investors with superior investment returns over the long term having regard to safety of capital," used by the Altamira Equity Fund. In other words, Frank Mersch, manager of the Altamira Equity Fund, can do just about anything he wants as long as he invests in Canadian equity. Others prefer to tighten the rules with descriptions like "the fund's principal investment objective is the long-term growth of capital with resultant increase in potential income," used by the Imperial Growth Canadian Equity Fund.

Some equity funds prefer to use more complex mission statements to explain their rationale for their fund. For example, the Bullock Optimax USA "A" fund attempts "to achieve long-term capital appreciation primarily by seeking to provide investment results that exceed the performance of equity securities in the aggregate, as represented by the S&P 500 Index, while reducing overall investment risk. The fund will invest in a dynamic portfolio of large and medium capitalization stocks selected from the S&P 500 through a sophisticated computer optimization program."

Then, of course, we have managers who focus on small-cap stocks, such as the Altamira Special Growth Fund which "invests primarily in emerging growth companies with small market capitalization," or the Marathon Equity Fund which attempts to "maximize growth of capital through common shares and other equity securities of Canadian exchange listed issuers. [It] contains some small-cap stocks with potential for significant appreciation. [It] may also invest in U.S. and other foreign securities." Of course, since the Marathon Equity Fund is RRSP eligible, the managers cannot commit more than 20% of their portfolio to foreign companies. The Sceptre Equity Fund follows a different small-cap investment style by maintaining "a portfolio of high-quality holdings." The manager "invests according to fundamental analysis and value orientation."

As well, many Canadian equity funds focus on specific sectors of the economy. The Royal Canadian Growth Fund, for example, seeks "above-average rates of return and long-term capital appreciation through investments in quality small- and medium-size Canadian corporations involved in industries such as telecommunications and resources." The All-Canadian Consumer Fund looks for "long-term preservation and growth of capital. [It] invests primarily in securities serving consumer interests, but may invest majority of assets in Treasury bills, bonds debentures or other monetary instruments as required by prevailing conditions."

The bottom line is that most fund managers will spend a lot of time explaining the rationale behind their particular approach and why their approach is worth consideration in your portfolio, but few will explain the difference in styles and why that may be significant.

We're not here to defend any particular management style. Quite frankly, we are not really convinced that, over the long haul, one approach is any better than another. However, there is evidence to show that different investment styles can be rewarded at different stages of the business cycle.

Given that, allow us to share some thoughts on just what each management style entails. We break down the numerous management styles into the following six basic categories:

- Top Down
- Bottom Up
- Value Method
- Market Timing
- Sector Rotation
- Indexation

The Top-Down Approach

A top-down manager generally begins with an overview of the economy. Are we headed for a period of slow growth with no inflation, or rapid growth with high inflation? Perhaps the economy is descending into a recession, which will impair earnings and push up the unemployment numbers. Or maybe we are moving into a period of expansion that will boost sales and lift earnings.

The top-down investment management team will weight each of the potential scenarios and assign a probability rank to each of them. The managers then focus on industries that are expected to profit under a specific macro-economic scenario. And within those industries, management seeks out the companies that look most promising.

The Bottom-Up Approach

A bottom-up manager is also interested in the outlook for the economy. It doesn't do much good to invest in stocks if we are about to enter a major recession that will impact on the profits of all companies. But rather than use the macro-economic scenario to determine investment choices, many bottom-up managers will use it to determine what percentage of the portfolio will be held in cash.

A true bottom-up philosophy seeks out companies that are 1) undervalued, and 2) have exciting long-term potential. The best company is one the manager can buy and never sell. Some bottom-up managers will focus on specific industries and then choose stocks that look particularly interesting at a point in time. Clearly, the technology industry is an example of just such a philosophy in today's market.

The Value Method

Most value managers follow the traditions of Benjamin Graham and Warren Buffet. Graham, the author of *Security Analysis* and *The Intelligent Investor,* is viewed by many as the architect of value investing. Warren Buffet is a strong follower of Graham's philosophy.

Value investing is a defensive approach, as these managers usually seek out long-term investments in out-of-favor companies—stocks that are often overlooked by the general investing public. Ideally, a value investor buys shares in a company that has a strong balance sheet and solid earnings growth at a time when its value on the stock market is less than its break-up value. Most value investors use a bottom-up selection process and often employ a buy-and-hold strategy.

Market Timing

Most market timers usually follow a technical approach to stock selection. A technician or chartist believes that a picture is worth a thousand words, and will often buy a stock or a number of stocks in a specific industry, or a basket of stocks representing a cross-section of the market, on the basis of a breakout or a change in a particular technical pattern.

Market timers pay particular attention to momentum, believing that when a stock or industry or the market itself moves in a particular direction—representing strong momentum—its path of least resistance will be in that same direction. Buy-and-sell signals are based on the degree of momentum and changes in that momentum.

Generally speaking, market timers are an aggressive group. Their funds are usually higher risk, and the returns reflect that. The market timer may use a few or many indicators to make an investment decision. And while the number of indicators is not that important, how often those indicators signal a change in direction is. There is a cost associated with frequent trading in and out of the market, which impacts on the MER of the fund. We prefer market timers who stick with positions for long periods, believing that the costs associated with frequent buy-and-sell signals eat away at most of the potential profits.

Sector Rotation

A sector rotator normally focuses on specific industries within the overall market. Most generally, a manager following this philosophy uses a top-down approach. The idea is to follow the ups and downs of the economy, moving from one industry to another at different stages of the business cycle.

During the expansion phase of the business cycle, sector rotators usually seek cyclical companies (i.e., referred to as cyclicals), like the auto industry, transportation stocks and consumer durables. These are industries that tend to profit during upturns in the economy and suffer the most during an economic slowdown.

During periods of economic contractions, a sector rotator will move into defensive industries like pharmaceuticals and health care—sectors whose profit margins are not tied as closely to changes in the business cycle.

Indexation

The goal of an index fund manager is to simply track the market. For example, the Mutual Canadian Index Fund attempts to mirror the performance of the Toronto 35 Index. The manager will simply buy all 35 stocks, weighting each purchase similarly to the benchmark index. Index fund managers, then, are more concerned with *tracking error* than they are with performance. Tracking error simply defines how closely the performance of the index fund mirrors the performance of the benchmark index. The strong selling point of the index fund is its low cost, since there is no buy-and-sell decision to make.

Summary

As you might expect, managers may employ a number of investment styles when running a portfolio. Frank Mersch at Altamira is a classic example. Some managers follow a top-down philosophy that focuses on sector rotation for the core of the portfolio. That same manager may take a small percentage of the portfolio and employ some good old bottom-up value methodology to select a stock he may choose to hold for long periods.

One manager we recently spoke with followed a top-down philosophy, but his largest position in the portfolio was the Loewen Group, a company that manages funeral homes. He bought this stock because 1) he liked the company's style of management, 2) he noticed the company had a very strong balance sheet and 3) he could see the long-term profit potential in the company's main line of business. Of course, the Loewen Group has just come through a nasty lawsuit brought against it in the state of Mississippi. Whether the company will continue to prosper as it has in the past will depend to a large extent on whether any further civil actions come out of the U.S. Lawsuits have a nasty way of changing the way we view "value" situations.

Stock Market Cycles

One of the concerns most investors face when looking at specific equity funds is the degree to which an equity fund will fluctuate in value from one year to the next. When equity funds are hot, the performance numbers sparkle; during not-so-hot years, the numbers can ruffle the feathers of even the most patient investor.

That equity funds traditionally ride a very steep roller coaster is hardly a revelation to the average investor, and for the more experienced investor is a basic investment tenet. History tells us that stocks move in cycles. The question, then, is not that cycles exist, but how to translate each cyclical phase into investment decisions. How well we fare in terms of our long-term performance numbers depends, to a large extent, on how well we interpret each phase of this so-called stock market cycle—a cycle, most analysts agree, that encompasses eight definable stages: three bear market phases and five bull market phases (see Figure 5.1).

The challenge, of course, is to determine where we are on the cycle, which, to be fair, is like trying to find your way through a maze without a map, and quite clearly is more art than science. However, using some historical benchmarks, we can offer a guide that at the very least provides an overview of the investment maze. If nothing else, it should serve to reassure investors that for every ride on the downside there follows another to the top.

Figure 5.1: THE EIGHT PHASES OF THE STOCK MARKET CYCLE

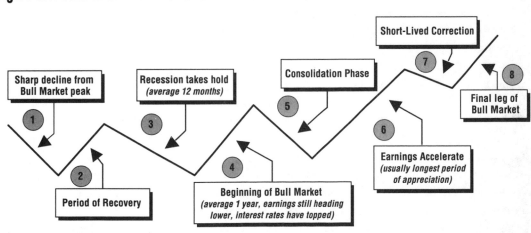

Chart courtesy of Royal Bank International

The Bear Market Stage

Stock market cycles begin with Phase 1—a bear market. We like to think of this phase as the market's wake-up call—a sharp, relatively short-lived collapse, just when you were starting to feel good about yourself. After a period of strong rallies, where picking the right fund was as easy as throwing darts at the wall, the bubble bursts. In a classic market blow-off, driven in most cases by panic selling, stocks fall sharply.

But don't look for signs of an economic slowdown, because a stock market decline is considered a leading economic indicator. A recession may not begin for another six months to two years. October 1987 was a classic example of just such a market.

While the October 19, 1987, blow-off saw stocks lose 23% of their value in one day, the decline actually began shortly after the August 1987 peak. After "Black Monday," the U.S. Federal Reserve quickly eased interest rates, effectively delaying the onset of a recession, which didn't come for another 18 months. In retrospect, the FED made the right decision. Delaying the recession no doubt prevented Wall Street's version of economic Armageddon.

The next step in the bear market cycle is Phase 2, which for lack of a better term is the stock market's recovery room. Your stay depends on the severity of the initial decline. Look for stocks to recover 50% to 100% of the initial Phase 1 sell-off. Investors believe that stocks are cheap relative to the recent highs, and prices are supported by rising earnings. Moreover, confidence remains in the system, because the underlying economic fundamentals remain firm and never did support the sell-off.

Phase 3 represents the next wake-up call. At this point, the economy is clearly in recession and stock prices begin to reflect the fallout. Stock prices usually bottom about three to six months before the recession ends. The extent of the decline in Phase 3 is also linked to the severity of the recession. For the record, 1990 looks like a classic Phase 3 sell-off.

Finally, we turn the corner. Phase 4 is not what you would call a bull stampede, but stocks prices begin to rise, and before you know it they have recovered all of the ground lost by the previous bear market. Surprisingly, stocks are rising while earnings continue to fall and most prognosticators are predicting doom and gloom. What's driving stock prices at this phase is lower interest rates. Which if you think sounds a lot like the period from 1991 through 1993, you're probably right.

Phase 5 is a consolidation period, which can push stock prices down by a third to half of what they gained in Phase 4. The Phase 5 contraction probably took place in 1994, when the U.S. Federal Reserve began to raise interest rates, and stocks and bond funds both lost money.

Fortunately, Phase 5 is soon—some would say not soon enough—followed by another, more sustained, rally: Phase 6. Here we see definite signs that the economy is expanding and earnings are accelerating. It is also a period of high volatility, as earnings become the driving force rather than interest rates. We saw some of that volatility in the technology sector, when high-tech stocks fell as much as 20% in the first three weeks of July 1996.

Based on these observations we are, in late 1996, probably in Phase 6 of this bull market. And this is a period when more of the major gains are made. It can last for as long as three years, and from our perch, there looks to be sufficient steam in this market to take us well into next year.

Now, we come to Phase 7, another short-lived consolidation. How can it be anything but short-lived? At this point in the stock market cycle, investors are really bullish, believing that nothing can stand in the way of continued prosperity. Even bad news is given a positive spin.

Which leads us to the ultimate blow-off, known as Phase 8. That's a point when stock prices rise with no fundamental justification. The outlook for earnings is beyond any rational expectation, and when companies fail to meet those lofty goals, prices fall . . . hard!

Equity Mutual Funds in a Bear Market

A raging bull market is an exciting event, especially if you are in the business of selling mutual funds. Since 1981 (save for the 1987 correction), the equity markets around the world have chalked up record post-war gains. For the most part, equity investors have enjoyed the ride.

While the 1987 stock market crash all but destroyed the retail brokerage business, it only dented the growth in the sales of equity mutual funds. The mutual fund industry continues to be a true growth industry and will probably remain so through to the end of this century.

There's little doubt that this growth has been good for the financial industry. However, there is some question whether the money invested in equity mutual funds is as safe as some people think.

For example, many investors in the 1980s were convinced that they should buy mutual funds with borrowed money. It does, after all, make perfect sense when the stock market is rising. How could you lose? Borrowing money at 10% in order to invest in an equity fund that had grown an average 15% per year seemed as easy as taking cash from a money tree. All that extra growth doesn't even take into consideration the tax benefits. The interest on the borrowed money is deductible, while capital gains have a 25% exclusion.

Unfortunately, those performance numbers have been based in large part on the fact that the market has been in a solid long-term uptrend. While the mutual fund prospectuses, as well as the advertising slogans, are filled with fine print telling you that "past performance is not necessarily indicative of future results," most investors buy with the belief that what was, will continue to be.

The first question is whether equity mutual funds will be able to live up to investors' expectations. Given that equity funds have had such a stellar performance in recent years, investors' expectations may be too high. How much longer can stocks continue to chalk up 15% annual gains?

In a bear market, individual fund holders may want to exit quickly. That means massive redemptions, which in a bear market environment could add fuel to the fire. It was, after all, one of the contributing factors to the October 1987 collapse.

What's more, given the fact that mutual funds have been volatile investments in the past, their explosive growth over the past 10 years may make them even more of a factor in the future. In short, a falling market could be accentuated by the presence of large redemptions, because portfolio managers will be forced to unload shares at any price.

All of which leads us to an even more important question. If and when the stock market takes a prolonged slide, will mutual fund investors be hit harder than direct shareholders? The evidence seems to suggest that they will. In 1984, for example, the U.S. stock market, as measured by the Dow Jones Industrial Average, showed a return of 1.3%, including reinvested dividends. However, mutual funds during the same period showed an average loss of 2.9%.

To be fair, the mutual fund numbers included some pretty steep losses—as much as 30% in some cases—that were absorbed by the more speculative funds. The hardest hit group were those mutual funds that dealt in smaller, less established companies, whose shares are not as easy to resell when the market is falling. What's clear is that 1984 was not unique; the same problems surfaced again in 1987.

Still, the popularity of these speculative funds suggests that not everyone believes that the redemption-forced liquidation syndrome is necessarily a greater problem for mutual fund investors than for individual shareholders. After all, traders will argue that when mutual funds are unloading their shares, they depress the price for everyone.

In a bear market, mutual funds, like individual shares, become more volatile. But our asset allocation model that we will discuss in Chapter 9 actually thrives on this type of environment. Why? Because it provides more opportunities to re-balance the portfolio during market shake-ups.

Take a look at the chart patterns of the Dow Jones Industrial Average since 1929, and they very closely follow the phases we have just described, proving once again that a picture is worth a thousand words. Examine the accompanying chart for the Standard and Poor's 500 Average since July 1987, and you will see similar results (Figure 5.2).

Figure 5.2: S&P 500 COMPOSITE INDEX

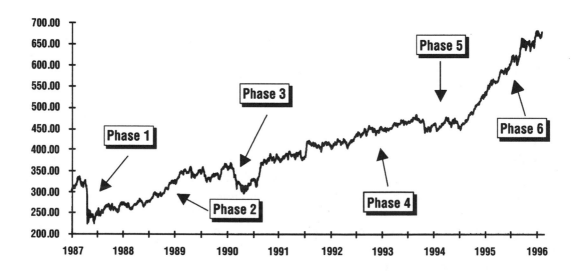

So, where are we now?

If you buy into the eight phases of the stock market cycle, it does appear that October 1987 signaled the end of economic expansion and the high stock market valuations so familiar in the 1980s. If we then assume that 1989 was the beginning of the North American recession, followed by the double dip of 1990, then the rally in late 1991—a rally driven by falling interest rates—was anticipating the end of the recession, an end that officially came in mid-1992.

After a series of rallies, the party abruptly ended in February 1994, when the U.S. Federal Reserve Board raised short-term interest rates by 25 basis points (i.e., 0.25%). What followed were seven additional interest rate hikes that finally ended in February 1995.

Those interest rate hikes were enough to cause some shock waves in the equity markets, to the point that more than a few analysts were talking bear! After a shaky start to 1995, through the end of February, the equity markets have recovered nicely. And now, with the odds stacked against further interest rate cuts, further advances in the stock market will have to be supported by higher earnings.

Moreover, inflation seems to be in check, at least according to the latest figures on the Producer Price front, which would seem to set the stage for continued expansion. From all accounts, we think this looks a lot like a Phase 6 expansion, which could take the Dow Jones Industrial Average and TSE 300 Composite Index well above the 6,000 level.

This rally will have some further bumps along the way, but we think that this expansion phase could last through 1996 and perhaps into 1997. A correction of 10% or more, we think, would be needed to signal an end of this phase, which would lead us directly into the Phase 8 blow-off, and that's a point where you should consider reducing the equity component of your portfolio and begin concentrating on lower-risk bond funds and some value-oriented equity funds.

CHAPTER SIX

Bond Funds

The "Bond" in Canada Savings Bonds

Here's a question: Why do Canada Savings Bonds (CSBs) that mature in 2005 yield about 5.75%, while Government of Canada bonds maturing in the same year yield about 7.5%? The same government issues both bonds. They have the same term-to-maturity (i.e,. they both mature in nine years). The quality of the investments is the same, in that you will receive the face value of the bonds at maturity. So why the disparity in yield?

It is these kind of questions that serve to confuse the average investor. For a subject that you would think is relatively straightforward—i.e., you buy a bond, you receive interest and, at maturity, your principal investment is returned—there have been volumes written about it. The problem, of course, is not so much for investors who want to buy a bond and hold it to maturity. The problems result when investors buy a bond and want to sell it prior to maturity. Or more commonly, buy a bond fund thinking that it is an alternative to GICs, only to find the value of the bond fund fluctuates with changes in the level of interest rates.

In this chapter we will examine the differences between CSBs and government bonds, explain some terms, and help you understand the relationship between long-term bonds, bond funds and interest rates. More specifically, we will focus on what makes a good bond fund and what to look for when buying either Canadian or global bond funds. Think of this chapter, then, as your "fixed-income primer."

Setting the Record Straight

Before entering the fixed-income maze, let's clear up the discrepancy between Canada Savings Bonds and Government of Canada bonds. In point of fact, the investment community is using a loose interpretation of the term "bond" when applying it to CSBs. Having the ability to redeem a CSB any time and receive the full face value plus accrued interest[2] is not how we define bonds. That is how we define cash.

The loose interpretation stems from the fact that while CSBs mature at some point in the future—maturing in 2005 using our hypothetical example—the interest payable is not fixed. The rate payable is adjusted on a needs basis to reflect changes in the rate of interest being paid on savings accounts, one-year guaranteed investment certificates, short-term Treasury bills and money market funds. Again, these are investment comparisons that are normally associated with cash assets.

Bonds are fixed-income instruments. The term "fixed income" refers to the interest or *coupon rate*, which is fixed for the life of the bond. The coupon rate is simply the rate of interest the bond issuer promises to pay as a percentage of the bond's *face value*. For example, if the Government of Canada issues a $1,000 (we refer to the $1,000 as the bond's face or par value) bond with a coupon rate of 12.25%, the government promises to pay to the bondholder $122.50 ($1,000 face value multiplied by 12.25% = $122.50) in interest each year, and that rate is fixed for the life of the bond. The notion that a bond's coupon rate is fixed is the primary difference between our pure definition of a bond and the rather weak inclusion of the word bond in CSBs.

Making Liberal Use of Examples

Having cleared up the first part of our discussion, let's continue with some hypothetical examples. Consider a Government of Canada bond, with a 12.25% coupon, maturing in September 2005. We'll refer to this bond as a GOC 12.25% / 2005. What we have, then, is a bond issued by the Government of Canada that promises to pay to the holder 12.25% per year until September 2005. The coupon rate is paid semi-annually, which simply means half of the 12.25% interest is paid in March and the other half in September. For the record, almost all bonds pay interest semi-annually.

Here's where it gets interesting. Our GOC 12.25% / 2005 pays 12.25% per year while similar government bonds maturing in 2005 are yielding 7.5%. This would appear to be a once-in-a-lifetime investment opportunity. The line forms to the left.

However, before standing too long in this line, realize that as with all aspects of life, there ain't no free lunch. Obviously, for this bond to be available at all, its true yield will have to fall well below the 12.25% compound rate.

For some thoughts on this, we return once again to the simplicity of this CSB example. You can cash in your CSB at any time for its full face value. You can do that because, when interest rates change, the rate payable on the CSB also changes, reflecting the current interest rates available on competing investment vehicles. In short, then, the value of the CSB is unchanged (i.e., you can cash it at any time for its full face value). Only the rate of interest the CSB pays will change.

With our GOC 12.25% / 2005, we know the rate is fixed for the life of the bond. We also

---

[2] *When you cash your CSB, you are eligible to receive interest for each full month you owned the CSB. As such, you should always wait until the end of the month before cashing a CSB, in order to be eligible to receive interest in that month.*

know that our GOC 12.25% / 2005 should effectively yield the same as other comparable instruments—approximately 7.5%—maturing at the same time.

The question, of course, is how do we get our GOC 12.25% / 2005 fixed coupon bond to yield only 7.5% compounded annually. Since we can't change the coupon rate, the only alternative is to change what we pay for the bond. And there again lies a significant difference between real bonds and CSBs. With CSBs, the rate of interest changes, but the price is fixed. With bonds, the rate of interest is fixed, but the price of the bond fluctuates.

To buy $1,000 face value of the GOC 12.25% / 2005, we will have to pay a premium, or a price higher than the $1,000 face value. Based on our calculations, which we'll explain in a moment, you should expect to pay approximately $1,320 for every $1,000 face value. Of course, if you talk to a professional bond trader and ask him for the price, you will get a response like $132. This is part of that technical bond market language that serves to confuse most investors. Suffice it to say, bond prices are quoted as a percentage of face value. The $132 price simply means 132% of face value.

Even though you pay a premium, this still looks like an attractive investment. After all, you will earn $122.50 in annual interest. Divide the annual interest by the price of the bond and the yield is 9.28%, a calculation that we refer to as the bond's *current yield*. What's interesting about this example is that the current yield is still more attractive than the average yield of 7.5% for other government bonds maturing in 2005. Confused? Still waiting in the line to buy? Before you do, consider the next step along this road.

If you hold the GOC 12.25% / 2005 bond to maturity, you will only receive the $1,000 face value. And there's the rub. Because you paid $1,320, your portfolio will suffer a $320 capital loss over the next nine years. That capital loss has to be factored into your total return, which is what bond traders do when they calculate *yield-to-maturity*.

And while the calculation may be a bit more complicated, the yield-to-maturity is the one measure that allows for an apples-to-apples comparison of all bonds regardless of maturity, coupon rate or price. The yield-to-maturity calculation accounts for all of the facets in the bond's total return, including the semi-annual interest payments as well as the repayment of principal. The yield-to-maturity calculation simply assigns a present-day value to all of the future cash flows including the principal repayment.

For example, if we purchase our GOC 12.25% / 2005 bond about the middle of August 1996, we will receive our first interest payment—$61.25 per $1,000 face value—one month later. Since we also know that similar government bonds maturing in 2005 have a yield-to-maturity of 7.5%, we use this rate to discount our payments to their present value.

Current Date		Aug-96
Face Value:		$1,000
Discount Rate:		7.50%
Payment Date	**Payment**	**Present Value of Payment**
Sep-96	$61.25	$60.84

The present value of our first $61.25 semi-annual interest payment then is $60.84. We can then apply the same calculation to the next semi-annual interest payment due in March 1997, the third payment due in September 1997 and so on up to and including the principal repayment due in September 2005. If we add the present values of all future semi-annual interest payments from Table 6.1, the total works out to $823.61. The present value of the principal repayment due September 2005 is $496.85. Add those two figures and we end up with the bond's current price $1,320.46 (i.e., $132 for short).

Table 6.1: GOVERNMENT OF CANADA 12.25% BOND DUE SEPTEMBER 2005—7.5% DISCOUNT

Date		Aug-9
Face Value:		$1,000
Discount Rate:		7.50%
Payment Date	**Interest**	**Present Value of Payment**
Sep-9	$61.20	$60.80
Mar-9	$61.20	$56.90
Sep-9	$61.20	$54.20
Mar-9	$61.20	$52.80
Sep-9	$61.20	$50.90
Mar-9	$61.20	$49.10
Sep-9	$61.20	$47.30
Mar-9	$61.20	$45.60
Sep-9	$61.20	$43.90
Mar-9	$61.20	$42.90
Sep-9	$61.20	$40.80
Mar-9	$61.20	$39.30
Sep-9	$61.20	$37.90
Mar-9	$61.20	$36.50
Sep-9	$61.20	$35.20
Mar-9	$61.20	$33.90
Sep-9	$61.20	$32.70
Mar-9	$61.20	$31.50
Sep-9	$61.20	$30.40
Total		**$823.60**
	Principal	**Present Value of Payment**
Sep-05	$1,000.00	$496.80

Present Value of Principal and Interest $1,320.40

Stating this another way, if we pay $132 to buy our GOC 12.25% / 2005 bond, our yield-to-maturity will be 7.5%. The yield-to-maturity approximates—after accounting for the decline in the bond's current price—the market rate for similar bonds maturing in 2005. The yield-to-maturity, then, is the principal (pardon the pun) measure used by professional bond traders when comparing fixed-income assets having similar risk factors and maturities. There is one caveat to this discussion. The yield-to-maturity calculation assumes by default (again excuse the pun) that you are able to reinvest those semi-annual interest payments at the 7.5% rate.

When you think about it, with a government bond, there is no real risk of default. Having removed default risk from the discussion means that the only factor impacting the price of the bond will be interest rates. That bond prices are inexorably linked to interest rates lays the foundation for the remainder of our discussion on domestic fixed-income assets. In short, when interest rates rise, bond prices fall, and conversely, when interest rates are falling, bond prices rise. We think of this inverse relationship as the fixed-income teeter-totter (Figure 6.1), with bond prices at one end and interest rates at the other.

Figure 6.1: THE FIXED-INCOME TEETER-TOTTER

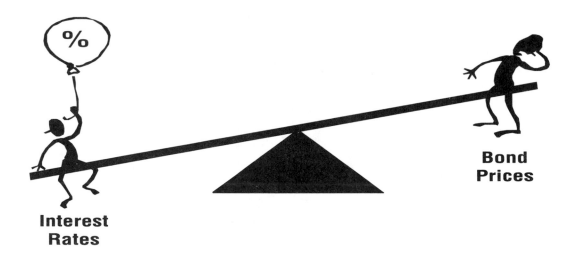

Interest Rates

Bond Prices

The Term-to-Maturity

When we talk about a bond being long term or short term, we are really talking about the bond's *term to maturity*. In August 1996, our GOC 12.25% / 2005 bond had a term-to-maturity of nine years and one month. A bond maturing in 2021 has a term-to-maturity of 25 years give or take a month or two, and one maturing in August 1997 has a term-to-maturity of one year.

The longer the term-to-maturity, the larger a factor the semi-annual interest payments play in the bond's total return. Indeed, from Table 6.1, you can see that the present value of the interest payments were almost twice as important in the bond's overall price than was the present value of the $1,000 principal repayment due in nine years.

Compare that to a government bond that has, say, a 10% coupon, matures in September 1998 and is discounted at 6.75%, the going rate for similar quality bonds with the same three-year maturity. From the calculations in Table 6.2, we see that the present value of the principal repayment carries a much greater weight in the bond's total price than does the stream of semi-annual interest payments.

Table 6.2: GOVERNMENT OF CANADA 10% BOND DUE SEPTEMBER 1998—6.75% DISCOUNT

Date	Aug-96
Face Value:	$1,000
Discount Rate:	6.75%

Payment Date	Interest	Present Value of Payment
Sep-96	$50.00	$49.70
Mar-97	$50.00	$46.79
Sep-97	$50.00	$45.26
Mar-98	$50.00	$43.78
Sep-98	$50.00	$42.35
Total		$227.88
	Principal	Present Value of Principal
Sep-98	$1,000	$847.08

Present Value of Principal and Interest $1,074.96

Term-to-maturity, then, is significant in terms of portfolio management. The longer the term-to-maturity, the more dramatic will be the shifts in the price of the bond given a change in interest rates.

To understand that, let's return to Tables 6.1 and 6.2, only this time we will assume interest rates have gone up by 1%, which alters our discounting factor. We will discount the GOC 12.25% / 2005 bond by 8.5% rather than 7.5%, and in Table 6.2 we will discount the bond by 7.75% rather than 6.75%. The price of both bonds will decline. The question is one of degree (see Tables 6.3 and 6.4).

Table 6.3: GOVERNMENT OF CANADA 12.25% BOND DUE SEPTEMBER 2005—8.5% DISCOUNT

Date	Aug-96
Face Value:	$1,000
Discount Rate:	8.50%

Payment Date	Interest	Present Value of Payment
Sep-96	$61.25	$60.78
Mar-97	$61.25	$56.36
Sep-97	$61.25	$54.06
Mar-98	$61.25	$51.86
Sep-98	$61.25	$49.74
Mar-99	$61.25	$47.71
Sep-99	$61.25	$45.77
Mar-00	$61.25	$43.90
Sep-00	$61.25	$42.11
Mar-01	$61.25	$40.40
Sep-01	$61.25	$38.75
Mar-02	$61.25	$37.17
Sep-02	$61.25	$35.65
Mar-03	$61.25	$34.20
Sep-03	$61.25	$32.81
Mar-04	$61.25	$31.47
Sep-04	$61.25	$30.19
Mar-05	$61.25	$28.96
Sep-05	$61.25	$27.78
Totals		**$786.66**

	Principal	Present Value of Principal
Sep-05	$1,000	$453.48

Present Value of Principal and Interest $1,243.14

The GOC 12.25% / 2005 bond went from $132 ($1,320 for every $1,000 face value) to approximately $124 ($1,240 for every $1,000 face value), a decline of 6.06%.

Table 6.4: GOVERNMENT OF CANADA 10% BOND DUE SEPTEMBER 1998—7.75% DISCOUNT

Date	Aug-96
Face Value:	$1,000
Discount Rate:	7.75%

Payment Date	Interest	Present Value of Payment
Sep-96	$50.00	$49.65
Mar-97	$50.00	$46.34
Sep-97	$50.00	$44.61
Mar-98	$50.00	$42.95
Sep-98	$50.00	$41.34
Total		$224.89

	Principal	Present Value of Principal
Sep-98	$1,000	$826.88

Present Value of Principal and Interest $1,051.77

The 10% Government of Canada bond maturing in 1998 went from $107.40 ($1,070.40 for every $1,000 face value) to approximately $105.10 ($$1,051 for every $1,000 face value), a decline of 2.14%.

The term-to-maturity, then, has a dramatic affect on how a bond's price will change given a change in the level of interest rates. The longer the term-to-maturity, the more volatile the bond's price will be. Using our playground analogy, the longer the term-to-maturity, the greater the movement at each end of the teeter-totter.

The Yield Curve

Bondholders expect a long-term bond to offer higher yields than shorter-term bonds. We saw this in our examples from Tables 6.1 and 6.2. Note that the bond maturing in 2005 was discounted by 7.5% versus a discount rate of 6.75% for the government bond maturing in three years. Generally, we would expect bonds with longer maturities to offer higher yields in order to compensate investors for the increased volatility in the bond's price given a shift in the level of interest rates.

The relationship between interest rates and the term-to-maturity is graphically displayed in the *yield curve* (see Figure 6.2). The yield curve is really just a line on a graph that plots the interest rate paid by bonds with similar risk characteristics but different terms-to-maturity.

There are many yield curves. For example, there is a yield curve for federal government bonds, another for provincial bonds, another for AAA rated corporate bonds, another for AA rated corporate bonds, and so on. The most widely followed yield curve is the one that graphs Government of Canada bonds ranging from maturities of one month to 30 years. There are a couple of reasons for this yield curve's popularity: 1) government bonds, as we said, have no default risk to distort the relationship between term-to-maturity and interest rates, and 2) federal government bonds are the most actively traded sector of the fixed-income market, thus providing an up-to-the-minute unbiased measure of the bond market's psychology.

The horizontal axis represents the term-to-maturity, while the vertical axis on the left of the graph represents different levels of interest rates. Note that in June 1996, three-year government bonds are currently yielding 6.75% (see also Table 6.2) while nine-year government bonds are yielding 7.75%. We refer to this as a normal sloping yield curve, in that the rate generally rises from left to right as the term-to-maturity lengthens.

Figure 6.2: YIELD CURVE (JUNE 1996)

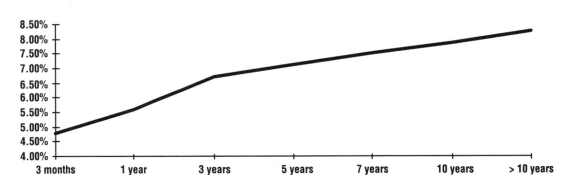

Interestingly, not all yield curves slope up from left to right. And the fact that occasionally the shape of the yield curve changes can tell you a great deal about where the market believes interest rates are headed. And from our perspective, being able to read and understand the yield curve can help us make intelligent choices when investing in fixed-income assets.

In effect, the yield curve paints a picture of the trade-off between risk and reward. It acts as a guide to help investors decide whether it makes more sense to buy bonds offering higher yields but with longer terms-to-maturity. Or perhaps, given some trepidation on the part of the investor, it makes more sense to opt for lower rates on a bond that matures within, say, the next three years. The key is understanding how to read the mood of the market from the yield curve. After all, the yield curve tells us how bond market investors view the future at any given moment. It may not be correct, but it is unbiased, because the participants are painting the picture with their own money.

The Shapes of the Yield Curve

We know in a normal yield curve the line slopes gently upward from left to right. We also know why. The higher interest rates simply compensate the investor for the risks associated with longer-term bonds. The fundamental risk is inflation, which over time will eat away at the real return of your bond.

When the yield curve slopes downward from left to right, it said to be inverted. This does not happen often, the most dramatic example in recent memory being the 1981 yield curve (see Figure 6.3), when short-term yields breached 20% while 30-year bonds yielded about 16%. Looking back, earning 16% for 30 years seems almost unbelievable, yet there were few investors willing to risk their capital for that length of time. The 1981 inverted curve reflected the market's belief that the long-term risk of inflation was much less than the short-term threat. The last time this happened, although much less dramatically, was in 1989.

Figure 6.3: INITIAL YIELD CURVE (1981)

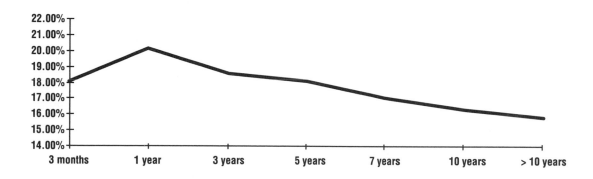

When both short- and long-term interest rates are roughly the same, the curve is said to be flat. An unusual situation to be sure, but one that closely resembles the curve in March 1995, when three-year government bonds yielded 8.24% versus 8.78% for 30-year government bonds. That such a small spread between the 2- and 30-year government bonds existed, implied that the market was not anticipating any serious long-term inflationary pressures.

The yield curve in March 1995 was quite different from the one we saw in 1994, when the spread between 3- and 30-year government bonds was 1.25 percentage points, and the spread between the 3-month Treasury bills and the 30-year bond exceeded 2.64% percentage points (see Figure 6.4).

Figure 6.4: FLAT YIELD CURVE (MARCH 1985)

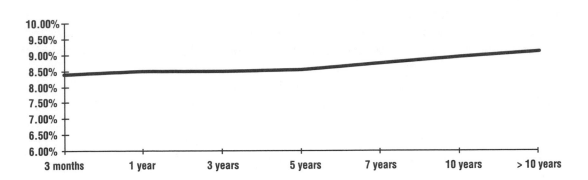

The change in the Canadian yield curve was driven primarily by actions south of the border. This illustrates how closely linked our two economies are, and how dramatic an impact the U.S. Federal Reserve Board (FED) can have on Canadian interest rates, especially when Chairman Alan Greenspan gets antsy about the U.S. economy and inflation.

Between February 1994 and February 1995, the Federal Reserve Board raised short-term interest rates seven times, pushing the yield on 3-month U.S. Treasury bills from 3.03% to 6%, while the yield on 30-year U.S. government bonds went from 6.23% to around 7.86% in a year. This is what gave us the predominantly flat curve we had in January 1995.

One other telling feature that needs to be examined can also be seen from Figure 6.3. Notice the bump, or if you prefer the technical term—"hump"—in the three-year maturity spectrum. Typically you find these so-called humps at the point along the yield curve where investors find the ideal combination of the highest yield with the least perceived risk.

And you wanted to trade bonds?

Having read this far, you have now probably come to the conclusion that there is more to fixed-income investing than meets the eye, which is why many investors turn to the professional money management offered by Canadian bond funds.

A bond fund, as the name suggests, simply invests in a portfolio of bonds. A high-grade Canadian bond fund would invest in a portfolio of secure bonds. In fact, some bond fund managers only invest in government bonds and ignore high-grade corporate bonds. Other bond fund managers prefer a mixture of government and high-grade corporate bonds.

Professional bond fund managers practice many different styles to meet the dual objectives of growth and income. (We will discuss styles later in this chapter.) It is important to understand that the return you get from any high-grade bond fund will be determined, for the most part, by the average term-to-maturity of the fund's portfolio.

If interest rates are high, and are expected to fall, bond managers generally lengthen their average term-to-maturity. They want to get the biggest bang for the buck, and from our previous examples, longer-term bonds will rise more dramatically than bonds with a shorter maturity.

If interest rates are low and the manager expects rates to rise, he will tend to shorten the average term-to-maturity of the bond portfolio so that the value of the fund will not fall as far as would be the case with longer-term bonds. A good bond fund manager is able to delicately balance this trade-off between performance and risk.

Caught between Performance and Risk

Those of you who bought Canadian bond funds in 1994 came face to face with two conflicting points of view: 1) wanting a percentage of the portfolio allocated to fixed-income investments to provide income and balance for the overall asset mix, versus 2) a concern that based on 1994's dismal performance numbers, the risks were too high.

To address the first issue, let's understand why domestic fixed-income assets—defined as Canadian bond funds—should be part of your portfolio. Simply stated, bond funds add stability. And since most bond funds automatically reinvest periodic interest distributions, they compel investors to systematically engage in dollar-cost averaging.

The concept of reinvestment is a key issue, and demands emphasis, particularly if you held bond funds throughout 1994. Thanks to FED Chairman Greenspan, the net asset value of almost every bond fund with at least a three-year track record declined. The average loss among Canadian bond funds was 4.6%.

Among the pieces that make an average, there was the Altamira Bond fund that fell more than 9% for the full year. Other funds, like the Trimark Government Income Fund, fell only marginally (-0.7%). At the end of the day, the result was the same. Massive bond fund redemptions took place during the 1995 RRSP season—just about the time the U.S. Federal Reserve Board was beginning to feel good about itself.

It bears repeating just how important it is to remain calm when riding the ups and downs of the interest rate cycle. February 1995 turned out to be the low water mark for Canadian bond funds. Interest rates had finally stopped climbing, and from that point they began a rather dramatic descent that turned 1994's worst performers into 1995's best performers. Unfortunately, most fixed-income investors had cashed in their chips just as the rally began.

Finding a Silver Lining

If there is a silver lining to the 1994 performance numbers, it is in the exception and not the rule. The exception in this case is the Dynamic Income Fund, the only fund with at least a three-year track record to spin a positive return. Not only did Dynamic Income Fund defy 1994's law of negative gravity, it did so with a vengeance, up 6.4% on the year. A good performance by any measure, and an outstanding performance relative to its peers in 1994.

Pointing out Dynamic Income's rather dynamic performance in 1994 establishes a foundation for understanding what drives bond fund performance in general. And we think that's important (why else would we have spent so much time laying a foundation for pricing bonds earlier in the chapter?) because it helps investors account for performance numbers in any given year. That's more useful than shrugging your shoulders, rolling your eyes and complaining about a manager who didn't live up to expectations.

We think by understanding the cause-and-effect relationship between interest rate cycles and bond fund performance, you will be accorded a measure of comfort through the bad years, which will keep you in the game to profit from the good years. You shouldn't be selling at exactly the wrong time.

We also believe that understanding the past helps us acquire the skills to make sound investment decisions for the future. Depending on your personal tolerance for risk, we can help you construct a portfolio of bond funds that takes advantage of the current interest rate cycle (more on that in Chapter 12 where we present our fearless forecast for 1997).

Of course, if you get an uneasy feeling whenever the Minister of Finance presents a budget laden with rosy economic forecasts, you may be better served with a bond fund portfolio that virtually eliminates all of the risks associated with economic predictions. We have a recipe for that as well. We like to think of this as our way of bringing "insurance" back into the investment management game.

Laying the Groundwork

To start a discussion on what drives bond fund performance, allow us to introduce some hard-nosed bond fund facts.

Fact #1

Solid performance numbers, steady cash flow and reasonable risk make Canadian bond funds an ideal long-term RRSP investment. We mention RRSPs because, as Canadians, we pay a higher tax rate on interest income. Given that, it makes sense to shelter as much of it as possible, hence bond funds inside an RRSP.

Fact #2

A bond fund's net asset value (NAV) will fluctuate. Canadian bond funds, then, are not an alternative to guaranteed investment certificates (GICs).

Fact #3

Bond funds, and some would say, bond fund managers, do not mature. The fund managers dictate the term-to-maturity of the portfolio, which presumably reflects the manager's view about interest rates within the context of the fund's stated objectives.

Fact #4

There's more to investing in a bond fund than meets the eye, which begs the question: "Will bond fund returns over the next three years match the longer-term historical numbers (five-year performance of the average Canadian bond fund equals 8.9% compounded annually), or will they reflect the dismal performance of 1994?" Like all investments, the answer probably lies between these two extremes.

What drives bond fund performance?

Interest rates drive the performance of a high-grade bond fund. We emphasize the "high-grade" trademark to distinguish between bond funds that invest in government or high-grade corporate bonds from those so-called "high-yield" bond funds that invest in what investment analysts refer to as "junk bonds."

A high-yield bond fund manager will invest in bonds issued by companies that may or may not be able to repay the principal at the end of the term. Therefore, in a high-yield bond fund, there is a risk of default, which adds another dimension to the performance numbers.

However, because we are not supporters of any investment strategy that has the term "junk" associated with it, we will only be recommending high-grade bond funds for your portfolio. As mentioned earlier, these high-grade bond funds invest primarily in government bonds, where the risk of default is not a major concern.

With that in mind, we expect a bond fund's NAV will move inversely to a change in the level of interest rates. If interest rates are rising, the NAV of the bond fund will decline; if interest rates are falling, a bond fund's NAV will rise. Knowing that a teeter-totter relationship exists is one thing; what's more important is knowing how high and low the teeter-totter will go. We need to know this in order to determine just how much of an impact a change in interest rates will have on the NAV of the bond fund.

What we need to know, then, is the bond fund's *average term-to-maturity*. We say average, because unlike the bond examples at the beginning of this chapter, a bond fund does not mature. Moreover, bond fund managers constantly change the bonds within the portfolio, either lengthening or shortening the portfolio's average term-to-maturity. Fund companies keep track of the average term-to-maturity for each of their bond funds, and that information is available to investors and financial advisors for the price of a phone call to the mutual fund's marketing department. In terms of price action, then, the longer the average term-to-maturity, the longer the potential teeter-totter and the more volatile the bond fund will be.

The Tale of Two Bond Funds

Since bond funds invest in bonds and interest rates drive bond prices, we now have some interpretive tools that help explain the difference in the 1994 performance numbers for the Dynamic Income Fund on the one hand, and the Altamira Bond Fund on the other.

Dynamic Income Fund's 6.4% return in 1994 was driven by two important investment decisions. First, Dynamic's managers—Goodman and Company Ltd.—invested about 40% of the portfolio in Canadian foreign pay bonds and foreign-denominated bonds. Even today, about 30% of the current portfolio is in Canadian foreign pay and another 19% in foreign bonds.

Foreign pay bonds, for those not familiar with the product, are bonds issued by provincial or federal governments and other government agencies that are denominated in a foreign currency—usually in U.S. dollars. Since these bonds are issued by Canadian entities, they are not considered a foreign investment, which allows Dynamic Income to remain 100% RRSP eligible. In 1994, the Canadian dollar fell sharply against the U.S. dollar, and thus the value of those foreign pay bonds increased.

Second, and from our perspective the most telling aspect of the 1994 performance numbers, was the decision by Goodman and Co. Ltd. to shorten the average term-to-maturity of the bond portfolio early in 1994. That provided a cushion against losses resulting from the rise in interest rates.

At the other end of the spectrum is the Altamira Bond Fund, whose dismal performance in 1994 was the direct result of the fund's long term-to-maturity. The Altamira Bond Fund had a portfolio with an average term-to-maturity in excess of 15 years in 1994. But rather than cashing in their chips, Altamira went into 1995 with a term-to-maturity of 25.9 years.

The rise in interest rates that predominated the financial markets in 1994 had a major impact on the Altamira Bond Fund. When interest rates went up, the value of the Altamira Bond Fund declined. You might say, then, that our tale of two bond funds demonstrates the long and short of it, and supports the rationale behind Fact # 3.

A Bond Fund's Duration

When you think about it, assuming a bond fund only invests in high-grade bonds, the term-to-maturity becomes the most important decision the manager has to make. And where the manager places the fund on the yield curve (i.e., invests in short-, medium- or long-term bonds), defines how sensitive the fund will be to changes in interest rates.

We can define that sensitivity, something we do for all bond funds in this book, by calculating a bond fund's duration. Not to complicate the issue with another statistical tool, suffice it to say that duration is a more precise calculation than the average term-to-maturity when measuring a bond fund's sensitivity to interest rates. That's because duration takes into account the portfolio's average coupon (i.e., interest paid by the various bonds in the portfolio), the frequency of interest payments and the current price of the bonds in the portfolio. In mathematical terms, duration tells you how long it will take, in years, to recover your initial investment. Duration is almost always less than the bond fund's average term-to-maturity.

More importantly, from our perspective of wanting the best information at the fingertips of each investor, knowing a bond fund's duration will tell us how much a bond fund should rise or fall given a specific change in the level of interest rates.

Duration is most accurate when used to forecast a bond fund's change in value, given a 100-basis point (i.e., 100 basis points equals 1%) rise or fall in interest rates. For example, if interest rates were to fall by 1%, a bond fund with a duration of 10 years would be expected to rise by approximately 10%. Conversely, a 1% rise in interest rates would approximate a 10% decline in the value of the fund.

While the process of calculating duration can be quite complicated, it is not something you need worry about. For one thing, most bond funds do the calculation for you, and you can usually find out the fund's current duration for the price of a phone call.

Of course, there are exceptions to this. There are still a few fund companies where a phone call to the marketing department gets a puzzled response when asked to supply the bond fund's duration and average term-to-maturity. If you get that response, buy another bond fund.

There are also, of course, international or global bond funds that rarely calculate duration which in this case makes sense, because the duration number can be rendered meaningless by fluctuations in the foreign exchange rate. (See Chapter 8, where we discuss borderless shopping.)

For our purposes, we need to know how duration helps us quantify a bond fund's potential risk. Looking at risk in terms of volatility, duration will tell you how much the value of your bond fund will change, given a change in interest rates.

Obviously, duration is one of the issues we will look at when recommending specific bond funds. Bond funds with a long average term-to-maturity (i.e., longer than, say, 10 years) would be considered a long-term fund, and we would expect that fund's duration to be anywhere from 5 to 8 years. Bond funds with an average term-to-maturity of, say, 3 to 9 years would be considered medium term (duration would be anywhere from 2 to just less than 5 years), and bond funds with an average term-to-maturity of less than 3 years (duration less than 2 years) would be considered short term.

The idea, of course, is to buy bond funds with long durations in an environment where interest rates are expected to decline (i.e., lower interest rates, higher bond prices), and look for shorter duration bond funds when anticipating a rise in interest rates. But as you might expect, that's easier said than done.

And the last shall be first!

Constructing an econometric model to predict the direction of interest rates is like trying to write a computer program that will predict Wayne Gretzky's next move based on past performance—the answer may be somewhat better than a blind guess, but it is hardly worth the effort.

Fortunately, knowing the next move in interest rates is not as important as making a judgment call on the long-term trend. In January 1994, when U.S. short-term interest rates were at 3.5%, common sense told us that rates would not go too much lower. We simply weren't that far from zero. The point is, you are never going to pick the bottom or top in interest rates—just try to be as close to one end or the other when making an investment decision.

Similarly, when the U.S. Federal Reserve Board raised interest rates seven times between February 1994 and February 1995, that was probably overkill, especially with inflation running at less than 2% annually.

So 1995 would have been the ideal time to buy aggressive bond funds like the Altamira Bond Fund. Obviously, when interest rates begin to decline, bond funds whose main portfolio includes a healthy dose of long-term bonds will produce the biggest bang for your investment dollar. Dramatic changes in interest rates turned some of 1994's worst-performing bond funds into 1995's best performers. During 1995, for example, the Altamira Bond Fund returned 27.5% and was the number-one performing bond fund over that period, reinforcing the notion that "the last shall be first." For the record, the Dynamic Income Fund returned 14.5% in 1995.

Adding ZIP to Your Fixed-income Portfolio

The prospectus of most major bond funds will talk about an active management philosophy. If a manager is not actively trading the bonds in the portfolio to enhance your bottom line, you have to wonder how many investors would be willing to pay the management-expense ratios associated with Canadian bond funds. By the way, the average management-expense ratio for all Canadian bond funds is 1.63%. Interestingly, we notice that among larger bond funds, the management-expense ratio is often below the average. The implication, in the fixed-income fund market at least, is that bigger is usually better.

The goal for most bond fund managers is to outperform some fixed-income benchmark, the most common being the ScotiaMcLeod Bond Universe. The ScotiaMcLeod Bond Universe[3] is simply an index that measures a hypothetical portfolio of high-grade short-, medium- and long-term bonds.

As we have already stated, in a high-grade bond fund, managers normally add value by shifting the average term-to-maturity of their portfolio. And since they are usually measured against the ScotiaMcLeod Bond Universe, more often than not, bond fund managers will maintain an average term-to-maturity that is close to the average term-to-maturity of the benchmark index.

Despite any self-imposed limitations, most domestic bond fund managers have a rather broad mandate in terms of where they can position the portfolio along the yield curve. There are exceptions, of course. And in terms of how we view portfolios, those exceptions can be useful.

As an example, we cite the Green Line Short Term Bond Fund which "invests in Canadian government and corporate fixed-income securities with maturities of less than three years." Not much room for this manager to maneuver along the yield curve. However, knowing that makes this low-risk bond fund a good choice if you want something to complement a position in a more aggressive actively managed bond fund.

Of course, as was evident with our Dynamic Income example, bond fund managers can also add value holding foreign pay bonds within the portfolio. This provides a currency kicker, so to speak, which can add value in addition to any gains that might be associated by shifts in domestic interest rates.

Fixed-income Management Styles

We know that domestic bond fund managers attempt to beat the average or benchmark index. They want to do well against their peers, relative to other funds in the same category. While

---

[3] There is also a ScotiaMcLeod long-bond index, a ScotiaMcLeod medium-term index and a ScotiaMcLeod short-term index.

these domestic bond fund managers all have the same goal, they accomplish it using different means. From our perspective, there are basically six management styles associated with both domestic bond fund managers and global bond fund managers.

Top Down: Most bond fund managers use a top-down approach. That's because most bond fund managers attempt to predict the direction of interest rates and set their average term-to-maturity to take advantage of interest rate shifts. Predicting interest rates is a top-down job which includes an analysis of such macro-economic forces as inflation, jobs and GDP growth. Interestingly, a top-down manager would also be sensitive to another macro-economic condition such as currency fluctuations, and might buy or sell foreign pay bonds to take advantage of any weakness or strength in the Canadian dollar.

Bottom-up managers are not, at least from our perspective, as commonplace as top-down bond fund managers. A bottom-up manager will normally look for opportunities among corporate or provincial bonds. The idea is to find opportunities at different points—the "hump"—along the yield curve.

Value: Bond fund managers who practice a value style generally work from the premise that the portfolio should maintain a consistent duration and credit quality. In other words, the manager might purchase only medium-term high-grade corporate bonds, or only long-term high-grade government bonds. The idea is to buy undervalued bonds for yield and capital appreciation within the context of a specific term-to-maturity and credit quality.

Sector Rotation: We normally associate this style with equity managers. And to be fair, the term sector rotation may be somewhat misleading when applied to bond fund managers. However, we think of sector rotation as a style that engages in "spread trading." The goal is to examine current yields spreads between bonds in different sectors (i.e., what is the spread between Government of Canada five-year bonds and, say, Province of Ontario five-year bonds). The manager compares these spreads with historical spreads in similar interest rate environments, and then seeks out the most attractive sectors, coupons and credit ratings. This is an active management style that generally, although not always, begins with a bottom-up point of view.

Market Timing: Most top-down bond fund managers follow a style known as interest rate anticipation. We have simply chosen to define interest rate anticipation in the FundLine (see Chapter 11) as market timing. Predicting changes in the shape of the yield curve, and then altering the average term-to-maturity to profit from those changes, is the goal of market timers. From our work, we note that most domestic bond fund managers follow a management style defined as top down/market timing.

Indexation: We offer a more liberal interpretation when it comes to defining whether or not a bond fund manager is operating an indexed portfolio. Obviously, for a pure indexed bond fund like the Green Line Canadian Government Bond Fund that "tracks the ScotiaMcLeod Government Bond Index," the distinction is clear. However, there are cases where bond fund managers always maintain the average term-to-maturity of their portfolio within close proximity to their benchmark index. For example, in the case of a long-term bond fund that always maintains its average term-to-maturity within, say, one year of the ScotiaMcLeod Long Bond Index, we would consider that a long-term bond fund with an indexed management style (note in the FundLine we have a slot to define whether the bond funds average term-to-maturity is short, medium or long term). Similarly, a fund like the Green Line Short-Term Income Fund is, for all intents, indexed to the ScotiaMcLeod short-term bond index, or some other short-term barometer. It is our opinion, because the manager has so little room to maneuver, that this is an indexed management style.

Some Misconceptions about Yield

A *FundLetter* Perspective on MacKenzie Industrial Income

At first blush, categorizing the MacKenzie Industrial Income Fund as a balanced fund seems like a contradiction in terms. The intent is to generate consistent quarterly distributions, providing the unitholders with steady cash flow. The managers accomplish this goal with a portfolio that has close to 90% of its assets invested in government and corporate fixed-income instruments and preferred shares. The implication here is that the fund isn't just another balanced fund that shifts the asset mix in order to profit from changes in the business cycle.

The fund provides unitholders with a $1.00 per year distribution. Given a net asset value per share of $8.14, this implies an annual yield of 12.28%. With guaranteed investment certificate rates in the 6% range, Industrial Income looks like an appealing investment.

Investors evidently agree. Assets grew by 23.3% over the past year to $2.634 billion, making this the sixth-largest open-end fund (and the largest balanced fund) available to Canadian investors.

The annual distribution includes dividend and interest income generated by the assets in the portfolio, as well as any capital gains resulting from purchases and sales within the fund. Nothing unusual about that. In the last couple of years, however, so as to maintain the $1.00 annual distribution, the Industrial Income fund has been forced to dip into principal. In other words, part of the distribution is really just a return of your original principal investment. In 1995, for example, of the $1.00 per unit distribution, 62.5 cents was a return of principal, about 34.25 cents was interest income and 3.25 was dividend income.

The point is, when we divide the income by the current net asset value per share, the resulting yield is misleading. Investors buying on that basis will find that the performance numbers will not live up to their billing. And with Industrial Income's huge size, the impact of the distribution will affect a lot of investors.

Does that mean you should avoid the MacKenzie Industrial Income Fund? Not at all! I am simply saying you have to understand what it is you're buying. And it looks to me that you are buying an income fund that promises steady cash flow by practicing what amounts to a systematic withdrawal program.

A systematic withdrawal program is not all that different from a regular contribution program, except that the money leaves the fund company and goes to the unitholder, rather than from the unitholder to the fund company. Most fund companies offer a systematic withdrawal service.

To get up to speed on this, it helps to understand some alternatives to a fund-sponsored systematic withdrawal program. Suppose you have $100,000 to invest, and you want to draw an income of $12,000 per year. You have a number of options available to you. You could, for example, invest the $100,000 into a bond yielding, say, 8% based on current rates. However, during the year, you would receive only $8,000 in interest income ($100,000 multiplied by 8% = $8,000). In order to meet your $12,000 in total income, you would have to sell $4,000 worth of the bond. That's what we mean when we talk about the return of principal.

Repeat the process each year and the principal in your investment diminishes until you no longer have any principal left to reinvest. (That's also a description of the way an annuity works.)

The systematic withdrawal program is really the mutual fund industry's answer to the annuity, only in this case you invest the $100,000 in a mutual fund and the sponsoring fund company pays you a set amount each month. Just how well your mutual fund performs will determine how long you will receive income and what percentage of that income is return of principal and what percentage is income.

Say you had invested $100,000 in, say, the Trimark Canadian five years ago (January 1, 1991) and had withdrawn $12,000 each year. Because the Trimark Canadian Fund returned 14.95%, at the end of five years your portfolio would be worth slightly less than $123,000. That's the type of example many fund companies use when setting up systematic withdrawal programs. The argument, of course, is that you should utilize an equity fund when entering a systematic withdrawal program, because an equity fund should earn sufficient returns to maintain your principal for a longer period of time.

Which brings me back to the MacKenzie Industrial Income Fund. Of course, it would prefer to earn sufficient returns to pay out the set rate of income without taking anything out of the principal. Easier said than done when you hold a portfolio of mostly fixed-income investments at a time when we have single-digit interest rates.

Bottom line is the MacKenzie Industrial Income Fund can be used for investors who want a set rate of income and understand that part of that income is simply a return of principal. The component of the income that is a return of principal is not subject to any tax liability, a selling feature for investors who are drawing a retirement income.

— R. C.

Global Bond Funds

Having spent most of our time discussing domestic fixed-income funds, it is time we looked beyond our domestic borders, specifically to global bond funds that hold a portfolio of bonds from around the world issued by foreign countries. Unlike a fund that holds domestically issued foreign pay bonds, these funds can only be purchased within an RRSP as part of the 20% foreign content rules.

Looking at the big picture, global bond funds bring to the table another form of diversification. They might, for example, invest in bonds of other countries where interest rates are perhaps higher than in Canada, and that can add some spice to your income needs.

That being said, global bond funds expose the investor to risks not associated with domestic bond funds that do not have any significant foreign pay holdings. The risk that can be present in a global bond fund is foreign currency exposure. We say "can" because some global bond funds actually try to hedge their foreign currency exposure, exposing the investor only to the potential income and capital gains from the bond portfolio. However, there is a cost to currency hedging and that will have some impact on the performance numbers.

Is currency hedging good or bad? We don't come down on one side or the other in this debate. However, we're not certain that currency hedging should be a major concern for global bond funds, because we believe that one of the reasons an investor looks to a global bond is to get some exposure to a foreign currency and use that as a hedge against the Canadian dollar.

Some Thoughts on Mortgage Funds

Mortgage funds are considered low-risk fixed-income assets, and the statistics bear this out. For example, the average three-year standard deviation for mortgage funds is 1.05% versus a three-year average standard deviation for Canadian bond funds of 1.96%.

Because mortgage funds carry less risk, they are often seen as an alternative to GICs. But as we explained in our section on money market funds, perception is quite different from reality. While it is true that mortgage funds are not as risky as bond funds, the price of a mortgage fund can still fluctuate. In 1994, our watershed year for Canadian bond funds, the average mortgage fund lost only 0.04%, well below the 5.8% average loss for Canadian bond funds.

But for a GIC investor that is not appropriate, because a negative return regardless how small, is not acceptable.

Finally, for the Record—a GIC Substitute

Having talked about why fixed income funds should not be considered as GIC substitutes, allow us to suggest the mutual fund market's alternative to GICs—the money market fund. Money market funds invest in low-risk Treasury bills, or certificates of deposit issued by major corporations, all of which provide steady, albeit low, monthly returns.

The monthly returns are usually reinvested into additional units of the fund, which effectively suggests that money market funds are all created equal. Given that, the real issue when scouting potential money market funds comes down to the cost of administration and management. Fort the record, the average management-expense ratio for all Canadian money market funds is 0.69%, which includes trading and administrative costs.

In terms of how a GIC investor views the world, the net asset value of a money market is, in most cases, fixed at $10 per unit. Money market funds can be cashed quickly at the $10 per unit price, and that addresses the investor's perception about the variability of returns.

Assuming the GIC investor's primary consideration is variability of return, then the alternative to a GIC is not a fixed-income fund, but the mutual fund industry's equivalent of cash.

CHAPTER SEVEN

The Basics of Cash

Cash Assets

From our perspective, cash assets are represented by any investment in which there is no real risk of losing your principal. It is any security that can be readily sold or turned into cash with very little bother or cost, and generally has a term-to-maturity of less than one year.

A number of assets fit in this category. Bank savings accounts are probably the most common form of cash, but savings accounts may not be an attractive option. For one thing, some savings accounts pay interest on the lowest balance during any particular month. Some pay interest that is compounded daily, while others compound interest weekly, monthly or even semi-annually. Remember, the less frequent the compounding, the lower your return. Second, the interest rates paid on savings accounts are seldom generous. There are other, more attractive, alternatives.

Canada Savings Bonds

Almost every Canadian is familiar with Canada Savings Bonds (CSBs). CSBs have been issued by the federal government every year since 1946. Now, more than 40 years after their introduction, CSBs make up an important component of the federal government's annual financing plans. More important, they make a great deal of sense for the average Canadian investor.

CSBs go on sale every October and the sale usually lasts for about two weeks. They have a number of popular features in that they are:

- backed by the Canadian government and thus are considered risk-free investments;
- easy to buy; you can walk into any bank, trust company or credit union and line up at the CSB wicket, or you can buy the bond in the fall and pay for it over the year through a payroll deduction plan;

- fully registered in the name of the holder. That means that every year you will receive a statement from Revenue Canada that calculates the amount of interest income you must declare on your tax form;
- cashable at any time for their full face value, which, in terms of defining CSBs as cash, is the most important feature. A trip to your local bank and you can receive cash plus any accrued interest within minutes. However, it is always best to wait until the first of the month before cashing your CSB or you will lose some of interest earned on your bond. If you decide on February 16 to cash a CSB, you should wait until March 1 or you will receive only the interest earned until the end of January. You will not be credited with any interest for the 16 days during which you held the bond in February. If you hold on to your bond, interest will be paid every November unless you buy a compound bond. With a compound bond, the interest is not paid out to you but is left to compound at the same interest rate as your principal.

Are CSBs the investment of choice for the cash component of our asset allocation model? (See Chapter 9.) A great deal depends on the interest rate of the CSBs. To decide, compare the yield with the rates being offered on T-bills or by financial institutions on GICs. In 1990, for example, CSBs were issued at 10.75%, between 0.25% to 0.75% below the rates available on GICs, and 1.25% below prevailing T-bill rates.

Treasury Bills

Treasury bills are the debt of the federal government. Original issues are delivered every Thursday by auction at the Bank of Canada. T-bills do not pay interest; instead, they are sold at a discount to their face value. The difference in the price you pay and the value of the bill at maturity represents the yield over the term of the T-bill.

For example, a $5,000 90-day T-bill might cost $4,925. At the end of three months you would receive $1,000, a return that represents an annual yield of about 6%. T-bills carry terms of 30, 60, 90, 180 or 360 days. You can also purchase nonstandard terms in the secondary market, which is maintained by investment dealers. T-bills can be bought and sold at any time.

T-bills have become very popular in the past few years, particularly since investment dealers relaxed the rules for purchases. At one time, you had to put down between $100,000 and $250,000 to buy a T-bill, but in the past few years investment dealers have been dividing the T-bills issued by the government into smaller offerings, sometimes as little as $5,000. Often there is no commission charge.

T-bills, unlike CSBs, come in bearer form, meaning they are not registered in your name, and you will not receive any information from Revenue Canada regarding the amount of interest you earned during the year in T-bills. Revenue Canada depends on the honesty of the taxpayer to claim the amount of interest earned on the tax form for the appropriate year.

Money Market Funds

One of the most versatile investment vehicles is the money market fund. These unique funds invest in money market securities of various maturities, including Treasury bills issued by the Government of Canada and the provinces, bankers' acceptances, short-term government and high-quality corporate bonds and the promissory notes of companies with very high credit ratings, a product called commercial paper. These are all considered low-risk investments, for which the possibility of a default is relatively remote.

The investor is entitled to a *pro rata* share of the interest earned on the fund's portfolio as well as any capital gains (losses) incurred in the fund's trading of securities before their maturity.

The money market fund is a hybrid between a traditional "mutual fund" and a savings instrument, and is a derived product that was fashioned to meet specific needs. The money market fund has a number of features that are consistent with traditional mutual funds in that it is a pooled, professionally managed, diversified product with normally small dollar entry requirements, dividend reinvestment plans, periodic purchase plans and no secondary market.

Money market funds debuted in Canada in 1983, although consumer interest appeared to materialize in 1985. In 1987, under amendments to the Bank Act, banks were permitted to manage and sell all categories of mutual funds, including money market funds, without restrictions.

However, unlike traditional mutual funds, Canadian money market funds (with a few exceptions) attempt to maintain a fixed net asset value per share (NAVPS) by using various accounting and trading techniques to accomplish this purpose. For money market funds, instead of a fluctuating NAVPS, it is the interest that fluctuates on a daily basis.

Money market funds only pay interest, so all distributions are likely to be treated as interest income. Normally, income is distributed through additional shares or units rather than through cash payments.

For example, if you bought 100 shares of a money market fund at $10 per share, your total investment would be $1,000. If the yield on the fund was, say, 6%, you would earn approximately 0.5% per month in interest distributions. In most cases you would simply receive a one-half share for each 100 shares held (100 x 0.005 = 1/2 share). At the end of one month, the net asset value of the mutual fund would still be $10 per share, but you would now own 100.50 shares.

Because you could purchase most of the investments that the money market fund will purchase for you, there is normally no fee for buying or selling the shares. The management fees on money market funds are also low relative to other funds. The research and analysis required to buy a basket of money market instruments is not intense or expensive. The management fees cover the administration of the fund and should not be any higher than 0.5% of the funds assets. Some money market mutual funds offer cheque-writing services, which can be an attractive feature.

Money market funds are liquid; you can receive cash for your fund almost immediately, at any time, with no penalty or fees in most cases. You might also consider buying a money market fund that is in the same family as your fixed-income and equity funds. This will make it easier to switch between funds if your changes to your portfolio dictate a change in asset weightings.

Investors use money market funds either as a place to park their money temporarily as they wait for other investment opportunities or as a permanent part of their portfolio.

There are four very good reasons to include money market funds in your portfolio:

1. **Capital Preservation:** Since they invest in very low risk, short term-to-maturity securities, your capital is quite safe with money market funds. You may want to use them as an alternative to a savings account, since you can cash out at any time at the fixed net asset value per share. Only under extremely unusual circumstances would a fund be unable to hold its fixed NAVPS at the $10 per share level.
2. **Competitive Yields:** Money market funds have traditionally provided returns that keep pace with changes in short-term interest rates. You will normally find that the returns are higher than that earned on bank deposits, although often lower than on term deposits. Yields are based on current interest-rate movements and will change with the changing interest-rate environment.
3. **Convenience:** The money market fund may be a more convenient product and offer economies of commission and bulk buying over the direct purchase of T-bills or other money market securities. They can be cashed out at any time at the net asset value per share, normally fixed at $10. Your monthly interest payments can be conveniently reinvested in new units. These are ideal as a result for RRSPs or other tax-sheltered plans since you can park small amounts of income temporarily in a money market fund until you decide what to do with it! We recommend that all RRSP investors have a money market fund as part of their plan.
4. **Collateral:** Since they are so stable, money market funds represent excellent collateral for loans.

GICs—Cash or Fixed Income?

This is one of the most hotly debated issues among investors and financial planners. Should we classify guaranteed investment certificates as cash assets or fixed-income assets when constructing an investment portfolio?

The notion that GICs are really fixed-income assets is driven by two major considerations: 1) the so-called accessibility issue, and 2) the maturity spectrum. The fact is, when we think of cash, we think in terms of accessibility: how quickly can you "cash" out your investment? In that sense, CSBs, money market funds and even government Treasury bills can be cashed out within 24 hours, and so defining them as cash assets is relatively easy.

Coupled with the accessibility issue is the investment's term-to-maturity. Again, we think of cash assets as short-term investments, with maturities ranging from 30 days to one year.

Looking at GICs from this perspective makes it difficult to define them as cash assets.

When you buy a GIC, you usually lock in your money for periods ranging from one to seven years. In terms of accessibility, you may have the ability to cash out your investment (depending on what interest rates have done in the meantime), but usually in such cases only after absorbing a severe penalty.

Again, following this same theme, we have the term-to-maturity factor. Any investment that ties up your assets for more than a year is hard to define as cash, even more so when you are locking in your assets for five to seven years. So from these perspectives, it is not surprising that investors view GICs as they would fixed-income investment. And there, in our opinion, lies the problem.

Investor perception can be a dangerous thing. In the fall of 1994, after an investment planning presentation, a retired lady approached us and asked what we thought about mortgage funds. For some historical perspective, this was about six months after the U.S. Federal Reserve and the Bank of Canada had begun pushing up interest rates. At this point in the cycle, the value of most mortgage funds had slipped badly.

We found out that this lady, an individual who had always held GICs, had recently rolled her maturing GIC portfolio into a mortgage fund on the advice of her financial advisor.

The advisor had told her—correctly—that she could enhance her yield. The problem was that the advisor also told her that mortgage funds were an alternative to GICs, because both were fixed-income investments. And to some extent the advisor was right. But what she did not understand was that the value of a mortgage fund could fluctuate, something that does not occur in a GIC, at least, not on the surface. Having invested a sizable portion of her portfolio (about $100,000) into this mortgage fund, she was now distraught to learn that the value of her portfolio had declined sharply.

The same holds true for bond funds. In fact, the variability of return in a bond fund is more dramatic than is the case with mortgage funds. And despite that, we continue to hear of cases where financial advisors recommend a bond fund as an alternative to a GIC, without explaining that a bond fund can fluctuate. And for a long-term investor, perception is everything.

From our perspective, an investor's perception of risk is the primary consideration when classifying investments. We think of cash as a riskless asset. That, too, is the perception of GICs, assuming, of course, they are purchased at a CDIC-insured institution. The GIC principal is guaranteed, and will be repaid with interest, on the maturity date.

The second important perception is the variability of return over the holding period. Cash assets, by definition, do not fluctuate in value. On the surface—i.e., there is no active secondary market or price quotes—neither do GICs. The notion that GICs should be viewed as cash, then, comes down to investor perception. And the view that investors and financial advisors should hold, in our opinion, is that short-term GICs are an alternative to cash, but not an alternative to fixed-income investments.

CHAPTER EIGHT

Borderless Shopping

There are major power shifts occurring in the investment world, signaling permanent and elemental changes in how financial planning and investment portfolio building is carried out. The most important implication is that you now need a global orientation to compete successfully in this rapidly changing environment.

There is a relentless march toward globalization of world markets and 24-hour trading. Geographical boundaries have blurred and trading pacts are proliferating. The Internet and electronic trading systems have linked the world in a manner totally unforeseen two decades ago. This globalization process has been marked by securities deregulation, by instant telecommunications and information flows and increased mobility of capital, all of which have served to foster international investing opportunities. Economic growth is shifting toward poorer countries, and knowledgeable investors are becoming increasingly interested in emerging or developing countries. The trend toward free markets, free trade, foreign investment and market deregulation has propelled capital resources to high-growth and low-per-capita GDP, as well as low-wage countries.

As a result, global investment has become an integral part of the investment asset allocation process. And with good reason. There are tens of thousands of different financial products traded in the world's some 500 bond, stock and derivatives markets. If you limit yourself to only the Canadian market, you are shutting yourself off from rich investment opportunities elsewhere. The Canadian domestic market represents a mere fraction of the world's investment opportunity set.

Investors who constrain their analysis and selection to domestic instruments severely limit their opportunities. And those investors who do venture forth into the international arena may be discouraged when they discover that their broker or advisor knows less than they do about foreign securities. However, the international investment process, although fraught with pitfalls, is by no means a daunting task.

The Benefits of Global Investment

The smaller the local market, the greater the rewards of global investing. Although Canada is a major investment center, ranking next to the first-tier giants of the United States, Japan and the United Kingdom, it still, as is pointed out so frequently in the financial press, represents only about 2% to 3% of the world, according to how much money is invested here.

There are a number of compelling reasons for investing abroad. Global portfolio investment offers enhanced returns, reduced portfolio risk through the arithmetic of diversification, increased investment opportunities, foreign exchange risk exposure, not to mention the psychic enjoyment of wandering through the global marketplace. But be forewarned. Many foreign markets are volatile and erratic. This underscores the value of concentrating on long-term diversification through a strong, strategic, asset allocation policy.

Enhanced Returns

Canada is one of the world's major industrialized countries and has well-developed capital markets, including the seventh-largest stock exchange in the world, the Toronto Stock Exchange. However, longer-term performance of Canada's equity markets can only be described as fair.

Canadian stocks are subject to a set of domestic economic, political and social factors that cannot be diversified away no matter how large the stock portfolio. These systematic effects, given the relatively tight policies followed by the Bank of Canada in recent years, have conspired to keep Canadian stock returns relatively low. For example, over the recent period 1986 to 1996, world security markets recorded solid returns, most of them far outstripping Canada. In fact, from a select sample of major markets, Canada ranked near the bottom, ahead of only a handful of markets. While the New York Stock Exchange was registering a return of about 14.7% per year over this period, the Canadian market turned in a more modest 8.0 % per annum performance. The leading index of world market performance, the Morgan Stanley Capital International's World Index of 25 major countries, recorded a 15.9% compounded return over that same 10-year period.

In a study published in the *Canadian Investment Review* in 1991, Harry Marmer, a respected researcher and commentator on the global investment scene with the William M. Mercer consulting firm, indicated that over the previous 12 years, using data from 1978 through 1989, non-U.S. foreign stocks as measured by the Morgan Stanley Capital International Europe Asia and Far East (MSCI EAFE) Total Return Index in U.S. dollars were the top-performing asset class, followed by U.S. stocks, Canadian stocks, Canadian bonds, foreign bonds and Canadian T-bills. Of particular interest was his finding that the correlation between Canadian stocks and non-U.S. foreign stocks was .40. This means that, more often than not, Canadian and non-U.S. stocks are moving independently, reflecting the different forces that drive them.

The bottom line is that global investors realized considerably higher rates of returns than those who confined their investments to strictly Canadian financial products. In a recent study, Keith Ambachtscheer, a well-known chronicler of asset returns and institutional investment strategies and performance, recently pointed out that equity exposure to an investment portfolio increases the potential for greater return without adding to overall risk. Marmer's 1991 study showed that non-U.S. foreign stocks realized 5.4% per annum higher returns than Canadian stocks, with a 2.6% per annum lower volatility.

Diversification

Diversification, as we have pointed out repeatedly in previous chapters, is the cornerstone of successful long-term investing. In simple terms, diversification means that you are selecting securities that do not always move together. Securities with low correlations are valuable diversification products.

Many leading lights in investment finance, including Nobel prizewinners Harry Markowitz and James Tobin, have shown that efficient diversification reduces the risk of a portfolio, assuming that risk is measured by the variance about the returns on the component securities and the portfolio. They have demonstrated that the degree of risk reduction offered by each security added to the portfolio reflects the security's co-variance or co-movement with either the portfolio or an appropriate market index. Therefore, securities that have a low co-variance with the portfolio of securities or a market index are valuable in reducing risk. Thus on any given day, some of your investments may rise and some may fall, and so the chances of major losses are substantially reduced.

This principle of diversification applies quite powerfully to international portfolio diversification. Numerous studies indicate that the correlation between individual stock market indexes and the world stock market index is relatively low. A high degree of the variance in stock indexes is due to unsystematic (or unique) risk of each country and can therefore be diversified away in an international portfolio of securities.

Bruno Solnik was the first to publish results on the value of global diversification. Using weekly price data for the period 1966 to 1971, he constructed securities portfolios of various sizes from the U.S., the U.K., France, West Germany, Italy, Belgium, the Netherlands and Switzerland, as well as an international portfolio. He concluded that "The gains from international diversification are substantial. In terms of variability of return an international well-diversified portfolio would be one-tenth as risky as a typical security and half as risky as a well-diversified portfolio of U.S. stocks [with the same number of holdings]." An important caveat is that you have to be prepared stick it out over the long term because the markets take turns. In general, given differing political and social policies, the longer-run correlations remain low.

Japan and the U.K. are relatively large markets and ideal candidates for internationally diversified portfolios for Canadian investors, based on their low degree of co-movement with Canadian markets.

Concentration on emerging markets is also useful. Since inflation/deflation/recession cycles are normally non-universal, the inclusion of countries with different economic systems and outlooks is valuable. Emerging countries are essentially uncorrelated among themselves and have low correlations with Canadian markets. Emerging countries with particularly low correlations include Argentina, Brazil, China, Greece and India.

The U.S. is the least valuable candidate for Canadians looking for global diversification. Auger and Parisien, in a study published in the *Canadian Investment Review* in the spring of 1989, showed that although stocks on the Toronto Stock Exchange had relatively low correlation with global asset classes, their correlation with U.S. stocks was relatively high. Their findings were as shown in the table below:

Table 8.1: STOCK CORRELATION

	S&P 500 Unhedged	S&P 500 Hedged	EAFE Unhedged	EAFE Hedged
TSE 300	.70	.70	.40	.50
Canadian Bonds	.50	.50	.30	.30

Are the Global Effects Diminishing?

A strategy of investing globally is to reduce risk. But equity markets are becoming increasingly globalized and homogenous. This has facilitated financial correlation between countries, reduced the effectiveness of domestic monetary policy, and made financial markets more rotational. Increased interdependence between markets means that shocks (good and bad) are transmitted much more quickly in domino-type effects. Could common factors cause all markets to act the same way? And, if so, could the value of global diversification be diminishing?

Well, there is bad news and good news. The bad news is that markets tend to move together during economic or political shocks (such as the 1987 global market crash or the 1990 invasion of Kuwait). It seems that when the volatility of global markets rises, the correlation between markets increases. So very short-term diversification effects may be limited. However, the good news is that, in general, given differing political and social policies, the longer-run correlations remain low. Overall, the diversification benefits long extolled for global investing remain intact.

Expanded Investment Opportunities

Global investment also expands your investment opportunities. Many foreign securities have features not available with Canadian domestic investments. Some industries that are at the mature stage in Canada are still at the sunrise level in Europe or Latin America or the Far East. There are numerous securities issued abroad that have different risk/return characteristics from domestic securities or that offer special features not available with Canadian investments. Examples of these include:

- the food and wine industries in Europe
- the efficient textiles and electronics industries of Hong Kong
- the mining industry of Australia
- the robotics, computer and other high-tech industries of Japan
- specialized automobile manufacturing in South Korea

Many investment instruments are readily available—if you know about them! For example, there are a large number of closed-end investment funds traded on the New York and American Stock Exchanges that offer opportunities to trade in single countries such as Chile or Thailand or in regions such as the Far East or Latin America.

Global Leverage

Don Reed, the president of Templeton International in Canada, recently talked about oil consumption in China averaging one barrel per person per year. Doubling that number would increase world oil production by over one billion barrels! Just imagine the leverage associated with this.

Currency Exposure

Global investment means foreign currency exposure. Over the past two decades, the Canadian dollar has fluctuated widely against all major currencies. Investors who hold all of their wealth in Canadian dollars have discovered that as the dollar weakens, the cost of a trip to New York or goods imported from Tokyo has correspondingly risen. If you want to guard against adverse currency fluctuations, you have to hold some of your wealth in something other than Canadian dollars.

For many Canadians, the most important is U.S. dollar investments. If you are looking to hold U.S. dollars, the best bets on the fixed-income side are U.S. dollar-denominated Eurobonds, closed-end bond funds and preferred shares.

U.S. dollar Eurobonds pay periodic interest (normally semi-annually) and mature at their par or face value. Unlike conventional U.S. bonds, they are sold outside the U.S. Eurobonds normally offer higher yields than term deposits, bank deposits and similar instruments. The yields on foreign and Eurobonds are sometimes higher than on domestic bond issues as well, although interest-rate parity means that the foreign currency is expected to depreciate at a rate that offsets the differential.

If you are interested in holding other currency-denominated assets such as Swiss francs, you can buy Eurobonds denominated in most major currencies. Eurobonds are relatively easy to buy and provide the highest yields among foreign currency fixed-income investments. You can buy and sell Eurobonds through your brokerage firm. You should also shop around at a few bond dealers at brokerage firms for the best quotes, as they can vary widely.

An important feature about Eurobonds is that the interest income is not subject to withholding tax at source. You simply include the annual receipts as interest income in the equivalent

Canadian dollars on your Canadian tax return. If you sell the bonds before maturity, you will trigger a capital gain (or loss), which is subject to the 75% capital gain inclusion rule.

Eurobonds issued by a Canadian government, corporation and certain international organizations such as the World Bank are RRSP-eligible.

Closed-end bond funds are investment fund units that, like their counterpart, the mutual fund, invest their portfolio assets in a portfolio of bonds and other fixed-income securities according to an investment plan or strategy. A healthy selection of bond funds holding U.S. dollar-denominated bonds are traded on the New York Stock Exchange.

U.S. pay-preferred shares are denominated in U.S. dollars and pay their dividends in U.S. dollars. Because the shares are issued by a Canadian-controlled private corporation, they are eligible for the dividend tax credit. If you sell them for a gain (loss) this will create a capital gain (or loss), which is subject to the 75% capital gain inclusion rule. Foreign exchange gains are taxable, since your purchase price and proceeds of disposition are ultimately translated into Canadian dollars. The first $200 of income attributed to foreign exchange fluctuations are exempt in a taxation year. The shares are eligible for inclusion in an RRSP if they are issued by a Canadian-controlled private corporation, and they are not subject to the foreign property rule.

Does Currency Matter?
You Bet It Does!
In a recent column, a reporter who should know better indicated that the TSE, in recording an 11.86% gain in 1995 (not including dividends) "didn't cut it." He pointed out that many markets outperformed Canada, citing, for example, Caracas—up 51%—and Mexico City—up 17%. He went on to say that currency fluctuations would have affected returns for Canadians, but in most cases currency levels don't change the fact that we could have done better elsewhere. Well, here's the truth. Currency fluctuations matter—a lot. When measured in Canadian dollars, Mexico actually recorded a loss of 23.7% in 1995, and Caracas had a loss of 26.2%.

To Hedge or Not To Hedge?

International diversification is important in enhancing the return and reducing the risk associated with your portfolio. One consideration is whether to keep the foreign currency component of your investments exposed or hedged. It depends on what you want. For some, it's the foreign currency exposure; for others, the diversification. It all comes down to demand for foreign currencies—yours. If you travel, buy imported goods or possibly intend to buy a foreign vacation property, then in addition to global diversification, you will also want the currency exposure. If, for example, you have current and future plans to travel in the United States and Europe, then you will want to hold some of your investments denominated in U.S. dollars and, say, Swiss francs.

On the other hand, if your spending outlook is domestic, but your investment attitude is global, you will want to manage all or some of the foreign currency exposure, particularly if the foreign currency component is large. Look at the impact on a Canadian investor of a foreign currency change on a U.S.$70,000 (Cdn$100,000) portfolio. If the Canadian dollar were to rise from Cdn$1.40 (i.e., U.S.$.7142) to Cdn$1.30 (U.S.$.7692), the value of U.S.$70,000 in Canadian dollars would drop from $98,000 to $91,000, assuming no other change in the underlying portfolio. This amount is worth hedging. But at what cost?

There are a number of products that can be used in portfolio risk management or, as it is commonly called, "hedging." These products, commonly classified as derivatives, include call options, futures, forwards and swaps. The first two are the most likely to be of interest to you.

Education

Let's not ignore a final and important consideration in global investing. There can be great psychic enjoyment associated with global investment. Following political developments in Mexico, reading about the change in government in South Korea and assessing the implications of the Indian market reform movement can be highly entertaining and informative in their own right. You can get hooked very quickly on the international economic and market scene.

Global Investment Is Not An Easy Task, However . . .

The idea of international investing in emerging countries is compelling. But it isn't easy to do, at least directly. It's hard enough keeping up with the stocks traded in Canada, let alone the tens of thousands of companies traded on developed and emerging markets.

There are some obvious and severe impediments to foreign investing. These "frictions" include lack of quality information, different accounting and reporting standards, variable transaction costs, withholding and other taxes, liquidity problems, foreign currency risks, political or sovereignty risk, delivery and settlement delays and foreign investor restrictions. The existence of these barriers makes the task of selecting individual foreign securities a difficult one.

There are a number of roadblocks. To invest intelligently in foreign companies, you need access to good-quality information. But current and valuable information on companies in foreign countries can be both expensive and difficult to obtain. Differing accounting and reporting standards make comparisons difficult. On many markets there are no restrictions on insider trading and little protection against manipulative practices. And some markets are completely blocked to small investors.

These and other barriers make it difficult for retail investors to invest directly in foreign securities. For all but the truly dedicated investor, the most efficient route to portfolio diversification is through global, international and specialty country mutual funds.

One of the problems is that large institutional investors are often excluded from trading because they are required to have a custodial bank handle their investing (separation of client funds from management). Many banks refuse to handle investment overseas markets. There are other reasons, including prudent lending standards and industry practices that exclude many institutions. Without institutional participation, the price discovery process is impeded and prices may not reflect value. Coupled with the often rudimentary market structure, weak regulatory environment and lack of local participants, foreign markets are often highly inefficient.

Market inefficiencies include:

1. **Lack of Investor Protection**
   Traders and shareholders are not afforded the same degree of protection as found on developed markets. In many countries there is little protection against trading abuses and market manipulation. Shareholders are often not protected against insider trading and other shady dealings by management. Many countries do not have coattail provisions for minority shareholders on takeovers. In some places there is little or no opportunity for redress if you are treated improperly by a broker.

2. **Lack of Availability and Quality of Information**
   There is very little technical and marketing information on companies published in many emerging countries. The variance in quality, quantity and release of information results in disparate search costs for the investor and the analyst.

3. **Different Accounting and Reporting Standards**
   Accounting standards vary across countries, making the task of comparative analysis on a consistent basis a difficult one. The substantial differences in reporting criteria and timing of releases by corporations add to the complexity of comparative investment analysis. Sometimes notices of rights offerings, special dividends, etc., may not reach the Canadian investor. The most severe challenges are in the area of accounting standards and policies. The quality and quantity of available information vary widely, and differing accounting and reporting standards make comparisons difficult.

4. **Transaction Costs**
   Transaction costs of trading include *visible* costs such as brokerage and institutional fees, stock turnover taxes, exchange taxes, transmittal fees and other miscellaneous agency costs, and *implicit* costs such as bid/ask spreads and impact costs. These levies vary widely by type of investment and country. The issue is complicated by the fact that in some countries, commissions are negotiated and determined by the investor's own bargaining prowess. Most countries levy withholding taxes on interest and dividend income earned by nonresidents on domestic investments. The existence of reciprocal tax conventions between Canada and many countries mitigates the impact, as investors will be eligible for a foreign tax credit for the taxes paid to foreign governments. The withholding tax on dividends in most countries is 15%. To recover it, you have to file a foreign tax return or ask for a special tax credit when filing your tax return.

   Bid/ask spreads are, in general, inversely related to size of market and can be as much as 50% to 100% in some very thin markets! Supply and demand imbalances occur with some regularity on smaller foreign markets.

5. **Liquidity Problems**

   Liquidity, or the ability of an investor to dispose of his or her holdings quickly at market at a reasonable cost, can be a particular problem of investing in emerging countries. Secondary markets in some countries are not particularly active and there can be particular problems involved in selling securities. Wide spreads between the bid/ask prices may exist, sometimes so wide as to render trading impractical. The lack of market makers is often an underlying cause of poor liquidity.

6. **Settlement and Delivery Problems**

   Settlement periods and processes vary widely. Trades made in Canada are normally settled in three business days from the date of the transaction, with theoretical delivery at that time. Trades made in the emerging countries can take weeks or even months to settle. In many countries, a custodian bank or other financial institution is required.

7. **Political and Sovereignty Risk**

   Political risk is the danger of a government taking action that will reduce the value of an investor's assets, either held in that country or invested in that country's resources. The danger extends not only to the existing government, but also to a new one as a result of an election or revolution. The degree of political risk differs greatly across countries, but must be viewed as a major concern when building an international portfolio. With careful portfolio selection, political risk can be sharply reduced through diversification.

8. **Foreign Investor Restrictions**

   Some countries impose restrictions on foreign investing in their domestic markets. These restrictions include position limits that constrain the dollar, unit or percentage amount that a foreigner can invest in a particular security, commodity or investment class; special taxes or levies placed on foreign investors; trading and delivery constraints and outright prohibitions on trading by nonresidents. (India and Pakistan are examples of restricted markets.)

All of these barriers make it difficult for retail investors to invest directly in foreign market securities. The best approach, then, is to invest in investment funds.

Global Investing—Your Various Avenues

Global investing need not be substantially more difficult to the typical investor than is any other means of reaching for profits in securities. There are numerous vehicles available to carry you on to the global stage, many of which require the investment of only a few hundred dollars.

Investors who wish to diversify their portfolios internationally can either trade directly in interlisted securities on domestic markets, securities on foreign markets, or indirectly through American Depositary Receipts and global, international or specific country mutual funds. These methods are briefly described.

Direct Dealings Overseas

There are a number of sources and methods by which you can buy or sell foreign securities directly. These include:

1. **Canadian Brokerage Firms**
   Full-service Canadian brokerage firms will place buy-and-sell orders for clients for foreign securities, typically for a relatively large commission that will reflect the commission schedule on the foreign stock market, plus an increment for the Canadian broker. Investors should expect some time delays, as the broker may have to wire abroad for a quote on the security. One- and two-day lags between the time the order is placed and a confirmation from the broker are not at all uncommon for foreign security transactions. Canadian brokerage firms can buy or sell American Depositary Receipts (ADRs) for clients, as well. ADR holders receive their dividends denominated in U.S dollars minus the depository's fee (typically U.S. $.01 per share).

   ADRs are often cheaper to buy than the stocks themselves. For example, the transaction costs associated with the direct purchase of Australian stocks can at times be more expensive than those associated with an Australian company ADR purchased on the New York Stock Exchange. Morgan Guaranty Trust, a major U.S. source for ADRs, also issues International Depositary Receipts, which are similar to ADRs but designed for foreign investors who wish to hold U.S. securities. IDRs, for example, are available in Europe for U.S. equities.

2. **Foreign Banks and Brokerage Firms**
   The more adventurous global investor can open accounts with overseas banks or brokerage firms. Some brokerage firms will allow nonresident clients to trade securities listed on Japanese, Hong Kong, Australian and certain European bourses. Investors who wish to trade directly should contact local branches of foreign banks or trade embassies for the names of reputable banks or brokerage firms. In general, however, this is a cumbersome method of trading in foreign securities, as it will require the search for a reputable firm, making appropriate custody arrangements and foreign currency conversions, and other such annoyances.

3. **Domestic Branches of Foreign Banks**
   The domestic branches of foreign banks will normally handle foreign security transactions for clients, including initial foreign currency conversions, delivery and custody arrangements and currency conversion at time of sale. Typically, however, the banks set minimum transaction amounts at $100,000.

Picking Global and International Funds

Investors who wish to diversify their portfolios internationally can either trade directly in securities on foreign markets, interlisted securities on domestic markets, or indirectly through American Depositary Receipts and indexed products. However, given the barriers and restrictions, we suggest that all but the truly dedicated should capture their global portfolio portion through global and international mutual funds. There are now literally hundreds of such funds domiciled in Canada with varying objectives, track records, load options and portfolios.

Types of Investment Funds

In the global framework, there are a number of global fixed-income funds, including money market and bond funds, with a wide array of objectives and target portfolios.

In the equity category, there are four types of funds. *Global funds* invest their assets in equities of various countries, including their own, while *international funds* invest only in securities of different countries (sometimes limited to a few specific regions) not including their own. *Regional funds* invest in stocks from specific regions of the world. *Specific country funds* invest in securities of a single foreign country.

Single country closed-end specialized mutual funds have proliferated in recent years. Their introduction and continued popularity mirror three distinct developments in world capital markets: namely, the increased interest of investors in global or foreign equity markets; the strong performance of some of the smaller markets (such as Chile, Korea, Taiwan) relative to the giants (U.S., Japan, U.K.), even after foreign currency adjustments to the investor's currency denomination; and the trend to innovative products and packaging, primarily by major North American and European brokerage firms.

The majority of the closed-end funds trade at discounts to their net asset values (NAVs), a phenomenon common to closed-end investment companies.

Some will sell at premiums to their NAV, particular during strong equity markets. The specialty country funds that invest in smaller countries, and in particular those countries whose markets are blocked or restricted to nonresidents, are valuable investments in that they offer both investment opportunities for globally minded investors and "market completion" devises for fund managers. Closed-end funds, on the other hand, have a fixed capital structure in that shares are initially sold to the public and the proceeds invested in a portfolio of securities according to a set of objectives. Like the open-ended fund, the management of the closed-ended fund is paid a fee to manage the portfolio, which may be subject to constant revisions. However, unlike the open-ended fund, new shares in the closed-ended fund are only issued in specific cases (such as a new investment opportunity or a takeover), and then only with the approval of the appropriate regulatory bodies. The shares of closed-end funds are traded on stock exchanges in the same manner as shares of public companies.

Investment Strategies

Canadian-based Foreign Mutual Funds

There are hundreds of global and international mutual funds domiciled in Canada. Funds can be described by investment objectives categories (safety, income, growth, aggressive growth); geographical orientation (single country, region, global and international); investment philosophy (active vs. passive); investment style (value vs. growth); bottom-up versus top-down; portfolio structure (small vs. medium vs. large capitalization). There are some 105 or so Canadian funds specializing in the United States alone with management-expense ratios ranging from 1.5% to about 3.0%, with the typical fund being about 2.5%.

The 12 Rules of Global Investing

1. Diversify your global portfolio.
2. Invest in countries whose markets have relatively low correlations with those of Canada.
3. Be aware that the U.S. is the least valuable diversification candidate for a Canadian investor.
4. Direct global investing is hazardous to your health. Buy global or international investment funds.
5. Timing probably won't work. Don't be constantly switching from country to country in the search for undervalued securities. The danger is you will miss out on the correlation effects and the advantages of diversification.
6. Select investment funds whose managers build portfolios that really match the stated objectives.
7. Select investment funds whose performance generally remains within a specific risk category.
8. Hold some securities denominated in foreign currency.
9. Always negotiate loads for load funds. Back-end loads are often not the best choice.
10. Review the "hedge or not to hedge" decision.
11. Select management styles (active versus passive; value versus growth) that match your tastes.
12. Don't base your selection on the absence of load fees or the size of the management-expense ratio. These are important but by no means critical factors.

---

1. Investment Objectives Categories

There are foreign funds available in Canada in virtually all of the investment objectives categories. These include money market funds, bond and income funds, balanced funds and equity funds.

Type	Number
Money market	22
Income	68
Balanced	27
Equity	374
Total	491

2. Geographical Orientation

Funds specialize in countries, regions, the world excluding Canada (international funds) and the world including Canada (international funds).

The general categories are the U.S., Japan, Europe, the Pacific Rim: Latin America, emerging countries, international and global.

Geographic Focus	Number
U.S. Money Market	14
International Money Market	8
U.S. and Global Income	68
U.S. and Global Balanced	27
U.S. Equity	95
North American Equity	19
Global Equity	61
International Equity	97
Asia Pacific Rim Equity	67
European Equity	35
Total	491

3. Investment Style—Active versus Passive

Active management represents the search for undervalued securities and individual selection. Passive investing focuses on index investing.

The History of Passive Investing

In the middle and late 1950s securities research was dominated by the search for undervalued securities, the predominant investment philosophy of the day. Retail investors—reflecting rising household incomes and general postwar prosperity—started to "play the market" and accounted for nearly 50% of trading volume on the secondary equity market. At the same time, institutional investors expanded their horizons from simple buy-and-hold strategies to a more active trading approach using more sophisticated analytic tools. In 1952, Harry Markowitz, a financial economist, published a paper on diversification techniques and portfolio selection. His theory was called "Portfolio Theory" and forever changed the security analysis process.

The modern era of security markets was launched. The 1960s ushered in the era of growth stocks, the so-called go-go period. The focus among portfolio managers shifted to investment performance from their previous emphasis on safety and security. "Beating the market" became the catchword of the day.

In the 1970s a theory called the "Efficient Markets Hypothesis" came into vogue. This theory held that securities are fairly priced, reflecting at least past and publicly available information. Acceptance of this theory led to a shift to portfolio management and market aggregates from fundamental analysis of individual securities. The theory compared stock prices changes to a giant roulette wheel. Like the wheel, which has no memory—the size and direction of the next market move—so the theory goes—is independent of the previous move. The theory is that stock prices follow a process called a "Random Walk." Do you remember your examination of small particles under a microscope in your chemistry classes? How the particles careered in seemingly random manner with no predictable direction? That's called the "Law of Brownian Motion" and Efficient Markets Theory says that's how stocks move, as well.

In the early 1980s, as an outgrowth of Portfolio Theory, Efficient Markets and the desire to build diversified portfolios, index funds debuted, with the objective of tracking or replicating the performance the whole stock market as measured by an index such as the Standard and Poor's 500 Index or the Toronto Stock Exchange 300 Composite Index. Thus we can see the genesis of index investing.

A further impetus came from the deregulation of commissions on May 1, 1975, in the U.S. (1983 in Canada), which shifted the emphasis of portfolio management from return performance to cost minimization, particularly for fund managers pursuing a passive or index-replicating strategy. Suddenly the sloughed-off transaction cost issue became paramount and there was a marked shift from the return component to the cost component of investment management. If a fund manager believes that expected return is primarily passive and uncontrollable, he might shift emphasis to the cost structure of the fund.

What can explain the proclivity of so many investors to choose active over passive management investment—the odds are often against them? Peter Bernstein calls it lottery risk—no one likes to pass up the chance of finding the big return! Could it be . . . better unsafe than sorry? The road to regret is paved with unsure intentions.

There are only a few passive global funds available in Canada.

— E. K.

4. Investment Style—Value vs. Growth

Value and growth have represented the two basic approaches to investing. Two standard demarcations in distinguishing the two are the price/book value and the price/earnings ratios. Benjamin Graham defined value as the lowest third of the DJIA, while managers focusing on growth will pick high P/E stocks. Another approach using two major benchmark indexes of S&P—Barra and Russell 1000 Index—is to designate stocks below the midpoint as value stocks, and those above it as growth stocks. Managers employing a value approach will focus on low price/book and low P/E stocks, often small-cap ones, as well.

Although studies indicate that the value approach seems to outperform growth, value investing may mean unusually high volatility and poorly diversified portfolios. One reason the value approach has yielded higher return in the long run reflects the principle of "mean reversion," a finding that important factors tend to revert or regress to an average or mean value. For example, low P/E multiple stocks will tend to rise toward the average of all stocks over time, while high P/E multiple stocks will regress to the average. This provides at least one explanation for why low P/E stocks will outperform high P/E stocks.

5. Investment Style—Bottom Up vs. Top Down

Portfolio orientation includes bottom up and top down. The bottom-up approach assumes that the entire universe of eligible securities should be monitored and the fund manager will select the securities that he believes offers the best value or prospects. The top-down approach assumes that the best approach is to search for undervalued countries and then select the securities with the best value from that group.

The secret is to diversify by country or region rather than picking individual country stocks. Furthermore, it has been shown that about 85% or so of total global returns are generated by country indexes—currency and individual stock movements have only a small effect on performance. Studies demonstrate that the country factor is the most important in emerging country investments and that it dominates world, currency and industry systematic influences.

Investing in Emerging Markets

Emerging markets offer potentially high returns and diversification benefits over established markets. But they are subject to occasional bubbles: liquidity risk, restricted access and settlement problems. By their very nature they are highly volatile. Accordingly, I believe strongly that they have a place in a diversified portfolio—in a long-term strategic asset allocation strategy. However, I do mean long-term; in the short run you will see all kinds of fluctuations.

Why do emerging countries generally perform so well—albeit erratically?

As growth in North America, Europe and Japan decelerates, capital from savings is flowing into emerging countries. Call it the "emerging country" syndrome.

One approach to finding ideal countries is to monitor emerging countries looking for new developments such as political progress, economic liberalization or capital markets developments. For example, political progress in South Africa through the prohibition of apartheid was the appropriate signal for evaluating South Africa investment. Other recent investment signals include the deregulation of markets in Korea, economic and political liberalization in Argentina and Chile and capital market development progress in China and India. Many emerging countries are limiting population growth;

are spending a much higher percentage on education; and are seeing the consumer sector rising sharply (the purchase of television sets in many emerging countries is taking place at an extraordinary rate). Over past 25 years the average rate of economic growth was 5.1% for emerging nations versus 3.5% for developed nations.

What Are the Emerging Countries?
There are some 50 to 60 emerging countries. The largest are Brazil, China and India. The most rapidly developing are Argentina, Chile, Korea, Malaysia, Mexico, the Philippines, Taiwan and Thailand. Others include Ghana, Greece, Jordan, Israel, Pakistan, Turkey and Zimbabwe.

Another way of looking at it is that emerging countries in general have the demographic and economic characteristics of North America in the growth era of the 1950s and 1960s. In fact, the United States was the leading emerging country/market at the turn of the century, as was Japan in the postwar period. Now the pattern should repeat with Argentina, Brazil, China, India, etc. In the 1970s and early 1980s, when we talked about emerging or developing countries it was normally in the context of poor central planning and concomitant debt escalation, inefficient banking systems and debt and currency crises. Now many emerging countries are concentrating on building and improving their equity markets and encouraging the financing of growth with equity issues. Argentina, Brazil, Chile, China, Mexico, Taiwan and Thailand are examples of countries focusing on economic growth through equity issues.

The capital markets of an emerging country in general are underdeveloped and inefficient. There are numerous barriers to trading. These barriers have paradoxical implications. On the one hand, they obviously result in increased search, analytic and monitoring "costs" for the investor. On the other hand, they also suggest the existence of market inefficiencies that can provide abnormal returns to the astute trader. The more barriers and problems, the more inefficient the market and the greater the opportunities for the skilled stock or (fund) picker!

— E. K.

Summary

The globalization process of the past two decades has meant a vast array of new and valuable opportunities for investors. The sheer size of the market and the limitless investment opportunities offered have meant that knowledgeable investors can come increasingly closer to the goal of efficient diversification.

Measured against its potential, globalization is still in its infancy. Over the next two decades, we can expect such developments as direct trading access to virtually all of the world's markets from a home video screen (or whatever replaces a screen), and through the next generation of Internet-type networks and a vastly expended investment opportunity set in the form of new and innovative financial products tied to employment, home ownership and daily life. Investor psychology will continue as a hot research topic, and much more will be learned about why we make the decisions we do. Financial planning will be transformed from a set of poorly connected notions into a science of how to tailor portfolios to closely align them with investment needs.

Global investing should mean higher portfolio returns, enhanced investment opportunities, more efficient diversification, foreign currency exposure or risk reduction and even enriched enjoyment in the investment process. The only limit to product design and new markets is our own imagination. Staying focused and informed as the events unfold will be essential to your investment success.

PART III

Building Your Own Mutual Fund Portfolio

CHAPTER NINE

Balancing Risk and Return

The Simple Case for Asset Allocation

Imagine a pie baked with 4 cups of flour and 10 pounds of sugar. Even those of us with a sweet tooth—something we have often been accused of—would find that a little rich! Unfortunately, we all too often find that investors are willing to mix their assets with the same regard for taste as was shown in our imaginary pie.

When portfolio managers talk about investments, they talk in terms of assets like equities, fixed income, cash, hedges, real estate, etc. If you own shares of the Altamira Equity Fund,[4] that would be considered an equity asset. Similarly, if you own shares in Northern Telecom, General Motors or IBM, these too would be considered equity assets. In short, then, equity assets are long on growth, can be quite volatile—more on that later— and, generally speaking, are not considered income-producing investments.

On the other hand, let's say you owned shares of the Dynamic Income Fund.[5] Since this fund invests in bonds and other fixed-income investments, it would be considered a fixed-income asset within our portfolio. As you can imagine, fixed-income assets produce income, generally have less risk—although many a bond fund manager might dispute that claim given the turmoil in the fixed-income markets in 1994—and, at times, fixed-income assets produce better-than-average capital gains.

In short, these so-called assets are nothing more than the "ingredients" of your portfolio. Just as with our imaginary pie, and so with your portfolio: choosing the right recipe—or asset

---

[4] *Altamira Equity Fund is an open-ended mutual fund that, for the most part, invests in good quality Canadian stocks.*

[5] *The Dynamic Income Fund invests in short, medium and long-term bonds of Canadian governments (federal and provincial) as well as investment-grade Canadian corporate bonds and debentures.*

mix—is the most important decision you and your manager will make.

When we talk about asset mix, we are really focusing on the percentage of a portfolio represented by each class of investment. For example, a portfolio mix might look something like "40% equities, 50% fixed income and 10% cash."

There is a reason for choosing that kind of description—and it's not because it's easier to say than "I'm holding $40,000 of the Altamira Equity Fund, 500 shares of General Motors, $50,000 in government bonds and $50,000 in GICs . . ." Managers describe portfolios in terms of asset mix because they understand the importance that asset mix decisions play on the portfolio's overall return.

Just how important? Studies have shown that 85% (some studies have suggested as much as 90%) of your overall return can be pegged to your asset mix decision, another 5% to 10% comes from market timing (i.e., shifting in and out of investments in response to economic changes), and the remaining 5% to 10% from selecting one specific security over another (i.e., buying IBM rather than General Motors, or Microsoft rather than Northern Telecom).

In other words, by determining what percentage of your portfolio is committed to fixed-income assets, what percentage to equity assets and what percentage to any other asset class, you have laid the basis for 85% of your total return.

To make the point, consider a hypothetical two-asset portfolio that includes equities (stocks) and fixed-income assets (bonds). We'll use the Toronto Stock Exchange (TSE) 300 Composite Total Return Index[6] to represent our equity assets, and the ScotiaMcLeod Bond Universe Total Return Index[7] to represent our fixed-income assets.

For the 10-year period between May 1986 and May 1996, the ScotiaMcLeod Bond Universe returned 10.7% compounded annually. A $10,000 investment, for example, in fixed-income assets went up 2.7 times over that 10-year period.

Now, over that same time frame, the TSE 300 Composite Total Return Index grew by 8.60% compounded annually. In other words, a $10,000 investment in an index representing Canadian stocks would have grown to just under $23,000 during that period.

Now, what we are going to do is to mix and match these two assets in a home-grown portfolio. Think of it as our version of investment taste testing. Based on Table 9.1, we'll examine a number of variations on this theme, hoping in the end to make the point about the importance of asset mix decisions.

---

[6] *The Toronto Stock Exchange 300 Composite Index measures the performance of 300 of Canada's largest companies. When we speak of total return, we are assuming that all the dividends received from those 300 companies are reinvested into the index, much like a dividend reinvestment program offered by many mutual funds.*

[7] *The ScotiaMcleod Bond Universe Index assumes the investor purchased an equally weighted basket of Canadian government bonds (i.e., Government of Canada bonds that mature in 3 years or less, an equal percentage that mature in 5 to 10 years and another group of long-term bonds that mature in 20 years), and that all interest payments were reinvested into the index.*

Table 9.1: IMPACT OF THE ASSET MIX DECISION

	Canadian Bond Funds	Canadian Equity Funds	Compound Annual Return	Value of $10,000
Portfolio A	100%	0%	10.70%	$27,636.07
Portfolio B	80%	20%	10.28%	$26,605.26
Portfolio C	60%	40%	9.86%	$25,609.20
Portfolio D	50%	50%	9.65%	$25,123.86
Portfolio E	40%	60%	9.44%	$24,646.82
Portfolio F	20%	80%	9.02%	$23,717.11
Portfolio G	0%	100%	8.60%	$22,819.09

Forgetting for the moment that fixed-income assets would have provided a decent retirement nest egg over our test period, we want you to look closely at Table 9.1 and note the impact of the asset mix decision.

If, for example, you modeled your asset mix based on Portfolio D—50% equities and 50% bonds—you would have locked in a base return of 9.65% without ever having selected a single security. Your $10,000 investment in May 1986 would have been worth $25,123.86 by May 1996.

Perhaps, rather than holding a Canadian equity fund whose returns matched the TSE 300 Composite Index, you practiced some nimble trading. If you were buying and selling individual securities at each phase of the business cycle, perhaps you could enhance those returns. For example, you might purchase financial stocks at the beginning of a cycle, then switch to cyclical stocks as the economic recovery picks up steam, and finally go into defensive stocks when the economy begins to peak.

Of course, that assumes you can consistently pick winning stocks and have the ability to recognize where we are on the business cycle. For most of us, that is simply too much to expect, especially since many professionals who are paid to forecast the current direction of the economy have difficulty being in the right place at the right time.

More importantly, we would argue, as do so many academic studies, that over the long haul the impact from that any trading strategy would be marginal at best, especially when compared with the asset mix decision.

Looking at Table 9.1, note what happens when you simply shift your asset mix from Portfolio D to Portfolio F. That one decision adds 0.63% compounded annually to your bottom line. And while that may not seem like much, on our $10,000 initial investment, it adds $1,481.40 to your pocket over a 10-year period.

But the incremental return that comes from the right asset mix goes beyond year-over-year excess returns. The reason? As was explained in Chapter 2, changes in compound return compound over time. The value of the $10,000 invested in Portfolio B is worth 5.9% more than Portfolio D at the end of the 10-year period.

If those returns remained consistent over the next 10 years, Portfolio F would be worth $70,784.01 compared with $63,120.83 for Portfolio D. That's a difference of 7,663.17, which means that Portfolio F would then be worth 12.14% more than Portfolio D. That's what we mean when we say returns compound over time, and explains a professional money manager's obsession with small improvements in annual rate of return.

It also speaks volumes about the importance asset mix plays in your long-range investment plan. Even modest changes in asset mix can lead to significant changes in return over the life of your portfolio. In our opinion, then, the asset mix decision is key to your financial well-being.

Normally, you should expect an asset mix that puts more emphasis on equities to outperform other investments over the long term—something, we might add, that didn't happen over our test period, but as we learned from the experience of Peter Lynch in Chapter 1, will occur over the long haul. On the other hand, if you cannot tolerate high levels of risk, then you should opt for an asset mix like portfolios A, B or C.

And don't forget, Canadian bonds and stocks are only two potential classes of investments. Your selection of portfolio ingredients might also include short-term, interest-bearing securities (referred to as "cash" or money market funds), U.S. and international equities, real estate, gold, etc.

Thus, conservative investors will probably add a generous dab of T-bills to provide additional safety. One low-risk asset mix might include 20% equities, 50% bonds and 30% cash. More speculative investors might choose a spicier mix, say, 5% cash, 25% bonds and 70% equities.

Having determined your asset mix, you should then look at particular securities, or better yet, specific funds, to represent each asset class. Unfortunately, if you're like most investors, you will probably reverse the process, focusing on security and/or fund selection to the exclusion of all other considerations. The result? When you add up the percentage committed to each asset class, you find that your asset mix has been determined by default. And that means that greater than 85% of your return has been determined without your conscious control, which is probably a recipe for disappointment.

Homemade vs. Store-bought Diversification

Diversification is, in our opinion, the cornerstone of successful long-term investing. It is the process of getting a suitable mix of safe, liquid assets such as savings accounts and money market funds, income-producing securities such as term deposits or bond mutual funds, and growth assets such as equity mutual funds and common shares into your combined personal and RRSP portfolio. The question is, how do you actually get your desired mix? Do you do it yourself, from the asset mix decision, right through to the security selection process, or do you simply buy it? We'll examine both approaches in this section.

If you have the knowledge and the time, you could even structure your own portfolio by hand-selecting the proper securities. You could, for example, attempt to structure a balanced portfolio by purchasing shares of, say, General Motors, Bank of Montreal and IBM. But understand this approach is very expensive and is not a simple procedure.

Remember, when buying stocks, you should purchase, at a minimum, a round lot. For most investors, a round lot is considered to be 100 shares. And to do it right, you will need to buy shares in more than the three companies we cite in our preamble. The Value Line Investment Survey, a well-respected U.S. advisory service, recommends that a well-diversified portfolio include at least 15 separate stocks in different industries. Other studies suggest you need at least 30 different stocks in your portfolio, which means that a properly diversified common stock portfolio could require upward of $40,000 to $50,000 in capital. And that is before you make any commitment to fixed-income assets or cash reserves.

On the other hand, you can buy diversification. One method is to simply buy a balanced mutual fund. These are funds that practice asset allocation by holding a portfolio of stocks and bonds. The balanced fund manager can then alter the weightings within the asset mix within the guidelines of the fund's prospectus. For example, the Sceptre Balanced Fund,[8] according to *Bell Charts*, "maintains a steady asset mix with equities at a maximum of 65% and a minimum of 35% of the portfolio." The *Southam Source Disk* goes on to add that "additional diversification is gained through the selection of foreign equities to a maximum of 20% of the fund."

Balanced fund managers, then, not only decide on which securities are held in the portfolio—i.e., how much General Motors, how much IBM and so on—they also allocate the percentage of the portfolio to be committed to any one asset class (i.e., equities, fixed income or cash).

When you think about it, balanced funds would seem to be the ideal approach. Let the portfolio manager decide not only the asset mix, but also the securities to buy within each asset class.

However, it isn't quite that straightforward. At the outset, you are leaving an asset mix decision to the portfolio manager, and that asset mix may not be suitable for your current situation and long-term goals. For example, if you are a conservative investor, your personal policy statement might be 20% equity, 65% fixed income and 15% cash. The balanced fund manager may be holding a portfolio that is 65% equity, 25% fixed income and 10% cash. The point is, the balanced fund manager is not reflecting your specific circumstances and we believe that may not be in your best long-term interest.

There are also some issues on the performance side. For some thoughts on that, we take you to Table 9.2, which looks at the average compounded return over the last 10 years (to May 1996) for Canadian balanced funds, Canadian bond funds, Canadian equity funds, Canadian money market funds and U.S. equity funds. We have weighted the returns on the basis of assets under management. In other words, a fund with $50 million under management will not carry as much weight in the calculation as a fund with, say, $200 million under management. The idea behind weighting the performance is to examine the numbers on the basis of the funds most often purchased by investors.

---

[8] *Sceptre Balanced Fund is managed by Sceptre Investment Counsel Limited in Toronto.*

Table 9.2: AVERAGE RETURNS AMONG VARIOUS FUND CATEGORIES

Canadian Balanced	Canadian Bond Funds	Canadian Equity Funds	Canadian Money Market	U.S. Equity Funds
8.90%	9.50%	8.40%	7.70%	11.70%

From Table 9.2, we know that the average Canadian balanced fund returned 8.9% compounded annually over the past 10 years (to May 31, 1996). What that means is a $10,000 investment made in the average Canadian balanced fund 10 years ago would be worth $23,457.34 by May 31, 1996.

Now let's examine what would have happened with a typical asset mix based on the personal policy statements from Chapter 3. Assuming your score was close to the average of most investors: say, 50% equity, 40% bonds and 10% cash. And since balanced funds can invest in markets other than Canada, we'll establish the following model portfolio:

Model Portfolio

Average Canadian Equity Fund	30%
Average U.S. Equity Fund	20%
Average Canadian Bond Fund	40%
Average Canadian Money Market Fund	10%
Total	100%

The question is, how did the performance of a model portfolio of average funds in each category compare with the performance of the average balanced fund over the past five years? If we assume you earned 30% (the weighting within the model portfolio) of the return from the average Canadian equity fund over the past five years (i.e., 8.4% x .30 = 2.52%), 40% of the return from the average bond fund (9.5% x .40 = 3.8%), 10% from the Canadian money market (7.7% x .10 = .77%), and 20% from the average U.S. equity fund (11.7% x .20 = 2.34%), your overall portfolio would return 9.43% (2.52% + 3.8% + .77% + 2.34%) compounded annually. A $10,000 investment that was made 10 years ago in this model portfolio would, today, be worth $24,624.31. When you compare this performance with the average balanced fund (i.e., 8.9% compounded annually) over the same 10-year period, you can see why we encourage you to design your own personal portfolio, and why we will give you the tools to do just that.

Moreover, by determining your personal asset mix, you tailor your investments to your personal policy statement. And coincidentally, the numbers tell us that by selecting funds to represent your own personal asset mix, you enhance your overall return. And that assumes you purchase only the average funds in each class, and make no changes to the asset mix for the 10-year holding period.

From our perspective, then, we think most investors are better off using mutual funds for their security selection. We believe that over the long haul, buying a Canadian equity fund makes more sense than trying to buy a portfolio of 30 Canadian stocks in different industries. Furthermore, the availability of dividend reinvestment programs make mutual fund investing more convenient, and the diversification that comes from an investment in a mutual fund is generally more cost-effective than you could achieve by purchasing your own handpicked portfolio.

We also believe that mutual fund managers add more value by bringing their stock picking or bond selection ability to the table than they do by arbitrarily deciding what asset mix makes the most sense at a point in the business cycle.

Basic Investment Planning

If you accept our notion that mutual funds should be used in place of security selection, then our most important decision once again comes down to the asset mix—the percentage of stocks, bonds and T-bills in the portfolio.

An investment strategy that allocates your financial resources among asset classes is referred to as asset allocation. And there are three basic formats your investment strategy can take:

1. Strategic Asset Allocation
2. Tactical Asset Allocation
3. Dynamic Asset Allocation

Strategic asset allocation means the process of apportioning the fund's investment portfolio among the broad investment classes—T-bills and other money market securities, fixed income, equities, real estate and international securities. The introduction of different types of securities, particularly those that are less than perfectly correlated with each other, will reduce the variability of the portfolio and increase the likelihood that the portfolio will earn the required rate of return.

When we talk about strategic asset allocation, we are talking about an investment philosophy where you structure a portfolio based on your personal investment objectives and risk tolerances. (Refer to the personal policy statement from Chapter 3.)

For most strategic investors, the range of appropriate asset allocation mixes is somewhere between 35%/65% to 65%/35% fixed-income assets relative to equity assets, spanning the very conservative to the highly aggressive.

Tactical or timing allocation is the sometimes controversial policy of changing the asset mix to capture perceived market cycle shifts or opportunities. Tactical asset allocation is practiced by a number of balanced funds, and in most cases these managers utilize sophisticated computer models to evaluate the relative value of equities to fixed-income investments to cash at a point in time. When, according to the computer model, equities are undervalued relative to bonds, for example, the manager will add stocks to the portfolio and reduce the commitment to bonds.

AGF Management practices tactical asset allocation and utilizes a computer model developed by the giant U.S. brokerage firm Paine Weber. This computer model draws on 70 years of historical performance statistics for stocks, bonds and cash, and evaluates the merits of one asset class relative to another at a point in time. Quite often, AGF will announce a major shift in its emphasis from stocks to bonds to cash, and when it does, it is newsworthy.

Obviously these managers believe they can identify market cycles, and thus can add value by adjusting the asset allocation mix by buying or selling equities, cash and bonds with the changing times. Tactical asset allocation is obviously an active strategy.

There are also passive approaches to asset allocation. For example, managers who believe in efficient markets where security prices reflect all information and are properly priced and that economic cycles cannot be accurately forecast don't spend time searching for undervalued securities or looking for changing economic cycles. Instead, they attempt to add value by constructing and maintaining the portfolio in the most cost-efficient manner.

Passive asset allocation strategies attempt to rebalance the portfolio at set intervals, say once a year or every six months, etc. The idea behind rebalancing is to bring the portfolio back to its original weighting. In other words, if equity funds outperformed the other assets over the preceding period, then equities would have a greater weight in the portfolio. In order to rebalance, you would sell some of the equity funds and buy more of the assets that underperformed. Think of it as a disciplined approach that forces you to buy low (i.e., assets that have underperformed) and sell high (i.e., assets that have outperformed).

On the question of which style we favor, we lean towards a combination approach. We believe in the "strategic" decision to structure an asset mix in line with your investment personality. But you will also note, from Chapter 3, that we provided a range for each asset class. That's to allow us the latitude to dynamically rebalance the asset mix while maintaining the long-term strategic intent of the portfolio.

We will make recommendations each time we update this book, as to whether you should over-weight, under-weight or maintain your policy statement during a particular year. These periodic changes in weighting attached to each asset class, based on our year-ahead view about the economy, is how we define the "dynamic" aspect of our asset allocation philosophy.

But we should point out that studies thus far have indicated that market timing is extremely difficult. The rewards of timing are high—but as Nobel prizewinner Paul Samuelson has pointed out, timing can be hazardous to your health.

The key is to choose the style you are most comfortable with and to stick with it. If you do not want to follow our dynamic model, then simply rebalance the asset mix once a year bringing it back in line with your policy statement. So, assess yourself honestly, stay within your comfort zone and stick by your convictions.

Defining Your Asset Mix

Having laid some of the foundation for asset allocation, we want to move into defining asset allocation as it pertains to the individual investor. Basically, there are four broad asset categories (see Figure 9.1):

1. Equity Assets
2. Fixed-income Assets
3. Cash Assets
4. Real Estate Assets

Figure 9.1: YOUR ASSET MIX

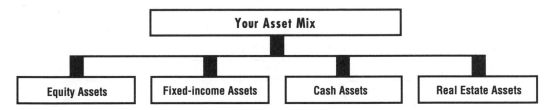

Most investors, at least from the ones we've talked with over the years, prefer to separate the family home from their investment portfolio. Indeed, we talked about that when formulating your personal investment profile. The fact is, most investors would prefer not to depend on the sale of their family home to provide for their retirement income. That's not to say they won't sell the home at retirement; we're simply saying that it's nice not to have to sell it. As such, when we talk about real estate assets, we're really talking about investments in real estate mutual funds, or perhaps an investment property, we're not talking about the family home.

There is also the question as to whether you should hold real estate assets at all. Real estate mutual funds, for example, have been at the bottom of the performance pile for some time, and some would suggest that the future doesn't look particularly bright.

Another factor which bears consideration is the so-called liquidity crisis that can prevent you from cashing out at a given point in time. We note, for example, the so-called "stabilization measures" imposed in August 1995 by two real estate funds managed by Roycom Advisors Inc.—Roycom-Summit TDF Fund and the Roycom-Summit Realty Fund. The goal, according to management, was to stem the tide of redemptions: "The stabilization process allows the funds to pay redemptions only out of money coming into the fund, which can result from new units being sold, or from rental income received on the properties in the fund's portfolio." (*The Globe and Mail*)

Without a provision of this sort, real estate funds would have to sell off properties at distressed prices, which could result in advantaging one group of unitholders to the detriment of others. Because real estate funds do not have the liquidity of a stock or bond fund, managers cannot move adeptly in and out of the market, and for investors who want the right to redeem, that's a risk factor.

Extending the Asset Mix

Having ascertained a reasonable asset mix from your personal investment profile, we find it helpful to broaden our definitions by extending the asset mix, effectively subdividing the assets by geographic region. Similarly, we want to segment our fixed-income assets into domestic fixed income and foreign fixed-income. How much in Canada, how much in the U.S. and how much overseas. In both cases, of course, we face some restrictions in terms of the foreign content rules within RRSPs.

The idea is to fine tune the portfolio, so that we can take advantage of our view about the world financial markets. Obviously, this is a judgment call, and for lack of a better term, represents the tactical aspect of our asset allocation model (see Figure 9.2 and Table 9.3).

Figure 9.2: EXTENDING YOUR ASSET MIX

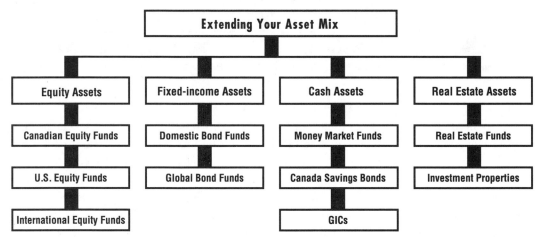

A couple of points come to mind. Holding U.S. equities is an important part of almost any investment package, simply because of the impact the U.S. economy has on the world stage and, more specifically on Canadian equities. Global equities provide us with further diversification and some negative correlation within the portfolio. In simple terms, global markets rarely move in sync. Often, one market will rise when another falls (i.e., negative correlation), which tends to stabilize the overall portfolio.

There are also advantages from the performance side. International diversification allows us more flexibility and provides an opportunity to enhance long-term returns without significantly altering our risk pattern. This is particularly useful when a sizable portion of the assets are held outside tax-sheltered plans. More about that in Chapter 11.

Table 9.3: A TYPICAL EXTENDED ASSET MIX

Asset Groups	Pct of Portfolio
Canadian Equity Funds	25%
U.S. Equity Funds	20%
International Equity Funds	10%
Total Equity Component	*55%*
Global Bond Funds	10%
Domestic Bond Funds	25%
Total Fixed-income Component	*35%*
Money Market Funds	10%
Total Cash Component	*10%*
Total Portfolio	*100%*

Security Selection

Equities

The final stage is the selection of securities to represent each of the asset classes, and ultimately each segment within that asset mix. Here you will decide which funds will provide the best fit in your portfolio. We will offer a number of potential funds, plus the necessary tools to mix and match these funds to give you the most *oomph* for your investment dollar, while always maintaining a tight rein on the risk side of the equation.

Fixed Income

In Canada, most bond funds invest in government securities. Since there is no default risk, the fixed-income manager focuses on the portfolio's duration or, put another way, the term-to-maturity. Portfolio managers lengthen the term-to-maturity if they feel interest rates will fall, and will generally shorten the maturity if they fear a rise in interest rates. Later on in this book, we'll be providing the tools to help you mix and match domestic and global bond funds in your portfolio.

Global bonds fall into a different category. Because size is a more important issue and exchange rate risk is a consideration, we believe that global bond fund managers bring an expertise that can add value to your investment decisions.

Cash

Cash is considered a hedge. It helps us smooth out the fluctuations in the overall portfolio and provides a buffer should we wish to add to any of our asset classes. There are three approaches to the cash component: money market funds, GICs, Canada Savings Bonds/Government of Canada Treasury bills.

More Risk—More Return

Having defined the typical makeup of an asset mix, and then extending that mix into various securities, we would like to once again return to Table 9.1. We simply believe that it is necessary to explain the rationale behind equity assets in a long-term growth portfolio, especially since our test period defies some long-standing investment truisms, specifically the relationship between risk and return. Equities, considered a higher-risk investment, underperformed lower-risk bonds, and more importantly, underperformed risk-free Treasury bills during the period 1986 to 1996.

If we told you in May 1986 that you had two investment choices—Government of Canada Treasury bills that would generate a compound annual yield of 8.43% with no risk, or Canadian equity funds that could generate an 8.60% return, with no guarantees—which would you choose?

And just for good measure, let us add another factor to this dilemma. With equity funds, there might be periods where you would earn nothing, and there is a good chance that you might even lose money in any given year! Using that as a sales pitch, equities would not look very attractive. Let's face it; who would be willing to risk their capital when investments with no risk offer better returns.?

And therein lies the rationale behind equity funds. Over the long haul, higher-risk equity investments must substantially outperform lower-risk investments. To suggest otherwise would mean that all investors, because we all fear financial risk, would simply buy risk-free assets. In the long run, risk capital would dry up. Based on our experience, 10 years is, in terms of risk, about as long a time horizon as most investors are comfortable with.

We believe that all portfolios should contain some equity securities. The appropriate amount or allocation varies, although the suggested range is normally 30% to 70% depending on your goals, tastes and financial plans.

What is the best way to achieve this? This depends to a large extent on your beliefs. Our view is that your investment philosophy should reflect your beliefs. If you think you can find undervalued securities, or that there are mutual funds managers who can, then you should pursue what is called an "active" strategy, searching for value by either hand-selecting your stocks, or by selecting equity mutual funds that pursue an active policy of searching for undervalued securities.

On the other hand, if you believe that markets are efficient and that stocks prices reflect all information, save the money and effort associated with stock and/or fund valuation, then take a "strategic" approach where you mix and match mutual funds within a portfolio where the asset mix is defined by your personal policy statement.

We believe that the financial markets will come full circle over the next decade. Indeed, over the next decade we will probably find ourselves in a very different environment, and with interest rates at 30-year lows, we can make a strong case that Canadian equities will once again resume their role as the dominant Canadian asset within your portfolio.

Which brings us one step farther down this road. There is a view expressed by some financial commentators that "because equities are the best long-term investment, why buy anything else?" And to be fair, given our views about equities for the next decade, individual investors who want to maximize their total long-term return, have no need for investment income and can accept a degree of risk, an all-equity portfolio may indeed be the answer.

However, for some thoughts on that, take a close look at Table 9.4 which looks at the annual returns of selected assets from the beginning of 1984 to the end of 1995. For six of the 10 years in question, Canadian equities produced double-digit returns. That is the attraction of equities. But again, while most of us like the potential of double-digit returns, not many can accept the risk associated with a major stock market correction. We point to the performance of 1987, and draw your specific attention to the performance of equities late in the year (see Figure 9.3). Could your pocketbook withstand that type of correction?

Interestingly, for the entire year, because of the strong performance of equities up to and including August 1987, Canadian and U.S. equities actually turned in a positive year-over-year return. More disturbing in terms of year-over-year performance was the 1990 bear market for equities, when U.S. stocks fell 4.09% (as measured by the S&P 500 Composite Total Return Index) and Canadian stocks fell 14.90% (as measured by the TSE 300 Total Return Index).

Table 9.4: PERFORMANCE OF SELECTED FINANCIAL ASSETS

Year	Canadian Equities $ Return	Canadian Equities % Return	U.S. Equities $ Return	U.S. Equities % Return	Canadian Bonds $ Return	Canadian Bonds % Return	Cash $ Return	Cash % Return
1/1/84	10,000		10,000		10,000		10,000	
1984	9,761	-2.39%	10,458	4.58%	11,466	14.66%	11,162	11.62%
1985	12,208	25.07%	13,614	30.18%	13,900	21.23%	12,267	9.90%
1986	13,301	8.95%	16,066	18.01%	15,944	14.70%	13,425	9.44%
1987	14,083	5.88%	16,861	4.95%	16,588	4.04%	14,558	8.44%
1988	15,643	11.08%	19,482	15.54%	18,212	9.79%	15,967	9.68%
1989	18,986	21.37%	25,463	30.70%	20,545	12.81%	17,982	12.62%
1990	16,176	-14.80%	24,421	-4.09%	22,094	7.54%	20,439	13.66%
1991	18,121	12.02%	31,640	29.56%	26,985	22.14%	22,370	9.45%
1992	17,861	-1.43%	33,852	6.99%	29,640	9.84%	23,896	6.82%
1993	23,675	32.55%	37,061	9.48%	35,017	18.14%	25,139	5.20%
1994	23,628	-0.20%	37,543	1.30%	33,511	-4.30%	26,496	5.40%
1995	27,054	14.50%	51,659	37.60%	40,448	20.70%	28,510	7.60%
Standard Deviation[1]		13.17%		13.70%		7.81%		2.65%

[1] Standard Deviation of Annual Returns

Of course, when we talk about the volatility of annual returns, we are talking about risk, which we defined in Chapter 4 as the standard deviation of those returns. By looking at Table 9.4, we can see that stocks were substantially more volatile than bonds over the period in question.

Indeed, the annual standard deviation of U.S. equities was 13.17% vs. 7.81% for Canadian bonds and 2.65% for Government of Canada Treasury bills. What that means, from our lesson in Chapter 2, is that we could expect the value of our U.S. equity funds to rise or fall within 13.17% (one standard deviation) of their mean 66% of the time.

Similarly, we would expect the value of a Canadian bond fund with a standard deviation similar to the ScotiaMcLeod Bond Universe to rise or fall within 7.81% of their mean 66% of the time. Interestingly, in support of the view that you should always expect the unexpected, we draw your attention to the performance of Canadian bond funds during the month of February 1994. For the record, in that one month, the average Canadian bond fund fell about 8%.

This just goes to show how performance numbers can get skewed when the unexpected happens. In this case, it was an unexpected hike in short-term interest rates by the U.S. Federal Reserve Board. And if you own a bond fund (see Chapter 6), rising interest rates mean lower bond prices.

Of course, Government of Canada Treasury bills have the lowest standard deviation of any asset. In the vernacular of the average investor, Treasury bills are low risk. That's not to suggest that the value of your money might not be eroded by the onset of inflation, which we contend is a significant risk factor. But in terms of repayment principal and interest, the annual standard deviation on Treasury bills suggests a risk-free asset.

Figure 9.3: ANNUAL RETURNS ON SELECTED FINANCIAL ASSETS

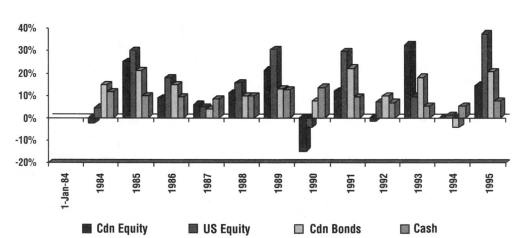

Figure 9.3 takes us another step along the road to asset allocation by graphically displaying the annual performance of all four of our selected assets. Note that all four assets had their

"day in the sun" over the past decade. It was, for each of these assets, "the best of times and the worst of times."

By spreading your investment dollars across all four financial assets, we are able to reduce the overall volatility in the portfolio. Taking that one step farther, because asset allocation reduces your overall risk, you need not be as concerned about the volatility of the funds you hold in the portfolio. You could, for example, buy an aggressive Canadian equity fund to represent your equity assets, and an aggressive bond fund to represent your fixed-income assets.

In portfolio management terms, by purchasing aggressive equity or bond funds, we are raising the beta of our portfolio. Now before we get caught up in another statistical concept, beta is not that complex. To review, beta simply measures the systematic risk of a fund, or more specifically, measures the performance of a particular fund relative to some benchmark index.

Most Canadian equity funds, for example, are measured against the TSE 300 Composite Index. And benchmark indexes, like the TSE 300 Composite Index, have a beta of 1.00. A Canadian equity fund with a beta of, say, 1.20 would be considered an aggressive equity fund.

We would expect, then, if the TSE 300 Composite Index went up 10%, our aggressive Canadian equity fund would rise by 12% (10% x 1.20 beta = 12%). So, in a rising market, the aggressive growth equity fund should outperform the benchmark index (i.e., the TSE 300 Composite Index), and conversely, in a down market, should underperform the benchmark.

This is a reasonable approach if we accept the basic tenet that diversification within the asset allocation model addresses our concern about volatility, allowing us to select individual funds on the basis of above-average performance. We can, then, buy so-called "aggressive growth funds" for the equity component of our asset allocation model because we have reduced our risk through diversification across a number of asset classes.

With that in mind, let's look at what happens to an asset allocation model from January 1, 1984 to December 31, 1995. In this case, we divided our model portfolio between equities (25% in Canadian equities, 25% U.S. equities), Canadian fixed income (25% domestic bonds) and cash (25% Government of Canada Treasury bills). We raised the beta on our equity assets from 1 to 1.2 by purchasing an aggressive Canadian equity fund and an aggressive U.S. equity fund. The returns and standard deviation are found in Table 9.5.

Table 9.5: ASSET ALLOCATION

Year	Cdn Equity	US Equity	Cdn Bonds	Cash	Portfolio
1/Jan/84	$10,000	$10,000	$10,000	$10,000	$10,000
1984	9,713	10,550	11,466	11,162	10,723
1985	12,635	14,370	13,900	12,267	13,293
1986	13,992	17,476	15,944	13,425	15,209
1987	14,980	18,514	16,588	14,558	16,160
1988	16,971	21,967	18,212	15,967	18,279
1989	21,323	30,059	20,545	17,982	22,477
1990	17,536	28,584	22,094	20,439	22,163
1991	20,066	38,723	26,985	22,370	27,036
1992	19,722	41,971	29,640	23,896	28,807
1993	27,425	46,746	35,017	25,139	33,582
1994	27,359	47,475	33,511	26,496	33,710
1995	32,119	68,895	40,448	28,510	42,493
Standard Deviation*	15.80%	16.44%	7.81%	2.65%	9.40%

* Standard deviation of annual returns.

Compare the performance of the asset allocation model portfolio (far right column in Table 9.5) with the performance of each of the assets in Table 9.4. In this case, the asset allocation portfolio outperformed Canadian equities, T-bills and Canadian bonds, and underperformed an all-U.S. equity portfolio.

However, and this is the point of the exercise, the risk associated with the asset allocation model portfolio in Table 9.5 was similar to the risk of the bond portfolio from Table 9.4, and substantially below the risk of either an all-Canadian or all-U.S. equity portfolio. That's because 25% of the asset allocated portfolio includes cash, which dramatically reduces the portfolio's overall risk.

An Intuitive View of Investing

Suppose you are holding three funds, each of which has a net asset value of $10. Let's call them fund A, B and C. Suppose that you paid $4, $10 and $12 respectively for each of the three.

What decisions should you make? Should you sell "A" to lock in a 150% gain? Should you sell "B" because it has done nothing for you? Should you sell "C" because you have lost 16.7% of your investment?

The answer is, none of the above. With the exception of a possible tax issue, none of the three choices makes sense as an independent decision. The point is, the portfolio of three funds is currently worth $30 against an initial cost of $26. The portfolio has risen by 15.4%. The relevant question is whether this portfolio is performing the way you had hoped and whether it is still suitable, given your objectives. This is the principle of mutual fund diversification, and the reason decisions should normally be made on a portfolio basis.

If we can get you to think of your portfolio as an all-weather vehicle, then you will become a longer-term investor who pays little attention to one-day, one-week, one-month or one-year fluctuations. You will hold a portfolio that gets you where you want to go, and does so while letting you sleep nights.

CHAPTER TEN

The Croft-Kirzner Indexes

The Ins and Outs of Performance Measurement

Suppose your portfolio earned 18% last year. Would this be good or bad? Without further information, you can't say. Knowing a quantity (how tall, how heavy, how much, etc.) tells us nothing about value. The only way to determine value is by comparing with something else. So, if you want to know whether you did well by earning 18% on your investments, you must find a yardstick against which to measure that return.

If, for example, a similar portfolio returned 22%, your portfolio may have been inferior. The purpose of portfolio evaluation or measures is to evaluate and contrast the returns realized by a fund manager with the returns that could have been obtained if an appropriate passive alternative portfolio had been selected. Absolute measures are insufficient; only relative returns count.

In other words, we must have some basis for comparison, because only by comparing a model portfolio with some benchmark index can we assess the merits of any strategy. The goal of a fund manager is to add value to your portfolio, beyond what you would get if you did not have a manager—and that's what the manager should be judged on.

In order to measure performance, then, we need to construct some benchmark against which the manager can be judged. You cannot compare, for example, a portfolio that is divided equally between stocks, bonds and cash with the TSE 300 Composite Total Return Index, or with the yield on risk-free Treasury bills, or any other single barometer. That would be like comparing apples and oranges.

So what makes a good benchmark? Most important, categories and benchmarks should reflect what managers do, rather than what they say they do! A benchmark, then, should be:

1. **Unambiguous**: The TSE 300 Composite Index is an unambiguous benchmark. Its composition is published, and investors know how it is comprised and how its value is determined.
2. **Investable**: The benchmark should represent a passive alternative to a money

manager. You should be able to actually trade it or a proxy for it. Could you have really have done it?

3. **Measurable**: The benchmark should be calculated and published periodically and subject to precise calculations.

4. **Appropriate**: The benchmark selected should match the investment. An index equity fund should be benchmarked by the index it replicates, whereas a small cap fund should be benchmarked by a small cap index.

To Measure Is to Know

There is a story about the great economist Frank Knight. He was walking around the University of Chicago campus and saw a plaque dedicated to Lord Kelvin that read: "That which cannot be measured cannot be known."

Knight, on seeing the plaque, said, "Oh, well, if you can't measure it, go ahead and measure it anyway."[9]

Even Knight, who was so accustomed to precision, was willing to accept the fact that something is better than nothing, which suggests that the search for the perfect performance measure is more like the search for the Holy Grail rather than the needle in the haystack. Both are about as hard to find, but at least the performance measure is worth the effort. And even if you can't find the perfect performance measure, the search is still worth the effort, because in the end, some measures are clearly better than others.

At the very least, performance measurements should be based on standardized time periods such as six months, one year, two years . . . up to 10 years. In fact, National Policy 39 (section 16) indicates that performance should be based on fresh numbers, prepared no more than 45 days after the end of the period in question.[10]

In Search of the Holy Grail

Using past performance to assess the future is a tricky business. Moreover, employing that past performance to distinguish skill from luck is also a challenging task. The following represent the various combination performance measures used:

- **Naive comparisons**: Compare the performance of your fund with randomly selected portfolios of equivalent risk. Note that these have no commissions or operating expenses.
- **Comparisons using capital market theory**

---

[9] *Recounted in Peter L. Bernstein, "Measuring the Performance of Performance Measurement," in* Performance Evaluation, Benchmarks, and Attribution Analysis *(New York: Association for Investment Management and Research, 1995), 70.*

[10] *National Policy 39 pertains to mutual funds doing business in Canada.*

Jensen's Alpha

Jensen's alpha measures the excess return realized by a fund manager above those reflecting the expected return for bearing market risk.

The computations underlying Jensen's alpha (α) are:

- Calculate the average T-bill rate for the period
- Calculate the average return on a market index
- Calculate the benchmark average return = ERp = Rf + (Rm - Rf) B
- Estimate a portfolio's ex post beta = B
- Calculate the realized return on portfolio = Rp
- Calculate α of portfolio = Rp - ERp

Rp - ERp = Rp - [(Rf + (Rm - Rf)B]

If α is positive, the fund manager realized an average return greater than the benchmark, indicating superior performance. Jensen's alpha is a crude but effective measure of the return realized from active portfolio management.

Legend
Rf = T-bill rate
Rp = realized return on portfolio
Rm = average return on market index
B = beta of portfolio
ERp = expected return on portfolio = Rf +(Rm-Rf)B

Example
Rf = T-bill rate = .06 or 6%
Rp = realized return on portfolio = .13 or 13%
Rm = average return on market index = .10 or 10%
B = beta of portfolio = 1.2
ERp = expected return on portfolio = Rf +(Rm-Rf)B = .06+ (.10-.06)1.2 = .108

α = Rp - [Rf+(Rm-Rf)B]
   = .13-[.06+(.10-.06)1.2
   = .022 or 2.2%

Treynor Reward to Volatility

The Treynor measure (T) is to identify a fund's excess return and divide by the fund's beta.

Treynor's formula is $T = (Rp - Rf)/B$ and it measures the excess return per unit of systematic risk. The value of T obtained for a specific period is then compared with a benchmark $(B) = (Rm - Rf)/1$. If T is greater than B, the fund over that time period provided a greater return per unit of systematic risk than the benchmark.

Jensen's α and Treynor's T must provide the same portfolio signals—positive or negative. However, they may **rank** funds differently.

- **Sharpe Reward to Variability**: The Sharpe measure (S) is calculated as the fund's return divided by the standard deviation. The formula is $S = (Rp - Rf)/op$. Sometimes this is expressed as the excess return (return above the risk-free rate) divided by the standard deviation of the excess return. This reward/risk ratio measures the past return per unit of risk undertaken and is a relative measure of risk. Comparisons among mutual funds and between the funds and a benchmark index are measures of past reward to variability. The Sharpe measure can provide different signals from the Jensen/Treynor model.

An Illustration of the Sharpe Measure

January 1996 through December 1996 data on Funds A and B

Fund A: The Growth Fund
Rf = T-bill rate = .06 or 6%
Rp = realized return on portfolio = .13 or 13%
op = standard deviation of portfolio = .08

$S = (.13-.06)/.08 = .875$

Fund B: The Supergrowth Fund
Rf = T-bill rate = .06 or 6%
Rp = realized return on portfolio = .22 or 22%
op = standard deviation of portfolio = .20

$S = (.22-.06)/.18 = .80$

Although Fund B realized a substantially higher return than Fund A, its lower Sharpe ratio indicates a smaller return per unit of risk undertaken. In other words, over this one-time period, Fund A outperformed Fund B based on return per unit of risk.

Introduction to the Croft-Kirzner Performance Index

What we have discussed so far has emphasized the need to look beyond one-dimensional rate-of-return calculations to assess the merits of any particular mutual fund.

That being said, we understand that a solid five-year track record will not guarantee good performance in the future. Moreover, when it comes to forecasting the performance of a particular fund, there is really no period return that will tell you what type of performance you can expect.

As a case in point, we cite the performance of the Universal Avenue Growth Fund, which to August 31, 1995, had a five-year compound return of 0.5%. A $10,000 investment in this fund five years ago would be worth $10,252.51 today. This pales in comparison with almost any investment, which includes socking money away in a savings account.

Not to single out the University Avenue Growth Fund, but it does serve as an excellent example of the problems associated with past performance. On January 7, 1993, this fund was merged into the Harvard Unit Trust, a memorandum-offered fund started in 1979 and managed by Douglas Davis. The funds Davis managed over the past five years brought in a return of 17.18% per annum. If, then, we are to focus on long-term performance as our sole criterion for future returns, whose record do we use? Let's add some additional grist to the performance mill.

Establishing Acceptable Benchmarks

The goal of the Croft-Kirzner Performance Index is to rank the performance of a fund manager relative to the fund manager's traditional benchmark, where both the manager's performance numbers and the performance numbers of the benchmark indexes are adjusted for risk.

When we talk about benchmark indexes, we are simply looking at some tool against which to measure a manager's performance. For example, Chip Morris runs the highly successful TD Green Line Science and Technology Fund. In 1995, the Science and Technology Fund returned more than 51.2%. If we were to judge Mr. Morris solely on the basis of his performance over the past year, we would rank him among the best money managers in the world. But would that be fair?

It depends, of course, on what benchmark we are using to judge Mr. Morris's performance numbers. If we are using the TSE 300 Total Return Index that returned 14.5% through 1995, then again, Mr. Morris would appear to have secured a place at the head table in the portfolio managers' hall of fame. Even to compare Mr. Morris's performance with that of the S&P 500 Total Return Index that returned 33.9% (adjusted for Cdn $) in 1995 demonstrates his ability to outperform by a wide margin. Again, is this fair?

Before you answer, consider some funds at the other end of the spectrum. For example, the performance of Canadian real estate funds. Royal LePage Commercial Real Estate Fund, the "top" fund in this category, returned 2.4% compounded annually over the past five years, which is dreadful. And that positive five-year return was due in large part to the 9.4% return the fund earned in 1995, one of its best years in recent history.

Based on those five-year performance numbers, Royal LePage Capital Property Services Ltd., the manager of the Royal LePage Commercial Real Estate Fund, would appear to be a very poor management team. Not only did they have a dreadful five-year compound return, but when compared with the TSE 300 Total Return Index or the S&P 500 Total Return Index, the underperformance is highlighted even more dramatically. Looking at the issue from this perspective, then, it is clear that the doors to the portfolio managers' hall of fame would not be open to Royal LePage Capital Property Services.

Judging a portfolio manager on the basis of the discussion to this point is like judging whether the seven-foot height of your son is a good or bad thing. We simply do not have enough information to make a rational judgment.

All we have done is define what sectors of the economy have been particularly profitable. We've said nothing about the manager's ability. Mr. Morris is mandated to invest his portfolio in shares of technology companies, which, as it turned out, was a hot property in 1995.

Royal LePage Capital Property Services, on the other hand, is mandated to invest in real estate, a sector where returns have not been particularly attractive over the past five years. The performance numbers of both managers, then, were driven by the performance of the markets they were mandated to invest in, not necessarily by their ability to function within their defined markets. Perhaps both managers added value to the process.

The first step is to define a reasonable benchmark against which to measure the portfolio manager. Specifically, we need a passive index that resembles the portfolio manager's mandated portfolio, and then we can compare one with the other. In the case of the TD Science and Technology Fund (the fund invests in U.S. technology companies), we should compare the performance numbers of Mr. Morris with the 1995 performance numbers of, say, the U.S. Computer and Technology Index, designed and maintained by the Philadelphia Stock Exchange—which, by the way, returned better than 43% (assuming reinvested dividends) in 1995.

Similarly, we should compare the performance numbers of Royal LePage Capital Property Services with, say, the Real Estate and Construction Index, published and maintained by the Toronto Stock Exchange. For the record, the TSE Real Estate and Construction Index had a negative return falling 18.98% (assuming reinvested dividends) in 1995.

Introducing fresh benchmarks that compare apples with apples is an important first step in making a judgment about the manager's ability. But we caution it is only the first step, because the benchmark only compares the performance or return side of the risk/return equation. We believe that only by measuring risk-adjusted returns do we get a clear picture of the manager's ability.

Understanding Risk-adjusted Returns

While most investors understand that a trade-off between risk and return exists, few know how to quantify that relationship. We know, for example, that an investment in pork belly futures could double or triple in a short period of time. We also know that speculating in commodity futures carries great risk, and we could lose our entire portfolio—and then some—in an equally short period of time.

On the other hand, we know that an investment in Canada Savings Bonds is, in terms of the principal investment, a risk-free exercise. We will receive a fixed rate of interest on our investment and our principal will be repaid in full when the CSBs are sold.

The decision to buy or not to buy either or both of these investments is driven by a subconscious assessment of the trade-off between risk and return—a trade-off that can only be made with certainty when looking at extreme situations.

Unfortunately, most investors and most investments fall somewhere between speculation in commodity futures and risk-free CSBs. As such, the trade-off between risk and return becomes blurred, and by extension, more difficult to quantify.

Again, let us return to fund managers and their benchmark indexes, and for this discussion we will look at two giant Canadian equity mutual funds: the Altamira Equity Fund and the Trimark Canadian Fund. Both have well over $1 billion Cdn in assets, and have diversified portfolios of Canadian stocks. Given that, we can assume a reasonable benchmark for both funds would be the TSE 300 Total Return Index.

If we were to look at the period returns for each fund and compare those performance numbers with the performance numbers for the TSE 300 Total Return Index over similar time periods, we have established a reasonable basis on which to judge a manager's performance.

Table 10.1 examines the one-month, three-month, one-year, three-year and five-year track records of the two funds relative to similar period returns for the TSE 300 Total Return Index. In each case, and through nearly all measurement periods, the fund managers outperformed the benchmark index. Based on our preliminary observations, it would appear that both fund managers added value, particularly over a five-year time period.

Table 10.1: RETURNS TO MAY 31, 1996

	1 month	3 months	1 year	3 years	5 years
Altamira Equity Fund	3.10%	6.70%	23.00%	13.70%	24.10%
Trimark Canadian Fund	1.70%	6.80%	17.30%	13.20%	13.40%
TSE 300 Total Return Index	2.10%	6.90%	20.60%	13.20%	11.20%

While we think this approach is a good first step, it still does not compare performance on a risk-adjusted basis. Remember, all that is being compared in Table 10.1 is the actual performance numbers of the fund manager against the actual performance of the benchmark index.

The three-year standard deviation for the Altamira Equity Fund is 3.38%, compared with 2.90% for the Trimark Canadian Equity Fund and 3.25% for the TSE Total Return Index. The Altamira Equity Fund, then,was more volatile over the past three years than the TSE Total Return Index, whereas the Trimark Canadian Equity Fund exhibited less variability of return than the benchmark index.

We know by definition that higher-risk portfolios ought to return more than lower-risk portfolios. The question, then, is how much of Frank Mersch's—manager of the Altamira Equity

Fund—superior performance numbers were the result of his ability to time the market, and how much were attributable to simply managing a more aggressive portfolio?

Along that same line, the performance of the managers of the Trimark Canadian investment committee (the committee includes Claude King, Robert Krembil, Rick Serafini and Phillip Taller) is particularly impressive when you consider that, over a five-year period, they actually outperformed the benchmark index, yet did so with a portfolio that was less risky than the benchmark index.

With that in mind, we set out to develop a model or rating system that measures whether a portfolio manager adds value based on his or her risk-adjusted performance numbers relative to the risk-adjusted performance numbers of the benchmark index. Our approach involves three steps.

Step 1: Establish an expected performance track

We believe that investors make investments anticipating a profitable outcome. Why else would anyone buy a mutual fund, or a stock, a bond, or even a GIC? Let's face it; no one who invests expects to lose money.

Assuming we make investments to earn positive returns, we start by establishing an expected rate of return given a specific level of risk, which we refer to as our *expected performance track*. The rate of return we should expect managers to deliver is based upon how much risk they are taking to generate that return. In other words, a manager with a three-year standard deviation of 4.50 should generate a higher return than a manager with a three-year standard deviation of 2.50. Just how much more is driven by the algorithm we use to calculate the expected performance track.

Within the expected performance track algorithm we:

1. establish a specific time period (i.e., monthly);
2. utilize the risk-free rate of return for that time period;
3. incorporate the three-year standard deviation of the fund adjusted for that time period; and
4. assume that all funds follow a lognormal distribution curve.

For the mathematically inclined, the assumption that mutual funds, or stock prices, or any other financial asset for that matter, follow a lognormal distribution is open to debate. However, we believe that because we are applying the same assumptions to all funds, the lognormal distribution most closely reflects a real-world compromise.

Without belaboring this point with mathematical mumbo jumbo, suffice it to say that a lognormal distribution establishes a set of price parameters that range from zero to infinity, and those parameters are defined by the standard deviation of those returns. In straight English, we are saying that the value of your mutual fund cannot fall below zero, but could, theoretically at least, rise to infinity, and that an expected performance track defines a range of positive returns that we would expect that particular fund to follow, based on the aforementioned criterion. A monthly positive rate of return is calculated for each fund using this criterion, which is what we define as the expected performance track.

It is important to understand that, to this point, all we have done is establish an expected performance track for each mutual fund with at least a three-year track record. (Note: We require the three-year standard deviation number to establish the expected return given that level of risk.) Table 10.2 displays the expected performance track for the Altamira Equity Fund and the Trimark Canadian Fund over a sample four-month period:

Table 10.2: EXPECTED MONTHLY PERFORMANCE TRACK*

	1	2	3	4
Altamira Equity Fund	2.23%	2.21%	2.22%	2.24%
Trimark Canadian Fund	1.96%	1.94%	1.95%	1.97%

* actual calculations go back 36 months from May 31, 1996

Of course, judging a fund manager against some expected performance track is unreasonable if we do not apply the same criteria to the index against which the fund manager is being benchmarked. If we have a Canadian equity fund, we use the same criteria to establish a monthly expected performance track for the TSE 300 Total Return Index. Table 10.3 displays the expected performance track for the TSE Total Return Index over a sample four-month period:

Table 10.3: EXPECTED MONTHLY PERFORMANCE TRACK*

	1	2	3	4
TSE 300 Total Return Index	2.15%	2.13%	2.14%	2.16%

* actual calculations go back 36 months from May 31, 1996

Step 2: Compare actual performance to expected performance

From Table 10.2, we know how much return we should expect each month given the level of risk assumed by the Altamira Equity Fund and the Trimark Canadian Fund. Obviously, we know that Frank Mersch or the Trimark management team will not always produce positive month-over-month returns. Nor are we suggesting that fund managers are not doing their jobs when they have negative monthly returns.

All we are really saying is that investors should reasonably expect, over the course of a business cycle (which on average can last anywhere from three to seven years), the portfolio manager to produce acceptable positive returns. Some months, managers will do much better than their expected performance track; other months they will underperform—sometimes dramatically.

In order to establish how well the manager has done month over month, we need to establish an actual performance track for the fund manager. Table 10.4 examines the actual monthly performance numbers for the Altamira Equity Fund and the Trimark Canadian Fund.

Table 10.4: ACTUAL MONTHLY PERFORMANCE NUMBERS*

	1	2	3	4
Altamira Equity Fund	3.09%	2.54%	0.98%	1.15%
Trimark Canadian Fund	1.71%	3.13%	1.86%	-0.12%

* actual returns go back 36 months from May 31, 1996

The Croft-Kirzner Performance Index ranks funds on the basis of return per unit of risk over the past three-year period. Obviously, we have to be careful not to infringe on the views set out at the beginning of this discussion—that no ideal time period on which to measure funds exists. However, since we decided to begin the discussion by looking at the risk side of the equation, we were drawn to the three-year standard deviation numbers widely available in the *Southam Source Disk.*

Quantity was also a factor. In the current *Source Book* and *Source Disk*, there are 622 funds with three-year track records, versus 537 funds with at least five-year records. By using the three-year numbers, we were able to rank more funds without, in our opinion, sacrificing the validity of the index. Because the risk measures in the *Source Book* and *Source Disk* are calculated using price and return data from the most recent 36 months, the three-year time period appears to be a reasonable compromise.

The second step in our calculation compares the fund's actual monthly performance with its expected performance. We simply divide the actual monthly performance numbers by the expected monthly performance numbers. Each month, we calculate a return per unit of risk value, which is really a monthly score (calculations are displayed in Table 10.5).

Table 10.5: ACTUAL RETURNS DIVIDED BY EXPECTED PERFORMANCE NUMBERS*

	1	2	3	4
Altamira Equity Fund	1.38	1.15	0.44	0.51
Trimark Canadian Fund	0.88	1.63	0.96	(0.06)

* actual calculations go back 36 months from May 31, 1996

We also calculate the actual monthly performance of the benchmark index and divide the actual monthly performance numbers by the benchmark index's expected monthly performance numbers (see Tables 10.6 and 10.7).

Table 10.6: ACTUAL MONTHLY PERFORMANCE NUMBERS*

	1	2	3	4
TSE 300 Total Return Index	2.13%	3.62%	1.03%	-0.53%

* actual returns go back 36 months from May 31, 1996

Table 10.7: ACTUAL RETURNS DIVIDED BY EXPECTED PERFORMANCE NUMBERS*

	1	2	3	4
TSE 300 Total Return Index	0.99	1.70	0.48	(0.24)

* actual calculations go back 36 months from May 31, 1996

Step 3: Compare the fund with the benchmark

At this stage, we have established, for lack of a better term, a monthly score for the fund and the comparable benchmark index. What we need to do is compare the monthly score of the fund with the comparable benchmark index. This allows us to compare the risk-adjusted performance of the fund against the risk-adjusted performance of the comparable benchmark index.

In step 3, then, we simply subtract the monthly score of the benchmark index from the monthly score for the fund whose manager is being evaluated. We then sum the results from the 36 monthly observation periods and add that result to a base value of 100. The calculations are displayed in Table 10.8.

Table 10.8: CALCULATIONS FOR THE CROFT-KIRZNER PERFORMANCE INDEX*

Returns from Table 10.5 less returns from Table 10.7					
	1	2	3	4	CKPI
Altamira Equity Fund	0.39	(0.55)	(0.04)	0.76	99.98
Trimark Canadian Fund	(0.11)	(0.07)	0.48	0.18	102.47

* actual calculations go back 36 months from May 31, 1996

From Table 10.8, we see that the Altamira Equity Fund scored 99.98, while the Trimark Canadian Fund scored 102.47. If the fund's index value is greater than 100, it means that the fund managers added value; a score of less than 100 indicates that the fund managers did not add value on a risk-adjusted basis over the past 36 months.

With the score just below 100, Mr. Mersch, despite a more aggressive investment style, was able to compensate investors with returns justified by the risks taken. Over the same time period, the Trimark investment committee outperformed the benchmark index, with less risk.

The CKPI tells us whether or not a fund manager added value when managed on a risk adjusted basis against a reasonable benchmark. All funds begin with a base score of 100. Any fund that scores a CKPI above 100, the manager has added value, while with funds that score below 100, the manager has not added value.

Note from our two fund examples, it appears that the Trimark management team added value on a risk-adjusted basis, even though Trimark's actual performance numbers were not as good as the numbers for the Altamira Equity Fund.

Breaking CKPI into Categories

Having established an index for each fund in each category, we are able to ascertain whether or not a portfolio manager added value. The next step is to rank the managers relative to the fund universe. In order to accomplish this, we divided the CKPI scores into five categories (ranked from 1 highest to 5 lowest) based on a normal distribution of a sampling of all funds with at least a three-year track record.

Funds that are in the top category (ranked 1) scored at least one standard deviation above the mean. Funds whose score ranked them in the lowest category (ranked 5) fell at least one standard deviation below the mean value of all fund scores.

Funds that ranked either 2, 3 or 4 were slotted into categories within one standard deviation of the mean of all fund values. In our example, both the Trimark Canadian Fund and the Altamira Equity Fund would have ranked in the "2" category.

Consistency, Consistency, Consistency

Some investors would argue that consistency is as important as performance. "Give me a fund manager whose portfolio closely tracks the benchmark index, and I'll be happy. After all, I should really be concerned about which asset class I am buying into because, as we have already learned, over the long term the fund manager is only going to add 10% to 15% to my bottom line."

We believe there is merit to that argument. But we think that you should look for fund managers who are consistently able to outperform. We see no advantage to a fund manager who consistently underperforms his or her benchmark index whether on a risk-adjusted or actual basis.

With that in mind, we want to add another dimension to this discussion—specifically, how consistent was the fund manager's risk-adjusted performance month over month? In other words, how much did the monthly scores vary in Table 10.8? Of course, the best way to calculate variance is to calculate the three-year standard deviation of the 36 monthly scores from Table 10.8. We refer to this calculation as the Croft-Kirzner Consistency Index (CKCI).

Table 10.9: CKCI CONSISTENCY RATING

		Rank
Altamira Equity Fund	1.82	4
Trimark Canadian Fund	1.55	4

We also divide the consistency scores into five categories, in the same way we divided the scores for the CK Performance Index. Funds that ranked best in the terms of consistency (i.e., most consistent risk-adjusted returns relative to their benchmark) are awarded a "5" rating. Funds that were not as consistent are ranked successively and would fall into the 4 through 1 categories, meaning a fund ranked "4" was more consistent than a "3" and so on.

Performance Measures—Uses and Abuses

Performance measures can be used to evaluate performance during both bull and bear markets. However, determining the appropriate benchmark and selecting an appropriate time frame is not a simple matter. Studies have shown that high-performing funds in one year are sometimes the big losers the next year. We cite our tale of two bond funds from Chapter 6.

Taking that analysis one step further, some funds outperform the averages in strong markets, but underperform when markets are weak. And more often than not, mutual funds on average do not outperform a randomly selected portfolio of securities. A key criterion in selecting a good fund is consistency of performance. How well does the fund perform in bad markets? In good markets? As a result, the fund's beta, variance and reward-to-risk measures are all important tools.

You should also examine the tenure of the fund's manager and whether the person who managed the fund's portfolio when it produced big gains is still at the helm, as our University Avenue Growth Fund example so aptly demonstrated. "Hot" managers are sometimes lured into a better-paying competitor's camp; "poor" managers often find themselves out of a job.

In other instances, the portfolio is managed by an advisory firm with a defined strategy. That can be a plus—it provides a degree of consistency at least, even when there's a coming and going of individual managers.

A mutual fund with a spectacular track record may not be a good bet for the future if there is a change in the management team or in the fund's objectives. Performance surveys list individual mutual fund managers and the number of years that they have been in charge (although some mutual funds are run by a team, and others refuse to disclose the manager). So you can track the performance of a particular manager or a fund's performance under different teams.

We believe, because we only track the most recent 36 monthly performance numbers, that the CKPI will incorporate a new manager's track record quickly into the model, particularly if the manager excels over a short period of time. However, when there is a change in management, there is usually a period of adjustment as the new manager rearranges the fund's portfolio to fit with his/her investment style. Assuming the new manager does a good job, that should begin to show up in the performance numbers, and ultimately be reflected in the trend of the CKPI.

At all costs, avoid the mistake of selecting funds strictly on the basis of recent quarterly or annual performance. The star performers this quarter or year may well be the laggards next period.

Some Thoughts on How to Use the CKPI Ratings

It is important to understand that the CK Performance Index measures whether or not the fund manager added value over the past 36 months, and how that manager stacked up against the fund's universe. As with any performance measure, it is not intended to be a guide for future performance. However, we would expect funds that consistently score high index values to give you the best bang for your investment dollar in terms of long-term returns per unit of risk.

We think investments ought to be approached from the top down. Rather than selecting funds on the basis of any measurement standard, investors should first look at how those funds fit within the context of their long-range objectives and risk tolerances.

The CK Performance Rating and the CK Consistency Rating are but two pieces of the puzzle. We believe investors should first decide what asset classes they want in their portfolio, as defined by their personal investment profile, and then purchase quality funds—based on the CK Performance and CK Consistency Rating—that provide optimum diversification across asset class, geographic regions, objectives and management style. In Chapter 11 we will introduce you to the FundLine, which will provide you with the only tool you will need to establish a well-balanced portfolio.

CHAPTER ELEVEN

The Croft-Kirzner FundLine

The Many Forms of Diversification

For most of us to maintain investments for the long term, we need a portfolio that will smooth the ride through the constant ebb and flow of the business cycle. The only way to achieve this is through diversification.

But diversification has no value if performance suffers. Our discussion in Chapter 10 provided a basis to mathematically quantify an expected rate of return for a given level of risk. In short, we know that lower-risk investments produce lower returns.

For diversification to add value, it has to be done in such a way as to magnify this relationship between risk and return. What we want, ideally, is a lower-risk portfolio that generates above-average returns.

What we suggest is a four-dimensional approach to diversification that includes:

1. Diversification by asset class or mix
2. Diversification by geographic region
3. Diversification by fund objectives
4. Diversification by investment style

Diversification by asset class was discussed in Chapter 9, and is the most important consideration when constructing a well-balanced portfolio. We can further reduce risk by extending the asset mix to include geographic regions, a topic we discussed in Chapter 10.

We believe that diversification by fund objectives and investment style is another important consideration. The purpose is not to judge the merits of any particular investment style, but rather to mix and match styles that bring a measure of balance to the portfolio. We discussed these elements in Chapter 5 on equity funds and Chapter 6 on bond funds.

In this chapter we will attempt to bring all of these elements together. We graphically display this four-dimensional approach to diversification in an easy-to-read format entitled the

FundLine. The FundLine provides an interpretive view of the risk-reduction elements a particular fund brings to your portfolio.

When you mix and match above-average funds, as measured by the Croft-Kirzner Performance and Consistency Ratings, with the diversification techniques characterized by the FundLine, you have all of the tools necessary to construct an optimally balanced portfolio—a portfolio that should, over the long haul, provide you with above-average risk-adjusted returns. And while this may not be the Holy Grail, any attempt to add value within the narrow definition of risk-adjusted return is certainly worth the effort.

The Croft-Kirzner FundLine

The goal of the Croft-Kirzner FundLine is to provide a graphic illustration of each mutual fund reviewed in this book. It is our way of streamlining the selection process so that all factors that affect the construction of a portfolio can be found in the FundLine. If you want to build an optimum portfolio, simply fill in the boxes.

The FundLine includes 24 boxes in three sections (see Figure 11.1). The first section, *Extended Asset Mix*, defines the asset class and geographic region in which the fund invests.

Figure 11.1: THE CROFT–KIRZNER FUNDLINE

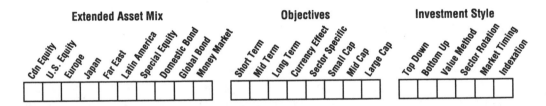

The second section, *Objectives,* broadly defines what investments the fund is emphasizing in the portfolio. For some funds, the objectives can change. For example, a bond fund manager who thinks interest rates are about to fall might have a large percentage of the portfolio invested in long-term bonds. As interest rates fall, that same manager may sell the long bonds at a profit and move the portfolio into short-term bonds. The attributes of a particular fund are categorized based on the portfolio at the time of writing.

The third section categorizes a number of different *Investment Styles*. Generally, the investment style of a successful fund will remain constant. No one really expects successful portfolio managers to change their approach to investing.

On the other hand, less successful portfolio managers tend to find themselves out of a job. And funds that remove a manager because of poor performance often seek out a new manager with a different approach. In that case, the investment style of a particular fund will change. Again, what investment style we attach to a specific fund is based upon our perception of style at the time this book went to press.

Extended Asset Mix

As you can see from the FundLine in Figure 11.1, we have subdivided—or extended—the asset classes into 10 broader categories. (Recall that in Chapter 9 we subdivided your asset mix into specific categories.) In the FundLine, we have simply broadened our international equity categories to include Canada, the United States, Europe, Japan, the Far East and Latin America. We have also included a special equity class that represents sector-specific funds, including real estate, precious metals, resources and any other special equity type of fund.

Fixed-income assets are also represented in the asset class section of the FundLine. In this case, we have subdivided the fixed-income component into domestic bond funds and global bond funds. The final category is money market, which simply represents any cash assets in your portfolio.

The idea that funds can be required to invest by asset class seems straightforward enough, but in actual practice, it is not as easy as it might seem. Global balanced funds offer an interesting perspective on this issue.

The Elliott & Page Global Balanced Fund invests in a diversified portfolio of equity and fixed-income investments from around the world. While David Boardman and Ian Henderson, the fund managers, have a mandate to invest anywhere in the world, they have recently focused their attention on equity and fixed-income investments in the U.S. and Japan. The fund, then, represents equity and fixed-income assets, as well as providing a measure of geographic diversification (see Figure 11.2).

Figure 11.2: FUNDLINE EXAMPLE

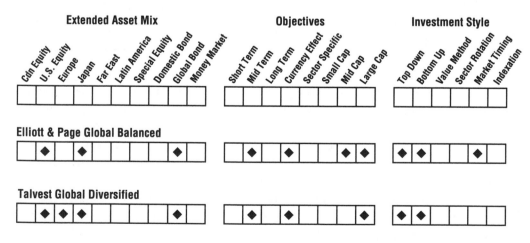

The Talvest Global Diversified fund also represents both equity and fixed-income investments, and has a mandate to invest worldwide. At the time of writing, fund manager Gordon Fyfe was focusing his attention on equity and fixed-income investments in the U.S., Europe and Japan. Theoretically, then, the Talvest Global Diversified Fund represents diversification in four categories within the extended asset class section of the FundLine.

Some Thoughts on One-Stop Shopping

In looking at the FundLine categories that pertain to global balanced (diversified) funds, an interesting question is raised. Is there an advantage to buying funds that offer many forms of diversification?

In Figure 11.2, for example, we see that the Elliott and Page Global Balanced Fund falls into 10 of the 24 categories in the FundLine, while the Talvest Global Diversified Fund provides exposure to nine FundLine categories. The mutual fund industry sees this as one-stop shopping. We see it as a handyman special that best serves small investors just starting out. It is not clear that global balanced (diversified) funds add value for investors who have the wherewithal to buy a diversified portfolio of six to eight quality mutual funds.

In terms of performance, we see advantages to buying good-quality funds that specialize in specific markets (i.e., equity funds, bond funds, international equity funds, small cap funds, etc.). Funds that strive to be all things to all investors suffer from what we like to think of as the "jack-of-all-trades-master-of-none" syndrome. The more diversification brought to the table by the fund manager, the less likely that manager will excel at any investment strategy that focuses on specific areas.

Balanced fund managers who are good at predicting which asset class to over-weight within the portfolio (i.e., mixing and matching the portfolio's weight between bonds, stocks and cash) are not always the best at selecting stocks to represent the equity component, or picking the term-to-maturity for the bond component.

Taking this one step further, global balanced (diversified) managers must determine the weights of each asset class within the portfolio (i.e., stocks, bonds and cash), decide which country offers the best opportunity for growth and select the right stocks and bonds within that geographic region. We think it is a stretch to expect a manager who is required to invest by asset mix and geographic region to also be adept at picking individual stocks and bonds that offer above-average performance.

In short, we concede that 85% to 90% of your overall return is dependent on your asset mix decision. And we concede that the asset mix decision is the core strategy of the balanced or global balanced (diversified) fund.

But in our opinion, purchasing a balanced fund or a global balanced (diversified) fund eliminates any possibility of finding a good manager who can add value for the other 10% to 15% of your overall performance numbers. We think the FundLine provides a solid, straightforward foundation on which to optimize your asset mix within your own personal guidelines, allowing you to then focus on the funds that specialize in certain investment areas.

The Fund's Objectives

The next section of the FundLine defines for us the makeup of the investments held by the individual funds. We're not talking about the specific stocks an equity fund might hold or the specific bonds in a bond fund. What we're focusing on is the general structure of the portfolio.

For example, a fund manager may focus specifically on large cap or small cap stocks. The Manulife Cabot Canadian Equity Fund has a clear Canadian large cap mandate, as the manager is restricted to the top 100 funds listed on the Toronto Stock Exchange. The Global Strategy Canadian Small Cap Fund, on the other hand, focuses attention entirely on shares of small cap companies.

Usually, we find that equity managers have a blended portfolio that includes, say, small and medium cap stocks, or medium and large cap stocks. Some managers will tell you they hold a blended portfolio that includes small, medium and large cap stocks.

However, we have found on closer examination that all fund managers express some bias in their selection process. As such, the bulk of any blended equity portfolio is usually weighted between two groups, say, small and medium-size firms, or medium and large cap companies.

We expect equity funds that focus on small cap stocks to, on average, be more volatile than equity funds with a large cap focus. In fact, the average three-year standard deviation for small cap Canadian equity funds is 3.77%, versus an average standard deviation of 3.14% for Canadian equity large cap funds.

While we do not endorse one type of fund portfolio over another, we do expect, over long periods of time, that small cap funds will outperform large cap funds. Higher returns simply compensate you for the increased risks, a position that the long-term performance numbers support. Using the average numbers from the two groups, 131 Canadian large cap funds had a three-year compound average return of 13.9%, compared with a three-year average compound return of 17.1% for small cap funds.

Like most issues when constructing an optimum portfolio, we suggest you balance your portfolio by including a small cap fund as well as a large cap fund.

Figure 11.3: A LARGE CAP FUND AND A SMALL CAP FUND

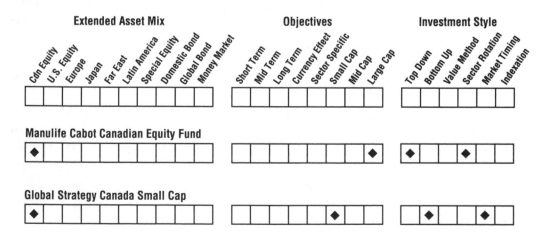

Fixed-income Portfolios

As is the case with equity funds, the FundLine provides three boxes that represent the portfolios of fixed-income managers. Fixed-income managers, whether mandated to invest globally or domestically, tend to pick their spots along the yield curve. These three categorizations are representative of virtually all fixed-income portfolios and, in short, pigeonhole the average term-to-maturity of the bond fund being analyzed.

You will recall from Chapter 6 that term-to-maturity and, more specifically, duration have a dramatic impact on the profitability of a bond fund, given a change in the level of interest rates. Simply stated, a domestic bond fund with a portfolio of long-term bonds will be more volatile, and offer greater capital gains potential, than a domestic bond fund with a short term-to-maturity.

For purposes of the FundLine, we define Short Term as those bond funds where the average term-to-maturity is three years or less. Mid Term is defined as a bond fund with an average term-to-maturity of three to 10 years, and Long Term represents fixed-income funds where the average term-to-maturity is greater than 10 years.

We have also included a box entitled "Currency Effect" in the middle of the *Objectives* section. This tells us whether the fund's performance will be affected by fluctuations in a foreign currency. Whether you view that box as currency risk or currency hedge depends on your point of view. If you go south every winter, you may look for funds that have a check mark under Currency Effect, viewing that as a tool to hedge yourself against changes in the value of the Canadian dollar.

Of course, the importance of currency effect in the fund's performance hinges on the type of investments held in the fund. For example, we would expect over most long periods that the bulk of the performance numbers generated by international equity funds are the result of the overall performance within a specific equity market, rather than from currency fluctuations. If the equity market in a particular country is doing well it usually means that the country's currency is also doing well.

This approach would seem to fly in the face of comments made in Chapter 9. Recall how currency fluctuations had such a dramatic impact on our Mexico Fund. Still, in general terms, an international fund (remember Latin American Funds have their own category) generally invests in mature markets (i.e., Europe, Japan and parts of the Far East) and, as such, the manager has the ability to hedge against currency fluctuations. As a result of that, we believe that the performance numbers from an international equity fund are driven largely by the performance of the stock market in the countries where the fund invests, and not as much by currency fluctuations.

In 1995, for example, the performance of the U.S. dollar vis-à-vis the Canadian dollar had some impact on the Canadian dollar-adjusted performance numbers generated by U.S. equity funds. However, the impact from changes in the U.S. dollar/Canadian dollar exchange rate paled in comparison with the returns produced by a hot U.S. equity market. On the other hand, exchange-rate risk has, in the past, played a major role in the performance of equity funds that invest in smaller markets, like Latin America.

Currency fluctuations also play a major role in the performance of global bond funds. There are periods where currency exchange has a greater impact on the global bond fund's performance than does the term-to-maturity of the fixed-income portfolio. In some cases, global bond fund managers actively manage currency exposure in an attempt of enhance returns from profitable currency trading.

For example, the Global strategy team, which is headed by Ceris Williams of the N. M. Rothschild Group in London, actively manages currency exposure to protect profits and enhance performance. Indeed, the Global Strategy Foreign Bond Fund and Global Strategy Diversified Bond Fund can use certain derivatives to meet those stated objectives.

Figure 11.4: A BOND FUND MIX

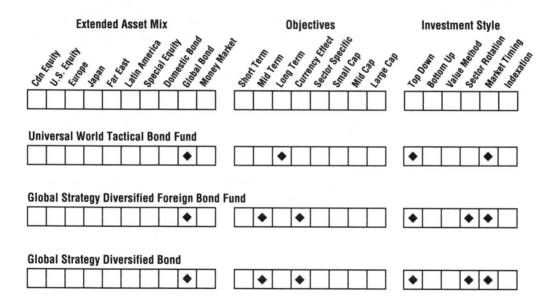

Other global bond funds go to great lengths to hedge against exchange-rate risk, which implies that most of the performance numbers from such funds will be the result of changes in the level of interest rates within a specific geographic region. An example is the Universal World Tactical Bond Fund, where the manager "uses active currency management to protect gains." Presumably, Mr. Williams is protecting the gains earned by actively managing the fixed-income part of the portfolio. If the manager actively hedges exchange rate fluctuations, we would not check off the Currency Effect box. Most U.S. and international equity funds, global bond funds and global balanced (diversified) funds are valued in Canadian dollars. There are exceptions, however, AGF being the classic example. AGF offers investors a choice. Many AGF funds can be purchased in U.S. or Canadian dollars.

Sector Specific Funds

Finally, under the *Objectives* section, we have a box entitled "Sector Specific," which represents funds that do not provide much in the way of diversification, but can add some real *oomph* to your bottom line. Funds that receive a check mark under Sector Specific will likely also have a check mark in the Special Equity box under the *Extended Asset Mix* section.

Investors should give careful consideration when using this box in constructing a portfolio. For example, the Green Line Science and Technology Fund, because of its narrow focus, would receive a check mark in the Special Equity and Sector Specific box. However, while we would expect a U.S. science and technology fund to be more volatile than the overall market, it will tend to move in the same direction as, say, the S&P 500 Composite Index, because the boom or bust in the technology sector is driven by the strength or weakness of the overall economy.

On the other hand, funds that specialize in precious metals or natural resources tend to move opposite to the general trend, and can provide reasonable diversification to the broader market. We would generally expect these types of special equity funds to perform quite differently from the broader equity market, perhaps rising when stocks are generally falling, and performing poorly—as has been the case in recent years—when the general market is rising. In 1995, for example, resource funds returned on average 4.5% for the year, while the average for precious metals funds was a surprising 8.6%. However, remove the stellar performance (+52.4%) numbers posted by the Royal Precious Metals Fund, and the average return in 1995 for this group falls to 2.5% However, because the Canadian economy is so dependent on natural resources, any Canadian equity fund will have some exposure to this sector, suggesting that it might not be necessary to have funds that specialize in precious metals or resources.

Using Special Equity Funds in Your Portfolio

They are the best of funds; they are the worst of funds. Check the three-month, six-month and one-year performance numbers, and at the top of the list you will usually find a special equity fund.

In fact, looking at the one-year numbers to April 30, 1996, the top three performers are special equity funds. Royal Precious Metals Fund (+131.49%) leads the pack, followed by Cambridge Resource Fund (+121.3%) and Prudential Precious Metals (+93.8%).

Check the same performance periods and at the bottom of the list you will usually find a special equity fund. In this case, the worst one-year performer was a special equity labor-sponsored fund, the Integrated Growth Fund (-19.2%). Next in line for the hall of shame, the second worst one-year performer, was another special equity fund, the Friedberg Double Gold Plus (-6.9%).

It is not surprising we find this much diversity among special equity funds. They do, after all, focus on a specific industry or economic sector. And in any given period, some sectors will be doing quite well—resources, metals and technology being cases in point—while other sectors are simply out of favor—real estate being an example of the latter. Critics of special equity funds see them as a collection of shooting stars, rocketing to the top of the charts one quarter, plummeting the next, seemingly going nowhere. The implication, then, is why take the risk?

And the risks are significant. The three-year standard deviation of the average special equity fund is 5.05%, compared with 3.90% for the average small cap fund, the next most volatile category. Special equity funds simply do not provide the risk-reduction advantages normally associated with an investment in mutual funds. And they don't profess to!

In most cases, special equity funds have more than 5% of their portfolio invested in a single stock. The Cambridge Resource Fund, for example, had 5.9% of the portfolio (as of March 31, 1996) invested in Profco Resources Ltd., and another 5.5% in America Mineral Fields Inc. If either of these companies falls sharply, so, too, does your special equity fund. Kind of like putting your eggs in one basket and watching them very, very carefully.

For the record, let's acknowledge that special equity funds are not a balanced mutual fund. What motivates an investment in special equity funds is performance. And with some careful selections, special equity funds can add value. Not as a stand-alone investment, mind you. But assuming you already have a well-balanced portfolio of funds, a carefully selected special equity fund can add nicely to your bottom line.

To get the extra kick from special equity funds, you need to focus on sectors that are likely to outperform the general market. Precious metals funds were typical examples of such investments during the first quarter. Longer term, however, you need a set of fundamental factors that will sustain the trend. The second quarter decline in gold prices has already taken some of the luster off precious metals funds.

Another consideration is the management expertise of the fund. Don't assume, when focusing on a specific sector, that all funds in that sector will perform the same. In the case of precious metals funds, for example, it depends on what percentage of the portfolio is invested in gold mining stocks and what percentage is in gold bullion. The Royal Precious Metals Fund has the bulk of its assets in mining companies; Friedberg Double Gold Plus has the bulk of its assets in gold bullion and/or gold futures.

In addition, how long do you want to hold the fund? In many cases, a good high-quality resource, technology or health-care fund could be a long-term hold. That being said, many special equity investments are viewed as cyclical in nature, because the stocks of many industry sectors tend to rise and fall as investors anticipate the expansion and contraction of the economy.

And finally, you need to understand how an investment in a special equity fund fits within your broader portfolio. Some funds, like precious metals or resource funds, might not be acceptable as stand-alone investments, but can be great additions to an already diversified portfolio. Adding funds that do not tend to move in sync with the broader market can actually reduce overall portfolio risk.

Of course, the amount of risk reduction depends on what other funds are already in your portfolio. For example, the Marathon Equity Fund is categorized as a small cap fund, but during May 1996, Wayne Deans had 40% of his assets invested in mining exploration companies. That total has since been reduced to 27%.

The point is, does a precious metals fund really make sense as an addition to a portfolio that already includes the Marathon Equity Fund? Special equity funds really make sense when they provide your portfolio with a better mix. Understanding that balancing act, special equity funds can fit in quite nicely.

The Importance of Investment Styles

To emphasize the importance of investment styles, we draw your attention to a study produced by the Altamira Group of mutual funds. At issue was whether three Altamira funds could meet the needs of investors pursuing three unique investment styles. To address this issue, Gordon Garmaise, president of Garmaise Investment Technologies of Toronto, analyzed the investment styles of Altamira's Capital Growth Fund, Altamira Equity Fund and the Altamira Special Growth Fund. As a consultant to Altamira, Garmaise examined these funds using three techniques:

Weighted Averages

First, he calculated the weighted average capitalization of each of our Canadian equity funds. "A fund holding a large number of small cap stocks will show a relatively low weighted average capitalization, while a large cap fund will show a high weighted average," Garmaise explained.

His calculations showed the Altamira Capital Growth Fund to be a large cap fund, the Equity Fund to be medium cap and the Special Growth Fund to be small cap. "Despite the perception in the investment community that all of Altamira's funds are small cap, clearly, we're dealing here with three very different types of funds," he said.

Size Weighting

Next, Garmaise compared the small and large cap exposure of the three mutual fund portfolios with that of the TSE, using a widely accepted statistical size weighting standard. "The extent to which a portfolio's size weighting exceeds or falls below the TSE's dictates whether it is small, medium or large cap," Garmaise explained. This approach again yielded results for the three Altamira funds similar to those obtained in the first test.

Index Comparisons

Finally, Garmaise compared the long-term returns of the three Altamira funds with the Burns Fry and Wood Gundy small cap indexes, as well as other measures. As expected, the Altamira Capital Growth Fund, shown earlier to be a large cap fund, had the least correlation of the three small cap indexes, while the small cap Special Growth Fund's returns were poorly correlated to large cap performance. The behavior of the Altamira Equity Fund was about halfway between the other two funds in its relationship with the small and large cap indexes. Thus, its performance was consistent with that of a medium cap fund. (Note: In the FundLine, we classify the Altamira Equity Fund as having exposure to medium and large cap stocks.)

Conclusion

"On the basis of all three of these measures, which produced remarkably consistent results," said Garmaise, "not only is the Altamira Capital Growth Fund clearly large cap, but in fact it is one of the most heavily oriented toward large cap investment of all Canadian mutual funds.

"On the other hand, the perception that the Altamira Special Growth Fund is a small cap fund is definitely correct. It has a very small weighted average capitalization and a significantly lower correlation to large cap indexes than any of its counterparts."

The Altamira Equity Fund falls clearly in the middle, as Garmaise also noted: "It demonstrates an average relation to the large and small cap indexes. For this fund, the values of the other two indicators that I've used—weighted average capitalization and the relative-size factor—also fall within the mid range."

Reprinted with permission from Altamira Investment Services Inc.

Investment Styles

In Chapters 5 and 6, we discussed investment styles in a general basis, particularly as they relate to equity and domestic bond funds. In this section, we want to expand the discussion to include some intricacies that may change the way you look at investment styles.

To expand this discussion, we will make liberal use of examples of investment styles as they relate to balanced funds, global balanced (diversified) funds, global fixed-income funds, international equity funds and money market funds. For the record, the six investment styles discussed in Chapters 6 and 7 are categorized at the far right of the FundLine.

When categorizing portfolio managers by their investment style, we came across some interesting concepts that need to be explained. For example, we generally assume that bottom-up equity fund managers focus most of their time ferreting out business opportunities and much less time predicting the short-term direction of the business cycle.

They buy a business because it is undervalued, based primarily on the long-term fundamentals, and second, because the economy is about to rebound. Given that position, we generally find that bottom-up managers are also value oriented, and practice a value style of investing.

Examples of that philosophy include the Trimark family of funds, where all of the equity funds are managed using a bottom up/value style. In fact, this is the investment philosophy in which Trimark prides itself and spends a great deal of money to market (see Figure 11.5).

Investment Styles of Trimark Equity Funds

When looking at the Trimark balanced (growth/income) funds, you'll see that the firm practices a top down/market timing philosophy to determine what percentage of the portfolio will be dedicated to stocks and what percentage to bonds over the course of the business cycle. At that point, the managers employ the traditional Trimark bottom up/value style to select individual stocks in the portfolio.

Figure 11.5: INVESTMENT STYLES OF TRIMARK EQUITY FUNDS

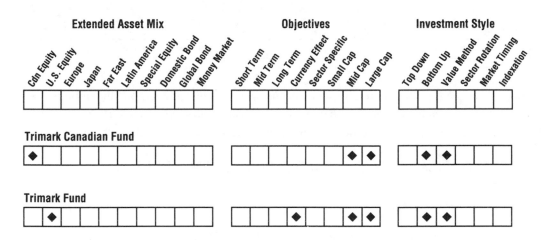

In a similar vein, global funds are difficult to pigeonhole in terms of investment style. A number of global equity fund managers, for example, will use a top-down investment approach to determine which country offers the best investment opportunities. Having settled on a specific country, some of those same managers will employ a bottom up/value style to select the individual stocks within that country. An example of this type of investment philosophy can be found in MacKenzie's Universal Emerging Growth Fund, which specializes in medium-size companies. Medium-size companies, as is the case with small cap stocks, require the managers to make some value judgments about the merits of a particular business, and that lends itself nicely to a bottom up/value style of investing to complement the top-down philosophy used to select the appropriate geographic regions.

Figure 11.6: INVESTMENT STYLES OF MACKENZIE UNIVERSAL EMERGING GROWTH FUND

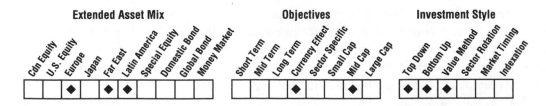

Another style that global fund managers use is "sector rotation." This is particularly well suited to global equity funds like Global Strategy's World Equity Fund, which uses a multi-manager approach focusing primarily on country selection and then on specific sectors within those countries.

Figure 11.7: INVESTMENT STYLES OF GLOBAL STRATEGY WORLD EQUITY FUND

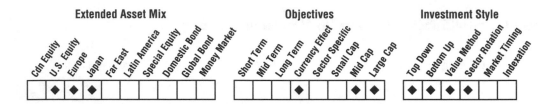

Indexation is a style that normally stands alone. We assume, for example, that money market funds employ an index style in that they attempt to track short-term interest rates. For our purposes, nearly all money market funds follow a FundLine similar to the one found in Figure 11.8.

Figure 11.8: INVESTMENT STYLES OF SELECTED MONEY MARKET FUNDS

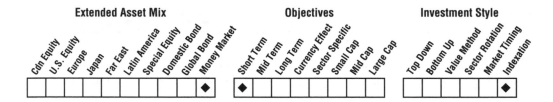

Keeping with the same theme, index fund managers are not normally associated with any other management style. As discussed previously, index fund managers are not market timers or sector rotators. When index fund managers talk about investment philosophy, they talk in terms of tracking error and matching an index's performance numbers; there is never any talk about outperforming the benchmark index.

However, that being said, there are global fund managers who we believe follow an indexation style, yet also practice some good old-fashioned top-down management. We cite as a case in point a number of the international equity funds from Global Strategy. In this case, the fund's managers employ a top-down philosophy to select which single country equity markets offer the most potential. Having selected a specific country, the managers will use derivatives (i.e., index futures contracts) to implement a position in that country. The manager seeks to match the performance of the index in that particular country. At the same time, the manager attempts to outperform other managers by profiting from currency fluctuations and by selecting the optimum country mix in which to be invested.

Another variation on that theme can be seen in the Global Strategy Europe Fund, where the managers actually purchase a number of good-quality large cap stocks—employing a top down/sector rotation management style—and then augment those selections with the purchase of index futures contracts on the various European bourses.

Figure 11.9: INVESTMENT STYLES OF GLOBAL STRATEGY DIVERSIFIED EUROPE FUND

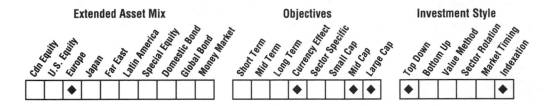

Market timing is a strategy well suited to bond funds. Bond fund managers refer to their style as interest rate anticipation (see Chapter 7). Fact is, most domestic fixed-income funds invest in high-grade government bonds, effectively eliminating default risk, and tying capital gains or losses to changes in the level of interest rates. The reason? A change in the level of interest rates is considered a macro-economic event that would, by definition, require the manager to follow a top-down philosophy. Simply stated, then, interest rate anticipators attempt to time the movement in interest rates, then take a position along the yield curve that will earn the maximum return should that scenario unfold. Examples of this type of fund managers can be found in Figure 11.10.

We also find some fixed-income fund managers who practice a bottom up/value style. Examples include a high-yield bond fund, where the manager looks for corporate bonds offering high rates of interest. However, when investing in a high-yielding corporate bond, you must accept the possibility of default.

High-yield bond fund managers diversify across a number of companies in different industries in order to reduce the risks associated with defaults. The point is, high-yield bond fund managers are keenly interested in the fundamentals underlying the company issuing the bond, because those fundamentals will dictate whether or not the company will be able to meet its obligations.

Figure 11.10: INVESTMENT STYLES OF SELECTED BOND FUNDS

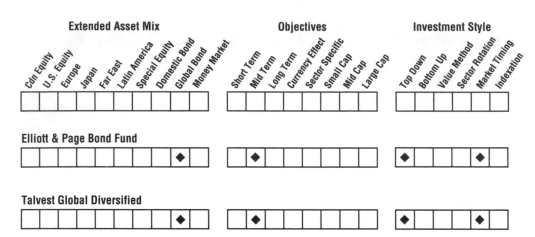

We have slotted most mortgage fund managers into a top down/value investment philosophy, even though they tend to invest in higher-grade mortgages. Contrary to that position, we view mortgage funds as an income vehicle. If you accept that premise, then mortgage fund managers should focus on maintaining a steady and reasonable monthly income for unit holders. Any potential capital gains resulting from the manager being able to time changes in the direction of interest rates will normally pale in comparison with the long-term goals of steady monthly income for the unit holder.

We also note that some balanced funds, like the MacKenzie Industrial Income Fund, practice a top down/sector rotation (spread trading)/market timing philosophy. In this case, the MacKenzie Fund management team attempts to provide unit holders with "a steady flow of income consistent with reasonable safety of capital. The portfolio consists mainly of corporate and government bonds, short-term notes, as well as common and preferred shares of established Canadian companies."

It is the last part of the objective statement—investments in large-established Canadian companies and different maturities—that brings sector rotation into the picture. We believe the sector rotation philosophy is a minor consideration in this fund's overall investment philosophy, with more emphasis being placed on the top down/market timing components of the investment plan.

Of course, many balanced fund and global fund managers use market timing when making investment decisions, particularly 1) when it comes to weighting the stock and bond components of the balanced portfolio, and 2) when it comes to country allocation and interest rate anticipation within specific countries for the global funds.

Figure 11.11: INVESTMENT STYLES OF SELECTED BOND/MORTGAGE FUNDS

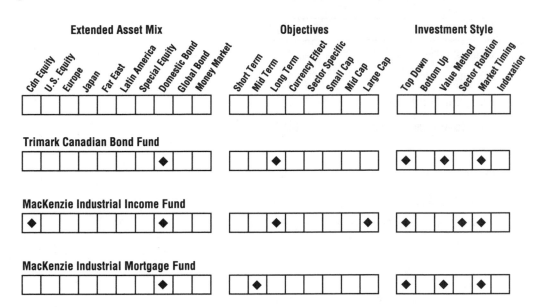

Putting It All Together

Having examined how we slot funds along the FundLine, you now have at your finger-tips all the information necessary to construct an optimal portfolio. You simply fill in the boxes using the highest-ranking funds from those we have included at the back of the book.

To see how easy the process is, consider the following hypothetical example. Suppose that Mr. Jones, after filling in the personal investment profile and based on his answers, had a score of 53. Given that score, Mr. Jones defines his personal policy statement and extended asset mix as follows:

Figure 11.12: MR. JONES' PERSONAL INVESTMENT PROFILE

				Growth			Score: 45 – 54	
	Equities			Fixed Income			Cash	
Min	**Policy**	Max	Min	**Policy**	Max	Min	**Policy**	Max
40%	**60%**	80%	20%	**30%**	40%	5%	**10%**	15%

Figure 11.13: MR. JONES' EXTENDED ASSET MIX

Asset Groups	Pct. of Portfolio
Canadian Equity Funds	30%
U.S. Equity Funds	20%
International Equity Funds	10%
Total Equity Component	**60%**
Global Bond Funds	10%
Domestic Bond Funds	20%
Total Fixed-income Component	**30%**
Money Market Funds	10%
Total Cash Component	**10%**
Total Portfolio	**100%**

Having arrived at an extended asset mix, the next step is security selection—specifically, which funds, representing each asset class, does Mr. Jones want in his portfolio? We'll assume, for simplicity, that Mr. Jones wants to hold no more than eight funds, with a goal of diversifying as broadly as possible.

We would begin, of course, with the best-ranked funds in each category (see Appendix). Now again, for clarification, let's assume that Mr. Jones has searched through our Best Bet Funds and has come up with the following 12 hypothetical candidates:

Figure 11.14: HYPOTHETICAL BEST BET FUNDS

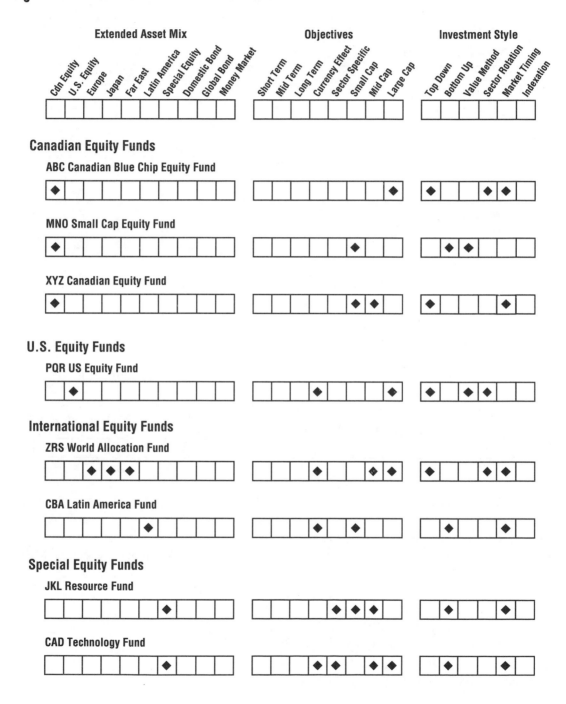

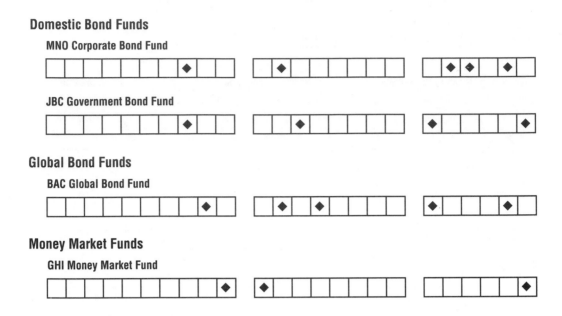

Domestic Bond Funds

MNO Corporate Bond Fund

JBC Government Bond Fund

Global Bond Funds

BAC Global Bond Fund

Money Market Funds

GHI Money Market Fund

The first thing we want to do is structure Mr. Jones' personal FundLine, which we do in Figure 11.15.

Figure 11.15: MR. JONES' PERSONAL FUNDLINE

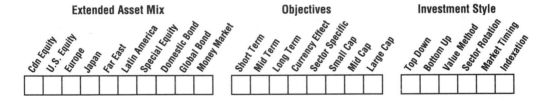

Having established a personal FundLine, Mr. Jones simply needs to select some funds—usually no more than seven funds are required—that 1) meet his ideal asset mix, and 2) provide measures of diversification, by filling in as many boxes along the FundLine as possible. (Note that boxes do not get checked off more than once.) For example, if Mr. Jones chooses the MNO Small Cap Equity Fund for his Canadian component, he would fill in four boxes along his FundLine:

1. under Extended Asset Mix, Canadian Equity
2. under Objectives, Small Cap
3. under Investment Style, Bottom Up
4. under Investment Style, Value Method

If his next selection was, say, the PQR U.S. Equity Fund, he would fill in another six boxes, five of which reflect new diversification:

1. under Extended Asset Mix, U.S. Equity
2. under Objectives, Currency Effect
3. under Objectives, Large Cap
4. under Investment Style, Top Down
5. under Investment Style, Value Method
6. under Investment Style, Sector Rotation

With these first two selections, Mr. Jones has filled in nine of the 24 potential boxes. If he then chooses the ZRS World Allocation Fund as his third selection, again he fills in nine boxes, six of which have not been filled before:

1. under Extended Asset Mix, Europe, Japan, Far East
2. under Objectives, Currency Effect
3. under Objectives, Mid Cap and Large Cap
4. under Investment Style, Top Down
5. under Investment Style, Sector Rotation
6. under Investment Style, Market Timing

Having made these selections, Mr. Jones has now completed 14 of the 24 potential boxes. If he then chooses the JBC Government Bond Fund for his domestic fixed-income asset and BAC Global Bond Fund for his global fixed-income component, he completes another eight boxes, including:

1. under Extended Asset Mix, Domestic Bond
2. under Extended Asset Mix, Global Bond
3. under Objectives, Mid Term
4. under Objectives, Long Term
5. under Objectives, Currency Effect
6. under Investment Style, Top Down
7. under Investment Style, Market Timing
8. under Investment Style, Indexation

Add the GHI Money Market Fund to this portfolio and you complete three more boxes, two of which—money market and short term—have not yet been filled in:

1. under Extended Asset Mix, Money Market
2. under Objectives, Short Term
3. under Investment Style, Top Down
4. under Investment Style, Indexation

We now have six funds in Mr. Jones' portfolio, and he has completed all but three of the boxes in the FundLine. The three remaining boxes are under *Extended Asset Mix*—Latin America and Special Equity—and *Objectives*—Sector Specific. Since 21 of the 24 boxes have been completed, Mr. Jones has a well-diversified portfolio. The next selection can probably be made simply on the basis of performance, which we'll assume the best performing of the remaining funds has been the CAD Technology Fund. The CAD Technology Fund represents another four boxes, two of which have not been completed:

1. under Extended Asset Mix, Special Equity
2. under Objectives, Currency Effect
3. under Objectives, Sector Specific
4. under Objectives, Small Cap
5. under Investment Style, Bottom Up
6. under Investment Style, Market Timing

Mr. Jones now has completed 23 of the 24 potential boxes, and we believe he has put together a well-diversified portfolio of solid funds. So you see, the idea with the FundLine is straightforward—complete as many boxes as possible with the number of funds you would like to purchase. If the final selection in Mr. Jones' portfolio is the CBA Latin America Fund, he is able to fill in the one remaining box (*Extended Asset Mix*—Latin America). With eight funds in his portfolio, Mr. Jones has completed all 24 boxes in the FundLine.

Figure 11.16: MR. JONES' PERSONAL FUNDLINE COMPLETED

Extended Asset Mix

Fund	Cdn Equity	U.S. Equity	Europe	Japan	Far East	Latin America	Special Equity	Domestic Bond	Global Bond	Money Market
(blank top row)										
MNO Small Cap Equity Fund	◆									
PQR US Equity Fund		◆								
ZRS World Allocation Fund			◆	◆	◆					
JBC Government Bond Fund								◆		
BAC Global Bond Fund									◆	
GHI Money Market Fund										◆
CAD Technology Fund							◆			
CBA Latin America Fund						◆				
Mr. Jones' Personal FundLine (completed)	◆	◆	◆	◆	◆	◆	◆	◆	◆	◆

Objectives

Fund	Short Term	Mid Term	Long Term	Currency Effect	Sector Specific	Small Cap	Mid Cap	Large Cap
(blank top row)								
MNO Small Cap Equity Fund						◆		
PQR US Equity Fund			◆					◆
ZRS World Allocation Fund			◆				◆	◆
JBC Government Bond Fund	◆							
BAC Global Bond Fund		◆	◆					
GHI Money Market Fund	◆							
CAD Technology Fund			◆	◆		◆		
CBA Latin America Fund			◆		◆			
Mr. Jones' Personal FundLine (completed)	◆	◆	◆	◆	◆	◆	◆	◆

Investment Style

Fund	Top Down	Bottom Up	Value Method	Sector Rotation	Market Timing	Indexation
(blank top row)						
MNO Small Cap Equity Fund	◆	◆				
PQR US Equity Fund	◆		◆	◆		
ZRS World Allocation Fund	◆			◆	◆	
JBC Government Bond Fund	◆					◆
BAC Global Bond Fund	◆				◆	
GHI Money Market Fund	◆					◆
CAD Technology Fund		◆		◆		
CBA Latin America Fund		◆		◆		
Mr. Jones' Personal FundLine (completed)	◆	◆	◆	◆	◆	◆

CHAPTER TWELVE

The FundLine Forecast

A common thread throughout this book is the notion that forecasting is more of an art than a science. That we are making our best guesses as to what to expect from financial markets in 1997 does not change our view that the forecasters' hall of fame is, at best, a small room.

Few forecasters can predict the direction of the economy on any consistent basis, and those who have had some success still go through periods when they mis-read signals. The problem, of course, is they tend to mis-read those signals at about the same time you are ready to follow their advice.

Given what we've said so far, you can be excused for thinking that this forecasting exercise is a contradiction in terms. But doing so, we think, misses the point. The point in this case is to help investors stay invested, rather than encourage them to time the market. Here's how we see it.

We know that individual investors usually sell their funds after short periods of poor performance. They get caught up in the short-term hype, often making panic-driven decisions while in an information vacuum. In essence, they are seeing the trees, but not the forest.

Our approach is to focus on the macro issues, and by doing so, hopefully provide you with a degree of confidence when short-term corrections in the marketplace occur. History tells us that short-term corrections do not normally change the long-term trend. Indeed, the volatility in the equity markets during July 1996 reinforced that position. Corrections of this magnitude come with such fury that they are often over before the individual investor has an opportunity to react, providing still more evidence about the risks of trying to time the market.

If you have at your fingertips a long-term economic overview—which is what we see our forecast as being—then you have a gauge to measure the impact of short-term corrections. In other words, is a correction the result of any change in the long-term fundamentals, or is it simply the market shaking out some less-informed investors?

To drive the point home, consider the following example. Interest rates and corporate profits are two macro issues that could have an effect on our forecast over the coming year. We expect—and will spell out why in this chapter—that long-term interest rates will not likely increase or decrease "materially" from current levels. The question is one of degree. Long-term Canadian interest rates might rise by a percentage point over the coming year; indeed, they may decline by a percentage point over the coming year. But within those parameters, we would not expect that to have a significant impact on our year-over-year forecast.

If we can get you to see both the trees and the forest—because you can compare what's happening in the market with our long-term position—we think you will be able to make decisions that are more informed. And in that context, you will likely find that the best decision is to remain invested. Perhaps you may even see a market correction as an opportunity to buy more fund units.

We also believe that any decisions must be made within the context of your overall portfolio. Don't sell one fund and buy another simply because one went up and another down. The question is really what impact did changes to the net asset value per share of either fund have on the total value of your portfolio. A top-down evaluation of the portfolio makes more sense than a bottom-up assessment of individual funds.

And finally, we think that providing an overview of the economy and a best guess forecast for the year ahead is a useful exercise for new investors. But here again, it must be used within the parameters of the personal asset mix described in Chapter 3.

Recall that your personal investment profile provided the foundation on which to build a personal policy statement, which in turn defined your ideal asset mix. Within that framework, we allowed some latitude in terms of the minimum and maximum percentage weights that could be applied to each asset class. This forecast simply lays a foundation on which to define those weightings for the year ahead, within the minimum and maximum parameters.

In summary, if this process adds value over the long term, it is not because we are superior prognosticators, but rather because our forecast talks in terms of what we see, and why we see things in that way. And knowing the why along with our expectations, we think, will provide some comfort during periods when equity markets are experiencing short-term volatility. If you can permit us some uncharacteristic flair for the dramatic, think of our forecasts as an investment roadmap, designed to soften your ride down the road to financial freedom.

In the years ahead, as we update this book, we will take a critical look at our performance, specifically measuring actual performance and trends against our predictions. Never wanting to be too sure of our position, we will take credit when we make the right choice, accept the blame when we are wrong, and expect, over time, to be right about 50% of the time.

Such are the inherent dangers of hanging from a limb. But having collectively provided recommendations for more than 30 years, we recognize that the best fruit lies at the extreme end of that limb. And so, we think, the risks are justified by the goal.

And finally, if you are concerned about the possibility that our long-term forecast will change, check us out in the monthly issues of the *FundLetter*, where we quite often discuss the macro issues within the context of short-term market performance.

The Structure of Our Forecast

We have divided our forecast into three distinct sections. First, we will look at where we are now. At least, were we are at the time of writing this forecast (July 1996). Second, we will provide an overview for the year ahead, based on an outlook for the Canadian and U.S. economies, and then a global perspective that includes a discussion of Latin America, Europe and, of course, the Asia Pacific basin. Third, we will look at what happened to the various asset classes for all of 1995 and for the first six months of 1996. We will make some suggestions as to where to invest in 1997, and in doing so provide you with an extended asset mix for each of the six investor categories defined at the end of Chapter 3.

We also provide two fundamental portfolios for each investor category—one for a taxable account (i.e., outside an RRSP) and the other for a portfolio that is entirely inside an RRSP. The reason for providing a specific asset mix for an RRSP has more to do with government restrictions than with particular merits of the investment. As you know, at least 80% of an RRSP portfolio has to be Canadian content.

Assuming you have sufficient capital to have both an RRSP portfolio and a portfolio outside the RRSP, then we suggest you combine the assets and follow the taxable investment plan. To demonstrate by way of an example, we will look at the personal policy statement for the Growth/Income portfolio that breaks down the asset mix as follows (see Figure 12.1).

Figure 12.1: PERSONAL POLICY STATEMENT

Growth/Income Asset Mix

	Equities			Fixed Income			Cash	
Min	**Policy**	Max	Min	**Policy**	Max	Min	**Policy**	Max
30%	**50%**	70%	25%	**40%**	55%	5%	**10%**	15%

If our recommendations were based on your personal policy statement, we might extend your asset mix for both an non-RRSP and RRSP portfolio as follows (see Figure 12.2). Notice how the percentage weightings for the RRSP portfolio have been altered to fit within Revenue Canada guidelines.

Figure 12.2: EXTENDED ASSET MIX FOR GROWTH/INCOME PORTFOLIO

	Non-RRSP	RRSP
Canadian Equity	20%	30%
U.S.Equity	15%	10%
International Equity	15%	10%
Total Equity Assets	**50%**	**50%**
Domestic Bond	30%	40%
Global Bondy	10%	0%
Total Fixed-income Assets	**40%**	**40%**
Money Market	10%	10%
Total Cash Assets	**10%**	**10%**

Now, suppose an investor had $100,000 to invest—$50,000 inside an RRSP and another $50,000 outside the RRSP. We suggest that the investor allocate those funds as if there was one big portfolio. In order to accomplish that and still remain invested within Revenue Canada's guidelines for an RRSP, we would suggest you break the portfolio down as shown in Figure 12.3.

Figure 12.3: SAFETY/GROWTH COMBINED RRSP–NON-RRSP PORTFOLIO

	Non-RRSP	Pct	RRSP	PCT
Canadian Equity	$10,000.00	20%	$10,000.00	20%
U.S.Equity	10,000.00	20%	5,000.00	10%
International Equity	10,000.00	20%	5,000.00	10%
Total Equity Assets	**$30,000.00**	**60%**	**$20,000.00**	**40%**
Domestic Bond	$5,000.00	10%	$25,000.00	50%
Global Bond	10,000.00	20%		0%
Total Fixed-income Assets	**$15,000.00**	**30%**	**$25,000.00**	**50%**
Money Market	$5,000.00	10%	$5,000.00	10%
Total Cash Assets	**$5,000.00**	**10%**	**$5,000.00**	**10%**
Total Portfolio Value	**$50,000.00**		**$50,000.00**	

Having provided an example of how to combine a taxable and non-taxable portfolio, the next step is to begin building a personal portfolio of funds using six to eight of our Best Bet Funds (see Appendix). So much for the structure—now on to the forecast.

Outlook 1997

The Investment Landscape

As we move into 1997, a number of interrelated issues will affect the way Canadians invest their money, most notable among them:

- Government Deficits
- Interest Rates
- Inflation
- Canadian Dollar
- Economic Growth

The Battle of the Deficit Bulge

Governments at all levels seem to have gotten the message. The majority of Canadians want to make deficit spending obsolete. Governments can accomplish this goal three ways: 1) they can raise taxes, 2) cut spending, or 3) provide a combination of tax increases and spending cuts. What we have been seeing over the past three years is a conscious decision by governments to move away from tax increases and onto spending cuts as the solution of choice for deficit reduction.

We applaud these efforts, and believe that economic growth will hinge on how well governments at all levels manage their spending cuts and deficit targets. We are convinced that high taxes, or more importantly the fear of an ever-increasing tax burden, have left consumers shell shocked. This probably explains why some Canadian "think tanks," and some provincial governments, have decided it's time to practice some good old-fashioned Canadian-style "Reaganomics."

Without getting caught up in a Canadian/U.S. debate on which is the right way to kickstart the Canadian economy, allow us the latitude to explain some of the positive attributes of supply side economics.

Milton Friedman, the well-known U.S. economist, who was President Reagan's economic advisor in 1981, first introduced the notion of supply side economics at the national level. Thought to be a radical position at the time, Friedman argued that by giving American consumers a tax cut, they would be encouraged to spend. So far so good, but how does giving a tax cut help solve the deficit problem? The answer is simple if you accept Friedman's extreme position: consumer spending would actually enhance tax revenue.

In the end, the jury is still out on just how successful that venture was. All through the Reagan years, U.S. deficits and total debt continued to rise. However, a large percentage of those deficits can be blamed on Reagan's insistence that there would be no cuts to defense spending. Whether the collapse of communism during his tenure was the result of his position that "strength," not "peace," was the antithesis to war, will be left for historians to decide. What did come about, as Friedman had argued, was a dramatic increase in tax revenue.

While the notion that lower taxes can produce more revenue seems like a contradiction in terms, it makes sense when you understand how tax revenue is generated. In short, tax revenue comes from every source in the Canadian economy. If you buy something you pay tax; in turn, the person or business from which you made the purchase will buy new products or supplies and too will pay tax. The economy is really one big wheel that turns from buyer to seller to buyer to seller. Each time the wheel turns, taxes are spinning off. And the faster the wheel turns, the greater the tax revenue that spins off. How fast money revolves through the system (i.e., how fast the economy is growing) is more important in terms of how much tax is collected than is the rate at which tax is charged.

Arthur Laffer, a prominent supply side economist at the University of Southern California, has vigorously defended this view and developed an economic model known as the "Laffer Curve" (see Figure 12.4). What the Laffer Curve depicts is the diminishing returns produced by higher taxes. The basic notion is that, as tax rates increase from zero to 100% ("x" axis), tax revenue ("y" axis) will increase from zero to some maximum level at "M". Tax revenues begin to decline after that point, presumably because the tax rate begins to "discourage consumption," or perhaps more appropriately, "encourage cash transactions."

Figure 12.4: THE LAFFER CURVE

"Tax Cuts = More Tax Revenue!"

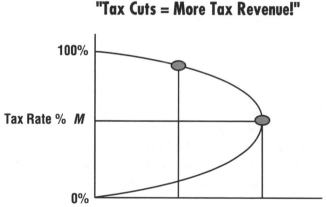

Looking at the extreme positions makes Laffer's assumptions more palatable. If the tax rate were zero, obviously the government would collect no revenue. At the other extreme, if the tax rate were 100%, the government would also fail to generate any revenue. People would simply have no incentive to work.

We bring this to the table because of the debate currently raging in the Province of Ontario. The "common sense revolution" platform that got Premier Mike Harris elected promised a number of things, most notably cutting the deficit while, at the same time, cutting taxes.

The Ontario premier is betting his political future, as President Reagan did in 1981, on the power of supply side economics. If he is correct, the increased economic activity should allow the treasury to recoup the lost revenue within a short period of time (i.e., by the end of his first term). And since Premier Harris does not have to fund a war machine that hindered President Reagan's goal of deficit reduction, we may get our first real test of the effectiveness of the supply side theory.

If supply side theory works, and consumers re-think their spending plans in an environment of tax stability, we believe it will pay huge dividends in the long term, particularly in the context of job creation, economic growth, low interest rates and moderate inflation.

Deficit Reduction Summary

What is particularly interesting about the current situation in the Province of Ontario is the way financial decisions are being made. They appear to be motivated by economic necessity rather than political correctness. So bad are the finances within the Province of Ontario that Premier Harris is operating under a siege mentality. That has allowed him to withstand attacks from special-interest groups and opposition parties, while apparently gaining grass-roots support from the majority of Ontario taxpayers.

In fact, looking at the polls, that is a position that is shared by most Canadian taxpayers. When asked, the silent majority of Canadians believes that government efforts to tackle the deficit have, if anything, not gone far enough. A poll commissioned by *Maclean's* magazine asked Canadians whether "Ottawa's efforts to reduce the deficit [had] gone too far." Only 10% agreed with that statement, while 66% said that Ottawa had not gone far enough. The results were similar when Canadians were asked whether any provincial government had gone too far in their deficit reduction efforts. Sixty-three percent said that none had gone too far!

While Harris has received much of the national attention on the issue of deficit cutting, he is only one of several premiers who have become fiscally responsible. By the end of 1996, we expect at least seven provinces—perhaps as many as eight depending on how well Newfoundland deals with its fiscal calendar—to come in with balanced budgets.

We also think the federal deficit will be lower than expected, perhaps as much as $5 billion below expectations, by mid-1997. And while that is noteworthy, we think the federal deficit picture is being painted by lower-than-anticipated interest rates and faster-than-expected economic growth, rather than deeper-than-expected fiscal cuts.

The Interest Rate Debate

If we are correct about the resolve of governments to continue their cost-cutting efforts, then we will continue to see the benefits in the form of lower interest rates. It will simply become a question of supply and demand. As government deficits come down, there is less demand for borrowed money, and on the supply side, there is an abundant stockpile of capital from baby boomers who are saving for retirement. More capital + less demand from borrowers = lower interest rates.

That being said, it's important to understand that investors are always looking to the future. Professional investors are making decisions now, on the basis of what they expect to see six months from now. Hence the position of a forecaster.

Figure 12.5 and Table 12.1 examine the yields on various Government of Canada bonds with different maturities, as well as our target for the coming year. We don't expect 1997 to be a big year for fixed-income investors. There just doesn't seem to be much room to lower rates significantly from this level, particularly at a time when the U.S. economy is running in high gear.

Table 12.1: YIELDS FOR SELECTED GOVERNMENT OF CANADA BONDS

Term	Current Yield	Croft-Kirzner Target Range	
1 month	4.87%	4.50%	5.31%
3 months	5.04%	4.66%	5.49%
6 months	5.28%	4.88%	5.76%
1 year	5.58%	5.16%	6.08%
2 years	6.13%	5.67%	6.68%
3 years	6.42%	5.94%	7.00%
5 years	6.98%	6.46%	7.61%
7 years	7.35%	6.80%	8.01%
10 years	7.56%	6.99%	8.24%
> 10 years	8.10%	7.49%	8.83%

Figure 12.5: YIELD CURVE AND CROFT-KIRZNER TARGETS

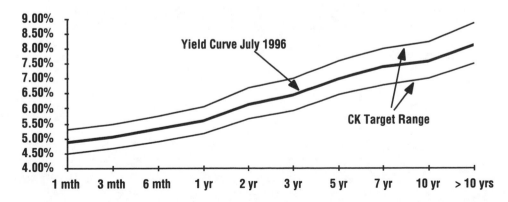

As with any interest rate forecast, there are risks. Clearly, low interest rates are premised on a low inflation scenario and a strong Canadian dollar. On the inflation front, much depends on the outlook for economic growth. We think Canadian GDP growth will come in somewhere between 2% and 2.5% for all of 1996. As for 1997, look for Canadian GDP growth to slow somewhat, probably coming in at 2% year over year.

Growth at that level is considered moderate, and would imply, based on historical standards, an inflation rate that is within the Bank of Canada's accepted target range. The Bank of Canada's inflation targets are set between 1% and 3% right through 1998 (see Figure 12.6 and Bank of Canada Monetary policy box).

With that in mind, don't look for double-digit yields on GICs anytime soon. In fact, we may not see double-digit GIC rates through to the turn of the century. A more likely scenario will see interest rate stability with rates unlikely to breach either end of our target range. As long as interest rates remain subdued, investors will look elsewhere to enhance their returns. Much of that money will find its way into the equity markets, and that should provide some real oomph to the Canadian and U.S. equity markets over the coming year.

Figure 12.6: BANK OF CANADA INFLATION TARGETS

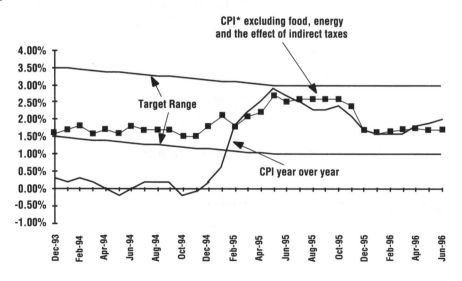

*CPI–Consumer Price Index

Bank of Canada Monetary Policy

Monetary policy is about money. The Bank of Canada is concerned with how much money circulates in our economy and how much that money is worth. The ultimate objective of the Bank of Canada, working through monetary policy, is to enhance the standard of living of Canadians. To this end, the Bank seeks to protect the value of our currency and to provide money that can be used with confidence—money whose value is not eroded by inflation.

In a period of inflation, too many people lose. The costs do not fall equally on all members of the population, since some are better able than others to protect themselves against rising prices.

Individuals on fixed incomes are among the most vulnerable: at 4.5% inflation, a fixed pension will lose half its value in just over 15 years. By focusing on price stability, monetary policy tries to promote, in the best way it can, good overall economic performance.

Bank of Canada Inflation Goals

A program to preserve the value of our money was articulated in a joint announcement by the Bank of Canada and the Minister of Finance in February 1991, when targets for reducing inflation were introduced. The targets illustrate for Canadians the clear downward path for inflation towards which monetary policy is being directed over the medium term.

In December 1993, inflation-control targets were defined to the end of 1998. The target is a band of 1% to 3% by the end of 1995, and this same inflation-control range will be maintained until 1998. By that time, the Bank is committed to having defined more precisely what price stability means in terms of the rate of increase of the consumer price index.

The targets contribute to the goal of achieving and maintaining price stability by making more explicit the commitment of the Bank and the government to that goal. As well, the targets make the Bank's monetary policy actions more understandable to financial market participants and to the general public. Having an explicit objective for monetary policy provides a better basis for judging the performance of the Bank, thereby improving its accountability.

(Source: Bank of Canada Review)

Concerns about Growth

From the discussion to this point, it is clear we are not concerned about the Canadian economy growing too fast forcing up inflation and higher domestic interest rates. The real fear is that the U.S. economy will overheat, and the impact from that will spill over into Canada. If U.S. Federal Reserve (FED) were to tighten U.S. interest rates in an effort to slow down the U.S. economy, that would have a negative impact on our rates.

There are a couple of reasons why our rates are impacted so dramatically by U.S. interest rates. Obviously, there is the close proximity of our two economies, but less obvious is a longstanding position that Canadian interest rates must be higher than U.S. rates to compensate investors for the risks uniquely associated with Canada.

To understand this so-called "risk compensation," we must look at things from the viewpoint of a foreign investor. Foreign investors who make a commitment to buy Canadian want to make sure that any positive returns from Canadian stocks or bonds are not lost in the currency translation. In other words, they do not want to see a weaker Canadian dollar.

So when we talk about risks unique to Canada, we are talking about issues that are beyond the control of the Bank of Canada. For example, there is a risk that Quebec may separate. That political risk has an effect on the Canadian dollar, and all the Bank of Canada can do is react in an attempt to protect our currency. And to do that, the Bank will intervene in the foreign exchange market—buying Canadian dollars from investors who want to sell—and perhaps by raising short-term interest rates.

And this political uncertainty, we think, is a major concern among foreign investors. Supporting that position is the Canadian dollar which, in terms of purchasing power parity, is significantly undervalued relative to the U.S. dollar.

Purchasing power parity, for the record, defines an equilibrium price at which a similar product or service can be purchased by one currency relative to another. *The Economist*, a well-known financial magazine, developed its own purchasing power methodology which we have borrowed to make an economic case for the Canadian dollar. Think of it as the "Big Mac Attack."

To make our point about purchasing power parity, we compared a similar product that is widely available in the U.S. and Canada—the Big Mac hamburger. We took a random sample that contrasted the pre-tax cost of a Big Mac in Buffalo, and compared that to the cost of the same Big Mac in Toronto.

In Buffalo, it cost $2.09 (US$) to buy a Big Mac; in Toronto, the cost was $2.65 (Cdn$). If we divide the U.S. Big Mac dollar value into the Canadian figure, the result is $0.789. In other words, for Canadian consumers to purchase a Big Mac in the U.S. at a price equivalent to what it costs in Canada, the Canadian dollar would have to be valued at 78.9 cents U.S. Since the Canadian dollar is, at the time of writing, valued at 72.8 cents U.S., we believe it is undervalued.

Obviously, a weak Canadian dollar is positive for Canadian companies that export their products to the U.S., a position that has not been lost on U.S. congressional leaders. There is a growing Republican anti-free trade faction in the U.S. Congress that has lobbied and won concessions from Canadian companies. The congressional route of choice is to claim unfair trade practices and then tack on punitive import duties. That forces our government to take the issues before a tribunal that attempts to resolve the problems. In the meantime, industries like softwood lumber and more recently, steel suffer. If the Canadian dollar remains substantially undervalued relative to the U.S. dollar, we will likely see more of these protectionist positions in the near future.

The ideal solution, from the Canadian perspective, is to see the value of our dollar move closer to its real purchasing power parity, which despite the simplicity of the Big Mac example, is probably around 79 cents U.S.

We do not expect the Canadian dollar to reach that level in 1996 and we are unlikely to see it at that level in 1997. Unless there is a definitive resolution to the Quebec sovereignty issue, it is not likely the Canadian dollar will ever reach real purchasing power parity with the U.S. dollar—at least not in this century.

However, during 1997, we think the Canadian dollar will move towards the 74 to 76 cent U.S. level. Given that position, the Canadian dollar should not impede efforts to maintain interest rate stability and, in fact, could provide support for a made-in-Canada interest rate policy.

While Canada Simmers, U.S. Growth Sizzles!

The North American economies were supposed to exhibit tepid growth this year. Estimates at the end of 1995 forecast 1.9% growth for all of 1996, slow and steady improvement with no real threat of inflation.

In actual fact, U.S. economic growth came in at 2.3% in the first quarter, and at the time of writing, looked as if we could see better than 3% year-over-year gains by the end of 1996. Moreover, there may be sufficient momentum to maintain those numbers well into the first quarter of 1997, if for no other reason than to replenish depleted inventories.

Now, you would think that an economic boom would buoy stock prices. Not so! In July 1996, North American stocks in particular were plummeting in what was a major cyclical correction. At the time, professional investors were concerned about interest rates, and so were carefully watching the U.S. Federal Reserve. The FED is not always happy when growth exceeds expectations, because Chairman Greenspan looks at that growth and sees the weeds rather than the flowers. The largest weed in this garden is inflation.

As you might imagine, growth forecasts have gone through a number of major revisions since the second quarter of 1996. Industrial production in the U.S. went up sharply in the first half of 1996, with a 0.7% increase in April (1996) and another 0.7% increase in May (1996). But that number that really got everyone worried was the sharp rise in U.S. non-farm payrolls at the end of June 1996.

Reports showed that the U.S. economy created 239,000 new jobs, well ahead of expectations. Bank of Canada Governor Theissen would welcome such a robust job report, but with U.S. unemployment already down to 5.3%, and factories operating near capacity, those stronger-than-expected employment numbers foreshadow future wage demands which could result in higher consumer prices. Such was the rationale for a sell-off in U.S. stocks, an example, we think, of short-term correction without any fundamental change in the long-term direction, and the ensuing spillover effect on Canadian equities.

Despite the surge in employment, there still does not appear to be any hardcore evidence of a pickup in inflation. And that's interesting. The fact that inflation remains subdued sets this expansion apart from many similar periods. And we think there are two possible explanations for this: 1) consumers' staunch resistance to price increases, and 2) incremental gains in productivity that have kept unit labor costs in check.

The increase in employee productivity, we think, is the result of improvements in technology. North American companies have been spending a fortune to stay at the leading edge of technological change, and they haven't spent all that money simply to look good. Buying solid technology improves efficiency, lowers costs and, by extension, improves a company's profit margin. In short, companies can still report record profits without having to necessarily raise prices. And if we're right about this, then the bull market for stocks that has been rolling virtually unchecked since 1992 may still have some snort left in it.

If those factors continue playing to the market, then the 1996 inflation numbers may well remain below 3% in the U.S., and perhaps below 2% in Canada. With that in mind, we think it is unlikely the FED will make any significant move on short-term U.S. interest rates in 1996, although 1997 may raise some additional concerns.

Such dramatic growth in the U.S. means that a recession in 1997 is less likely. That's good! But it also means that we will not likely see a return to slow and steady growth in the U.S., as the FED might like. We will face instead a cycle of boom and bust.

As for U.S. economic growth, don't expect any real slowdown until the fourth quarter of 1996 or perhaps not until the first quarter of 1997. That being said, we will likely see a slight rise in long-term U.S. mortgage rates by the first quarter of 1997, which will have a dampening effect on disposable income. Bring that to the table at a time when U.S. consumers are already tapped out, and that will slow down this expansion. It won't likely halt the economy in its track, but it will provide enough braking power to give the markets some pause in 1997. Like we said, boom and bust cycles.

All in all, a slight slowdown in 1997 would be healthy. The real danger is inflation which, if the U.S. continues on its current path, could spook the bond market. In that event, U.S. bond yields could head above 7.5%, forcing the FED to hike rates faster than planned.

A Separate Canadian Agenda?

The Canadian economy is in a much better position to deal with higher-than-expected economic growth without putting upward pressure on prices. Supporting that theory were the most recent unemployment numbers. Based on numbers from the end of June 1996, 10% of the Canadian labor force was looking for work, which is the highest percentage in 20 months.

To some investors, those unemployment numbers paint a bleak picture for the Canadian economy. But to be fair, we think that position may be too harsh. Before writing off the Canadian economy, investors would do well to look beyond any single statistic or at least scrutinize those statistics that give cause for concern.

The abrupt change in Canadian unemployment during June 1996 stemmed from an influx of 36,000 people into the job market, mostly students seeking summer employment. At the same time, Canada's economy shed 56,000 jobs, and 70% of those jobs—41,000 positions— were lost in Quebec. Like it or not, the political uncertainty is weighing on the minds of both domestic and foreign investors.

Still, such a dramatic turnaround in the Canadian employment numbers has to be seen as a short-term blip rather than a change in the longer-term trend. The trend remains positive, because Canada's employment growth, even with the lapse at the end of June 1996, is still significantly higher than the average for the G-7 countries in 1996. Employment growth is expected to remain above average well into 1997.

Looking at the big picture, we find ourselves in agreement with the position of Bank of Canada Governor Thiessen that the combination of low inflation, falling deficits and debt as a percentage of gross domestic product has put the nation on its best economic footing in 20 years.

Clearly, as the unemployment numbers tell us, Canadian industry is operating at nowhere near capacity (about 82.5% capacity utilization), and could sustain higher-than-expected economic growth without putting any upward pressure on prices.

Another positive factor is that Canadians are growing more optimistic about the economy. According to an Angus Reid/Southam News poll conducted in the spring of 1996, 48% of Canadians believed the national economy was in good shape, up from 40% in March 1996 and 37% in January 1996.

Keeping the growth fires burning during the long Canadian winter will mean keeping a lid on deficits. But again, Canada is expected to lead the pack, with the lowest deficit to GDP ratio among G-7 countries by the end of 1997.

Employment growth, steady progress in the fight against deficits, low inflation and low interest rates are powerful economic engines that should drive the Canadian economy into a significant growth spurt over the coming year. And, thankfully, without the resident boom and bust cycles expected to hinder the U.S. economic landscape.

Where to Invest in 1997

Having provided an economic overview, the next step is to examine the various mutual fund categories for Canadian investors. Think of it as an investment blueprint for 1997. Figure 12.7 graphically displays the performance of the various fund categories. The top bar along each category represents the average return for 1995. The second bar represents the 1996 year-to-date (six months ended June 30) performance of each mutual fund category. Categories are weighted by asset size.

Figure 12.7: PERFORMANCE COMPARISONS 1995 TO MID-1996

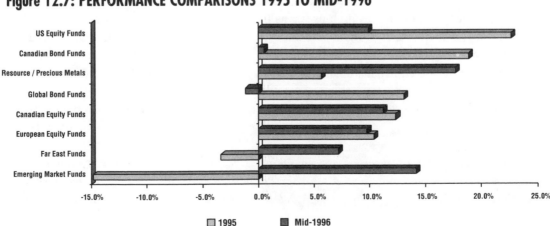

Canadian and U.S. Equity Funds

Clearly, 1995 was a stellar year for U.S. equity funds, as they set the pace among all fund categories. But interestingly, while these funds topped the pack in terms of performance, most of them underperformed the S&P 500 Composite Index (the U.S. benchmark equity index). In other words, not many U.S. equity managers were able to beat a passive index portfolio. By the midpoint of 1996, it was clear we would not see such dramatic gains in U.S. equity funds in 1996, and we're not certain we can expect such stellar gains in 1997 either.

Looking at traditional measures like dividend yield and earnings yield, stocks are overvalued, to the point that some analysts, like noted Elliott Wave theorist Robert Prechtor, are predicting a major correction. Prechtor, with his flair for the dramatic, thinks we are at the end of a major bull cycle that will eventually push stock prices down by as much as 35%. That position, we think, overstates the risk!

Traditional measures, while valid, cannot be viewed in a vacuum. Consider, for example, the 2.5% dividend yield on the Standard and Poor's 500 Composite Index as of July 1996. That has historical significance, because analysts have traditionally viewed 3% as a sort of demarcation line (yields above 3% make stocks a buy; if below 3%, investors should be net sellers), citing the mini-crash on October 13, 1989 as the most recent example. The dividend yield on the S&P 500 during October 1989 was 2.9%.

However, to accept the view that dividends dictate equity values, assumes that investors buy equity funds because of their yield. That might be true for dividend funds, but the argument has questionable merit when viewed in terms of the average equity fund. Most would argue that equity funds represent the growth component of a portfolio.

Not to diminish the importance of dividends, but to accept the notion that stock investors are motivated by income, means that you have to compare the yield on stocks with what those investors could earn buying, say, Treasury bonds. Using that as our criteria, the demarcation line begins to blur. In October 1989, the yield on U.S. bonds[11] (i.e., bonds maturing within 10 years) was 8.5%, or 5.6% (8.5% bond yield less 2.9% dividend yield = 5.6% spread) above the dividend yield on U.S. stocks.

The current spread between the dividend yield on U.S. stocks and U.S. T-bonds is enough to make you nervous, but not as high as it was in 1989. With the dividend yield at 2.5% and the yield on U.S. T-bonds at about 6.5%, the spread is 4% (6.5% bond yield less 2.5% dividend yield = 4% spread). That is not, in our opinion, a significant enough spread to dictate a 35% correction in the equity markets. It is, however, significant enough to hold the reins on any dramatic surge in U.S. stock prices.

Price-to-earnings ratios tell a similar story. The price-to-earnings measure is simply the stock

---

[11] *In this analysis, we are comparing the yield on bonds that mature within 10 years to the dividend yield on stocks. We use mid-term bonds to make this comparison, because we are examining cash flows, as opposed to earnings, and we believe this provides a more valid apples-to-apples comparison.*

price divided by the earnings per share. If, for example, ABC company earns $1.00 per share, and the stock is currently trading at $16 per share, ABC is said to have a price-to-earnings ratio of 16, which for the record is the current price-to-earnings ratio on the S&P 500 Composite Index.

At 16 times current earnings—as of July 1996—the S&P 500 Composite Index hardly supports the analysis of the "doom and gloom" set, especially when viewed in terms of current interest rates.

In order to avoid "vacuum block," let's compare the earnings yield with U.S. long-term Treasury bonds[12] to the earnings yield. The earnings yield, which is simply the number "1" divided by the price-earnings ratio (16), was 6.25%. When compared to the 7.05% (as of July 1996) yield on U.S. government long-term bonds (i.e., bonds with at least 30 years to maturity), the difference between the earnings yield and the bond yield is 0.80% (7.05% 30-year bond yield less 6.25% earnings yield = 0.80% spread).

Now for some historical benchmarks. Consider the spread between earnings and interest rates in mid-1996 with, say, October 1987, when the S&P 500 Composite Index was trading at 22 times earnings, for an earnings yield of 4.55%. In October 1987, long-term government bond yields were 9.80%. The difference between the earnings yield and the yield on long-term Treasury bonds was 5.25% (9.80% 30-year bond yield less 4.55% earnings yield = 5.25% spread), or more than six times higher than is the case now. So in our opinion, U.S. stock prices, while not cheap, are not at levels that suggest a stampede for the exits.

Another factor that weighs on everyone's mind is the fact that small investors are pouring money into equity funds at a record clip, a sure sign that the end is near. But to buy that argument implies that we are seeing the first signs of a speculative frenzy. Most investors we talk with are buying equity funds in search of returns that can beat the GIC rates offered at their local bank, and not because they expect double-digit returns from a rip-roaring bull market.

The fact that so much pessimism exists provides another interesting spin to this market. Proving once again that all cycles are different, this is the first time in recent memory where individual and institutional investors have become more cautious as stocks moved higher. As can be seen in most of the sentiment polls, skepticism, while not rampant, is clearly at healthy levels. And while stocks do not climb straight up a wall of worry, they rarely come crashing down.

Of course, if we point to sentiment indicators and suggest that all is well, we would be as guilty as those who look for bear traps in fundamental measures. What we need to do is understand our current environment and where equity funds fit within that mix.

The facts are that we have low interest rates; inflation is, at present, a non-issue; and the North American economy continues to grow at a healthy pace. We have lean companies, with a more productive labor force, and wages remain at bearable levels. All of these point to healthy profit margins, which should continue to support the current bull cycle. Not dramatic maybe, but definitely sustainable.

---

[12] *In this example we are comparing corporate earnings to U.S. 30-year Treasury bonds, as opposed to the previous analysis that compared dividend yields to U.S. Treasury bonds maturing within 10 years. The objective here is to compare earnings, which we believe drive stock prices over the longer term, to a longer-term fixed-income investment. Again, we are attempting to provide an apples-to-apples comparison.*

Assuming U.S. bond yields remain between the 6.5% and 7.75% levels for all of 1997, and assuming U.S. corporate earnings can produce another year of double-digit growth, an upside target for the S&P 500 Composite Index in 1997 would be 700 to 725. That represents a healthy, if not spectacular, year-over-year return.

Canadian Equity Funds

The case for the Canadian equity market mirrors our view about the U.S. equity market. Although the Canadian equity market is not blessed—or depending on your point of view, cursed—with many forecasters telling us exactly when to buy and sell, we are not normally driven to panic.

Given that position, we think 1997 will be a good year for the Canadian equity market. We don't believe that the low domestic interest rates have been fully discounted by the Canadian equity market. And we think by the close of 1996 that Canadian corporate earnings will come in better than expected.

We are looking for earnings on the TSE 300 Composite Index to come in at about $350 to $400. Assuming the price-to-earnings ratio remains constant, and accounting for Canadian interest rates (i.e., rates on long term—over 10 years—government bonds) to ease down to 7.5% from about 8.2%, the TSE 300 Composite Index could see 6,000 by the end of 1997.

International Markets

Most of the rewards of global investing consist of striking a good portfolio balance (for example, 40% in Europe, 30% in the United States and 30% in the Far East) and then sticking with it. A large portion of the variance in overall stock prices is due to the unique risk of each country and can therefore be mitigated through the use of a broadly diversified equity portfolio as in a mutual fund. Nevertheless, when it comes to international investing, changing world patterns cannot be ignored and some rotation is essential.

The Asian Markets: Japan

Japan is certainly the economic miracle of the past four decades. Double-digit returns were the norm on the Tokyo Stock Exchange in the 1980s making it the darling of global investors. The Japanese economy was considered the model of the industrialized world with controlled inflation, low interest rates, and a responsive labor and business sector.

At the time, productivity rates were also the highest in the world. A major investment boom sent real estate and security prices to unprecedented heights. Accordingly, when the global recession hit, it hit Japan the hardest, and the country has suffered through its worst downturn since World War Two.

To make matters worse, Japan's long-standing ability to be a major exporting nation remained intact, and because of that, the *yen* continued to strengthen despite the recession. That's when Japanese investors felt the domino effect of a deflationary spiral, which began with a breakdown in the bloated real estate market, followed by a collapse in security prices. Plunging real estate prices, a weak stock market and virtually no economic growth for more than five years set off a host of bankruptcies.

A major initiative launched in the summer of 1995 has reversed the economic situation. The Bank of Japan, through a major liquidity injection program, forced interest rates lower, encouraged investors to invest abroad and sent (purposely) the *yen* tumbling. Japan began to work its way out of its problems by exporting its surplus through the purchase of foreign bonds, resulting in a weakening *yen*.

Japan's Ministry of Finance continues to pursue an aggressive monetary policy designed to stimulate the economy and help keep interest rates down. A plan designed to resolve Japan's bad debt problems and a "resolution trust" type agreement allowing banks to write off some bad loans should provide a healthy boost as well. Japan could again become a major buyer of high-yield global bonds providing important support for the world bond market. At this stage, Japan has the lowest inflation rate, the lowest interest rates (nominal and real), the lowest unemployment rate and the highest per-capita GNP of the leading industrialized countries.

Such a revival in Japan has implications for the global economy, but not all of them are good! As the Japanese economy recovers, profits rise and, over time, interest rates will start to rise as well. This could cause a severe outflow of funds and send rates higher in the U.S. Such is the other side of the coin.

Japan is a key target both for investment and as a harbinger of the future. At present, Japanese investors are buying North American and European securities for their high yields and to provide some protection against the declining *yen* (Japanese short-term interest rates are below 1%). As the Japanese economy improves and stock and real estate prices eventually rebound, Japanese investors will start to repatriate their capital. And therein lies a potential threat. If anything could bring a halt to the current North American/European bull market, it would be a reversal of capital flows back into Japan. Such a reversal would buoy the Japanese equity markets, but could have a negative impact on the global equity markets. This is all the more reason why an investment in Japanese securities provides an important hedge to your global portfolio.

You might even spin some decent profits in the process. The outlook for Japan is buoyant. The Japanese economy is expanding at a rate of about 3.2% and should continue to maintain this pace in 1997. The recovery is reaching the self-sustaining stage—the only worry is the pressure that could be placed on interest rates. So make certain that any international equity fund you consider has a weighting in Japan.

The Rest of Asia: Taiwan, Korea, Malaysia and Singapore

The entire Pacific Rim is making noises. Loud and clear, the area is open for business. We note a marked change in the political climate, deregulation becoming a buzzword. For example, in mid-1996 both Malaysia and Korea announced changes that will allow foreign companies to list on their respective exchanges.

The major Asian countries are showing substantial real growth with relatively low inflation rates. The Taiwan economy remains a model for emerging countries. It is running a fiscal surplus and, despite a high rate of growth, inflation is is well under control at about 4%.

The situation isn't quite as buoyant in South Korea. The country is running a small current account deficit. Interest rates are rising, reflecting the government's strong interventionist stance as well as the current 7% inflation rate. Add to that the real or imagined threat from North Korea, which makes the Quebec sovereignty issue seem tame by comparison, and you can see why the South Korean markets will continue to haunted by uncertainty.

Europe

The legacy of the prolonged 1992-93 European recession is high unemployment and lower inflation. The latter has meant lower interest rates and greater competitiveness, although the former means a continued threat to the political and social stability of the continent.

The 14 members of the European Community (including the new 1995 members—Austria, Finland and Sweden) continue to move toward implementation of the terms as set out in the 1992 Maastricht Treaty. The EC is moving towards monetary union, and a common currency is scheduled to come into effect by 1999.

It is the growing pains along the road to a monetary union that have created many of the problems facing EC members. A particularly thorny issue is the restrictive rules the Maastricht Treaty imposes on fiscal and monetary restraint among EC members.

The treaty signed in Maastricht in 1992 by the then members of the European Community set out a number of eligibility conditions for individual countries that want to participate in monetary union. These conditions include a stable currency for two years; budget deficits that are limited to a maximum of 3% of GDP; long-term interest rates and inflation rates that are under control; and gross government debt of no more than 60% of GDP.

Far and away, the most important provision limits national budget deficits, since this clearly represents the resolve to maintain strict fiscal conservatism. Interestingly, the average EC budget deficit has risen to over 7% in the 1990s, moving a number of countries out of eligibility range at present.

The currency unification plan is literal. In 1999, conversion exchange rates will be frozen, and a single currency introduced for paper transactions. Eventually, that currency will be used in day-to-day monetary transactions. Countries already running large deficits will either have to employ severe deficit-cutting tactics, and risk either severe recession or to be shut out of the union.

The 1995-96 interest rate cutting cycle among the key European countries has promoted a period of slow but steady economic growth and solid equity market returns. Economic growth should improve in 1997. The long-term outlook for the leading European countries, including Germany and Switzerland, is very strong. Europe is likely to be a major economic power for years to come. International equity funds with a European presence will probably be an important component in your portfolio during 1997.

Emerging Countries: Latin America

The major Latin America investment markets are "The Big Four"—Argentina, Brazil, Chile and Mexico, as well as Peru and Venezuela. These countries and their markets are still at the developing stages.

The free-market initiatives undertaken, including the abolition of price controls, removal of trade barriers and privatization of telecommunications and utilities have created a constructive investment climate.

Additionally, Latin America countries have been steadily removing foreign restriction barriers, allowing for freer flow of capital. On the development front, a young population (about 55% of the South America population is below 25 years of age), democratic reforms, and advances in managing the huge supplies of natural resources have meant dramatic economic growth in recent years, to the point where economic growth in Latin America has far outstripped rates experienced in North America and Europe.

But as events in the wake of the December 1994 January 1995 *peso* crisis have underscored, this is a difficult and sometimes perverse region. Two steps forward and one step (sometimes two or three steps) back.

Politics remain questionable. Political scandals surface with even greater regularity and greater intensity than in Europe. In Latin America, the underground economy and influence peddling are still an integral part of life.

But these elements notwithstanding, take a long-term view of this region where stocks are trading at low price-to-earnings levels (i.e., price of the stock as a multiple of the earnings per share), and low price-to-book values (i.e., price of the stock relative to the break up or book value of the company). The strongest growth in this region will likely be seen in Brazil and Chile. Brazil is emerging from a three-year recession, while the Chilean economy is expanding at a rate of 6% to 7% per year.

The outlook for Mexico, the third partner in the North America Free Trade Agreement, is particularly good. Economic reforms implemented in 1995 has been relatively successful. Confidence is being restored as investors seem to be buying into the reform packages. That has been good news for Mexican stocks: the Bolsa Mexicana de Volores, Mexico's only stock exchange, has recorded substantial gains this year.

Mexico's future, although tarnished, remains bright. You have to realize that financial crises are not new to Mexico. Looking back, financial crises have come in six-year waves, as the *peso* was devalued in 1976, 1982 and 1988 and again in 1994! We think there is time before the next wave hits.

Outlook 1997—Summary

This forecast for 1997 is to be used as a guideline for your portfolio. This so-called blueprint is meant to be part of a larger picture and is intended to help you balance your asset allocation model to take advantage of the world according to Croft and Kirzner.

That being said, each investor has a different tolerance for risk, and by extension, a different asset mix. Remember, the discussion in this blueprint is designed to work within the context of your personal asset mix.

Recommended Asset Mixes for 1997

Safety Portfolio

	Non-RRSP	RRSP
Canadian Equity	10%	10%
U.S. Equity	5%	5%
International Equity	5%	5%
Total Equity Assets	**20%**	**20%**
Domestic Bond	50%	50%
Global Bond	10%	10%
Total Fixed-Income Assets	**60%**	**60%**
Money Market	20%	20%
Total Cash Assets	**20%**	**20%**

RECOMMENDED 1997 ASSET MIX

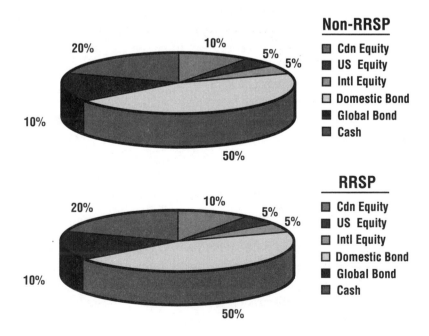

Figure 12.8

Safety/Income Portfolio

	Non-RRSP	RRSP
Canadian Equity	10%	10%
U.S. Equity	10%	10%
International Equity	10%	10%
Total Equity Assets	**30%**	**30%**
Domestic Bond	40%	50%
Global Bond	10%	0%
Total Fixed-Income Assets	**50%**	**50%**
Money Market	20%	20%
Total Cash Assets	**20%**	**20%**

RECOMMENDED 1997 ASSET MIX

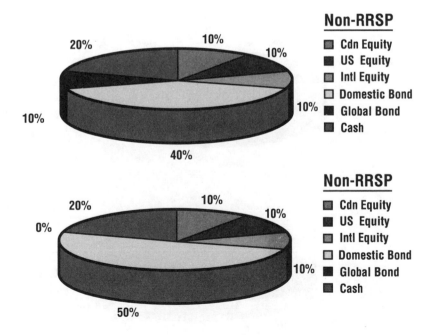

Figure 12.9

Income/Growth Portfolio

	Non-RRSP	RRSP
Canadian Equity	15%	25%
U.S. Equity	15%	10%
International Equity	15%	10%
Total Equity Assets	**45%**	**45%**
Domestic Bond	30%	40%
Global Bond	10%	0%
Total Fixed-Income Assets	**40%**	**40%**
Money Market	15%	15%
Total Cash Assets	**15%**	**15%**

RECOMMENDED 1997 ASSET MIX

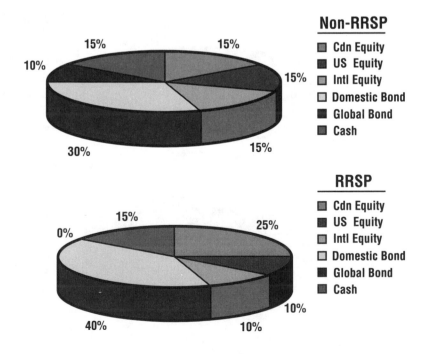

Figure 12.10

Growth/Income Portfolio

	Non-RRSP	RRSP
Canadian Equity	20%	40%
U.S. Equity	20%	10%
International Equity	20%	10%
Total Equity Assets	**60%**	**60%**
Domestic Bond	30%	30%
Global Bond	0%	0%
Total Fixed-Income Assets	**30%**	**30%**
Money Market	10%	10%
Total Cash Assets	**10%**	**10%**

RECOMMENDED 1997 ASSET MIX

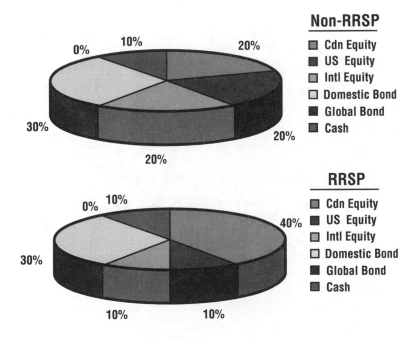

Figure 12.11

Growth Portfolio

	Non-RRSP	RRSP
Canadian Equity	30%	50%
U.S. Equity	20%	10%
International Equity	20%	10%
Total Equity Assets	**70%**	**70%**
Domestic Bond	20%	25%
Global Bond	5%	0%
Total Fixed-Income Assets	**25%**	**25%**
Money Market	5%	5%
Total Cash Assets	**5%**	**5%**

RECOMMENDED 1997 ASSET MIX

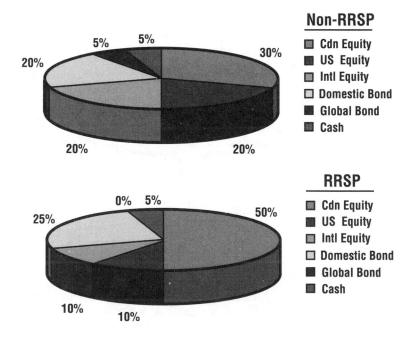

Figure 12.12

Aggressive Growth Portfolio

	Non-RRSP	RRSP
Canadian Equity	35%	65%
U.S. Equity	25%	10%
International Equity	25%	10%
Total Equity Assets	**85%**	**85%**
Domestic Bond	5%	10%
Global Bond	5%	0%
Total Fixed-Income Assets	**10%**	**10%**
Money Market	5%	5%
Total Cash Assets	**5%**	**5%**

RECOMMENDED 1997 ASSET MIX

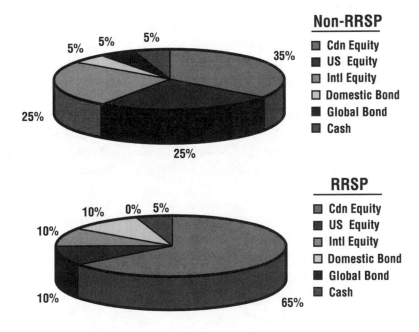

Figure 12.13

Your Guide to the Best Bet Funds

The Worksheet

This appendix provides in-depth information about our Best Bet Funds that you might consider for your portfolio. Most of these funds require only small initial investments, usually between $500 and $1,000. However, some in our list, like the ABC Fundamental Value Fund which has a $150,000 minimum, will only be suitable for certain investors. From our Best Bet list you will be able to find funds that cover all but one of the boxes in the Fundline—the "long term" box, which represents bond funds whose average term-to-maturity is greater than 10 years. There simply were not many fund managers holding long-term bonds, suggesting that few managers are willing to bet that interest rates will decline substantially in the coming year.

To begin your search through the the Best Bet list, we have included a blank worksheet. Fill it out based on your investor category. Then set your asset mix using the recommended weightings discussed in Chapter 12, or by using your own pre-selected weightings. But remember, use weightings that fit within the minimum and maximum parameters of your personal investment profile.

The Fund Review

As for the full-page review of specific funds, we have included a number of mutual funds from the following categories:

- **Equity Assets**
  Canadian Equity Fund
  Canadian Small Cap Funds
  International Equity Funds
  U.S. Equity Funds
  Special Equity Funds

- **Fixed-income Assets**
  Canadian Bond Funds
  Canadian Mortgage Funds
  Global Bond Funds

- **Balanced Funds**
  Canadian Balanced Funds
  International (Global) Balanced Funds

Our Best Bet list of funds is by no means complete. Indeed, there are some funds that scored in the first performance quintile, yet because they are closed to new investors, are not included in the list. The Marathon Equity Fund, for example, ranked in the first quintile for performance. However, it was recently capped at $300 million and as such is not open to new investors. Another is the highly regarded Phillips, Hager & North Vintage fund, also ranked "1" for performance, but it too is closed to new investors.

Croft-Kirzner Performance and Consistency Ratings
The Croft-Kirzner Performance Rating (CKPR) and Consistency Rating (CKCR), expressed on a scale of 1 (best) to 5 (worst), form a comprehensive evaluation system that asks a very basic question: "Is the manager or management team adding value?"

While the CKPR and the CKCR are useful analytical tools, they should be used as an initial screen, not as a conclusion. The ratings describe how well a fund manager or management team has balanced risk and return in the past, but should not be seen as predictive measures nor as a recommendation to buy or sell.

The Croft-Kirzner Performance Rating
The CKPR is a two-step process that measures a fund manager's performance based on:

1. the fund's return after accounting for risk, and
2. against a risk-adjusted passive benchmark index.

A Canadian equity fund, for example, is measured on a risk-adjusted basis against the TSE 300 Total Return Index. The TSE 300 Total Return Index is a passive benchmark that tracks the total return (including dividends) of a cross-section of 300 large Canadian companies.

To ascertain a fund's CKPR, we first determine what performance the fund should deliver given its risk. We plot a three-year expected performance track based on the fund's risk. The higher the risk, the higher the expected performance. We then measure, on a month-to-month basis, the fund's actual performance against its expected performance.

We also plot a three-year expected performance track for the passive benchmark index and measure, on a month-to-month basis, the actual return of the passive benchmark index against its expected performance track. We compare the results.

The second step in determining the CKPR is to measure on a month-to-month basis (for the previous 36 months) the fund's risk-adjusted performance against the risk-adjusted performance of the passive benchmark index.

The results for each fund are plotted along a bell curve to determine the fund's rating for the previous 36 months. Generally, although not always, we would expect 10% of the funds measured to receive a "1" rating (highest). Approximately 22.5% of funds would be expected to receive a "2" rating (above average), roughly 35% would receive a "3" rating (neutral or average), another 22.5% a "4" rating (below average), while funds normally scoring in the bottom 10% or so, would receive a "5" rating (lowest).

It is important to understand that the CKPR views a fund in isolation and not as part of a portfolio. In that context, studies have shown that it is rare for a manager or management team to outperform their benchmark index over long periods. We would expect managers in the top quintile during any measuring period to fall into lower quintiles over subsequent measuring periods.

The Croft-Kirzner Consistency Rating

The CKCR measures how consistently the fund's risk-adjusted performance tracked the risk-adjusted performance of the passive benchmark index (the second step in the CKPR). In this case, we are asking whether the fund manager, on a risk-adjusted basis, consistently outperformed or consistently underperformed the passive benchmark index.

This measure is most useful when looking at mutual funds within the context of a portfolio rather than in isolation. Investors, for example, may want to hold lower-risk bond funds in order to add stability within a portfolio. Most bond funds are average performers when measured against a passive fixed-income benchmark. But given the objective of adding stability, consistency of performance may be more important than actual risk-adjusted performance.

The CKCR for each fund is also plotted along a bell curve to determine the fund's consistency over the previous 36 months. Generally, although not always, we would expect 10% of the funds measured to receive a "1" rating (most consistent). Approximately 22.5% of funds would be expected to receive a "2" rating (above average), roughly 35% would receive a "3" rating (neutral or average), another 22.5% a "4" rating (below average). Funds normally scoring in the bottom 10% or so, would receive a "5" rating (inconsistent). Both the CKPR and the CKCR are recalculated monthly.

What we have attempted to do is provide a list of funds, with various minimum investments, that are open to new investors and ranked in the first, second or third quintile based on the Croft-Kirzner Performance Index (see Figure 1).

Figure 1: CROFT-KIRZNER RATINGS: FROM 1 (BEST) TO 5 (WORST)

Performance Rank	1	Consistency Rank	1

We also provide an in-depth review of a few funds which we think deserve honorable mention, but they will not be ranked using the Croft-Kirzner Indexes. There are a couple of reasons: 1) the fund may not have been around for at least three years, but invests in an area we think has long-term potential (i.e., the Green Line Science and Technology Fund is a case in point), or 2) Fund Data—the company that does the rankings—has yet to determine an appropriate benchmark index against which to measure a particular fund category.

The Canadian balanced funds and the international balanced funds are examples of fund categories where an appropriate index is still under development. In each case, the benchmark is a combination of a number of other indexes. For example, the benchmark for Canadian Balanced Funds might be 40% TSE 300 Total Return Index, 10% S&P 500 Composite Index, 40% ScotiaMcLeod Bond Universe and 10% Canadian T-bills. In these categories—Canadian balanced and international balanced funds—we provide honorable mentions without actually providing a ranking number.

In each of the fund reviews, we provide the sponsor's address and telephone number. The numbers are usually 1-800 numbers, although most fund companies have a direct line if you live in the province where the fund's head office is located. (A visit with your financial planner can help you locate potential investments for your portfolio.) We also tell you if this is a load or no-load fund (Figure 2). Note that most load funds offer negotiated commissions, and investors can purchase with the option of a front or deferred load.

Figure 2

Sales Fee	Load
Sales Fee	No-Load

Whether or not the fund is eligible as an RRSP investment is also important. If we answer "yes" to the RRSP eligibility question, there are no restrictions on the fund (Figure 3). If the answer is "foreign," that means the fund cannot represent more than 20% of the assets within your RRSP.

Figure 3

RRSP Eligibility	Yes
RRSP Eligibility	Foreign

We also tell you the minimum initial investment depending on whether the fund is being purchased inside an RRSP or outside an RRSP (Figure 4).

Figure 4

Minimum Initial Investment
RRSP $1,000   Non-RRSP $1,000

Next, we acknowledge the fund manager—at least, the person who was managing the fund as of June 1996. Things could change by the time you read the book, and if a new manager has taken over, find out if the management style of the fund is expected to change. In some cases you may want a new style, particularly if the manager hasn't done his job. However, in the funds we review, all of the managers have done a good job, and as such, we would like to think the funds will continue to be managed as effectively.

Next comes the FundLine, which defines the elements of diversification a specific fund brings to the portfolio.

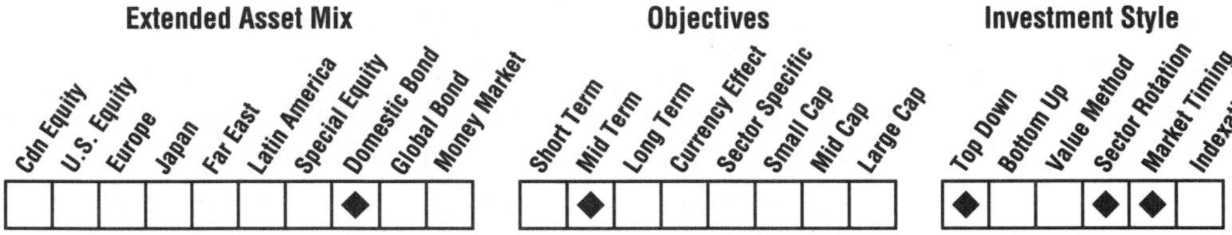

Under the FundLine and to the left of the sheet are three issues of interest to a prospective investor, specifically:

- *Risk*: We measure risk using the standard deviation of returns over the last three years. (Standard deviation was discussed in Chapter 2.) Suffice it to say, the higher the standard deviation (the number at the bottom of the bar chart), the more volatile the fund is likely to be. Conversely, we would expect that a fund with a low standard deviation will be less volatile. If no standard deviation is calculated for a particular fund, it simply means that the fund does not have at least a three-year track record. To have a basis for comparison, note that the extended lines on the bar chart represent the average standard deviation for funds in this particular category.

- *MER*: The management-expense ratio tells us how much it costs to operate the fund, including transaction costs and management and custodial fees. The MER is calculated as a percentage of the fund's assets. For example, a fund with $100 million in assets, that costs $2 million per year to operate, would have an MER of 2%. As with standard deviation, we also include an extended bar to define the average MER within that fund category.

- *Size*: The size of the fund simply defines the assets under administration. A fund with $100 million in assets would read as 100.0 under the size bar chart. Again, we provide an average size of funds within that category (see Figure 5).

Figure 5

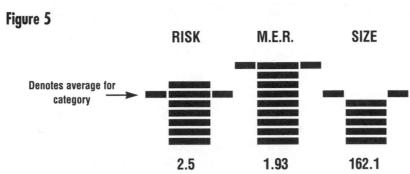

To the right of the bar charts, we present a line chart that shows the value of $1,000 invested in this particular fund from July 1993 to the end of June 1996. We assume the money was invested for three years, unless the fund has not been around that long. In cases where the fund has less than a three-year track record, we show the value of $1,000 invested at the fund's inception, and then tell you how long a period that was (Figure 6).

Figure 6

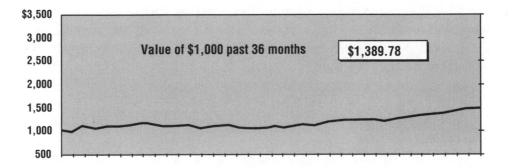

The final chart along the bottom of the page is a monthly performance chart. This chart graphs the fund's monthly percentage returns for the last three years, or from inception if the fund does not have a three-year track record. Each "Monthly Performance" chart is drawn to the same scale, which will provide a visual guide to how volatile the fund was in the past. Think of it as your visual guide to the standard deviation number. The longer the bars in the chart, the more volatile the fund is likely to be (Figure 7).

Figure 7

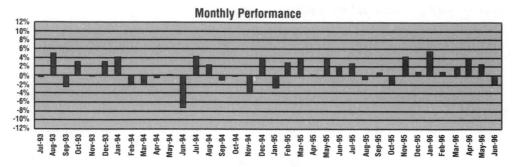

Finally, at the bottom of the page, you will see any pertinent notes about the fund. Notice, for example, that segregated funds have an asterisk by their name at the top of the page. At the bottom of the page, we simply tell you what the asterisk means.

The notes will also tell you anything unusual about the fund. For example, in some case the fund is only available to investors in the province where the fund resides. The notes at the bottom of the page will tell you that.

At the end of the appendix, we have a section exhibiting the individual FundLine for each of the funds in the largest fund families in Canada. It is quite likely you already hold one or more of these funds in your portfolio. As such, this information provides a tool to help you assess where each fund fits within your overall portfolio of funds and to determine the degree of diversification in your portfolio.

One thing you might notice, is that we provide no fundlines for MacKenzie's S.T.A.R. asset allocation service, Investors Group Portfolio funds and the Dynamic Managed Portfolio. These fund companies offer a portfolio of their funds in one easy-to-buy package. But since that is the goal of the FundLine, it didn't, in our opinion, add any value to include these services in the appendix.

In future editions of this book, we intend to expand the list of funds covered. In the meantime, if you can't wait, you can e-mail Richard Croft at Croftfin@aol.com, or call the R. N. Croft Financial Group at 1-416-751-6267 and we will send you a FundLine for any fund you might be considering.

Finally, if you don't have a financial advisor, we suggest you consider talking with one. This book provides you with an excellent foundation on which to establish a relationship with a financial advisor. You now have the tools to understand why a financial advisor has recommended specific mutual funds for your portfolio. And conversely, you have the tools to examine whether recommendations made by the financial advisor meet all the elements of diversification you have come to expect. We simply think an educated financial consumer is a better client.

And speaking of financial advice, we believe, it is well worth the cost. And the cost is not as much as you would think. Almost all funds—whether load or no-load funds—pay annual "trailer" fees to financial advisors to help them offset the cost of managing the day-to-day issues with the client. Those trailer fees are being paid whether or not you use a financial advisor or a discount broker, or if you buy the funds directly. Our view is simple: if you are going to pay the fees anyway, get some advice for your money.

Personal Worksheet

Investor Category _____

	Non-RRSP		RRSP	
Canadian Equity	$_____	_____%	$_____	_____%
U.S. Equity	$_____	_____%	$_____	_____%
International Equity	$_____	_____%	$_____	_____%
Total Equity Assets	$_____	_____%	$_____	_____%
Domestic Bond	$_____	_____%	$_____	_____%
Global Bond	$_____	_____%	$_____	_____%
Total Fixed-income Assets	$_____	_____%	$_____	_____%
Money Market	$_____	_____%	$_____	_____%
Total Cash Assets	$_____	_____%	$_____	_____%
Total Portfolio	$_____	_____%	$_____	_____%

Fund Name	Extended Asset Mix										Objectives								Investment Style					
	Cdn Equity	U.S. Equity	Europe	Japan	Far East	Latin America	Special Equity	Domestic Bond	Global Bond	Money Market	Short Term	Mid Term	Long Term	Currency Effect	Sector Specific	Small Cap	Mid Cap	Large Cap	Top Down	Bottom Up	Value Method	Sector Rotation	Market Timing	Indexation
_____																								
_____																								
_____																								
_____																								
_____																								
_____																								
_____																								
_____																								
_____																								
_____																								

Industrial Future Fund

CROFT–KIRZNER RATINGS:

Performance Rank	1	**Consistency Rank**	2

Sponsor   MacKenzie Financial Corporation
150 Bloor St. West, Suite M111
Toronto, Ontario, M5S 3B5

Phone   1-800-387-0615

Sales Fee   Load   **RRSP Eligibility**   Yes

Category   Canadian Equity

Portfolio Manager
John Rohr–MacKenzie Financial Corporation

Minimum Initial Investment

RRSP $500   Non-RRSP $500

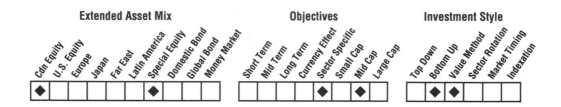

Extended Asset Mix — Objectives — Investment Style

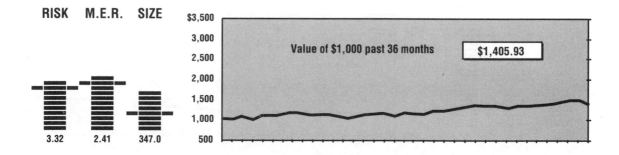

RISK	M.E.R.	SIZE
3.32	2.41	347.0

Value of $1,000 past 36 months $1,405.93

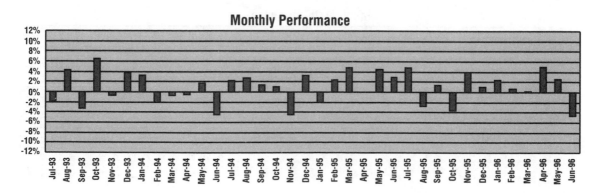

Monthly Performance

Ivy Canadian Fund

CROFT–KIRZNER RATINGS:

Performance Rank	1		**Consistency Rank**	3
Sponsor	MacKenzie Financial Corporation		**Category**	Canadian Equity
	150 Bloor St. West, Suite M111		**Portfolio Manager**	
	Toronto, Ontario, M5S 3B5		Gary Coleman–MacKenzie Financial Corporation	
Phone	1-800-387-0615		**Minimum Initial Investment**	
Sales Fee	Load **RRSP Eligibility** Yes		RRSP $500 Non-RRSP $500	

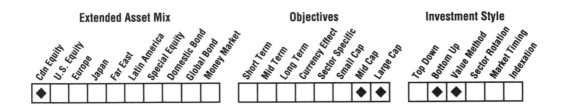

Extended Asset Mix · Objectives · Investment Style

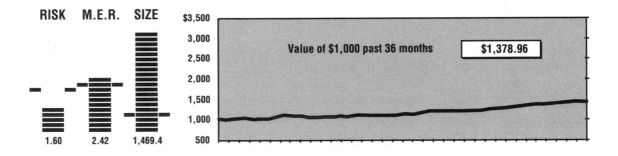

RISK 1.60   M.E.R. 2.42   SIZE 1,469.4

Value of $1,000 past 36 months $1,378.96

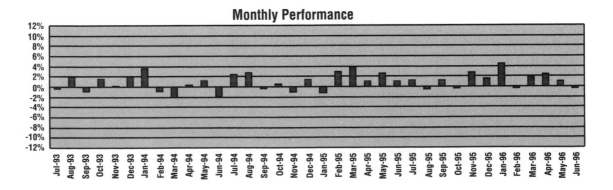

Monthly Performance

Scotia Excelsior Canadian Growth Fund

CROFT–KIRZNER RATINGS:

Performance Rank	1	**Consistency Rank**	3
Sponsor	Scotia Securities Inc.	**Category**	Canadian Equity
	40 King St. West, 5th Floor	**Portfolio Manager**	
	Toronto, Ontario, M5H 1H1	Denis Ouellet–Montrusco Associates	
Phone	1-800-268-9269	**Minimum Initial Investment**	
Sales Fee	No-Load **RRSP Eligibility** Yes	RRSP $500 Non-RRSP $500	

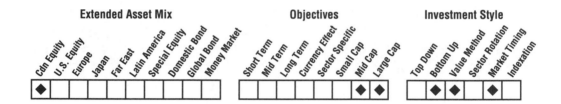

Extended Asset Mix — Cdn Equity, U.S. Equity, Europe, Japan, Far East, Latin America, Special Equity, Domestic Bond, Global Bond, Money Market

Objectives — Short Term, Mid Term, Long Term, Currency Effect, Sector Specific, Small Cap, Mid Cap, Large Cap

Investment Style — Top Down, Bottom Up, Value Method, Sector Rotation, Market Timing, Indexation

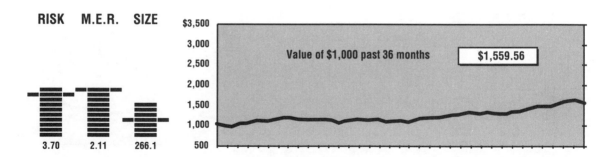

RISK M.E.R. SIZE

3.70 2.11 266.1

Value of $1,000 past 36 months $1,559.56

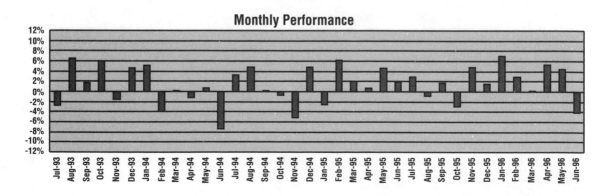

Monthly Performance

Tradex Equity Fund Limited

CROFT–KIRZNER RATINGS:

Performance Rank	1		**Consistency Rank**	3
Sponsor	Tradex Management Inc.		**Category**	Canadian Equity
	45 O'Connor St., Suite 1860		**Portfolio Manager**	
	Ottawa, Ontario, K1P 1A4		Phillips, Hager & North Investment Management	
Phone	1-800-567-3863		**Minimum Initial Investment**	
Sales Fee	No-Load **RRSP Eligibility** Yes		RRSP $500 Non-RRSP $500	

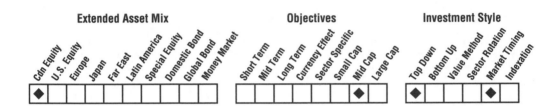

Extended Asset Mix — Cdn Equity ◆, U.S. Equity, Europe, Japan, Far East, Latin America, Special Equity, Domestic Bond, Global Bond, Money Market

Objectives — Short Term, Mid Term, Long Term, Currency Effect, Sector Specific, Small Cap, Mid Cap ◆, Large Cap

Investment Style — Top Down ◆, Bottom Up, Value Method, Sector Rotation ◆, Market Timing, Indexation

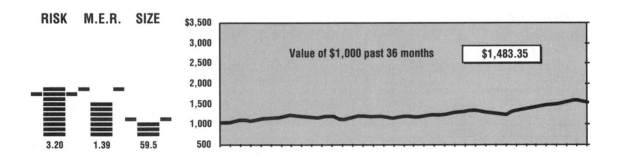

RISK 3.20   **M.E.R.** 1.39   **SIZE** 59.5

Value of $1,000 past 36 months $1,483.35

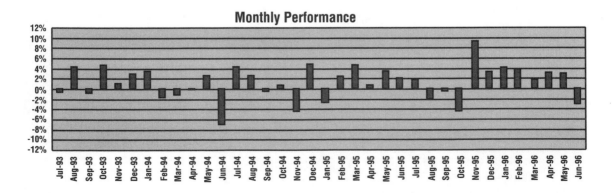

Monthly Performance

Equitable Life Segregated Common Stock*

CROFT–KIRZNER RATINGS:

Performance Rank	1	**Consistency Rank**	2
Sponsor	Equitable Life Insurance Company	**Category**	Canadian Equity
	1 Westmount Road North	**Portfolio Manager**	
	Waterloo, Ontario, N2J 4C7	Rick Brooks—P. H. & N. Investment Management	
Phone	1-800-387-0588	**Minimum Initial Investment**	
Sales Fee	Load **RRSP Eligibility** Yes	RRSP $1,000 Non-RRSP $1,000	

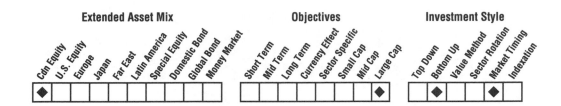

Extended Asset Mix — Cdn Equity ◆, U.S. Equity, Europe, Japan, Far East, Latin America, Special Equity, Domestic Bond, Global Bond, Money Market

Objectives — Short Term, Mid Term, Long Term, Currency Effect, Sector Specific, Small Cap, Mid Cap, Large Cap ◆

Investment Style — Top Down ◆, Bottom Up, Value Method, Sector Rotation ◆, Market Timing, Indexation

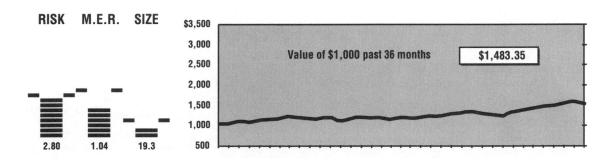

RISK   M.E.R.   SIZE
2.80   1.04   19.3

Value of $1,000 past 36 months $1,483.35

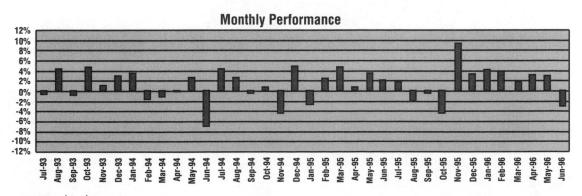

Monthly Performance

*Segregated Fund

National Life Equities Fund*

CROFT–KIRZNER RATINGS:

Performance Rank	1	**Consistency Rank**	2
Sponsor	National Life of Canada	**Category**	Canadian Equity
	522 University Ave.	**Portfolio Manager**	
	Toronto, Ontario, M5G 1Y7	James Blake–National Life	
Phone	1-800-242-9753	**Minimum Initial Investment**	
Sales Fee	Load **RRSP Eligibility** Yes	RRSP $500 Non-RRSP $500	

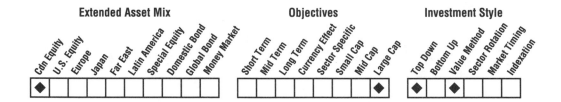

Extended Asset Mix | Objectives | Investment Style

RISK   M.E.R.   SIZE

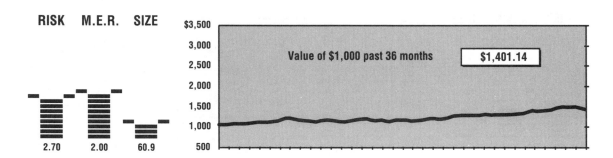

2.70   2.00   60.9

Value of $1,000 past 36 months $1,401.14

Monthly Performance

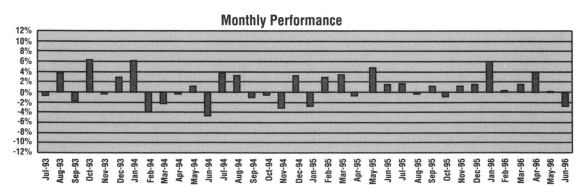

*Segregated Fund

Standard Life Ideal Investment Series Equity*

CROFT–KIRZNER RATINGS:

Performance Rank	1	**Consistency Rank**	2
Sponsor	Standard Life Assurance Co.	**Category**	Canadian Equity
	1245 Sherbrooke St. West	**Portfolio Manager**	
	Montreal, Quebec, H3G 1G3	Standard Life Portfolio Management Team	
Phone	1-800-567-3863	**Minimum Initial Investment**	
Sales Fee	Load **RRSP Eligibility** Yes	RRSP $1,000 Non-RRSP $1,000	

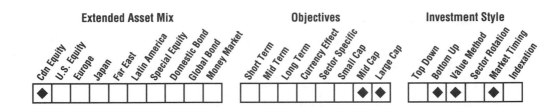

Extended Asset Mix / Objectives / Investment Style

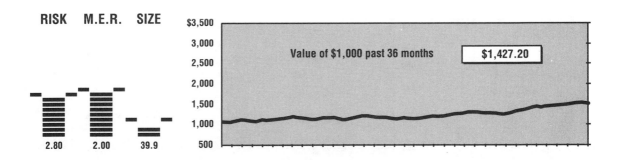

RISK M.E.R. SIZE
2.80 2.00 39.9

Value of $1,000 past 36 months $1,427.20

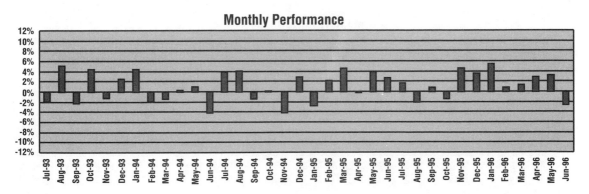

Monthly Performance

*Segregated Fund

Industrial Pension Fund

CROFT–KIRZNER RATINGS:

Performance Rank	1		**Consistency Rank**	3

Sponsor   MacKenzie Financial Corporation

150 Bloor St. West, Suite M111

Toronto, Ontario, M5S 3B5

Phone   1-800-387-0615

Sales Fee   Load   **RRSP Eligibility**   Yes

Category   Canadian Equity

Portfolio Manager

William Procter–MacKenzie Financial

Minimum Initial Investment

RRSP $500   Non-RRSP $500

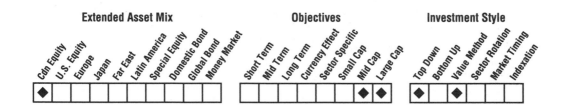

Extended Asset Mix / Objectives / Investment Style

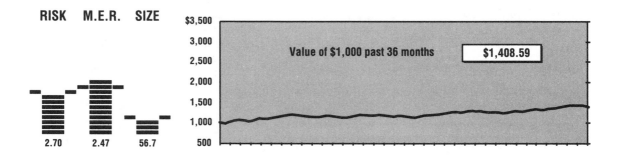

RISK   M.E.R.   SIZE

2.70   2.47   56.7

Value of $1,000 past 36 months $1,408.59

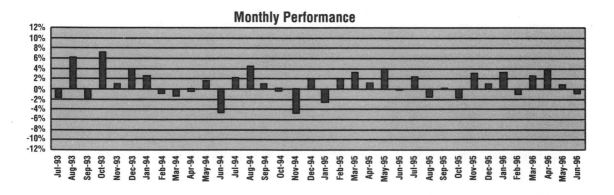

Monthly Performance

Investors Summa Fund

CROFT–KIRZNER RATINGS:

Performance Rank	1	**Consistency Rank**	3
Sponsor	Investors Group Inc.	**Category**	Canadian Equity
	One Canada Centre, 447 Portage Ave.	**Portfolio Manager**	
	Winnipeg Manitoba, R3C 3B6	Quinn Bamford–I.G. Investment Management	
Phone	1-204-943-0361	**Minimum Initial Investment**	
Sales Fee	Load **RRSP Eligibility** Yes	RRSP $500 Non-RRSP $500	

Extended Asset Mix | Objectives | Investment Style

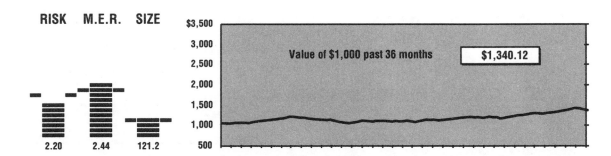

RISK   M.E.R.   SIZE

2.20   2.44   121.2

Value of $1,000 past 36 months $1,340.12

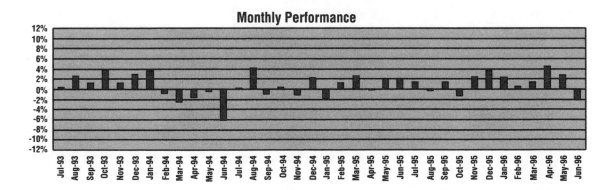

Monthly Performance

P.H. & N. RSP/RIF Equity Fund

CROFT–KIRZNER RATINGS:

Performance Rank	1	**Consistency Rank**	2
Sponsor	Phillips, Hager & North Ltd.	**Category**	Canadian Equity
	1055 West Hastings, Suite 1700	**Portfolio Manager**	
	Vancouver, B.C., V6E 2H3	Phillips, Hager & North Ltd.	
Phone	1-800-661-6141	**Minimum Initial Investment**	
Sales Fee	No-Load **RRSP Eligibility** Yes	RRSP $3,500 Non-RRSP $25,000	

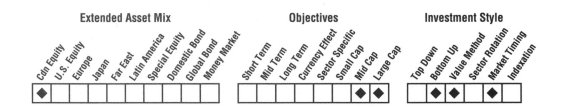

Extended Asset Mix — Cdn Equity ◆, U.S. Equity, Europe, Japan, Far East, Latin America, Special Equity, Domestic Bond, Global Bond, Money Market

Objectives — Short Term, Mid Term, Long Term, Currency Effect, Sector Specific, Small Cap, Mid Cap ◆, Large Cap ◆

Investment Style — Top Down, Bottom Up ◆, Value Method ◆, Sector Rotation, Market Timing ◆, Indexation

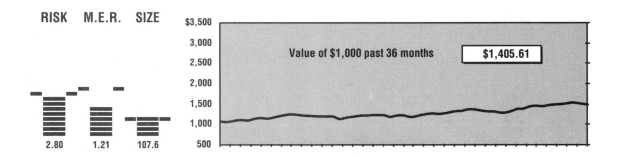

RISK M.E.R. SIZE

2.80 1.21 107.6

Value of $1,000 past 36 months $1,405.61

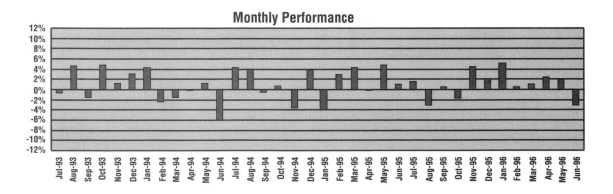

Monthly Performance

United Canadian Equity Fund

CROFT–KIRZNER RATINGS:

Performance Rank	2	**Consistency Rank**	2	

Sponsor   Spectrum United Financial Services

55 University Ave., 15th Floor

Toronto, Ontario, M5J 2H7

Category   Canadian Equity

Portfolio Manager

Catherine A. (Kiki) Delaney–Delaney Capital

Phone   1-800-263-1867

Minimum Initial Investment

Sales Fee   Load   **RRSP Eligibility**   Yes

RRSP $500   Non-RRSP $500

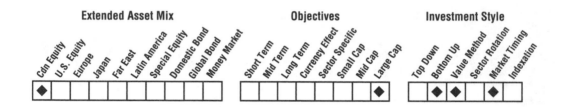

Extended Asset Mix — Cdn Equity ◆ / U.S. Equity / Europe / Japan / Far East / Latin America / Special Equity / Domestic Bond / Global Bond / Money Market

Objectives — Short Term / Mid Term / Long Term / Currency Effect / Sector Specific / Small Cap / Mid Cap / Large Cap ◆

Investment Style — Top Down / Bottom Up ◆ / Value Method ◆ / Sector Rotation ◆ / Market Timing / Indexation

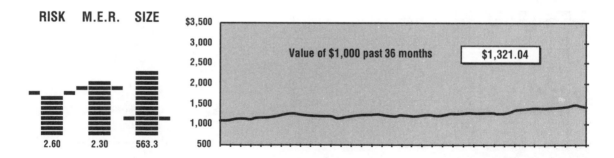

RISK   **M.E.R.**   **SIZE**

2.60   2.30   563.3

Value of $1,000 past 36 months $1,321.04

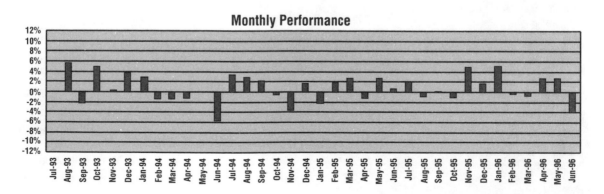

Monthly Performance

Trimark Canadian Fund

CROFT–KIRZNER RATINGS:

Performance Rank	2		**Consistency Rank**	2

Sponsor Trimark Investment Management Inc.
 1 First Canadian Place, Suite 5600, Box 487
 Toronto, Ontario, M5X 1E5

Category Canadian Equity
Portfolio Manager
Rick Serafini–Trimark Investment Management

Phone 1-800-387-9841

Minimum Initial Investment

Sales Fee No-Load **RRSP Eligibility** Yes

RRSP $500 Non-RRSP $500

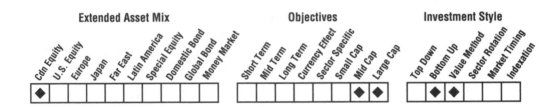

Extended Asset Mix — Cdn Equity, U.S. Equity, Europe, Japan, Far East, Latin America, Special Equity, Domestic Bond, Global Bond, Money Market

Objectives — Short Term, Mid Term, Long Term, Currency Effect, Sector Specific, Small Cap, Mid Cap, Large Cap

Investment Style — Top Down, Bottom Up, Value Method, Sector Rotation, Market Timing, Indexation

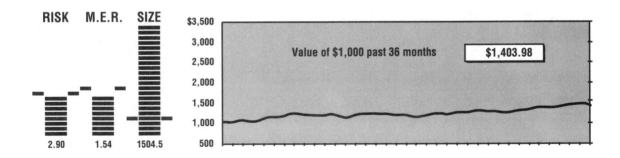

RISK 2.90 M.E.R. 1.54 SIZE 1504.5

Value of $1,000 past 36 months $1,403.98

Monthly Performance

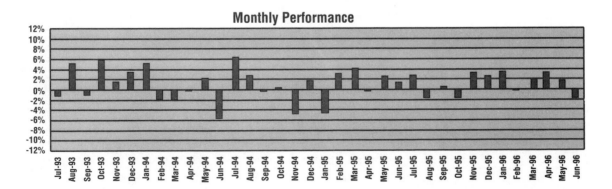

Bissett Canadian Fund

CROFT–KIRZNER RATINGS:

Performance Rank	2		**Consistency Rank**	2
Sponsor	Bissett & Associates		**Category**	Canadian Equity
	500 4th Ave. SW, Suite 1120		**Portfolio Manager**	
	Calgary, Alberta, T2P 2V6		Michael Quinn & Fred Pynn–Bissett & Associates	
Phone	1-403-266-4664		**Minimum Initial Investment**	
Sales Fee	No-Load **RRSP Eligibility** Yes		RRSP $5,000 Non-RRSP $5,000	

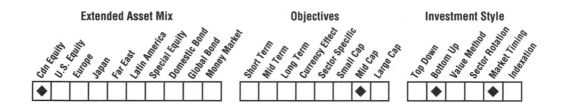

Extended Asset Mix — Objectives — Investment Style

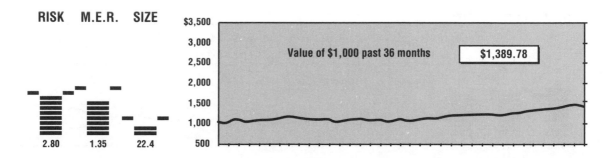

RISK M.E.R. SIZE

2.80 1.35 22.4

Value of $1,000 past 36 months $1,389.78

Monthly Performance

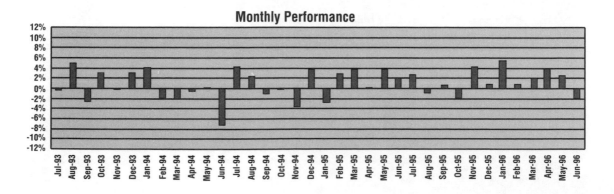

Elliott & Page Equity

CROFT–KIRZNER RATINGS:

Performance Rank	2		**Consistency Rank**	2
Sponsor	Elliott & Page Limited		**Category**	Canadian Equity
	120 Adelaide St. West, Suite 1120		**Portfolio Manager**	
	Toronto, Ontario, M5H 1V1		Nereo Piticco—Elliott & Page	
Phone	1-800-363-6647		**Minimum Initial Investment**	
Sales Fee	Load **RRSP Eligibility** Yes		RRSP $500 Non-RRSP $500	

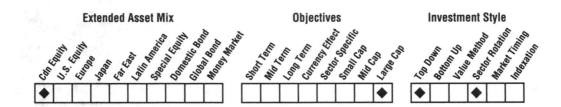

Extended Asset Mix — Objectives — Investment Style

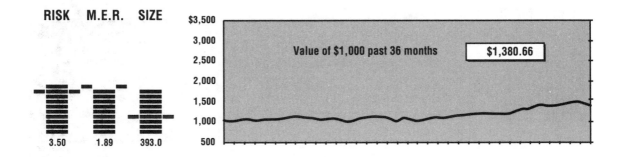

RISK M.E.R. SIZE

3.50 1.89 393.0

Value of $1,000 past 36 months $1,380.66

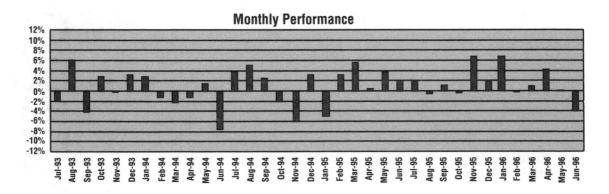

Monthly Performance

Sceptre Equity Fund

CROFT–KIRZNER RATINGS:

Performance Rank	1	**Consistency Rank**	3
Sponsor	Sceptre Investment Counsel Limited	**Category**	Canadian Small Cap
	26 Wellington St. East, Suite 1200	**Portfolio Manager**	
	Toronto, Ontario, M5E 1W4	Allan Jacobs–Sceptre Investment Counsel	
Phone	1-800-265-1888	**Minimum Initial Investment**	
Sales Fee	Load **RRSP Eligibility** Yes	RRSP $5,000 Non-RRSP $5,000	

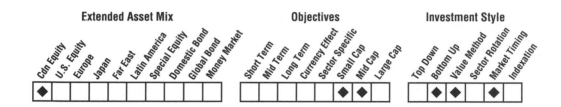

Extended Asset Mix — Cdn Equity ◆

Objectives — Small Cap ◆ Mid Cap ◆

Investment Style — Bottom Up ◆ Value Method ◆ Market Timing ◆

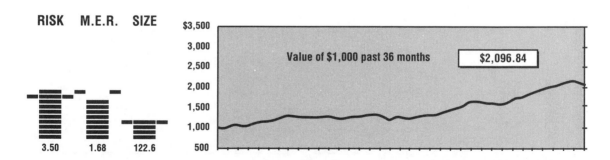

RISK   M.E.R.   SIZE

3.50   1.68   122.6

Value of $1,000 past 36 months $2,096.84

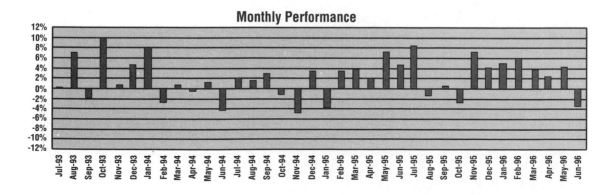

Monthly Performance

Navigator Value Investment Retirement Fund

CROFT–KIRZNER RATINGS:

Performance Rank	1		**Consistency Rank**	5
Sponsor	Navigator Fund Company Ltd.		**Category**	Canadian Small Cap
	444 St. Mary Ave., Suite 1500		**Portfolio Manager**	
	Winnipeg, Manitoba, R3C 3T1		Wayne Deans–Deans Knight	
Phone	1-800-665-1667		**Minimum Initial Investment**	
Sales Fee	Load **RRSP Eligibility** Yes		RRSP $51,000 Non-RRSP $10,000	

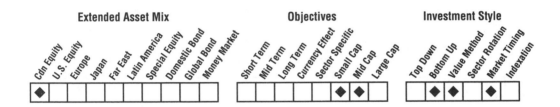

Extended Asset Mix — Objectives — Investment Style

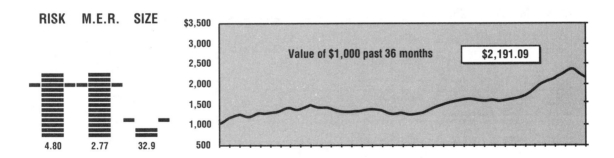

RISK   M.E.R.   SIZE
4.80   2.77   32.9

Value of $1,000 past 36 months $2,191.09

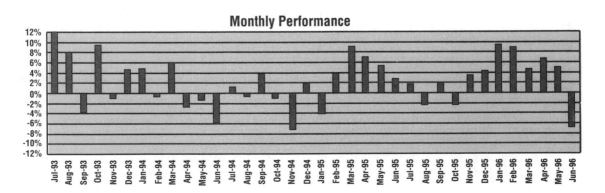

Monthly Performance

Cundill Security Fund

CROFT–KIRZNER RATINGS:

Performance Rank	1		**Consistency Rank**	5
Sponsor	Peter Cundill & Associates Limited		**Category**	Canadian Small Cap
	1100 Melville St., 1200 Sun Life Plaza		**Portfolio Manager**	
	Vancouver, B.C., V6E 4A6		Peter Cundill–Peter Cundill & Associates	
Phone	1-800-663-0156		**Minimum Initial Investment**	
Sales Fee	Load **RRSP Eligibility** Yes		RRSP $5,000 Non-RRSP $5,000	

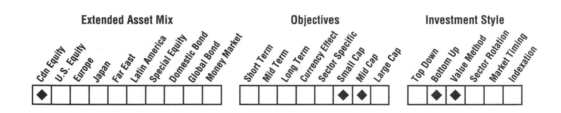

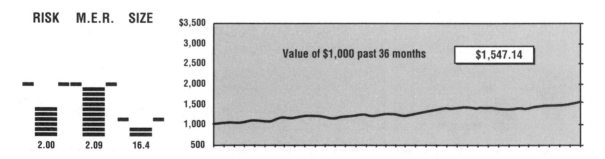

Value of $1,000 past 36 months $1,547.14

RISK 2.00 M.E.R. 2.09 SIZE 16.4

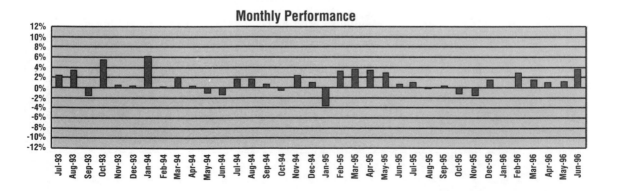

Monthly Performance

ABC Fundamental Value Fund

CROFT–KIRZNER RATINGS:

Performance Rank	1	**Consistency Rank**	4
Sponsor	I.A. Michael Investment Counsel Ltd.	**Category**	Canadian Small Cap
	8 King St. East, Suite 500	**Portfolio Manager**	
	Toronto, Ontario, M5C 1B5	Irwin Michael—I.A. Michael Investment Counsel Ltd.	
Phone	1-416-365-9696	**Minimum Initial Investment**	
Sales Fee	No-Load **RRSP Eligibility** Yes	RRSP $150,000 Non-RRSP $150,000	

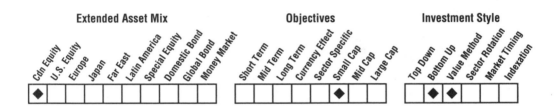

Extended Asset Mix — Cdn Equity ◆, U.S. Equity, Europe, Japan, Far East, Latin America, Special Equity, Domestic Bond, Global Bond, Money Market

Objectives — Short Term, Mid Term, Long Term, Currency Effect, Sector Specific, Small Cap ◆, Mid Cap, Large Cap

Investment Style — Top Down ◆, Bottom Up ◆, Value Method, Sector Rotation, Market Timing, Indexation

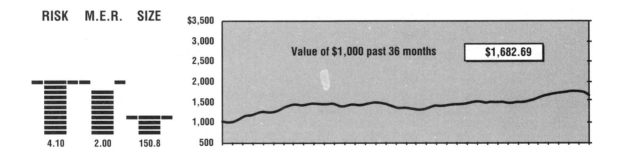

RISK M.E.R. SIZE

4.10   2.00   150.8

Value of $1,000 past 36 months $1,682.69

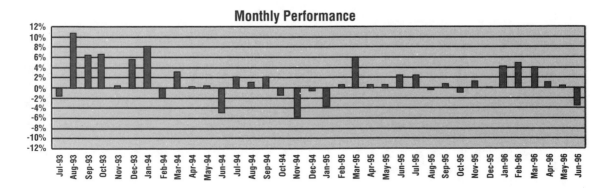

Monthly Performance

Multiple Opportunities Fund

CROFT–KIRZNER RATINGS:

Performance Rank	1	**Consistency Rank**	5
Sponsor	Canaccord Capital Corp.	**Category**	Canadian Small Cap
	609 Granville St., 20th Floor, Box 10379	**Portfolio Manager**	
	Vancouver, B.C., V7Y 1G8	C. Channing Buckland–Canaccord Capital	
Phone	1-800-663-6370	**Minimum Initial Investment**	
Sales Fee	Load **RRSP Eligibility** Yes	RRSP $500 Non-RRSP $500	

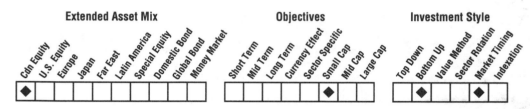

Extended Asset Mix — Cdn Equity, U.S. Equity, Europe, Japan, Far East, Latin America, Special Equity, Domestic Bond, Global Bond, Money Market

Objectives — Short Term, Mid Term, Long Term, Currency Effect, Sector Specific, Small Cap, Mid Cap, Large Cap

Investment Style — Top Down, Bottom Up, Value Method, Sector Rotation, Market Timing, Indexation

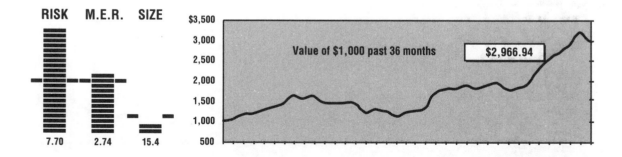

RISK M.E.R. SIZE

7.70   2.74   15.4

Value of $1,000 past 36 months $2,966.94

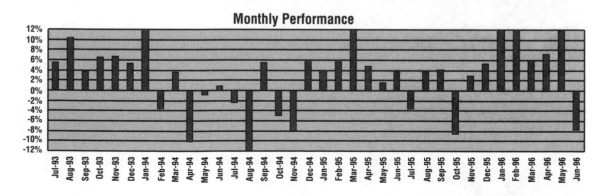

Monthly Performance

BPI Canadian Small Companies

CROFT–KIRZNER RATINGS:

Performance Rank	1		**Consistency Rank**	4

Sponsor BPI Capital Management Corporation
161 Bay St., Suite 3900
Toronto, Ontario, M5J 2S1

Category Canadian Small Cap
Portfolio Manager
Steven Misener—BPI Capital

Phone 1-800-263-2427

Minimum Initial Investment

Sales Fee Load **RRSP Eligibility** Yes

RRSP $500 Non-RRSP $500

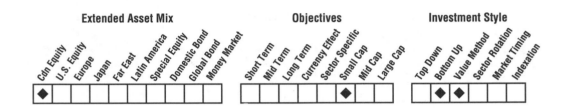

Extended Asset Mix — Objectives — Investment Style

RISK M.E.R. SIZE

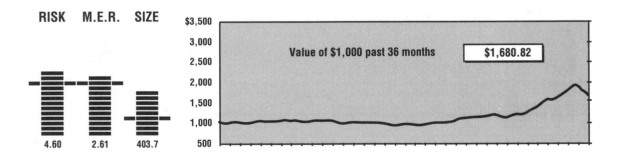

4.60 2.61 403.7

Value of $1,000 past 36 months $1,680.82

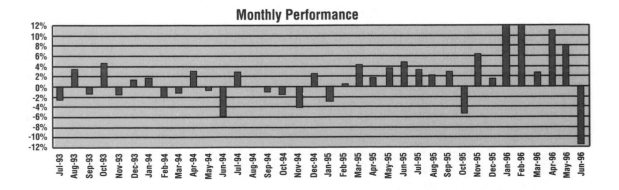

Monthly Performance

United Canadian Growth Fund

CROFT–KIRZNER RATINGS:

Performance Rank	1		**Consistency Rank**	3
Sponsor	Spectrum United Financial Services		**Category**	Canadian Small Cap
	55 University Ave., 15th Floor		**Portfolio Manager**	
	Toronto, Ontario, M5J 2H7		Lynn Miller–Delaney Capital Management	
Phone	1-800-263-1867		**Minimum Initial Investment**	
Sales Fee	Load **RRSP Eligibility** Yes		RRSP $500 Non-RRSP $500	

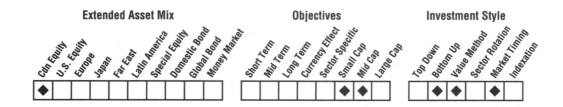

Extended Asset Mix — Objectives — Investment Style

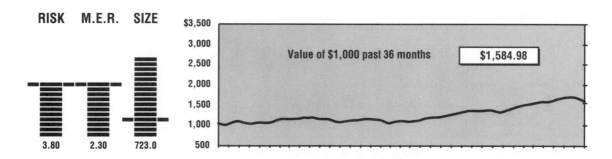

RISK M.E.R. SIZE
3.80 2.30 723.0

Value of $1,000 past 36 months $1,584.98

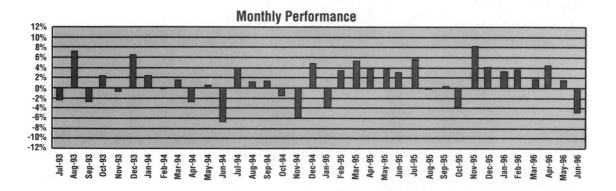

Monthly Performance

Guardian Enterprise Fund A

CROFT–KIRZNER RATINGS:

Performance Rank	1	**Consistency Rank**	3

Sponsor Guardian Group of Funds Limited
Commerce Court West, Suite 3100, Box 201
Toronto, Ontario, M5L 1E8

Phone 1-800-668-7327

Sales Fee Load   **RRSP Eligibility** Yes

Category Canadian Small Cap

Portfolio Manager
Gary Chapman–Guardian Capital

Minimum Initial Investment
RRSP $500   Non-RRSP $500

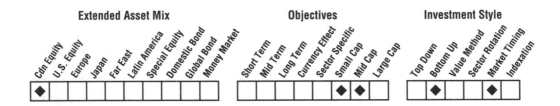

Extended Asset Mix: Cdn Equity, U.S. Equity, Europe, Japan, Far East, Latin America, Special Equity, Domestic Bond, Global Bond, Money Market — ◆ Cdn Equity

Objectives: Short Term, Mid Term, Long Term, Currency Effect, Sector Specific, Small Cap, Mid Cap, Large Cap — ◆ Small Cap, ◆ Mid Cap

Investment Style: Top Down, Bottom Up, Value Method, Sector Rotation, Market Timing, Indexation — ◆ Bottom Up, ◆ Market Timing

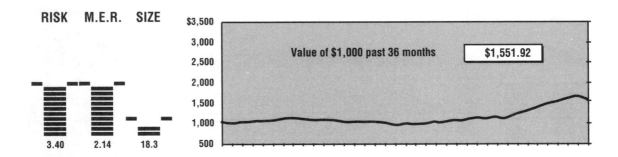

RISK   M.E.R.   SIZE
3.40   2.14   18.3

Value of $1,000 past 36 months $1,551.92

Monthly Performance

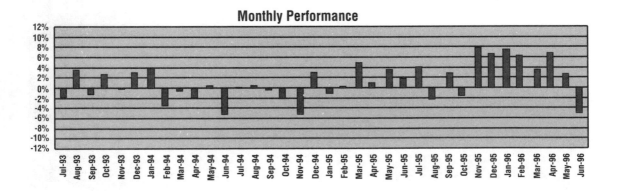

Mawer New Canada Fund

CROFT–KIRZNER RATINGS:

Performance Rank	1	**Consistency Rank**	4

Sponsor Mawer Investment Management
603-7th Ave. SW, Suite 600, Manulife House
Calgary, Alberta, T2P 2T5

Category Canadian Small Cap
Portfolio Manager
Leighton F. Pullen–Mawer Investment Management

Phone 1-403-262-4673
Minimum Initial Investment

Sales Fee Load **RRSP Eligibility** Yes
RRSP $25,000 Non-RRSP $25,000

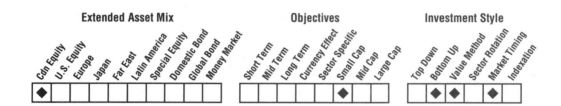

Extended Asset Mix — Cdn Equity, U.S. Equity, Europe, Japan, Far East, Latin America, Special Equity, Domestic Bond, Global Bond, Money Market

Objectives — Short Term, Mid Term, Long Term, Currency Effect, Sector Specific, Small Cap, Mid Cap, Large Cap

Investment Style — Top Down, Bottom Up, Value Method, Sector Rotation, Market Timing, Indexation

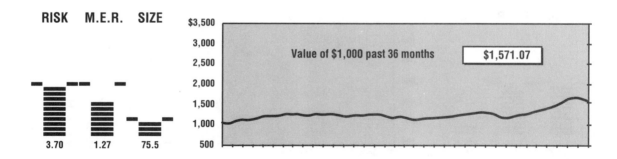

RISK M.E.R. SIZE
3.70 1.27 75.5

Value of $1,000 past 36 months $1,571.07

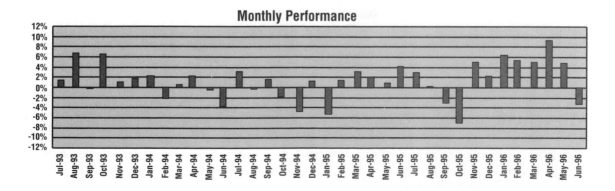

Monthly Performance

Bissett Small Cap Fund

CROFT–KIRZNER RATINGS:

Performance Rank	1		**Consistency Rank**	3

Sponsor Bissett & Associates

500 4th Ave. SW, Suite 1120

Calgary, Alberta, T2P 2V6

Phone 1-403-266-4664

Sales Fee No-Load **RRSP Eligibility** Yes

Category Canadian Small Cap

Portfolio Manager

David A. Bissett—Bissett & Associates

Minimum Initial Investment

RRSP $5,000 Non-RRSP $20,000

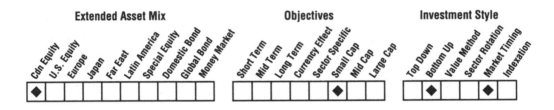

Extended Asset Mix — Cdn Equity, U.S. Equity, Europe, Japan, Far East, Latin America, Special Equity, Domestic Bond, Global Bond, Money Market

Objectives — Short Term, Mid Term, Long Term, Currency Effect, Sector Specific, Small Cap, Mid Cap, Large Cap

Investment Style — Top Down, Bottom Up, Value Method, Sector Rotation, Market Timing, Indexation

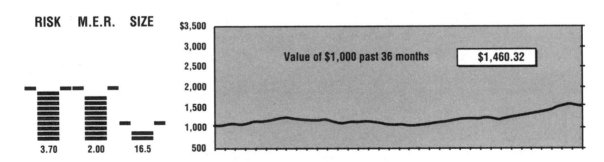

RISK M.E.R. SIZE

3.70 2.00 16.5

Value of $1,000 past 36 months $1,460.32

$3,500 / 3,000 / 2,500 / 2,000 / 1,500 / 1,000 / 500

Monthly Performance

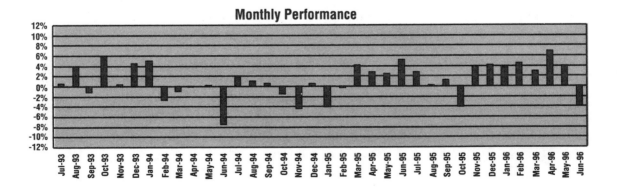

C. I. American Fund

CROFT–KIRZNER RATINGS:

Performance Rank	2		**Consistency Rank**	4
Sponsor	C. I. Mutual Funds		**Category**	U.S. Equity
	151 Yonge St.		**Portfolio Manager**	
	Toronto, Ontario, M5C 2Y1		Bill Priest–BEA Associates	
Phone	1-800-563-5181		**Minimum Initial Investment**	
Sales Fee	Load **RRSP Eligibility** Foreign		RRSP $500 Non-RRSP $500	

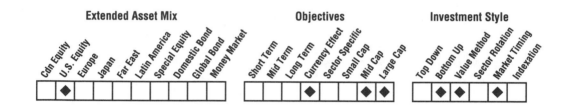

Extended Asset Mix — Cdn Equity, U.S. Equity ◆, Europe, Japan, Far East, Latin America, Special Equity, Domestic Bond, Global Bond, Money Market

Objectives — Short Term, Mid Term, Long Term ◆, Currency Effect, Sector Specific, Small Cap, Mid Cap ◆, Large Cap ◆

Investment Style — Top Down, Bottom Up ◆, Value Method ◆, Sector Rotation, Market Timing ◆, Indexation

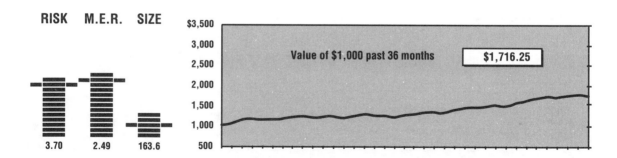

RISK	M.E.R.	SIZE
3.70	2.49	163.6

Value of $1,000 past 36 months $1,716.25

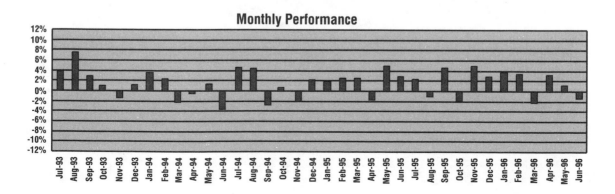

Monthly Performance

BPI American Small Companies

CROFT–KIRZNER RATINGS:

Performance Rank	2		**Consistency Rank**	5
Sponsor	BPI Capital Management Corporation		**Category**	U.S. Equity
	161 Bay St., Suite 3900		**Portfolio Manager**	
	Toronto, Ontario, M5J 2S1		M. Rome & E. Alexanderson–Lazard Freres	
Phone	1-800-263-2427		**Minimum Initial Investment**	
Sales Fee	Load **RRSP Eligibility** Foreign		RRSP $500 Non-RRSP $500	

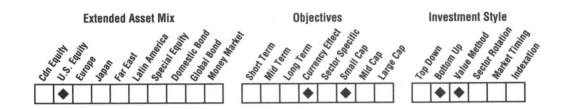

Extended Asset Mix / Objectives / Investment Style

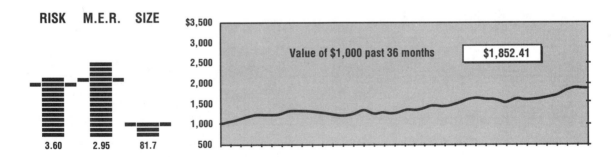

RISK   M.E.R.   SIZE

3.60   2.95   81.7

Value of $1,000 past 36 months $1,852.41

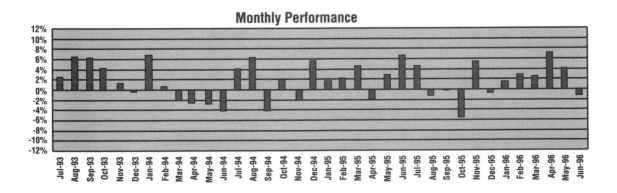

Monthly Performance

United American Growth Fund

CROFT–KIRZNER RATINGS:

Performance Rank	2		**Consistency Rank**	5
Sponsor	Spectrum United Financial Services		**Category**	U.S. Equity
	55 University Ave., 15th Floor		**Portfolio Manager**	
	Toronto, Ontario, M5J 2H7		John Ballen–MFS Asset Management Inc.	
Phone	1-800-263-1867		**Minimum Initial Investment**	
Sales Fee	Load **RRSP Eligibility** Foreign		RRSP $500 Non-RRSP $500	

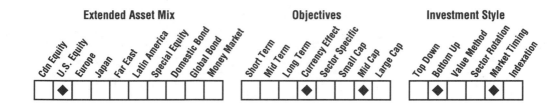

Extended Asset Mix | Objectives | Investment Style

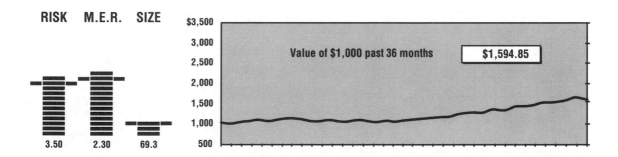

RISK   M.E.R.   SIZE

3.50   2.30   69.3

Value of $1,000 past 36 months $1,594.85

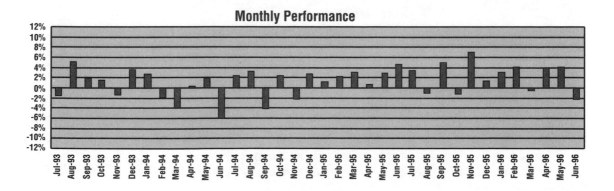

Monthly Performance

Universal U.S. Emerging Growth Fund

CROFT–KIRZNER RATINGS:

Performance Rank	2	**Consistency Rank**	5
Sponsor	MacKenzie Financial Corporation	**Category**	U.S. Equity
	150 Bloor St. West, Suite M111	**Portfolio Manager**	
	Toronto, Ontario, M5S 3B5	James Broadfoot–MacKenzie Financial	
Phone	1-800-387-0615	**Minimum Initial Investment**	
Sales Fee	Load **RRSP Eligibility** Foreign	RRSP $500 Non-RRSP $500	

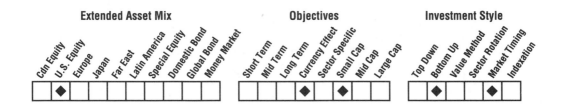

Extended Asset Mix — Objectives — Investment Style

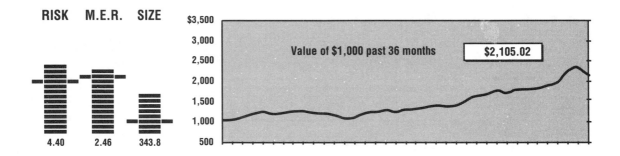

RISK   M.E.R.   SIZE
4.40   2.46   343.8

Value of $1,000 past 36 months — $2,105.02

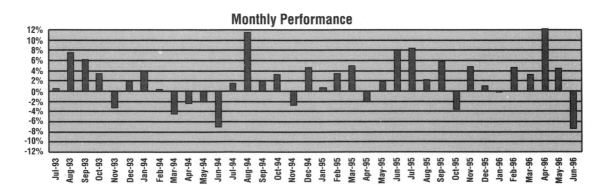

Monthly Performance

Zweig Strategic Growth Fund

CROFT–KIRZNER RATINGS:

Performance Rank	2	**Consistency Rank**	5
Sponsor	Royal Mutual Funds Inc.	**Category**	U.S. Equity
	Royal Trust Tower, 77 King St. West, 5th Floor	**Portfolio Manager**	
	Toronto, Ontario, M5W 1P9	D. Katzen & M. Zweig–Zweig Investors Inc.	
Phone	1-800-463-3863	**Minimum Initial Investment**	
Sales Fee	No-Load **RRSP Eligibility** Foreign	RRSP $500 Non-RRSP $500	

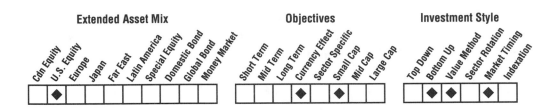

Extended Asset Mix — Objectives — Investment Style

RISK 2.00   M.E.R. 2.62   SIZE 159.6

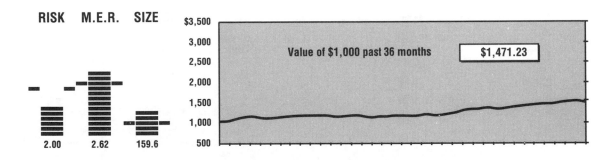

Value of $1,000 past 36 months $1,471.23

Monthly Performance

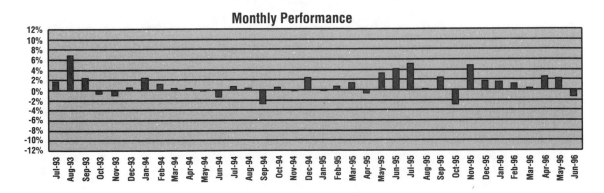

Phillips, Hager & North U.S. Equity Fund

CROFT–KIRZNER RATINGS:

Performance Rank	2		**Consistency Rank**	4

Sponsor   Phillips, Hager & North Ltd.

Category   U.S. Equity

1055 West Hastings, Suite 1700

Portfolio Manager

Vancouver, B.C., V6E 2H3

Phillips, Hager & North Ltd.

Phone   1-800-661-6141

Minimum Initial Investment

Sales Fee   No-Load   **RRSP Eligibility**   Foreign   RRSP $3,500   Non-RRSP $25,000

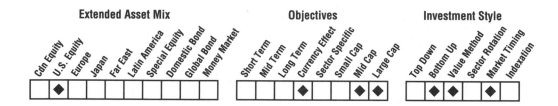

Extended Asset Mix — Objectives — Investment Style

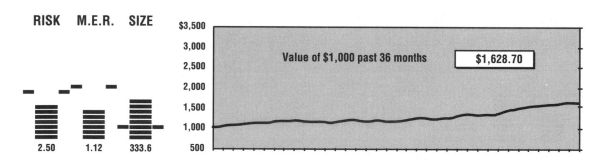

RISK M.E.R. SIZE   2.50   1.12   333.6

Value of $1,000 past 36 months $1,628.70

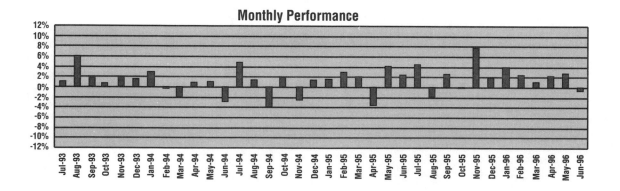

Monthly Performance

Mawer U.S. Equity Fund

CROFT–KIRZNER RATINGS:

Performance Rank	3	**Consistency Rank**	4

Sponsor Mawer Investment Management
603-7th Ave. SW, Suite 600, Manulife House
Calgary, Alberta, T2P 2T5

Category U.S. Equity

Portfolio Manager
Darrell Anderson—Mawer Investment Management

Phone 1-403-262-4673

Minimum Initial Investment

Sales Fee No-Load **RRSP Eligibility** Foreign

RRSP $25,000 Non-RRSP $25,000

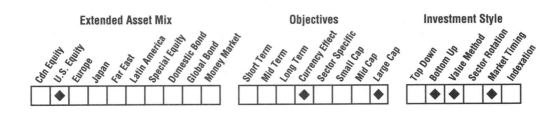

Extended Asset Mix / Objectives / Investment Style

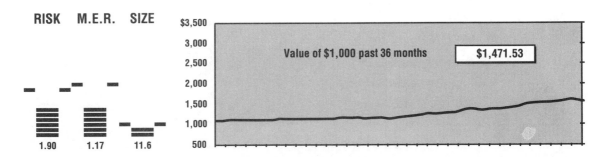

RISK M.E.R. SIZE
1.90 1.17 11.6

Value of $1,000 past 36 months — $1,471.53

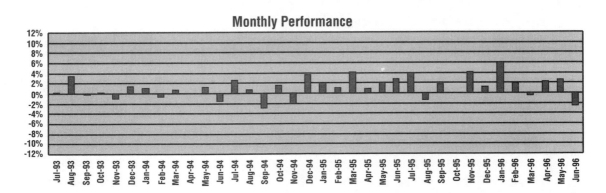

Monthly Performance

Green Line U.S. Equity Index Fund (US$)

CROFT–KIRZNER RATINGS:

Performance Rank	3	**Consistency Rank**	1
Sponsor	TD Asset Management Inc.	**Category**	U.S. Equity
	TD Center, Box 100, TD Bank Tower, 20th Floor	**Portfolio Manager**	
	Toronto, Ontario, M5K 1G8	TD Asset Management Inc.	
Phone	1-800-268-8166	**Minimum Initial Investment**	
Sales Fee	No-Load **RRSP Eligibility** Foreign	RRSP $100 Non-RRSP $2,000	

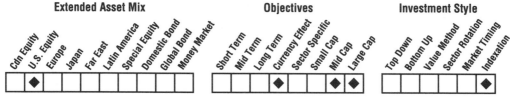

Extended Asset Mix — Objectives — Investment Style

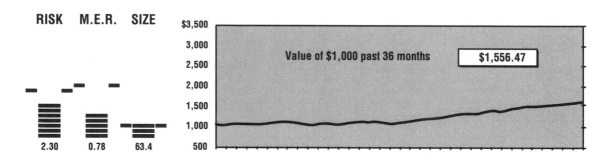

RISK   M.E.R.   SIZE

2.30   0.78   63.4

Value of $1,000 past 36 months $1,556.47

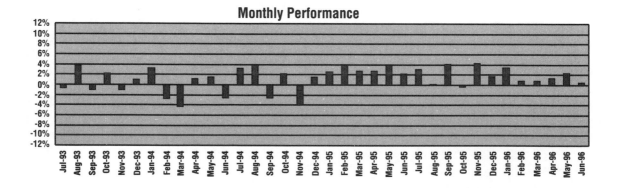

Monthly Performance

AGF American Growth Fund Ltd.

CROFT–KIRZNER RATINGS:

Performance Rank	3		**Consistency Rank**	4

Sponsor   AGF Management Ltd.
TD Bank Tower, 31st Floor, Box 50
Toronto, Ontario, M5K 1E9

Category   U.S. Equity
Portfolio Manager
Stephen Rogers—AGF Management Ltd.

Phone   1-800-268-8583

Minimum Initial Investment

Sales Fee   Load   **RRSP Eligibility**   Foreign   RRSP $1,000   Non-RRSP $1,000

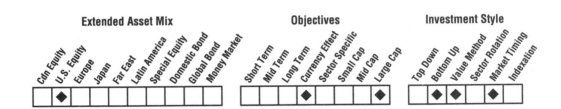

Extended Asset Mix — Cdn Equity, U.S. Equity ◆, Europe, Japan, Far East, Latin America, Special Equity, Domestic Bond, Global Bond, Money Market

Objectives — Short Term, Mid Term, Long Term ◆, Currency Effect, Sector Specific, Small Cap, Mid Cap, Large Cap ◆

Investment Style — Top Down, Bottom Up ◆, Value Method ◆, Sector Rotation, Market Timing ◆, Indexation

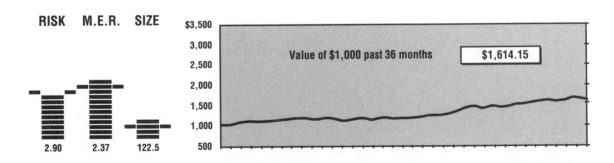

RISK	M.E.R.	SIZE
2.90	2.37	122.5

Value of $1,000 past 36 months $1,614.15

Monthly Performance

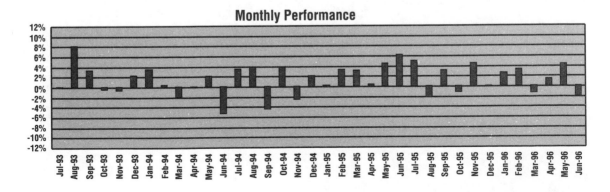

Investors U.S. Growth Fund

CROFT–KIRZNER RATINGS:

Performance Rank	2		**Consistency Rank**	5
Sponsor	Investors Group Inc.		**Category**	U.S. Equity
	One Canada Centre, 447 Portage Ave.		**Portfolio Manager**	
	Winnipeg Manitoba, R3C 3B6		Larry Sarbit—I.G. Investment Management	
Phone	1-204-943-0361		**Minimum Initial Investment**	
Sales Fee	Load	**RRSP Eligibility** Foreign	RRSP $500	Non-RRSP $1,000

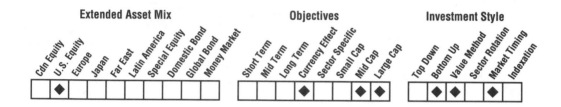

Extended Asset Mix — Objectives — Investment Style

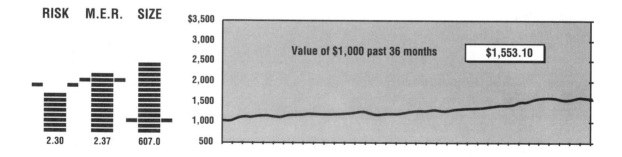

RISK 2.30 M.E.R. 2.37 SIZE 607.0

Value of $1,000 past 36 months $1,553.10

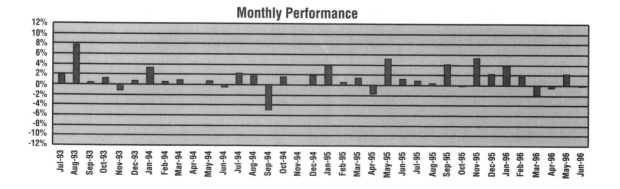

Monthly Performance

Trimark Fund

CROFT–KIRZNER RATINGS:

Performance Rank	2	**Consistency Rank**	4
Sponsor	Trimark Investment Management Inc.	**Category**	U.S. Equity
	1 First Canadian Place, Suite 5600, Box 487	**Portfolio Manager**	
	Toronto, Ontario, M5X 1E5	Angela Eaton & Richard Jenkins—Trimark	
Phone	1-800-387-9841	**Minimum Initial Investment**	
Sales Fee	Load **RRSP Eligibility** Foreign	RRSP $500 Non-RRSP $500	

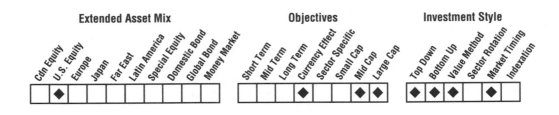

Extended Asset Mix — Objectives — Investment Style

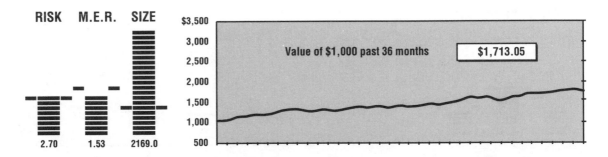

RISK 2.70 M.E.R. 1.53 SIZE 2169.0

Value of $1,000 past 36 months $1,713.05

Monthly Performance

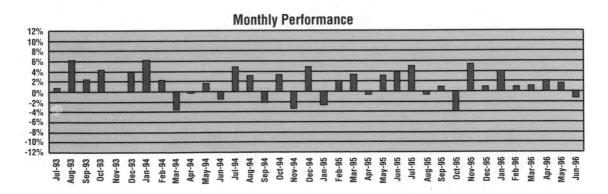

Ivy Foreign Equity Fund

CROFT–KIRZNER RATINGS:

Performance Rank	1	**Consistency Rank**	5
Sponsor	MacKenzie Financial Corporation	**Category**	U.S. Equity
	150 Bloor St. West, Suite M111	**Portfolio Manager**	
	Toronto, Ontario, M5S 3B5	Jerry Javasky–MacKenzie Financial Corporation	
Phone	1-800-387-0615	**Minimum Initial Investment**	
Sales Fee	Load **RRSP Eligibility** Foreign	RRSP $500 Non-RRSP $500	

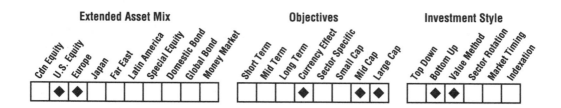

Extended Asset Mix — Cdn Equity, U.S. Equity, Europe, Japan, Far East, Latin America, Special Equity, Domestic Bond, Global Bond, Money Market

Objectives — Short Term, Mid Term, Long Term, Currency Effect, Sector Specific, Small Cap, Mid Cap, Large Cap

Investment Style — Top Down, Bottom Up, Value Method, Sector Rotation, Market Timing, Indexation

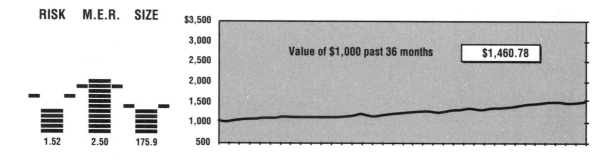

RISK   M.E.R.   SIZE

1.52   2.50   175.9

Value of $1,000 past 36 months $1,460.78

Monthly Performance

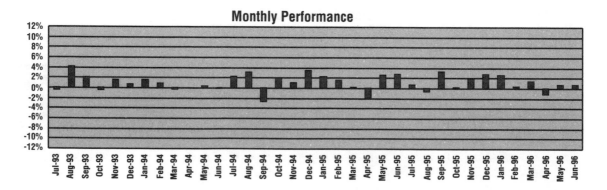

National Life Global Equities Fund*

CROFT–KIRZNER RATINGS:

Performance Rank	1	**Consistency Rank**	3
Sponsor	National Life of Canada	**Category**	International Equity
	522 University Ave.	**Portfolio Manager**	
	Toronto, Ontario, M5G 1Y7	James Fairweather–Martin Currie Inc.	
Phone	1-800-242-9753	**Minimum Initial Investment**	
Sales Fee Load	**RRSP Eligibility** Foreign	RRSP $500	Non-RRSP $500

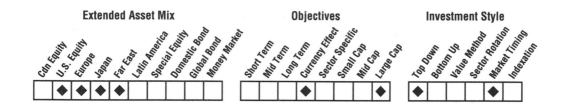

Extended Asset Mix — Cdn Equity, U.S. Equity ◆, Europe ◆, Japan ◆, Far East ◆, Latin America, Special Equity, Domestic Bond, Global Bond, Money Market

Objectives — Short Term, Mid Term, Long Term ◆, Currency Effect, Sector Specific, Small Cap, Mid Cap, Large Cap ◆

Investment Style — Top Down ◆, Bottom Up, Value Method, Sector Rotation ◆, Market Timing, Indexation

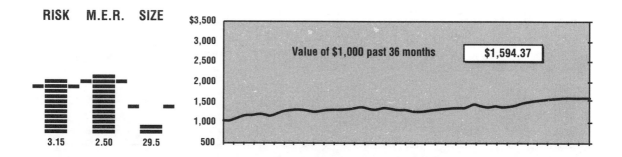

RISK M.E.R. SIZE

3.15   2.50   29.5

Value of $1,000 past 36 months $1,594.37

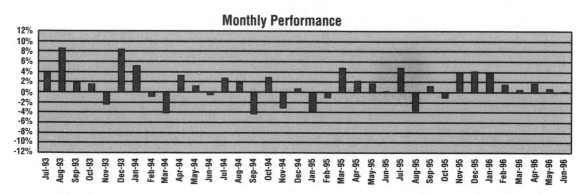

Monthly Performance

(Jul-93 through Jun-96)

*Segregated Fund

Saxon World Growth

CROFT–KIRZNER RATINGS:

Performance Rank	2	**Consistency Rank**	5
Sponsor	Saxon Funds	**Category**	International Equity
	20 Queen St. West, Suite 1904, Box 95	**Portfolio Manager**	
	Toronto, Ontario, M5H 3R3	Robert Tattersall—Howson Tattersall Inv. Counsel	
Phone	1-416-979-1818	**Minimum Initial Investment**	
Sales Fee	No-Load **RRSP Eligibility** Foreign	RRSP $5,000 Non-RRSP $5,000	

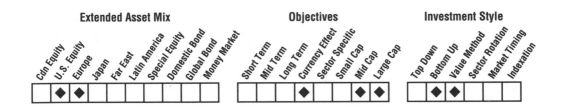

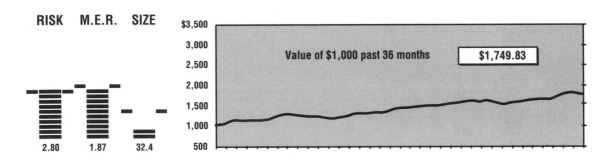

Value of $1,000 past 36 months $1,749.83

RISK   M.E.R.   SIZE
2.80   1.87   32.4

Monthly Performance

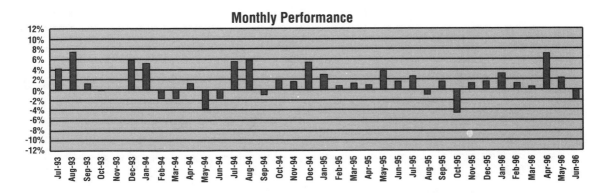

BPI Global Equity Fund

CROFT–KIRZNER RATINGS:

Performance Rank	1	**Consistency Rank**	4
Sponsor	BPI Capital Management Corporation	**Category**	International Equity
	161 Bay St., Suite 3900	**Portfolio Manager**	
	Toronto, Ontario, M5J 2S1	John Reinsberg–Lazard Freres	
Phone	1-800-263-2427	**Minimum Initial Investment**	
Sales Fee Load	**RRSP Eligibility** Foreign	RRSP $500	Non-RRSP $500

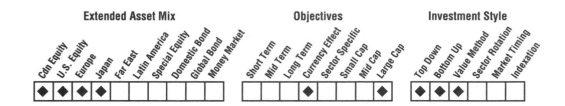

Extended Asset Mix — Objectives — Investment Style

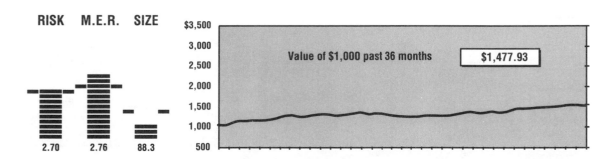

RISK 2.70 M.E.R. 2.76 SIZE 88.3

Value of $1,000 past 36 months $1,477.93

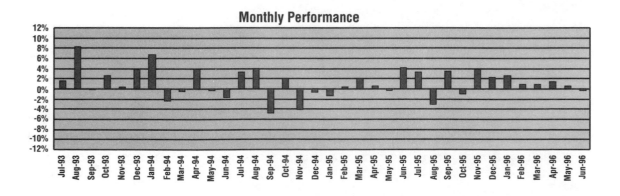

Monthly Performance

Templeton Global Smaller Companies Fund

CROFT–KIRZNER RATINGS:

Performance Rank	1	**Consistency Rank**	4
Sponsor	Templeton Management Limited	**Category**	International Equity
	4 King St. West, Box 4070, Stn A	**Portfolio Manager**	
	Toronto, Ontario, M5W 1M3	Marc. S. Joseph–Templeton Management	
Phone	1-800-387-0830	**Minimum Initial Investment**	
Sales Fee	Load **RRSP Eligibility** Foreign	RRSP $500 Non-RRSP $500	

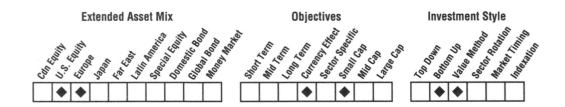

Extended Asset Mix

Cdn Equity | U.S. Equity ◆ | Europe ◆ | Japan | Far East | Latin America | Special Equity | Domestic Bond | Global Bond | Money Market

Objectives

Short Term | Mid Term | Long Term | Currency Effect ◆ | Sector Specific | Small Cap ◆ | Mid Cap | Large Cap

Investment Style

Top Down | Bottom Up ◆ | Value Method ◆ | Sector Rotation | Market Timing | Indexation

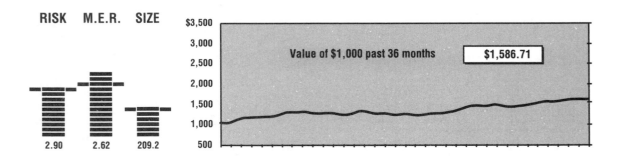

RISK M.E.R. SIZE

2.90   2.62   209.2

Value of $1,000 past 36 months $1,586.71

$3,500
3,000
2,500
2,000
1,500
1,000
500

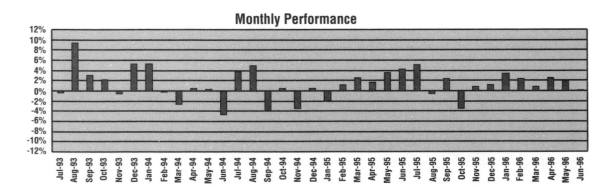

Monthly Performance

12%
10%
8%
6%
4%
2%
0%
-2%
-4%
-6%
-8%
-10%
-12%

Jul-93 Aug-93 Sep-93 Oct-93 Nov-93 Dec-93 Jan-94 Feb-94 Mar-94 Apr-94 May-94 Jun-94 Jul-94 Aug-94 Sep-94 Oct-94 Nov-94 Dec-94 Jan-95 Feb-95 Mar-95 Apr-95 May-95 Jun-95 Jul-95 Aug-95 Sep-95 Oct-95 Nov-95 Dec-95 Jan-96 Feb-96 Mar-96 Apr-96 May-96 Jun-96

Templeton Growth Fund

CROFT–KIRZNER RATINGS:

Performance Rank	1		**Consistency Rank**	4
Sponsor	Templeton Management Limited		**Category**	International Equity
	4 King St. West, Box 4070, Stn A		**Portfolio Manager**	
	Toronto, Ontario, M5W 1M3		Mark G. Holowesko–Templeton Management	
Phone	1-800-387-0830		**Minimum Initial Investment**	
Sales Fee	Load	**RRSP Eligibility** Foreign	RRSP $500	Non-RRSP $500

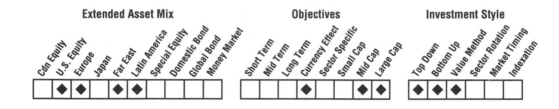

Extended Asset Mix — Cdn Equity, U.S. Equity ◆, Europe ◆, Japan, Far East ◆, Latin America ◆, Special Equity, Domestic Bond, Global Bond, Money Market

Objectives — Short Term, Mid Term, Long Term ◆, Currency Effect, Sector Specific, Small Cap, Mid Cap ◆, Large Cap ◆

Investment Style — Top Down ◆, Bottom Up ◆, Value Method ◆, Sector Rotation, Market Timing, Indexation

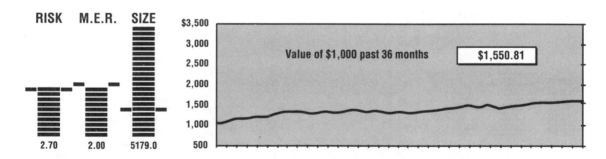

RISK 2.70   M.E.R. 2.00   SIZE 5179.0

Value of $1,000 past 36 months $1,550.81

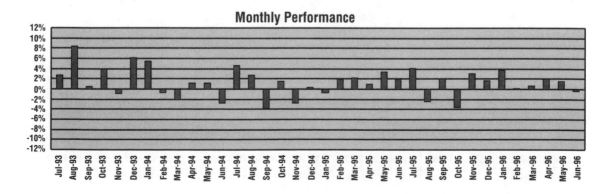

Monthly Performance

Jul-93, Aug-93, Sep-93, Oct-93, Nov-93, Dec-93, Jan-94, Feb-94, Mar-94, Apr-94, May-94, Jun-94, Jul-94, Aug-94, Sep-94, Oct-94, Nov-94, Dec-94, Jan-95, Feb-95, Mar-95, Apr-95, May-95, Jun-95, Jul-95, Aug-95, Sep-95, Oct-95, Nov-95, Dec-95, Jan-96, Feb-96, Mar-96, Apr-96, May-96, Jun-96

Templeton International Stock Fund

CROFT–KIRZNER RATINGS:

Performance Rank	1	**Consistency Rank**	4
Sponsor	Templeton Management Limited	**Category**	International Equity
	4 King St. West, Box 4070, Stn A	**Portfolio Manager**	
	Toronto, Ontario, M5W 1M3	Donald F. Reed—Templeton Management	
Phone	1-800-387-0830	**Minimum Initial Investment**	
Sales Fee	Load **RRSP Eligibility** Foreign	RRSP $500 Non-RRSP $500	

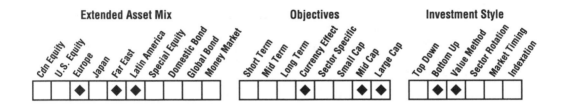

Extended Asset Mix / Objectives / Investment Style

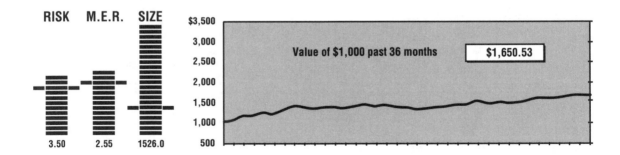

RISK 3.50 M.E.R. 2.55 SIZE 1526.0

Value of $1,000 past 36 months $1,650.53

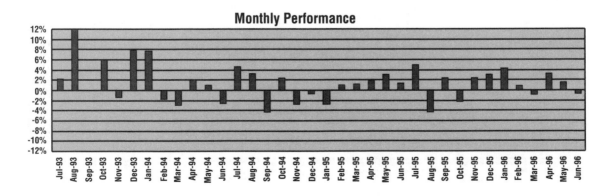

Monthly Performance

BPI Global Small Companies Fund

CROFT–KIRZNER RATINGS:

Performance Rank	1	**Consistency Rank**	5
Sponsor	BPI Capital Management Corporation	**Category**	International Equity
	161 Bay St., Suite 3900	**Portfolio Manager**	
	Toronto, Ontario, M5J 2S1	Eileen Alexanderson–Lazard Freres	
Phone	1-800-263-2427	**Minimum Initial Investment**	
Sales Fee Load	**RRSP Eligibility** Foreign	RRSP $500	Non-RRSP $500

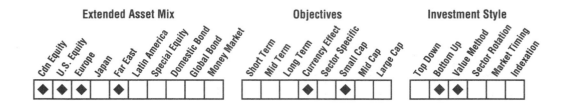

Extended Asset Mix — Objectives — Investment Style

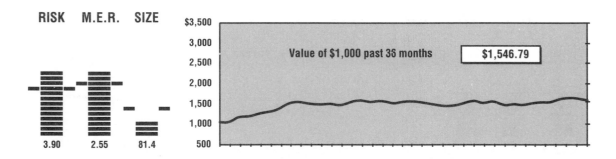

RISK 3.90   M.E.R. 2.55   SIZE 81.4

Value of $1,000 past 36 months $1,546.79

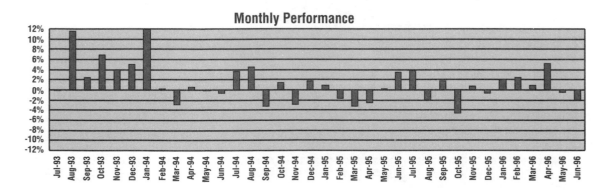

Monthly Performance

Cundill Value Fund

CROFT–KIRZNER RATINGS:

Performance Rank	1	**Consistency Rank**	5
Sponsor	Peter Cundill & Associates Limited	**Category**	International Equity
	1100 Melville St., 1200 Sun Life Plaza	**Portfolio Manager**	
	Vancouver, B.C., V6E 4A6	Peter Cundill–Peter Cundill & Associates	
Phone	1-800-663-0156	**Minimum Initial Investment**	
Sales Fee	Load **RRSP Eligibility** Foreign	RRSP $5,000 Non-RRSP $5,000	

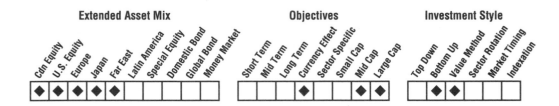

Extended Asset Mix — Objectives — Investment Style

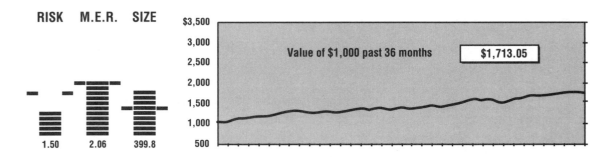

RISK M.E.R. SIZE

1.50   2.06   399.8

Value of $1,000 past 36 months $1,713.05

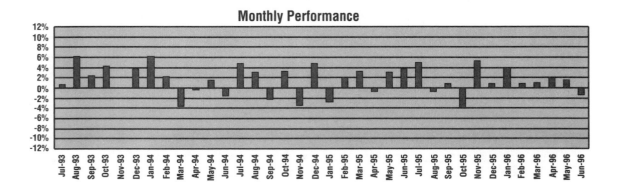

Monthly Performance

Investors Global Fund

CROFT–KIRZNER RATINGS:

Performance Rank	1	**Consistency Rank**	3
Sponsor	Investors Group Inc.	**Category**	International Equity
	One Canada Centre, 447 Portage Ave.	**Portfolio Manager**	
	Winnipeg Manitoba, R3C 3B6	Derek Smith—I.G. Investment Management	
Phone	1-204-943-0361	**Minimum Initial Investment**	
Sales Fee Load **RRSP Eligibility** Foreign		RRSP $500 Non-RRSP $1,000	

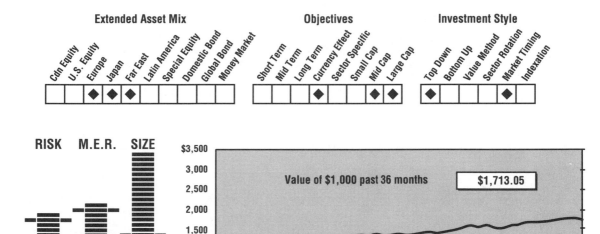

RISK 2.60 M.E.R. 2.43 SIZE 993.0

Value of $1,000 past 36 months $1,713.05

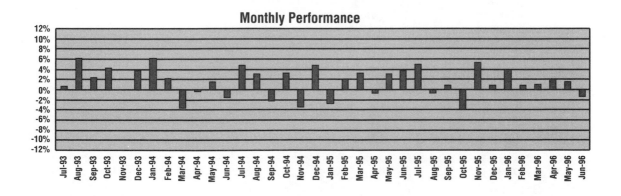

Monthly Performance

Fidelity International Portfolio Fund

CROFT–KIRZNER RATINGS:

Performance Rank	2		**Consistency Rank**	3

Sponsor Fidelity Investments Canada Limited
Ernst & Young Tower, 222Bay St., Suite 900
Toronto Ontario, M5K 1P1

Phone 1-800-263-4077

Sales Fee Load **RRSP Eligibility** Foreign

Category International Equity

Portfolio Manager
Dick Habermann—Fidelity Management

Minimum Initial Investment
RRSP $500 Non-RRSP $1,000

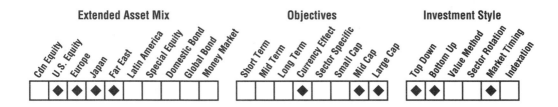

Extended Asset Mix — Objectives — Investment Style

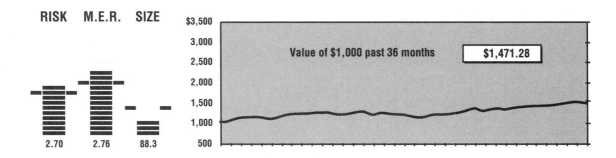

RISK 2.70 M.E.R. 2.76 SIZE 88.3

Value of $1,000 past 36 months — $1,471.28

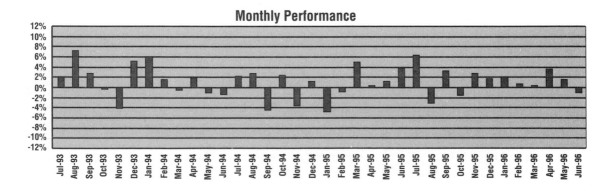

Monthly Performance

20/20 International Value Fund

CROFT–KIRZNER RATINGS:

Performance Rank	2	**Consistency Rank**	5
Sponsor	20/20 Funds Inc.	**Category**	International Equity
	690 Dorval Drive, Suite 700	**Portfolio Manager**	
	Oakville, Ontario, L6K 3X9	Charles Brandes—Brandes Investment Partners	
Phone	1-800-268-8690	**Minimum Initial Investment**	
Sales Fee	Load **RRSP Eligibility** Foreign	RRSP $500 Non-RRSP $500	

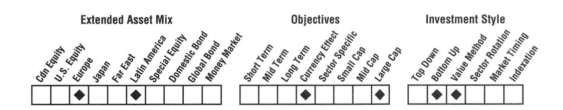

Extended Asset Mix — Cdn Equity, U.S. Equity, Europe ◆, Japan, Far East, Latin America ◆, Special Equity, Domestic Bond, Global Bond, Money Market

Objectives — Short Term, Mid Term, Long Term, Currency Effect ◆, Sector Specific, Small Cap, Mid Cap, Large Cap ◆

Investment Style — Top Down, Bottom Up ◆ ◆, Value Method, Sector Rotation, Market Timing, Indexation

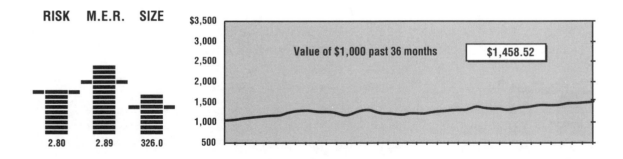

RISK 2.80 **M.E.R.** 2.89 **SIZE** 326.0

Value of $1,000 past 36 months $1,458.52

$3,500 / 3,000 / 2,500 / 2,000 / 1,500 / 1,000 / 500

Monthly Performance

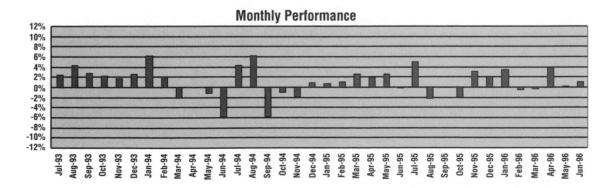

12% 10% 8% 6% 4% 2% 0% -2% -4% -6% -8% -10% -12%

Jul-93, Aug-93, Sep-93, Oct-93, Nov-93, Dec-93, Jan-94, Feb-94, Mar-94, Apr-94, May-94, Jun-94, Jul-94, Aug-94, Sep-94, Oct-94, Nov-94, Dec-94, Jan-95, Feb-95, Mar-95, Apr-95, May-95, Jun-95, Jul-95, Aug-95, Sep-95, Oct-95, Nov-95, Dec-95, Jan-96, Feb-96, Mar-96, Apr-96, May-96, Jun-96

Altamira Global Diversified Fund

CROFT–KIRZNER RATINGS:

Performance Rank	2	**Consistency Rank**	3

Sponsor	Altamira Investment Services Inc.	**Category** International Equity
	250 Bloor St. East, Suite 200	**Portfolio Manager**
	Toronto, Ontario, M4W 1E6	M-C Bernal & R. Rands–Wellington Management
Phone	1-800-263-2824	**Minimum Initial Investment**
Sales Fee	No-Load **RRSP Eligibility** Foreign	RRSP $1,000 Non-RRSP $1,000

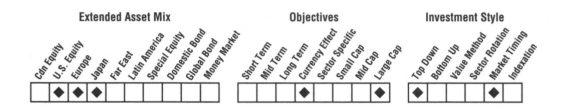

Extended Asset Mix — Cdn Equity, U.S. Equity ◆, Europe ◆, Japan ◆, Far East, Latin America, Special Equity, Domestic Bond, Global Bond, Money Market

Objectives — Short Term, Mid Term, Long Term ◆, Currency Effect, Sector Specific, Small Cap, Mid Cap, Large Cap ◆

Investment Style — Top Down ◆, Bottom Up, Value Method, Sector Rotation ◆, Market Timing, Indexation

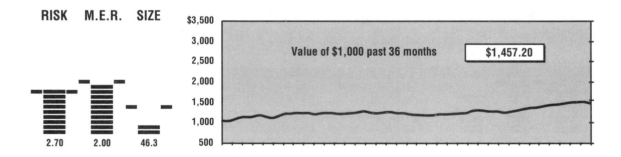

RISK 2.70   M.E.R. 2.00   SIZE 46.3

Value of $1,000 past 36 months $1,457.20

Monthly Performance

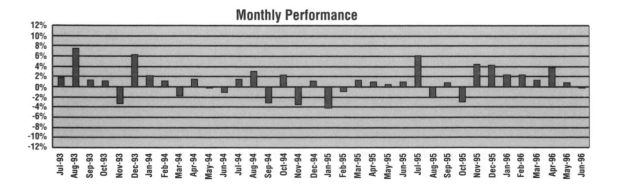

Royal Precious Metals

CROFT–KIRZNER RATINGS:

Performance Rank	1	**Consistency Rank**	5
Sponsor	Royal Mutual Funds Inc.	**Category**	Special Equity
	Royal Trust Tower, 77 King St. West, 5th Floor	**Portfolio Manager**	
	Toronto, Ontario, M5W 1P9	John Embry–Royal Bank Investment	
Phone	1-800-463-3863	**Minimum Initial Investment**	
Sales Fee	No-Load **RRSP Eligibility** Yes	RRSP $500 Non-RRSP $500	

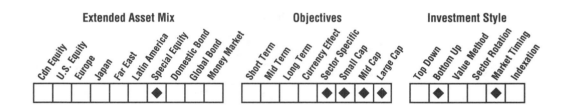

Extended Asset Mix — Objectives — Investment Style

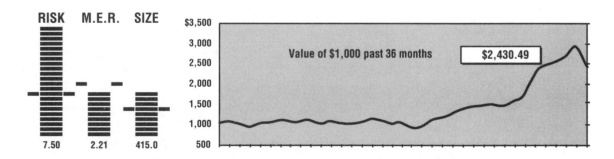

RISK 7.50 M.E.R. 2.21 SIZE 415.0

Value of $1,000 past 36 months — $2,430.49

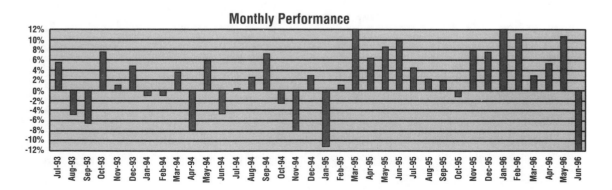

Monthly Performance

Prudential Precious Metals Fund

CROFT–KIRZNER RATINGS:

Performance Rank	1		**Consistency Rank**	5

Sponsor Prudential Family of Funds
200 Consillium Place, 6th Floor
Scarborough, Ontario, M1H 3E6

Phone 1-416-296-3287

Sales Fee Load   **RRSP Eligibility** Yes

Category Special Equity

Portfolio Manager
Martin Anstee—Prudential Fund Management

Minimum Initial Investment
RRSP $300   Non-RRSP $300

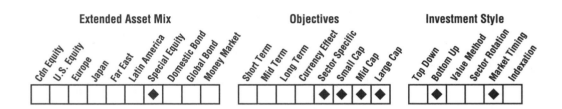

Extended Asset Mix — Objectives — Investment Style

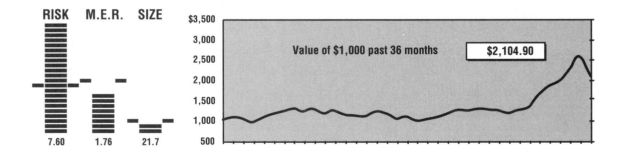

RISK 7.60   M.E.R. 1.76   SIZE 21.7

Value of $1,000 past 36 months $2,104.90

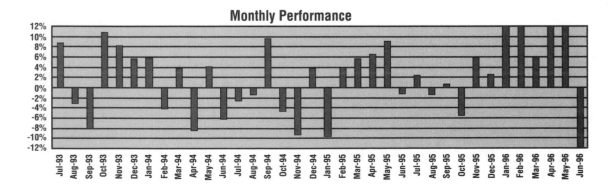

Monthly Performance

Prudential Natural Resource Fund

CROFT–KIRZNER RATINGS:

Performance Rank	1		**Consistency Rank**	5
Sponsor	Prudential Family of Funds		**Category**	Special Equity
	200 Consillium Place, 6th Floor		**Portfolio Manager**	
	Scarborough, Ontario, M1H 3E6		Martin Anstee—Prudential Fund Management	
Phone	1-416-296-3287		**Minimum Initial Investment**	
Sales Fee	Load **RRSP Eligibility** Yes		RRSP $300 Non-RRSP $300	

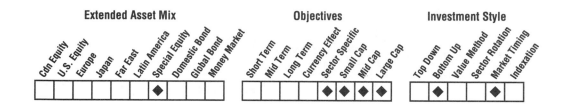

Extended Asset Mix — Cdn Equity, U.S. Equity, Europe, Japan, Far East, Latin America, Special Equity ◆, Domestic Bond, Global Bond, Money Market

Objectives — Short Term, Mid Term, Long Term, Currency Effect, Sector Specific ◆, Small Cap ◆, Mid Cap ◆, Large Cap ◆

Investment Style — Top Down, Bottom Up ◆, Value Method, Sector Rotation ◆, Market Timing, Indexation

RISK   M.E.R.   SIZE

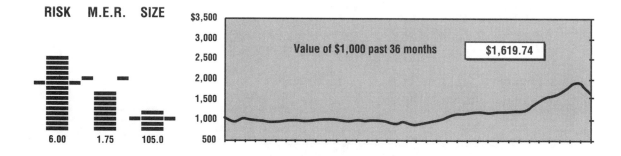

Value of $1,000 past 36 months $1,619.74

6.00   1.75   105.0

Monthly Performance

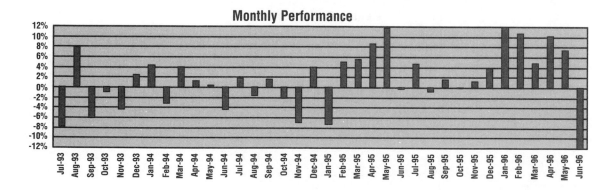

Dynamic Precious Metals Fund

CROFT–KIRZNER RATINGS:

Performance Rank	1		**Consistency Rank**	5

Sponsor Dynamic Mutual Funds
Scotia Plaza, 40 King St. West, 55th Floor
Toronto, Ontario, M5H 4A9

Phone 1-800-268-8186

Sales Fee Load **RRSP Eligibility** Yes

Category Special Equity

Portfolio Manager
Johnathan Goodman–Goodman and Co.

Minimum Initial Investment
RRSP $1,000 Non-RRSP $1,000

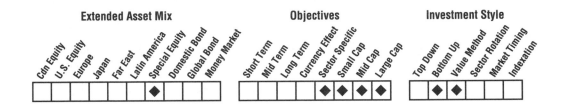

Extended Asset Mix

Cdn Equity, U.S. Equity, Europe, Japan, Far East, Latin America, Special Equity ◆, Domestic Bond, Global Bond, Money Market

Objectives

Short Term, Mid Term, Long Term, Currency Effect, Sector Specific ◆, Small Cap ◆, Mid Cap ◆, Large Cap ◆

Investment Style

Top Down ◆, Bottom Up ◆, Value Method, Sector Rotation, Market Timing, Indexation

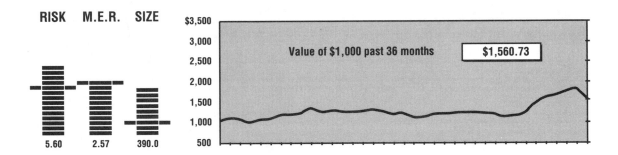

RISK 5.60 **M.E.R.** 2.57 **SIZE** 390.0

Value of $1,000 past 36 months $1,560.73

$3,500
3,000
2,500
2,000
1,500
1,000
500

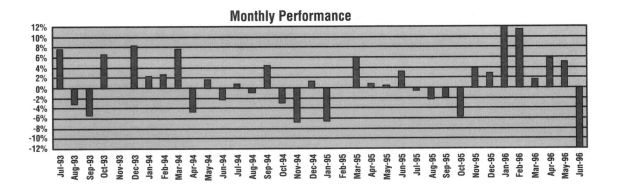

Monthly Performance

12%
10%
8%
6%
4%
2%
0%
-2%
-4%
-6%
-8%
-10%
-12%

Jul-93, Aug-93, Sep-93, Oct-93, Nov-93, Dec-93, Jan-94, Feb-94, Mar-94, Apr-94, May-94, Jun-94, Jul-94, Aug-94, Sep-94, Oct-94, Nov-94, Dec-94, Jan-95, Feb-95, Mar-95, Apr-95, May-95, Jun-95, Jul-95, Aug-95, Sep-95, Oct-95, Nov-95, Dec-95, Jan-96, Feb-96, Mar-96, Apr-96, May-96, Jun-96

Cambridge Resource Fund

CROFT–KIRZNER RATINGS:

Performance Rank	2		**Consistency Rank**	5

Sponsor Sagit Investment Management Ltd.   **Category**   Special Equity
789 West Pender St., Suite 900   **Portfolio Manager**
Vancouver, B.C., V6C 1H2   Raoul Tsakok–Sagit Investment Management Ltd.

Phone   1-800-663-1003   **Minimum Initial Investment**

Sales Fee   Load   **RRSP Eligibility**   Yes   RRSP $500   Non-RRSP $500

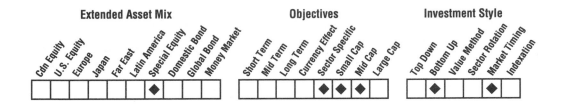

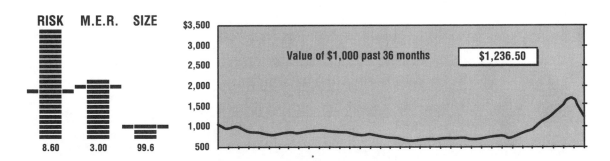

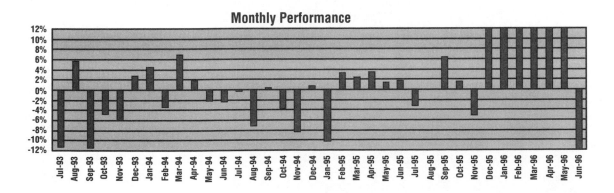

All-Canadian Resources Corporation

CROFT–KIRZNER RATINGS:

Performance Rank	3		**Consistency Rank**	5
Sponsor	All-Canadian Management Inc.		**Category**	Special Equity
	P.O. Box 7320		**Portfolio Manager**	
	Ancaster, Ontario, L9G 3N6		All-Canadian Management Team	
Phone	1-905-468-2025		**Minimum Initial Investment**	
Sales Fee	Load **RRSP Eligibility** Yes		RRSP $1,000 Non-RRSP $1,000	

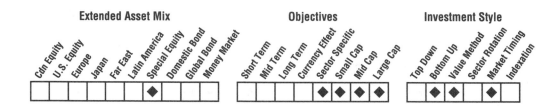

Extended Asset Mix — Objectives — Investment Style

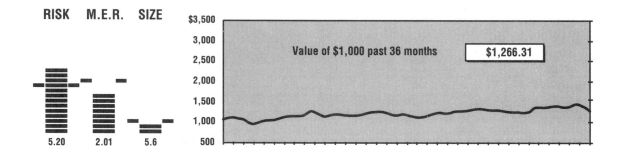

RISK M.E.R. SIZE

5.20   2.01   5.6

Value of $1,000 past 36 months $1,266.31

Monthly Performance

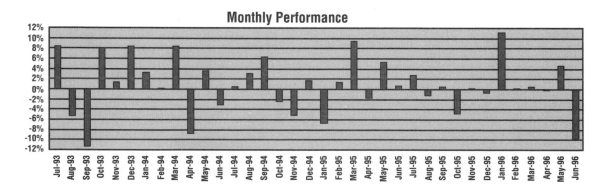

BPI Canadian Resource Fund Inc.

CROFT–KIRZNER RATINGS:

Performance Rank   3   **Consistency Rank**   5

Sponsor   BPI Capital Management Corporation   **Category**   Special Equity

161 Bay St., Suite 3900   **Portfolio Manager**

Toronto, Ontario, M5J 2S1   Frederick Dalley—BPI

Phone   1-800-263-2427   **Minimum Initial Investment**

Sales Fee   Load   **RRSP Eligibility**   Yes   RRSP $500   Non-RRSP $500

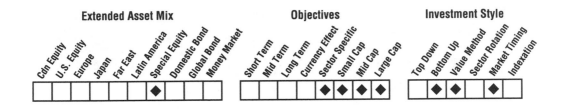

| Extended Asset Mix | Objectives | Investment Style |

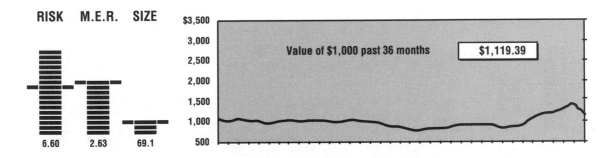

RISK	M.E.R.	SIZE
6.60	2.63	69.1

Value of $1,000 past 36 months $1,119.39

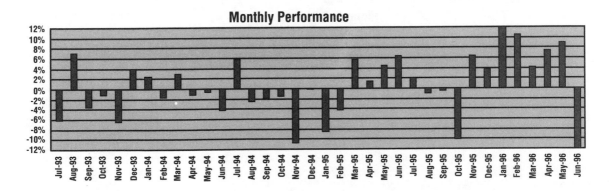

Monthly Performance

Admax Global Health Sciences Fund

CROFT–KIRZNER RATINGS:

Performance Rank	**N/A**	**Consistency Rank**	**N/A**
Sponsor	Admax Regent Group of Funds	**Category**	Special Equity
	150 King St. West, Suite 1802	**Portfolio Manager**	
	Toronto, Ontario, M5H 1J9	John Schroer–Invesco Trust Company	
Phone	1-800-463-3863	**Minimum Initial Investment**	
Sales Fee	Load **RRSP Eligibility** Foreign	RRSP $500 Non-RRSP $500	

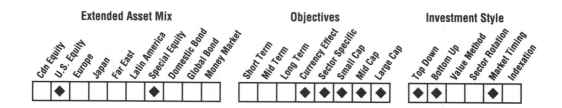

Extended Asset Mix — Objectives — Investment Style

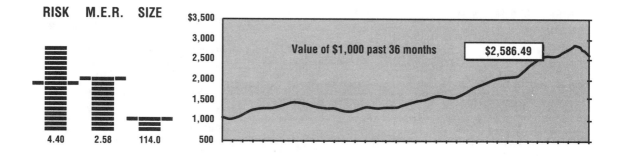

RISK   M.E.R.   SIZE
4.40   2.58   114.0

Value of $1,000 past 36 months $2,586.49

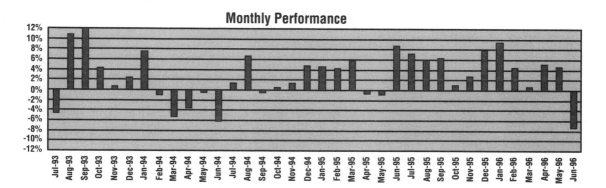

Monthly Performance

Green Line Science & Technology Fund

CROFT–KIRZNER RATINGS:

Performance Rank	**N/A**		**Consistency Rank**	**N/A**
Sponsor	TD Asset Management Inc.		**Category**	Special Equity
	TD Center, Box 100, TD Bank Tower, 20th Floor		**Portfolio Manager**	
	Toronto, Ontario, M5K 1G8		T. Rowe Price Investment Services	
Phone	1-800-268-8166		**Minimum Initial Investment**	
Sales Fee	No-Load **RRSP Eligibility** Foreign		RRSP $100 Non-RRSP $2,000	

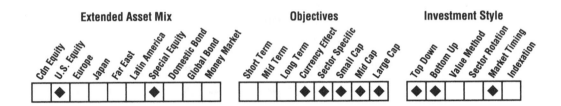

Extended Asset Mix · Objectives · Investment Style

RISK   M.E.R.   SIZE

N/A   2.64   155.1

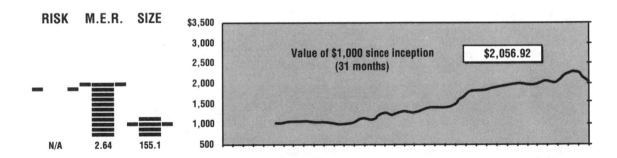

Value of $1,000 since inception
(31 months) $2,056.92

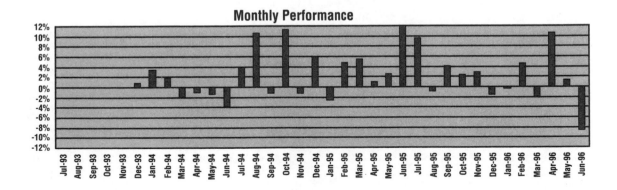

Monthly Performance

Universal World Precious Metals

CROFT–KIRZNER RATINGS:

Performance Rank	N/A	**Consistency Rank**	N/A

Sponsor MacKenzie Financial Corporation

150 Bloor St. West, Suite M111

Toronto, Ontario, M5S 3B5

Phone 1-800-387-0615

Sales Fee Load **RRSP Eligibility** Yes

Category Special Equity

Portfolio Manager

Fred Sturm–MacKenzie Financial

Minimum Initial Investment

RRSP $500 Non-RRSP $500

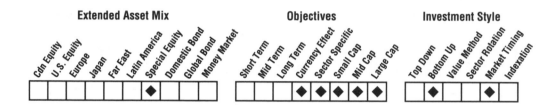

Extended Asset Mix: Cdn Equity, U.S. Equity, Europe, Japan, Far East, Latin America, Special Equity (◆), Domestic Bond, Global Bond, Money Market

Objectives: Short Term, Mid Term, Long Term, Currency Effect (◆), Sector Specific (◆), Small Cap (◆), Mid Cap (◆), Large Cap (◆)

Investment Style: Top Down (◆), Bottom Up, Value Method, Sector Rotation (◆), Market Timing, Indexation

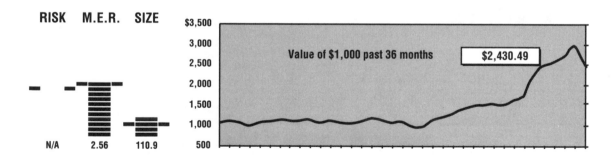

RISK **M.E.R.** **SIZE**

N/A 2.56 110.9

Value of $1,000 past 36 months $2,430.49

$3,500 / 3,000 / 2,500 / 2,000 / 1,500 / 1,000 / 500

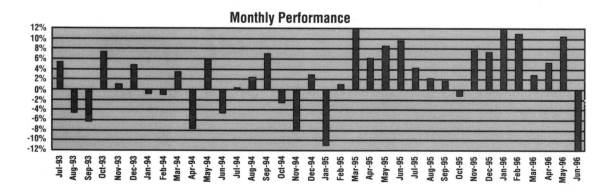

Monthly Performance

Jul-93, Aug-93, Sep-93, Oct-93, Nov-93, Dec-93, Jan-94, Feb-94, Mar-94, Apr-94, May-94, Jun-94, Jul-94, Aug-94, Sep-94, Oct-94, Nov-94, Dec-94, Jan-95, Feb-95, Mar-95, Apr-95, May-95, Jun-95, Jul-95, Aug-95, Sep-95, Oct-95, Nov-95, Dec-95, Jan-96, Feb-96, Mar-96, Apr-96, May-96, Jun-96

Dynamic Income Fund

CROFT–KIRZNER RATINGS:

Performance Rank	1	**Consistency Rank**	5
Sponsor	Dynamic Mutual Funds	**Category**	Canadian Bond
	Scotia Plaza, 40 King St. West, 55th Floor	**Portfolio Manager**	
	Toronto, Ontario, M5H 4A9	Norm Bengough–Goodman and Co.	
Phone	1-800-268-8186	**Minimum Initial Investment**	
Sales Fee	Load **RRSP Eligibility** Yes	RRSP $1,000 Non-RRSP $1,000	

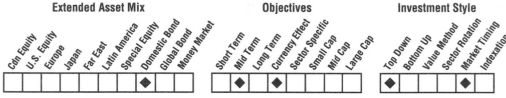

Extended Asset Mix: Cdn Equity, U.S. Equity, Europe, Japan, Far East, Latin America, Special Equity ◆, Domestic Bond, Global Bond, Money Market

Objectives: Short Term, Mid Term ◆, Long Term ◆, Currency Effect, Sector Specific, Small Cap, Mid Cap, Large Cap

Investment Style: Top Down ◆, Bottom Up, Value Method, Sector Rotation ◆, Market Timing, Indexation

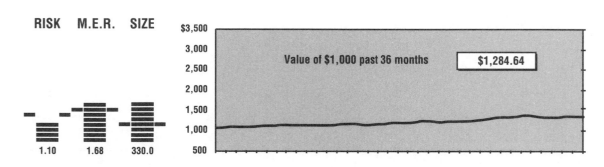

RISK   M.E.R.   SIZE

1.10   1.68   330.0

Value of $1,000 past 36 months $1,284.64

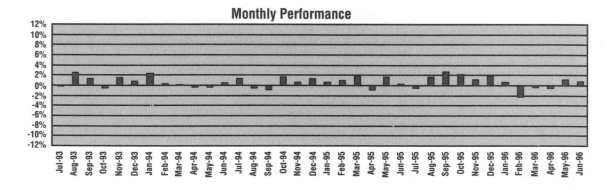

Monthly Performance

Bissett Bond Fund

CROFT–KIRZNER RATINGS:

Performance Rank	2		**Consistency Rank**	1
Sponsor	Bissett & Associates		**Category**	Canadian Bond
	500 4th Ave. SW, Suite 1120		**Portfolio Manager**	
	Calgary, Alberta, T2P 2V6		All-Canadian Management Team	
Phone	1-403-266-4664		**Minimum Initial Investment**	
Sales Fee	No-Load	**RRSP Eligibility** Yes	RRSP $5,000	Non-RRSP $5,000

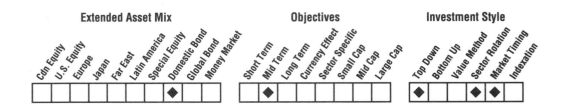

Extended Asset Mix: Cdn Equity, U.S. Equity, Europe, Japan, Far East, Latin America, Special Equity, Domestic Bond ◆, Global Bond, Money Market

Objectives: Short Term ◆, Mid Term, Long Term, Currency Effect, Sector Specific, Small Cap, Mid Cap, Large Cap

Investment Style: Top Down ◆, Bottom Up, Value Method, Sector Rotation ◆, Market Timing ◆, Indexation

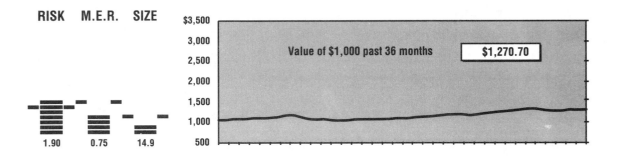

RISK 1.90 **M.E.R.** 0.75 **SIZE** 14.9

Value of $1,000 past 36 months $1,270.70

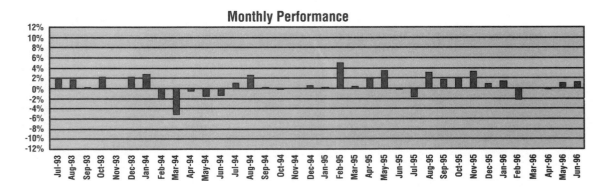

Monthly Performance

Talvest Income Fund

CROFT–KIRZNER RATINGS:

Performance Rank	2	**Consistency Rank**	2
Sponsor	Talvest Fund Management	**Category**	Canadian Bond
	The Exchange Tower, Suite 2200	**Portfolio Manager**	
	Toronto, Ontario, M5X 1B1	John W. Braive–T.A.L. Investment Counsel	
Phone	1-800-268-8258	**Minimum Initial Investment**	
Sales Fee Load	**RRSP Eligibility** Yes	RRSP $500 Non-RRSP $500	

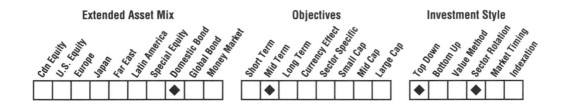

Extended Asset Mix — Objectives — Investment Style

RISK   M.E.R.   SIZE

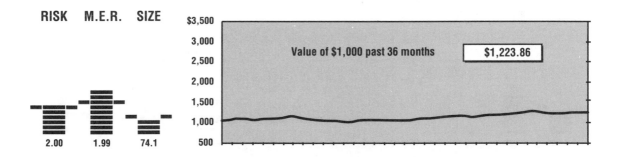

2.00   1.99   74.1

Value of $1,000 past 36 months $1,223.86

Monthly Performance

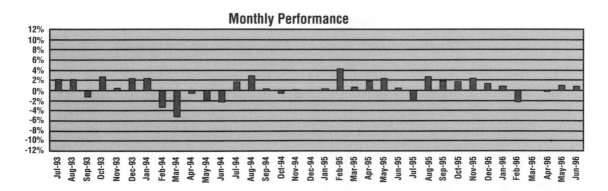

C. I. Canadian Bond Fund

CROFT–KIRZNER RATINGS:

Performance Rank	2	**Consistency Rank**	2

Sponsor	C. I. Mutual Funds
	151 Yonge St.
	Toronto, Ontario, M5C 2Y1
Phone	1-800-563-5181
Sales Fee	Load

Category Canadian Bond

Portfolio Manager
John Zechner–J. Zechner Associates

Minimum Initial Investment

RRSP Eligibility Foreign

RRSP $500   Non-RRSP $500

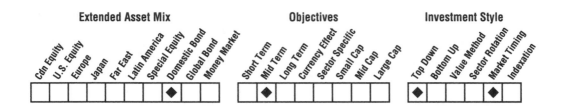

Extended Asset Mix — Cdn Equity, U.S. Equity, Europe, Japan, Far East, Latin America, Special Equity, Domestic Bond ◆, Global Bond, Money Market

Objectives — Short Term ◆, Mid Term, Long Term, Currency Effect, Sector Specific, Small Cap, Mid Cap, Large Cap

Investment Style — Top Down ◆, Bottom Up, Value Method, Sector Rotation ◆, Market Timing, Indexation

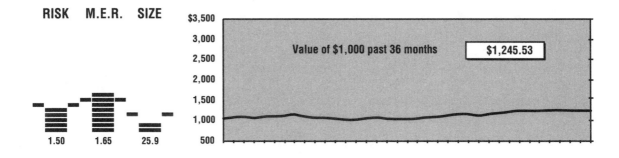

RISK **M.E.R.** **SIZE**

1.50   1.65   25.9

Value of $1,000 past 36 months $1,245.53

$3,500 / 3,000 / 2,500 / 2,000 / 1,500 / 1,000 / 500

Monthly Performance

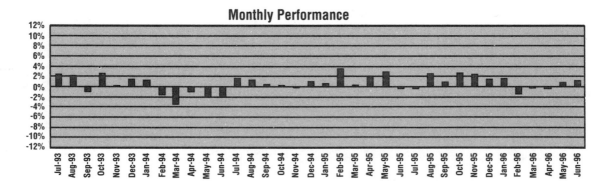

Jul-93 Aug-93 Sep-93 Oct-93 Nov-93 Dec-93 Jan-94 Feb-94 Mar-94 Apr-94 May-94 Jun-94 Jul-94 Aug-94 Sep-94 Oct-94 Nov-94 Dec-94 Jan-95 Feb-95 Mar-95 Apr-95 May-95 Jun-95 Jul-95 Aug-95 Sep-95 Oct-95 Nov-95 Dec-95 Jan-96 Feb-96 Mar-96 Apr-96 May-96 Jun-96

Royal Trust Bond

CROFT–KIRZNER RATINGS:

Performance Rank	3	**Consistency Rank**	1

Sponsor	Royal Mutual Funds Inc.
	Royal Trust Tower, 77 King St. West, 5th Floor
	Toronto, Ontario, M5W 1P9
Phone	1-800-463-3863
Sales Fee	No-Load

Category	Canadian Bond
Portfolio Manager	
Tom Czitron–Royal Bank Investment	
Minimum Initial Investment	

RRSP Eligibility Yes   RRSP $500   Non-RRSP $500

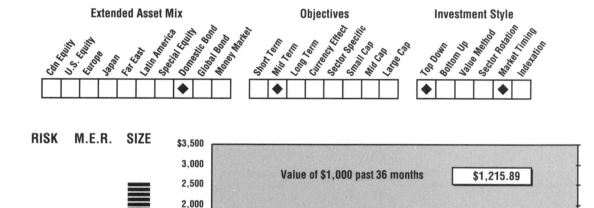

Extended Asset Mix — Cdn Equity, U.S. Equity, Europe, Japan, Far East, Latin America, Special Equity, Domestic Bond ◆, Global Bond, Money Market

Objectives — Short Term, Mid Term ◆, Long Term, Currency Effect, Sector Specific, Small Cap, Mid Cap, Large Cap

Investment Style — Top Down ◆, Bottom Up, Value Method, Sector Rotation ◆, Market Timing, Indexation

RISK 1.90 **M.E.R.** 1.39 **SIZE** 683.3

Value of $1,000 past 36 months $1,215.89

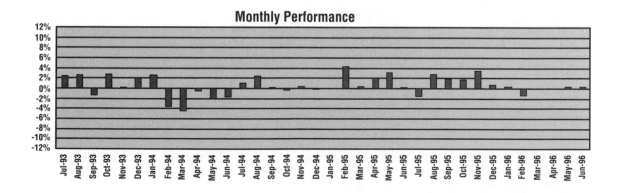

Monthly Performance

Scotia Excelsior Defensive Income Fund

CROFT–KIRZNER RATINGS:

Performance Rank	2	**Consistency Rank**	1
Sponsor	Scotia Securities Inc.	**Category**	Canadian Bond
	40 King St. West, 5th Floor	**Portfolio Manager**	
	Toronto, Ontario, M5H 1H1	Bruce Grantier–Scotia Investment Management	
Phone	1-800-268-9269	**Minimum Initial Investment**	
Sales Fee	No-Load **RRSP Eligibility** Yes	RRSP $500 Non-RRSP $500	

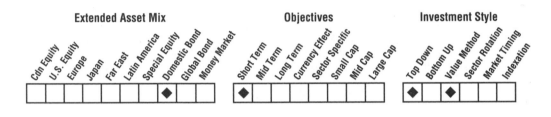

Extended Asset Mix — Cdn Equity, U.S. Equity, Europe, Japan, Far East, Latin America, Special Equity ◆, Domestic Bond, Global Bond, Money Market

Objectives — Short Term ◆, Mid Term, Long Term, Currency Effect, Sector Specific, Small Cap, Mid Cap, Large Cap

Investment Style — Top Down ◆, Bottom Up, Value Method ◆, Sector Rotation, Market Timing, Indexation

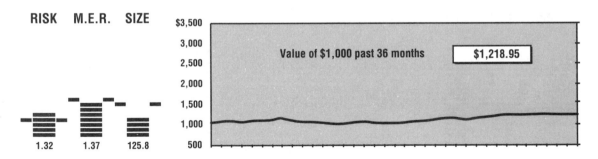

RISK   M.E.R.   SIZE

1.32   1.37   125.8

Value of $1,000 past 36 months $1,218.95

Monthly Performance

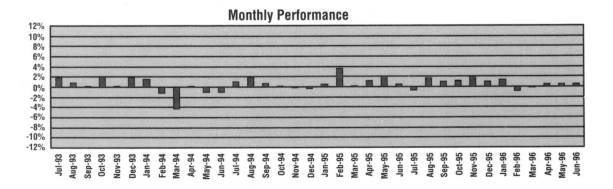

Hong Kong Bank Mortgage Fund

CROFT–KIRZNER RATINGS:

Performance Rank	1	**Consistency Rank**	2
Sponsor	Hongkong Bank of Canada Ltd.	**Category**	Canadian Mortgage
	885 West Georgia St., Suite 600	**Portfolio Manager**	
	Vancouver, B.C., V6C 3E9	Robert DeHart–M. K. Wong & Associates	
Phone	1-800-831-8888	**Minimum Initial Investment**	
Sales Fee	No-Load **RRSP Eligibility** Yes	RRSP $500 Non-RRSP $500	

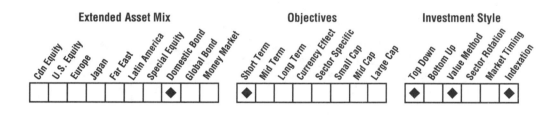

Extended Asset Mix / Objectives / Investment Style

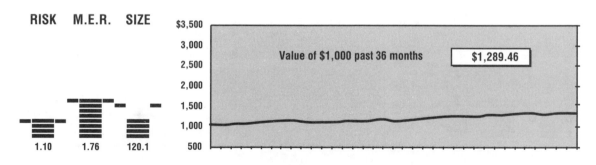

RISK   M.E.R.   SIZE

1.10   1.76   120.1

Value of $1,000 past 36 months $1,289.46

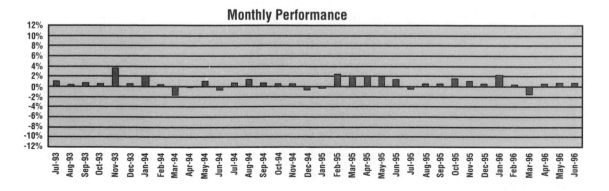

Monthly Performance

Canada Trust Everest Mortgage Fund

CROFT–KIRZNER RATINGS:

Performance Rank	1	**Consistency Rank**	2

Sponsor C. T. Fund Services Inc.
161 Bay St., 3rd Floor
Toronto, Ontario, M5J 2T2

Phone 1-800-386-3757

Sales Fee No-Load **RRSP Eligibility** Yes

Category Canadian Mortgage

Portfolio Manager
C. T. Investment Management

Minimum Initial Investment
RRSP None Non-RRSP $500

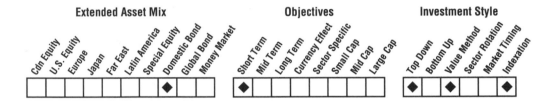

RISK M.E.R. SIZE

0.90 1.61 681.1

Value of $1,000 past 36 months $1,289.46

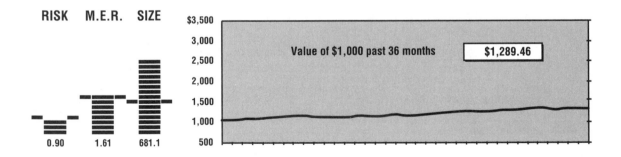

Monthly Performance

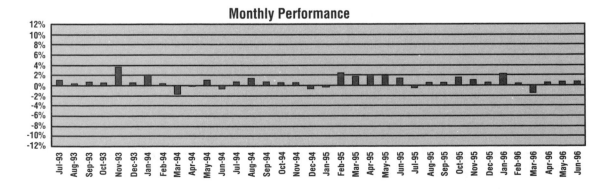

C. I. World Bond Fund

CROFT–KIRZNER RATINGS:

Performance Rank	3		**Consistency Rank**	4
Sponsor	C. I. Mutual Funds		**Category**	Global Bond
	151 Yonge St.		**Portfolio Manager**	
	Toronto, Ontario, M5C 2Y1		Gregg Diliberto—BEA Associates	
Phone	1-800-563-5181		**Minimum Initial Investment**	
Sales Fee	Load	**RRSP Eligibility** Foreign	RRSP $500	Non-RRSP $500

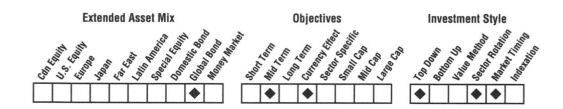

Extended Asset Mix — Objectives — Investment Style

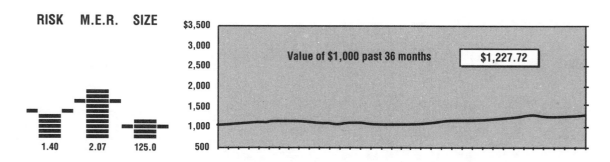

RISK	M.E.R.	SIZE
1.40	2.07	125.0

Value of $1,000 past 36 months $1,227.72

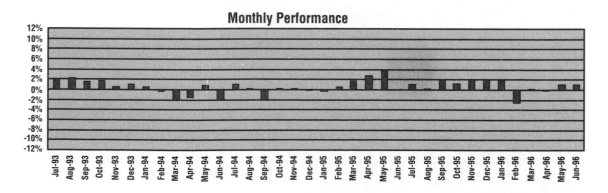

Monthly Performance

Dynamic Global Bond Fund

CROFT–KIRZNER RATINGS:

Performance Rank	3	**Consistency Rank**	4

Sponsor	Dynamic Mutual Funds	**Category**	Global Bond
	Scotia Plaza, 40 King St. West, 55th Floor	**Portfolio Manager**	
	Toronto, Ontario, M5H 4A9	Norm Bengough–Goodman and Co.	
Phone	1-800-268-8186	**Minimum Initial Investment**	
Sales Fee	Load **RRSP Eligibility** Yes	RRSP $1,000 Non-RRSP $1,000	

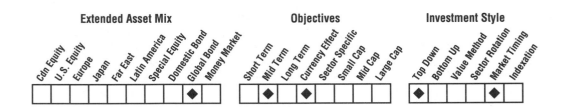

Extended Asset Mix: Cdn Equity, U.S. Equity, Europe, Japan, Far East, Latin America, Special Equity, Domestic Bond ◆ Global Bond, Money Market

Objectives: Short Term ◆ Mid Term, Long Term ◆ Currency Effect, Sector Specific, Small Cap, Mid Cap, Large Cap

Investment Style: Top Down ◆ Bottom Up, Value Method, Sector Rotation ◆ Market Timing, Indexation

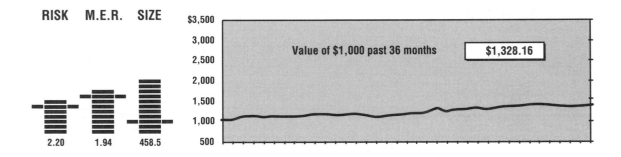

RISK	M.E.R.	SIZE
2.20	1.94	458.5

Value of $1,000 past 36 months $1,328.16

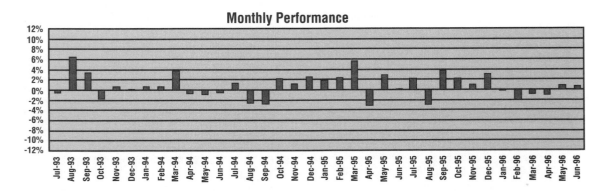

Monthly Performance

Templeton Global Bond Fund

CROFT–KIRZNER RATINGS:

Performance Rank	3	**Consistency Rank**	4
Sponsor	Templeton Management Limited	**Category**	Global Bond
	4 King St. West, Box 4070, Stn A	**Portfolio Manager**	
	Toronto, Ontario, M5W 1M3	Neil S. Devlin–Templeton Management Limited	
Phone	1-800-387-0830	**Minimum Initial Investment**	
Sales Fee	Load **RRSP Eligibility** Foreign	RRSP $500 Non-RRSP $500	

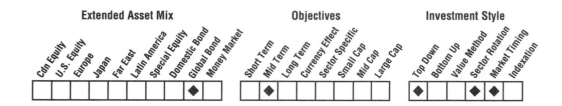

Extended Asset Mix — Objectives — Investment Style

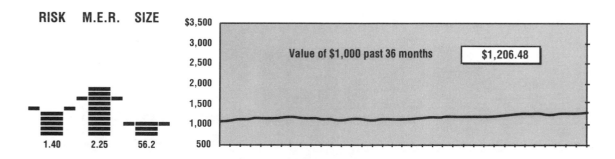

RISK   M.E.R.   SIZE

1.40   2.25   56.2

Value of $1,000 past 36 months $1,206.48

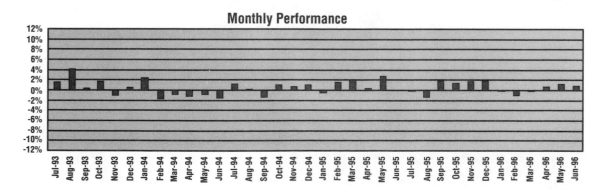

Monthly Performance

AGF Growth and Income Fund

CROFT–KIRZNER RATINGS:

Performance Rank	**N/A**	**Consistency Rank**	**N/A**
Sponsor	AGF Management Ltd.	**Category**	Canadian Balanced
	TD Bank Tower, 31st Floor, Box 50	**Portfolio Manager**	
	Toronto, Ontario, M5K 1E9	Clive Coombs & Stephen Uzielli–AGF	
Phone	1-800-268-8583	**Minimum Initial Investment**	
Sales Fee	Load **RRSP Eligibility** Yes	RRSP $1,000 Non-RRSP $1,000	

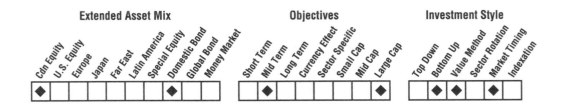

Extended Asset Mix · Objectives · Investment Style

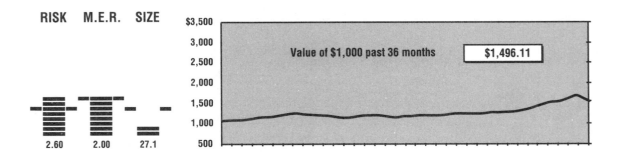

RISK	M.E.R.	SIZE
2.60	2.00	27.1

Value of $1,000 past 36 months $1,496.11

Monthly Performance

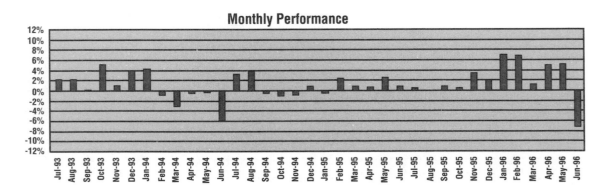

Elliott & Page Balanced Fund

CROFT–KIRZNER RATINGS:

Performance Rank	**N/A**	**Consistency Rank**	**N/A**
Sponsor	Elliott & Page Limited	**Category**	Canadian Balanced
	120 Adelaide St. West, Suite 1120	**Portfolio Manager**	
	Toronto, Ontario, M5H 1V1	Nereo Piticco—Elliott & Page	
Phone	1-800-363-6647	**Minimum Initial Investment**	
Sales Fee Load	**RRSP Eligibility** Yes	RRSP $500	Non-RRSP $500

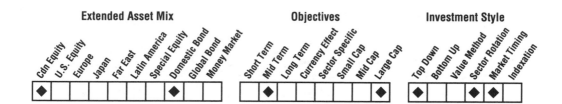

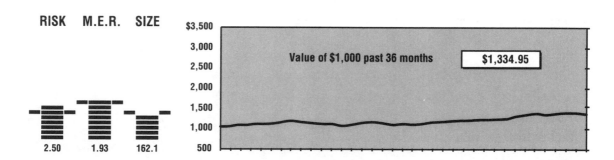

RISK   M.E.R.   SIZE

2.50   1.93   162.1

Value of $1,000 past 36 months $1,334.95

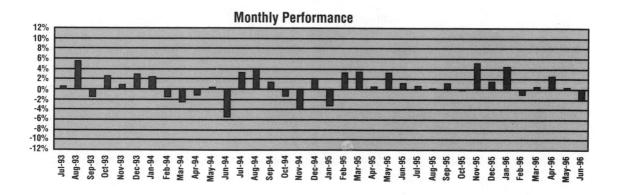

Monthly Performance

Sceptre Balanced Fund

CROFT–KIRZNER RATINGS:

Performance Rank	N/A	**Consistency Rank**	N/A
Sponsor	Sceptre Investment Counsel Limited	**Category**	Canadian Balanced
	26 Wellington St. East, Suite 1200	**Portfolio Manager**	
	Toronto, Ontario, M5E 1W4	Lyle Stein–Sceptre Investment Counsel	
Phone	1-800-265-1888	**Minimum Initial Investment**	
Sales Fee	Load **RRSP Eligibility** Yes	RRSP $5,000 Non-RRSP $5,000	

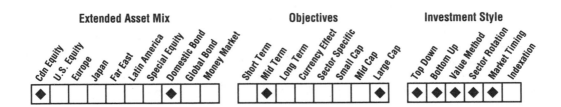

Extended Asset Mix — Objectives — Investment Style

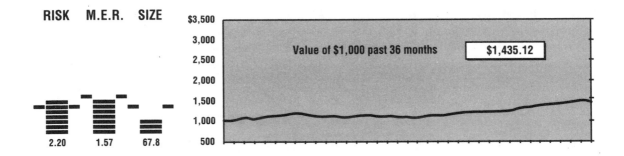

RISK	M.E.R.	SIZE
2.20	1.57	67.8

Value of $1,000 past 36 months $1,435.12

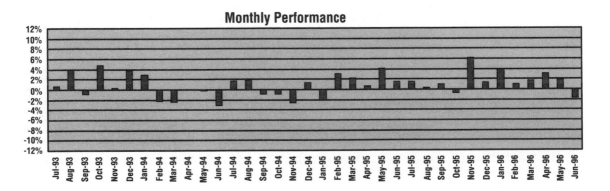

Monthly Performance

Universal World Balanced RRSP Fund

CROFT–KIRZNER RATINGS:

Performance Rank	N/A	**Consistency Rank**	N/A
Sponsor	MacKenzie Financial Corporation	**Category**	International (Global) Balanced
	150 Bloor St. West, Suite M111	**Portfolio Manager**	
	Toronto, Ontario, M5S 3B5	Lyle Stein–Sceptre Investment Counsel	
Phone	1-800-387-0615	**Minimum Initial Investment**	
Sales Fee Load	**RRSP Eligibility** Yes	RRSP $500	Non-RRSP $500

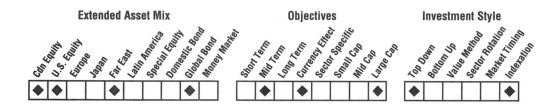

Extended Asset Mix — Cdn Equity, U.S. Equity, Europe, Japan, Far East, Latin America, Special Equity, Domestic Bond, Global Bond, Money Market

Objectives — Short Term, Mid Term, Long Term, Currency Effect, Sector Specific, Small Cap, Mid Cap, Large Cap

Investment Style — Top Down, Bottom Up, Value Method, Sector Rotation, Market Timing, Indexation

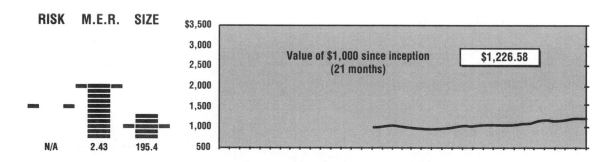

RISK   M.E.R.   SIZE

N/A   2.43   195.4

Value of $1,000 since inception
(21 months) $1,226.58

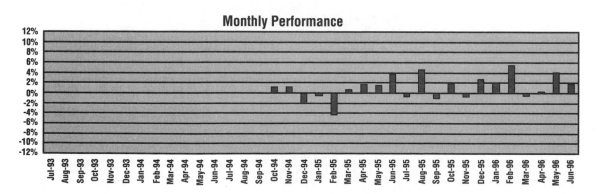

Monthly Performance

Dynamic Global Partners Fund

CROFT–KIRZNER RATINGS:

Performance Rank	N/A	**Consistency Rank**	N/A

Sponsor Dynamic Mutual Funds
Scotia Plaza, 40 King St. West, 55th Floor
Toronto, Ontario, M5H 4A9

Category International (Global) Balanced
Portfolio Manager
Ned Goonman & Norm Bengough

Phone 1-800-268-8186

Minimum Initial Investment

Sales Fee Load **RRSP Eligibility** Yes

RRSP $1,000   Non-RRSP $1,000

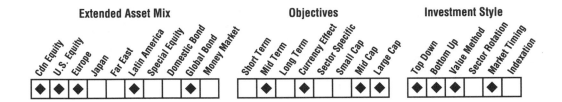

Extended Asset Mix · Objectives · Investment Style

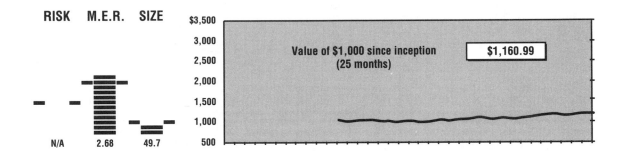

RISK   M.E.R.   SIZE

N/A   2.68   49.7

Value of $1,000 since inception (25 months) $1,160.99

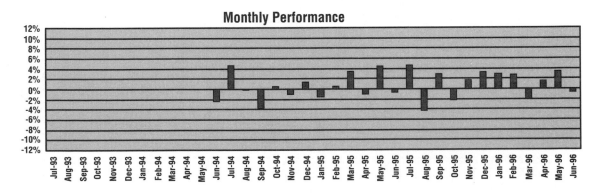

Monthly Performance

AGF FAMILY OF FUNDS

Column groups: **Extended Asset Mix** (Cdn Equity → Money Market), **Objectives** (Short Term → Large Cap), **Investment Style** (Top Down → Indexation).

Fund Name	Cdn Equity	U.S. Equity	Europe	Japan	Far East	Latin America	Special Equity	Domestic Bond	Global Bond	Money Market	Short Term	Mid Term	Long Term	Currency Effect	Sector Specific	Small Cap	Mid Cap	Large Cap	Top Down	Bottom Up	Value Method	Sector Rotation	Market Timing	Indexation
A.G.F. American Growth		◆											◆					◆			◆			
A.G.F. Asian Growth					◆								◆					◆	◆	◆				
A.G.F. China Focus					◆								◆					◆	◆	◆	◆			
A.G.F. European Growth			◆										◆					◆	◆	◆				
A.G.F. Germany			◆										◆					◆	◆		◆			
A.G.F. Japan				◆									◆					◆	◆	◆	◆			
A.G.F. World Equity		◆	◆	◆									◆					◆	◆		◆	◆		
A.G.F. Strategic Income								◆			◆								◆			◆		
A.G.F. US$ Money Market										◆	◆												◆	
A.G.F. US Income									◆		◆								◆			◆		
A.G.F. Canadian Bond								◆				◆							◆			◆		
A.G.F. Canadian Equity	◆												◆					◆	◆	◆	◆			
A.G.F. Canadian Resources							◆							◆	◆		◆		◆			◆		
A.G.F. Global Government Bond									◆		◆		◆						◆			◆		
A.G.F. Growth and Income	◆								◆		◆		◆						◆	◆	◆			
A.G.F. Growth Equity	◆												◆			◆			◆	◆				
A.G.F. High Income								◆			◆								◆				◆	
A.G.F. International Short Term								◆			◆								◆					
A.G.F. Money Market										◆	◆								◆				◆	
A.G.F. Special Fund Ltd.		◆											◆	◆				◆	◆	◆				

ALTAMIRA FAMILY OF FUNDS

Fund Name	Cdn Equity	U.S. Equity	Europe	Japan	Far East	Latin America	Special Equity	Domestic Bond	Global Bond	Money Market	Short Term	Mid Term	Long Term	Currency Effect	Sector Specific	Small Cap	Mid Cap	Large Cap	Top Down	Bottom Up	Value Method	Sector Rotation	Market Timing	Indexation
					Extended Asset Mix								Objectives								Investment Style			
Altafund Investment Corp.	◆																◆		◆		◆	◆		
Altamira Asia Pacific Fund				◆	◆								◆						◆			◆		
Altamira Balanced Fund	◆							◆			◆							◆	◆		◆	◆		
Altamira Bond Fund								◆					◆						◆			◆		
Altamira Capital Growth Fund	◆																	◆	◆		◆	◆		
Altamira Dividend Fund Inc.	◆							◆			◆							◆		◆		◆		
Altamira Equity Fund	◆																◆	◆	◆		◆	◆		
Altamira European Equity Fund			◆											◆			◆	◆	◆			◆		
Altamira Global Bond Fund									◆		◆			◆					◆			◆		
Altamira Global Discovery Fund			◆		◆			◆						◆			◆	◆	◆			◆		
Altamira Global Diversified Fund		◆	◆	◆							◆						◆	◆	◆		◆	◆		
Altamira Growth & Income Fund	◆							◆			◆						◆	◆	◆			◆		
Altamira Income Fund								◆				◆							◆			◆		
Altamira Japanese Opportunity				◆												◆				◆		◆		
Altamira North American Recovery	◆	◆													◆	◆	◆	◆		◆		◆		
Altamira Precious & Strategic Metal							◆									◆	◆	◆		◆		◆		
Altamira Resource Fund							◆								◆	◆	◆	◆		◆	◆	◆		
Altamira Science & Technology Fund							◆							◆		◆	◆	◆		◆		◆		
Altamira Select American		◆												◆		◆				◆		◆		

Altamira Short Term Global Inc

Altamira Short Term Government Bond

Altamira Special High Yield Bond

Altamira Special Growth Fund

Altamira U.S. Larger Company

BPI FAMILY of FUNDS

Fund Name	Cdn Equity	U.S. Equity	Europe	Japan	Far East	Latin America	Special Equity	Domestic Bond	Global Bond	Money Market	Short Term	Mid Term	Long Term	Currency Effect	Sector Specific	Small Cap	Mid Cap	Large Cap	Top Down	Bottom Up	Value Method	Sector Rotation	Market Timing	Indexation
	Extended Asset Mix										**Objectives**								**Investment Style**					
BPI American Equity Value Fund		◆											◆					◆	◆	◆	◆			
BPI American Small Companies		◆											◆			◆				◆	◆			
BPI Canadian Balanced Fund	◆							◆				◆						◆	◆	◆	◆			
BPI Canadian Bond Fund								◆				◆							◆			◆		
BPI Canadian Equity Value Fund	◆												◆					◆		◆	◆			
BPI Canadian Opportunities RSP	◆												◆			◆	◆			◆	◆			
BPI Canadian Resource Fund Inc.							◆						◆				◆	◆		◆	◆			
BPI Canadian Small Companies	◆												◆			◆				◆	◆			
BPI Global Balanced RSP Fund	◆								◆			◆	◆					◆		◆	◆			
BPI Global Equity Fund		◆	◆	◆									◆					◆		◆	◆			
BPI Global Opportunities Fund		◆	◆	◆									◆			◆	◆			◆	◆			
BPI Global RSP Bond Fund									◆				◆						◆			◆		
BPI Emerging Markets Fund			◆		◆	◆							◆					◆		◆	◆			
BPI Global Small Companies Fund		◆	◆	◆									◆			◆				◆	◆			
BPI Income Fund								◆				◆						◆		◆	◆			
BPI International Equity Fund			◆	◆									◆					◆		◆	◆			
BPI North American Balanced RSP	◆							◆				◆						◆		◆	◆	◆		
BPI T-Bill Fund										◆	◆													◆

C.I. FAMILY of FUNDS

Fund Name	Extended Asset Mix										Objectives								Investment Style					
	Cdn Equity	U.S. Equity	Europe	Japan	Far East	Latin America	Special Equity	Domestic Bond	Global Bond	Money Market	Short Term	Mid Term	Long Term	Currency Effect	Sector Specific	Small Cap	Mid Cap	Large Cap	Top Down	Bottom Up	Value Method	Sector Rotation	Market Timing	Indexation
C.I. Global		◆	◆	◆		◆								◆				◆	◆	◆				
C.I. Global Equity (RRSP)		◆	◆	◆		◆								◆				◆	◆					◆
C.I. Emerging Markets					◆	◆								◆			◆	◆	◆	◆				
C.I. Latin America						◆								◆			◆	◆	◆	◆				
C.I. World Bond									◆		◆			◆					◆				◆	
C.I. Global Bond (RRSP)									◆			◆		◆					◆					◆
C.I. New World Income									◆			◆		◆					◆			◆		
C.I. American		◆												◆			◆	◆		◆		◆		
C.I. International Balanced		◆	◆						◆			◆		◆				◆	◆	◆		◆		
C.I. International Balanced (RRSP)		◆	◆						◆			◆		◆				◆	◆					◆
C.I. Pacific					◆									◆				◆	◆	◆				
C.I. Emerging Asian					◆									◆		◆			◆	◆				
C.I. Canadian Growth	◆																	◆		◆	◆			
C.I. Canadian Balanced	◆							◆			◆						◆	◆		◆	◆	◆		
C.I. Canadian Income								◆			◆								◆			◆		
C.I. Canadian Bond								◆			◆								◆			◆		
C.I. Canadian Money Market										◆	◆													◆
C.I. U.S. Money Market										◆	◆			◆										◆
C.I. European Fund			◆											◆			◆	◆	◆	◆				

DYNAMIC FAMILY OF FUNDS

Fund Name	Cdn Equity	U.S. Equity	Europe	Japan	Far East	Latin America	Special Equity	Domestic Bond	Global Bond	Money Market	Short Term	Mid Term	Long Term	Currency Effect	Sector Specific	Small Cap	Mid Cap	Large Cap	Top Down	Bottom Up	Value Method	Sector Rotation	Market Timing	Indexation
	Extended Asset Mix										Objectives								Investment Style					
Dynamic American Fund		◆											◆					◆	◆	◆				
Dynamic Canadian Growth Fund	◆																◆	◆	◆	◆				
Dynamic Dividend Fund							◆					◆						◆	◆	◆				
Dynamic Dividend Growth Fund	◆						◆											◆	◆	◆				
Dynamic Europe Fund			◆										◆					◆	◆	◆				
Dynamic Far East Fund					◆								◆					◆	◆	◆				
Dynamic Fund of Canada	◆																	◆	◆	◆				
Dynamic Global Bond Fund									◆		◆		◆	◆					◆			◆		
Dynamic Global Green Fund	◆	◆	◆			◆							◆	◆			◆	◆	◆	◆				
Dynamic Global Partners Fund	◆	◆	◆			◆			◆		◆		◆	◆			◆	◆	◆	◆		◆		
Dynamic Global Resource Fund	◆	◆	◆				◆						◆	◆					◆	◆				
Dynamic Government Income Fund								◆			◆								◆	◆				
Dynamic Income Fund								◆				◆	◆					◆	◆	◆		◆		
Dynamic International Fund	◆	◆	◆										◆						◆	◆				
Dynamic Money Market Fund										◆	◆								◆				◆	
Dynamic Partners Fund	◆						◆					◆					◆		◆		◆			
Dynamic Precious Metals Fund							◆								◆	◆	◆	◆	◆	◆				
Dynamic Real Estate Fund							◆								◆		◆	◆	◆	◆				

ELLIOTT & PAGE FAMILY OF FUNDS

Fund Name	Extended Asset Mix										Objectives								Investment Style					
	Can Equity	U.S. Equity	Europe	Japan	Far East	Latin America	Special Equity	Domestic Bond	Global Bond	Money Market	Short Term	Mid Term	Long Term	Currency Effect	Sector Specific	Small Cap	Mid Cap	Large Cap	Top Down	Bottom Up	Value Method	Sector Rotation	Market Timing	Indexation
Elliott & Page Equity	◆																	◆	◆		◆			
Elliott & Page Balanced	◆							◆				◆						◆	◆			◆		
Elliott & Page Bond								◆				◆							◆			◆		
Elliott & Page Money Market										◆	◆												◆	
Elliott & Page T-Bill										◆	◆												◆	
Elliott & Page American Growth		◆											◆			◆	◆	◆	◆	◆				
Elliott & Page Global Balanced		◆		◆					◆			◆	◆			◆	◆	◆	◆	◆		◆		
Elliott & Page Global Equity		◆		◆									◆					◆	◆			◆		
Elliott & Page Global Bond									◆			◆	◆						◆			◆		
Elliott & Page Emerging Markets			◆		◆								◆			◆	◆	◆	◆			◆		
Elliott & Page Asian Growth					◆								◆			◆	◆	◆	◆			◆		

FIDELITY FAMILY OF FUNDS

Fund Name	\<Extended Asset Mix\> Cdn Equity	U.S. Equity	Europe	Japan	Far East	Latin America	Special Equity	Domestic Bond	Global Bond	Money Market	\<Objectives\> Short Term	Mid Term	Long Term	Currency Effect	Sector Specific	Small Cap	Mid Cap	Large Cap	\<Investment Style\> Top Down	Bottom Up	Value Method	Sector Rotation	Market Timing	Indexation
Fidelity Asset Manager	♦	♦							♦		♦							♦	♦			♦		
Fidelity Canadian Bond								♦			♦									♦	♦			
Fidelity Canadian Income								♦			♦									♦	♦			
Fidelity Capital Builder	♦																	♦		♦				
Fidelity Canadian Asset Allocation	♦							♦			♦							♦	♦	♦		♦		
Fidelity Canadian Growth	♦														♦	♦				♦	♦			
Fidelity Canadian Short Term										♦													♦	
Fidelity Emerging Markets Bond									♦			♦								♦	♦	♦		
Fidelity Emerging Markets Portfolio					♦	♦							♦				♦	♦	♦	♦		♦		
Fidelity European Growth			♦										♦				♦	♦		♦		♦		
Fidelity Far East Fund					♦								♦				♦	♦		♦		♦		
Fidelity Growth America		♦											♦				♦	♦	♦	♦		♦		
Fidelity International Portfolio		♦		♦									♦				♦	♦	♦	♦		♦		
Fidelity Japanese Growth				♦									♦				♦	♦		♦		♦		
Fidelity Latin America Growth						♦							♦					♦		♦		♦		
Fidelity North America Income								♦			♦		♦							♦	♦	♦		
Fidelity RRSP Global Bond								♦					♦							♦		♦		
Fidelity Small Cap America		♦											♦			♦				♦		♦		
Fidelity U.S. Money Market									♦		♦		♦											♦

G.T. GLOBAL FAMILY of FUNDS

Extended Asset Mix

Fund Name	Cdn Equity	U.S. Equity	Europe	Japan	Far East	Latin America	Special Equity	Domestic Bond	Global Bond	Money Market
G.T. Canada Growth Class	◆									
G.T. Global American Growth Class										
G.T. Global Growth & Income Class	◆	◆	◆					◆		
G.T. Global Infrastructure Class		◆					◆			
G.T. Latin America Growth Class						◆				
G.T. Global Natural Resource Class							◆			
G.T. Global Pacific Growth Class				◆	◆					
G.T. Telecommunications Class							◆			
G.T. Global World Bond Fund Class									◆	
G.T. Canada Income Class								◆		
G.T. Global Health Care Class							◆			
G.T. Short Term Income Class										◆

Objectives

Fund Name	Short Term	Mid Term	Long Term	Currency Effect	Sector Specific	Small Cap	Mid Cap	Large Cap
G.T. Canada Growth Class							◆	◆
G.T. Global American Growth Class			◆			◆	◆	
G.T. Global Growth & Income Class	◆		◆					◆
G.T. Global Infrastructure Class			◆				◆	◆
G.T. Latin America Growth Class			◆					◆
G.T. Global Natural Resource Class			◆				◆	◆
G.T. Global Pacific Growth Class			◆		◆	◆		
G.T. Telecommunications Class			◆					
G.T. Global World Bond Fund Class	◆		◆					
G.T. Canada Income Class		◆						
G.T. Global Health Care Class			◆		◆	◆	◆	◆
G.T. Short Term Income Class	◆							

Investment Style

Fund Name	Top Down	Bottom Up	Value Method	Sector Rotation	Market Timing	Indexation
G.T. Canada Growth Class		◆	◆			
G.T. Global American Growth Class		◆	◆			
G.T. Global Growth & Income Class	◆		◆			
G.T. Global Infrastructure Class		◆	◆			
G.T. Latin America Growth Class		◆	◆			
G.T. Global Natural Resource Class	◆		◆			
G.T. Global Pacific Growth Class	◆		◆			
G.T. Telecommunications Class		◆	◆			
G.T. Global World Bond Fund Class	◆		◆			
G.T. Canada Income Class	◆		◆			
G.T. Global Health Care Class	◆		◆			
G.T. Short Term Income Class	◆				◆	

GLOBAL STRATEGY FAMILY OF FUNDS

Fund Name	Cdn Equity	U.S. Equity	Europe	Japan	Far East	Latin America	Special Equity	Domestic Bond	Global Bond	Money Market	Short Term	Mid Term	Long Term	Currency Effect	Sector Specific	Small Cap	Mid Cap	Large Cap	Top Down	Bottom Up	Value Method	Sector Rotation	Market Timing	Indexation
Global Strategy Asia					◆								◆						◆		◆			
Global Strategy Bond								◆				◆							◆			◆		
Global Strategy Canada Growth	◆																◆	◆	◆		◆			
Global Strategy Canada Small Cap	◆												◆			◆			◆	◆				
Global Strategy Diversified Foreign Bond									◆			◆	◆						◆			◆		
Global Strategy Diversified Japan Plus		◆	◆	◆									◆					◆	◆				◆	
Global Strategy Diversified World Equity		◆	◆	◆									◆					◆	◆				◆	
Global Strategy Diversified Gold Plus							◆							◆	◆				◆	◆				
Global Strategy Diversified Growth		◆	◆	◆									◆					◆	◆			◆		
Global Strategy Diversified Asia					◆								◆				◆		◆				◆	
Global Strategy Diversified Bond								◆				◆							◆			◆		
Global Strategy Diversified Europe			◆										◆				◆	◆	◆		◆		◆	
Global Strategy Diversified Latin America						◆							◆						◆	◆				
Global Strategy Diversified Short Term Income										◆	◆								◆				◆	
Global Strategy Diversified Americas		◆				◆							◆				◆	◆	◆	◆				
Global Strategy Europe Plus			◆										◆						◆		◆			
Global Strategy Foreign Bond									◆			◆							◆			◆		
Global Strategy Income Plus	◆								◆			◆							◆			◆		
Global Strategy Japan				◆									◆				◆		◆			◆		

Column groups: **Extended Asset Mix** (Cdn Equity, U.S. Equity, Europe, Japan, Far East, Latin America, Special Equity, Domestic Bond, Global Bond, Money Market); **Objectives** (Short Term, Mid Term, Long Term, Currency Effect, Sector Specific, Small Cap, Mid Cap, Large Cap); **Investment Style** (Top Down, Bottom Up, Value Method, Sector Rotation, Market Timing, Indexation).

Global Strategy Latin America

Global Strategy Real Estate

Global Strategy T-Bill Savings

Global Strategy U.S. Equity

Global Strategy U.S. Growth

Global Strategy U.S. Savings

Global Strategy World Balanced

Global Strategy World Bond

Global Strategy World Equity

Global Strategy Emerging Markets

INVESTORS GROUP FAMILY of FUNDS

Fund Name	Cdn Equity	U.S. Equity	Europe	Japan	Far East	Latin America	Special Equity	Domestic Bond	Global Bond	Money Market	Short Term	Mid Term	Long Term	Currency Effect	Sector Specific	Small Cap	Mid Cap	Large Cap	Top Down	Bottom Up	Value Method	Sector Rotation	Market Timing	Indexation
Investors Asset Allocation Fund	♦							♦				♦						♦	♦			♦		
Investors Canadian Equity Fund	♦																	♦	♦		♦			
Investors Corporate Bond								♦			♦									♦	♦			
Investors Dividend Fund								♦									♦	♦		♦	♦			
Investors European Growth Fund			♦										♦				♦	♦	♦					
Investors Global Bond Fund									♦				♦					♦	♦			♦		
Investors Global Fund	♦	♦	♦	♦	♦								♦					♦	♦		♦			
Investors Government Bond								♦				♦	♦					♦	♦	♦		♦		
Investors Japanese Growth Fund				♦									♦				♦	♦	♦	♦				
Investors Money Market Fund									♦	♦	♦												♦	
Investors Mortgage Fund								♦				♦								♦				
Investors Mutual of Canada Fund	♦							♦				♦						♦	♦		♦			
Investors North America Growth Fund	♦	♦											♦				♦	♦	♦	♦	♦			
Investors Pacific International Fund					♦								♦				♦	♦	♦	♦	♦			
Investors Real Property Fund							♦							♦					♦					
Investors Retirement Mutual Fund	♦																	♦	♦		♦			
Investors Special Fund	♦	♦											♦					♦	♦		♦	♦		
Investors Summa Fund	♦	♦											♦					♦	♦		♦	♦		
Investors U.S. Growth Fund		♦											♦				♦	♦	♦	♦		♦		
Investors World Growth Portfolio	♦	♦	♦	♦	♦								♦				♦	♦	♦		♦	♦		

Extended Asset Mix — Cdn Equity, U.S. Equity, Europe, Japan, Far East, Latin America, Special Equity, Domestic Bond, Global Bond, Money Market

Objectives — Short Term, Mid Term, Long Term, Currency Effect, Sector Specific, Small Cap, Mid Cap, Large Cap

Investment Style — Top Down, Bottom Up, Value Method, Sector Rotation, Market Timing, Indexation

MacKENZIE FAMILY OF FUNDS

The table below groups each fund's attributes under three headings — **Extended Asset Mix**, **Objectives**, and **Investment Style**. A ◆ marks each applicable attribute.

Fund Name	Can Equity	U.S. Equity	Europe	Japan	Far East	Latin America	Special Equity	Domestic Bond	Global Bond	Money Market	Short Term	Mid Term	Long Term	Currency Effect	Sector Specific	Small Cap	Mid Cap	Large Cap	Top Down	Bottom Up	Value Method	Sector Rotation	Market Timing	Indexation
Industrial American		◆												◆			◆	◆	◆	◆				
Industrial Equity	◆															◆			◆	◆	◆			
Industrial Future	◆						◆								◆		◆		◆	◆				
Industrial Growth	◆																◆		◆	◆				
Industrial Horizon	◆																	◆	◆	◆				
Industrial Balanced	◆							◆					◆				◆	◆	◆		◆			
Industrial Pension	◆																◆	◆	◆	◆				
Industrial Dividend								◆				◆					◆		◆			◆		
Industrial Bond								◆					◆						◆	◆				
Industrial Income								◆					◆						◆			◆		
Industrial Mortgage								◆				◆							◆			◆		
Industrial Cash Management										◆	◆													◆
Industrial Short Term										◆	◆													◆
Ivy Canadian	◆																◆	◆	◆	◆				
Ivy Enterprise	◆															◆			◆	◆				
Ivy Foreign Equity			◆											◆			◆	◆	◆	◆				
Ivy Growth and Income	◆							◆				◆					◆	◆		◆				◆
Ivy Mortgage								◆				◆												◆
Universal Americas		◆				◆								◆			◆	◆	◆	◆	◆			

MacKENZIE FAMILY OF FUNDS

Fund Name	Cdn Equity	U.S. Equity	Europe	Japan	Far East	Latin America	Special Equity	Domestic Bond	Global Bond	Money Market	Short Term	Mid Term	Long Term	Currency Effect	Sector Specific	Small Cap	Mid Cap	Large Cap	Top Down	Bottom Up	Value Method	Sector Rotation	Market Timing	Indexation
	Extended Asset Mix										**Objectives**								**Investment Style**					
Universal Canadian Growth	◆																◆		◆	◆				
Universal Canadian Resources	◆						◆								◆	◆			◆			◆		
Universal European Opportunities			◆										◆			◆	◆		◆	◆				
Universal Far East					◆								◆				◆		◆		◆			
Universal Growth Fund		◆											◆				◆			◆				
Universal Japan Fund				◆									◆				◆		◆					
Universal U.S. Emerging Growth		◆											◆			◆			◆	◆				
Universal U.S. Money Market										◆	◆		◆										◆	
Universal World Asset Allocation	◆	◆	◆	◆				◆			◆		◆					◆	◆	◆		◆		
Universal World Balanced RSP	◆	◆	◆		◆			◆			◆		◆						◆	◆		◆		
Universal Emerging Growth		◆	◆		◆								◆				◆		◆	◆				
Universal World Equity		◆	◆	◆									◆				◆		◆	◆				
Universal Growth RRSP		◆	◆	◆									◆					◆	◆	◆			◆	
Universal Income RRSP									◆		◆		◆						◆				◆	
Universal Precious Metals	◆	◆				◆							◆	◆	◆	◆	◆			◆				
Universal Tactical Bond								◆				◆	◆						◆			◆		

MANULIFE CABOT FAMILY OF FUNDS

Extended Asset Mix

Fund Name	Cdn Equity	U.S. Equity	Europe	Japan	Far East	Latin America	Special Equity	Domestic Bond	Global Bond	Money Market
Cabot Blue Chip Fund	◆									
Cabot Canadian Equity Fund	◆									
Cabot Canadian Growth	◆									
Cabot Diversified Bond								◆		
Cabot Emerging Growth	◆									
Cabot Global Equity		◆	◆	◆						
Cabot Money Market										◆

Objectives

Fund Name	Short Term	Mid Term	Long Term	Currency Effect	Sector Specific	Small Cap	Mid Cap	Large Cap
Cabot Blue Chip Fund								◆
Cabot Canadian Equity Fund								◆
Cabot Canadian Growth						◆	◆	
Cabot Diversified Bond		◆						
Cabot Emerging Growth						◆	◆	
Cabot Global Equity							◆	◆
Cabot Money Market	◆							

Investment Style

Fund Name	Top Down	Bottom Up	Value Method	Sector Rotation	Market Timing	Indexation
Cabot Blue Chip Fund	◆			◆		
Cabot Canadian Equity Fund	◆		◆	◆		
Cabot Canadian Growth		◆		◆		
Cabot Diversified Bond	◆			◆		
Cabot Emerging Growth		◆		◆		
Cabot Global Equity	◆	◆		◆		
Cabot Money Market					◆	

O'DONNELL FAMILY OF FUNDS

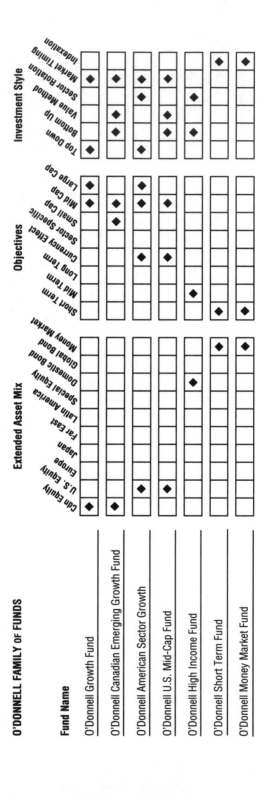

Fund Name	Extended Asset Mix										Objectives								Investment Style					
	Cdn Equity	U.S. Equity	Europe	Japan	Far East	Latin America	Special Equity	Domestic Bond	Global Bond	Money Market	Short Term	Mid Term	Long Term	Currency Effect	Sector Specific	Small Cap	Mid Cap	Large Cap	Top Down	Bottom Up	Value Method	Sector Rotation	Market Timing	Indexation
O'Donnell Growth Fund	◆																◆	◆	◆			◆		
O'Donnell Canadian Emerging Growth Fund	◆															◆	◆			◆		◆		
O'Donnell American Sector Growth		◆												◆			◆	◆	◆		◆	◆		
O'Donnell U.S. Mid-Cap Fund		◆												◆			◆			◆		◆		
O'Donnell High Income Fund								◆				◆								◆	◆			
O'Donnell Short Term Fund										◆	◆												◆	
O'Donnell Money Market Fund										◆	◆												◆	

SEGREGATED FUNDS

Fund	Extended Asset Mix										Objectives								Investment Style					
	Can Equity	U.S. Equity	Europe	Japan	Far East	Latin America	Special Equity	Domestic Bond	Global Bond	Money Market	Short Term	Mid Term	Long Term	Currency Effect	Sector Specific	Small Cap	Mid Cap	Large Cap	Top Down	Bottom Up	Value Method	Sector Rotation	Market Timing	Indexation
MANULIFE VISTA FAMILY OF FUNDS																								
Vista Fund American Stock		◆											◆				◆	◆		◆	◆	◆		
Vista Fund Bond								◆				◆							◆			◆		
Vista Fund Capital Gains Growth	◆															◆	◆	◆		◆	◆			
Vista Fund Diversified	◆							◆				◆					◆	◆	◆		◆	◆		
Vista Fund Equity	◆																◆	◆	◆		◆			
Vista Fund Global Bond									◆			◆	◆						◆	◆				
Vista Fund Global Equity			◆	◆	◆								◆				◆	◆		◆		◆		
Vista Fund Short Term										◆	◆													◆
NAL-INVESTOR FAMILY OF FUNDS																								
NAL-Investor Money Market										◆	◆												◆	
NAL-Investor Canadian Bond								◆				◆							◆			◆		
NAL-Investor Balanced Growth	◆							◆				◆						◆	◆	◆		◆		
NAL-Investor Canadian Diversified	◆							◆				◆						◆	◆	◆		◆		
NAL-Investor Equity Growth	◆						◆											◆	◆	◆				
NAL-Investor Canadian Equity	◆																	◆	◆		◆			
NAL-Investor US Equity		◆											◆				◆	◆	◆	◆				
NAL-Investor Global Equity		◆	◆	◆									◆					◆	◆		◆			

TALVEST FAMILY OF FUNDS

Fund Name	Cdn Equity	U.S. Equity	Europe	Japan	Far East	Latin America	Special Equity	Domestic Bond	Global Bond	Money Market	Short Term	Mid Term	Long Term	Currency Effect	Sector Specific	Small Cap	Mid Cap	Large Cap	Top Down	Bottom Up	Value Method	Sector Rotation	Market Timing	Indexation
	Extended Asset Mix										Objectives								Investment Style					
Talvest Bond								◆				◆							◆			◆		
Talvest Diversified	◆							◆				◆						◆	◆			◆		
Talvest Dividend								◆				◆						◆	◆	◆				
Talvest Foreign Pay Canadian Bond									◆					◆					◆			◆		
Talvest Global Diversified		◆	◆	◆					◆			◆		◆				◆	◆	◆				
Talvest Global RRSP		◆	◆	◆								◆		◆				◆	◆				◆	
Talvest Growth Fund	◆																	◆	◆	◆				
Talvest Income Fund								◆				◆							◆				◆	
Talvest Money Fund										◆	◆												◆	
Talvest New Economy Fund	◆													◆	◆	◆	◆	◆		◆				
Talvest U.S. Diversified		◆						◆				◆		◆			◆	◆	◆			◆		
Talvest U.S. Growth		◆												◆			◆	◆	◆		◆			

TEMPLETON FAMILY OF FUNDS

Fund Name	Extended Asset Mix										Objectives								Investment Style					
	Cdn Equity	U.S. Equity	Europe	Japan	Far East	Latin America	Special Equity	Domestic Bond	Global Bond	Money Market	Short Term	Mid Term	Long Term	Currency Effect	Sector Specific	Small Cap	Mid Cap	Large Cap	Top Down	Bottom Up	Value Method	Sector Rotation	Market Timing	Indexation
Templeton Balanced	♦						♦					♦						♦	♦			♦		
Templeton Canadian Asset Allocation	♦						♦					♦					♦	♦	♦		♦	♦		
Templeton Canadian Bond							♦					♦							♦		♦	♦		
Templeton Canadian Stock	♦																	♦		♦	♦			
Templeton Emerging Markets					♦								♦				♦			♦	♦			
Templeton Global Balanced		♦	♦						♦				♦					♦	♦	♦	♦			
Templeton Global Bond									♦			♦	♦						♦			♦		
Templeton Smaller Companies		♦	♦										♦			♦				♦	♦			
Templeton Growth		♦	♦										♦				♦	♦	♦	♦	♦			
Templeton International Balanced			♦		♦							♦					♦	♦	♦	♦	♦			
Templeton International Stock			♦										♦				♦	♦		♦	♦			
Templeton Treasury Bill										♦	♦													♦

TRIMARK FAMILY OF FUNDS

Fund Name	_ Extended Asset Mix: Cdn Equity	U.S. Equity	Europe	Japan	Far East	Latin America	Special Equity	Domestic Bond	Global Bond	Money Market	_ Objectives: Short Term	Mid Term	Long Term	Currency Effect	Sector Specific	Small Cap	Mid Cap	Large Cap	_ Investment Style: Top Down	Bottom Up	Value Method	Sector Rotation	Market Timing	Indexation
Trimark Americas		◆				◆								◆			◆	◆		◆	◆			
Trimark Advantage Bond								◆					◆							◆				
Trimark Canadian Bond								◆					◆						◆	◆		◆		
Trimark Canadian	◆																◆	◆		◆	◆			
Trimark Fund		◆												◆			◆	◆		◆	◆			
Trimark Government Income									◆			◆							◆	◆		◆		
Trimark Income/Growth	◆								◆				◆				◆	◆	◆	◆		◆		
Trimark Indo-Pacific				◆	◆									◆			◆	◆		◆	◆			
Trimark Interest										◆	◆												◆	
Trimark RRSP Equity	◆																	◆		◆	◆			
Trimark Selected Balanced	◆							◆					◆				◆	◆	◆	◆	◆	◆		
Trimark Canadian Growth	◆																	◆		◆	◆			
Trimark Select Growth		◆												◆				◆		◆	◆			

20/20 FAMILY OF FUNDS

Fund Name	Extended Asset Mix										Objectives								Investment Style					
	Can Equity	U.S. Equity	Europe	Japan	Far East	Latin America	Special Equity	Domestic Bond	Global Bond	Money Market	Short Term	Mid Term	Long Term	Currency Effect	Sector Specific	Small Cap	Mid Cap	Large Cap	Top Down	Bottom Up	Value Method	Sector Rotation	Market Timing	Indexation
20/20 Aggressive Growth Fund	◆	◆	◆										◆			◆	◆		◆	◆		◆		
20/20 American Tactical Asset Allocation		◆						◆			◆		◆					◆	◆			◆		
20/20 Asia Pacific Fund				◆	◆								◆				◆	◆	◆			◆		
20/20 Canadian Asset Allocation	◆							◆			◆								◆			◆		
20/20 Canadian Growth Fund	◆												◆				◆	◆	◆		◆	◆		
20/20 Dividend Fund	◆											◆	◆						◆			◆		
20/20 European Asset Allocation			◆					◆				◆	◆								◆	◆		
20/20 Foreign RSP Bond Fund								◆				◆							◆			◆		
20/20 Income Fund							◆						◆					◆	◆			◆		
20/20 India Fund						◆							◆					◆	◆	◆				
20/20 International Value Fund		◆	◆										◆					◆	◆	◆		◆		
20/20 Latin America					◆								◆					◆	◆	◆				
20/20 Money Market Fund									◆	◆	◆												◆	
20/20 Multi-Manager Emerging Markets					◆	◆							◆				◆	◆	◆			◆		
20/20 RSP Aggressive	◆												◆			◆	◆		◆	◆		◆		
20/20 RSP International Equity Allocation		◆	◆	◆									◆					◆	◆	◆		◆		
20/20 Short-Term High Yield Fund								◆			◆		◆						◆	◆		◆		
20/20 World Bond Fund				◆					◆			◆	◆						◆			◆		
20/20 World Fund			◆	◆					◆		◆		◆					◆	◆			◆		

BANK of MONTREAL FAMILY of FUNDS

Fund Name	Cdn Equity	U.S. Equity	Europe	Japan	Far East	Latin America	Special Equity	Domestic Bond	Global Bond	Money Market	Short Term	Mid Term	Long Term	Currency Effect	Sector Specific	Small Cap	Mid Cap	Large Cap	Top Down	Bottom Up	Value Method	Sector Rotation	Market Timing	Indexation
First Canadian Asset Allocation	◆							◆				◆						◆	◆			◆		
First Canadian Bond Fund								◆				◆								◆	◆			
First Canadian Dividend Income	◆							◆				◆						◆	◆	◆				
First Canadian Emerging Markets					◆	◆							◆				◆	◆	◆			◆		
First Canadian Equity Index	◆																	◆						◆
First Canadian European Growth			◆										◆					◆	◆		◆			
First Canadian Far East Growth	◆				◆								◆					◆	◆			◆		
First Canadian Growth Fund													◆					◆	◆	◆				
First Canadian International Bond									◆								◆	◆	◆			◆		
First Canadian International Growth			◆	◆									◆				◆	◆		◆	◆			
First Canadian Japanese Growth				◆									◆				◆	◆		◆	◆			
First Canadian Money Market										◆	◆												◆	
First Canadian Mortgage Fund							◆					◆								◆	◆			
First Canadian NAFTA Advantage	◆	◆				◆							◆				◆	◆	◆	◆		◆		
First Canadian Resource Fund							◆							◆		◆	◆	◆		◆		◆		
First Canadian Special Growth	◆															◆	◆			◆		◆		
First Canadian T-Bill Fund										◆	◆												◆	
First Canadian U.S. Growth Fund		◆											◆					◆	◆		◆	◆		

BANK OF NOVA SCOTIA FAMILY OF FUNDS

Fund Name	Cdn Equity	U.S. Equity	Europe	Japan	Far East	Latin America	Special Equity	Domestic Bond	Global Bond	Money Market	Short Term	Mid Term	Long Term	Currency Effect	Sector Specific	Small Cap	Mid Cap	Large Cap	Top Down	Bottom Up	Value Method	Sector Rotation	Market Timing	Indexation
Scotia CanAm Growth Fund		◆											◆					◆						◆
Scotia CanAm Income Fund								◆			◆		◆						◆			◆		
Scotia Excelsior Balanced Fund	◆						◆				◆							◆	◆			◆		
Scotia Excelsior Canadian Blue Chip Fund	◆																◆	◆	◆		◆			
Scotia Excelsior Canadian Growth Fund	◆																◆	◆	◆	◆		◆		
Scotia Excelsior Defensive Income							◆				◆								◆	◆				
Scotia Excelsior Dividend Fund	◆						◆				◆		◆						◆	◆				
Scotia Excelsior Global Fund									◆				◆						◆			◆		
Scotia Excelsior Income Fund							◆				◆								◆			◆		
Scotia Excelsior International Equity		◆	◆	◆									◆				◆	◆	◆	◆				
Scotia Excelsior Money Market									◆		◆												◆	
Scotia Excelsior Mortgage							◆				◆								◆	◆				
Scotia Excelsior Pacific Rim				◆	◆								◆				◆	◆	◆			◆		
Scotia Excelsior Premium T-Bill										◆	◆												◆	
Scotia Excelsior T-Bill fund										◆	◆												◆	
Scotia Excelsior Total Return	◆						◆				◆		◆				◆	◆	◆			◆		
Scotia Excelsior America Equity Growth		◆											◆				◆	◆	◆	◆	◆			
Scotia Excelsior Latin America	◆				◆								◆				◆	◆	◆			◆		
Scotia Excelsior Precious Metals	◆						◆								◆	◆	◆	◆		◆		◆		

CIBC FAMILY OF FUNDS

Fund Name	Cdn Equity	U.S. Equity	Europe	Japan	Far East	Latin America	Special Equity	Domestic Bond	Global Bond	Money Market	Short Term	Mid Term	Long Term	Currency Effect	Sector Specific	Small Cap	Mid Cap	Large Cap	Top Down	Bottom Up	Value Method	Sector Rotation	Market Timing	Indexation
	Extended Asset Mix										**Objectives**								**Investment Style**					
CIBC Balanced Income and Growth	◆							◆				◆						◆	◆	◆		◆		
CIBC Canadian Bond Fund								◆				◆							◆			◆		
CIBC Canadian Equity Fund	◆																◆	◆		◆		◆		
CIBC Canadian Income Fund								◆			◆	◆							◆	◆	◆			
CIBC Canadian Resources Fund							◆							◆		◆	◆		◆	◆		◆		
CIBC Canadian T-Bill										◆	◆												◆	
CIBC Capital Appreciation Fund	◆																◆	◆		◆		◆		
CIBC Emerging Economies					◆	◆							◆			◆	◆					◆		
CIBC Equity Income Fund	◆												◆				◆	◆	◆	◆		◆		
CIBC European Equity Fund			◆										◆				◆	◆		◆		◆		
CIBC Far East Prosperity Fund					◆								◆				◆	◆		◆		◆		
CIBC Global Bond Fund									◆			◆							◆			◆		
CIBC Global Equity Fund	◆	◆	◆	◆									◆				◆	◆	◆			◆		
CIBC Global Technology Fund	◆	◆					◆						◆	◆			◆	◆		◆	◆	◆		
CIBC Japanese Equity Fund				◆									◆				◆	◆		◆		◆		
CIBC Money Market Fund										◆	◆												◆	
CIBC Mortgage Investment Fund								◆				◆							◆			◆		
CIBC Premium T-Bill Fund										◆	◆											◆		
CIBC U.S. Dollar Money Market										◆	◆												◆	
CIBC U.S. Equity Fund		◆											◆					◆		◆		◆		
CIBC U.S. Opportunities Fund		◆											◆			◆	◆			◆		◆		

CANADA TRUST FAMILY OF FUNDS

Fund Name	Cdn Equity	U.S. Equity	Europe	Japan	Far East	Latin America	Special Equity	Domestic Bond	Global Bond	Money Market	Short Term	Mid Term	Long Term	Currency Effect	Sector Specific	Small Cap	Mid Cap	Large Cap	Top Down	Bottom Up	Value Method	Sector Rotation	Market Timing	Indexation
	Extended Asset Mix										**Objectives**								**Investment Style**					
C T Everest Amerigrowth		◆											◆					◆					◆	
C T Everest AsiaGrowth					◆								◆					◆					◆	
C T Everest Balanced Fund	◆						◆					◆						◆	◆			◆		
C T Everest Bond Fund	◆						◆						◆						◆			◆		
C T Everest Dividend Income	◆						◆					◆						◆	◆	◆				
C T Everest Emerging Markets					◆	◆							◆				◆		◆		◆			
C T Everest Eurogrowth			◆										◆					◆					◆	
C T Everest International Bond									◆			◆							◆			◆		
C T Everest International Equity			◆	◆	◆								◆				◆	◆	◆			◆		
C T Everest Money Market Fund										◆	◆												◆	
C T Everest Mortgage Fund							◆					◆								◆				
C T Everest North American Fund	◆	◆											◆				◆	◆	◆	◆		◆		
C T Everest Special Equity Fund	◆															◆	◆		◆	◆		◆		
C T Everest U.S. Equity	◆																◆	◆	◆	◆		◆		
C T Everest U.S. Equity		◆											◆					◆	◆	◆		◆		

ROYAL BANK FAMILY OF FUNDS

Legend: ◆ indicates the category applies to the fund. Column groups — **Extended Asset Mix**: Can Equity, U.S. Equity, Europe, Japan, Far East, Latin America, Special Equity, Domestic Bond, Global Bond, Money Market. **Objectives**: Short Term, Mid Term, Long Term, Currency Effect, Sector Specific, Small Cap, Mid Cap, Large Cap. **Investment Style**: Top Down, Bottom Up, Value Method, Sector Rotation, Market Timing, Indexation.

Fund Name	Can Eq	US Eq	Europe	Japan	Far East	Lat. Am.	Special Eq	Dom. Bond	Global Bond	Money Mkt	Short Term	Mid Term	Long Term	Currency Eff	Sector Spec	Small Cap	Mid Cap	Large Cap	Top Down	Bottom Up	Value Method	Sector Rot.	Market Timing	Indexation
RoyFund Bond Fund								◆				◆							◆	◆				
RoyFund Canadian Equity Fund	◆																◆	◆	◆			◆		
RoyFund Canadian Money Market										◆	◆													◆
RoyFund Canadian T-Bill Fund										◆	◆													◆
RoyFund Canadian Dividend Fund	◆							◆										◆	◆	◆				
RoyFund International Income									◆				◆						◆					
RoyFund Mortgage Fund								◆				◆							◆					
RoyFund US$ Money Market Fund										◆	◆													◆
RoyFund U.S. Equity Fund		◆											◆				◆	◆	◆		◆	◆		
Royal Asian Growth Fund					◆								◆				◆	◆	◆			◆		
Royal Balanced Fund	◆							◆				◆						◆	◆					
Royal Canadian Growth Fund	◆															◆		◆	◆			◆		
Royal Canadian Small-Cap Fund	◆															◆			◆			◆		
Royal Energy Fund							◆								◆				◆			◆		
Royal European Growth Fund			◆										◆				◆	◆	◆			◆		
Royal International Equity Fund			◆	◆									◆				◆	◆	◆			◆		
Royal Japanese Stock Fund				◆									◆				◆	◆	◆			◆		
Royal Latin America Fund						◆							◆				◆	◆	◆	◆		◆		
Royal Precious Metals Fund							◆						◆		◆	◆	◆	◆		◆		◆		
Royal Trust American Stock Fund		◆															◆	◆	◆	◆		◆		
Royal Trust Bond Fund								◆				◆							◆					

Royal Trust Canadian Money Market

Royal Trust Canadian StockFund

Royal Trust Canadian T-Bill Fund

Royal Trust Growth and Income

Royal Trust International Bond

Royal Trust Mortgage Fund

Royal Trust U.S. Money Market

TD GREEN LINE FAMILY of FUNDS

Fund Name	Cdn Equity	U.S. Equity	Europe	Japan	Far East	Latin America	Special Equity	Domestic Bond	Global Bond	Money Market	Short Term	Mid Term	Long Term	Currency Effect	Sector Specific	Small Cap	Mid Cap	Large Cap	Top Down	Bottom Up	Value Method	Sector Rotation	Market Timing	Indexation
	Extended Asset Mix										**Objectives**								**Investment Style**					
Green Line Asian Growth Fund					◆									◆			◆	◆	◆			◆		
Green Line Balanced Growth Fund	◆						◆					◆					◆	◆	◆			◆		
Green Line Balanced Income Fund	◆						◆					◆						◆		◆				
Green Line Blue Chip Equity Fund	◆											◆						◆		◆	◆	◆		
Green Line Canadian Index Fund	◆																	◆					◆	
Green Line Canadian Money Market										◆	◆												◆	
Green Line Canadian T-Bill Fund										◆	◆												◆	
Green Line Canadian Government Bond								◆				◆							◆		◆	◆		
Green Line Dividend Fund	◆						◆											◆		◆				
Green Line Emerging Markets Fund					◆	◆								◆			◆	◆	◆			◆		
Green Line Energy Fund	◆						◆									◆	◆	◆	◆	◆		◆		
Green Line European Growth Fund			◆											◆			◆	◆	◆			◆		
Green Line Global Government Bond									◆			◆		◆					◆			◆		
Green Line Global RRSP Bond									◆			◆		◆					◆					
Green Line Global Select Fund		◆	◆	◆										◆			◆	◆	◆			◆		
Green Line International Equity		◆	◆	◆										◆			◆	◆	◆			◆		
Green Line Japanese Growth				◆										◆				◆	◆	◆		◆		
Green Line Latin America Growth						◆								◆				◆	◆		◆	◆		
Green Line Mortgage Fund							◆				◆	◆								◆				
Green Line Mortgage Back Fund							◆				◆	◆								◆				
Green Line North America Growth Fund		◆												◆			◆	◆	◆	◆		◆		

Green Line Precious Metals Fund

Green Line Real Return Bond Fund

Green Line Resource Fund

Green Line Science and Technology Fund

Green Line Short Term Income Fund

Green Line U.S. Index Fund

Green Line U.S. Money Market Fund

Green Line Value Fund